Sri Sivabala Yogi
(24 Jan 1935 - 28 Mar 1994)

Laghu Guru Upanishad

Spiritual Teachings of Sri Sivabala Yogi

GURPRASAD

PARTRIDGE

To order additional copies of this book, contact
Partridge India
000 800 10062 62
orders.india@partridgepublishing.com

www.partridgepublishing.com/india

Contents

Chapter	Subject	Page No
Preamble		ix
A Note	(Reproduced from Guru Upanishad)	xi
1.	(Reproduced from Guru Upanishad)	1
	Invocation	1
	Introduction	1
2.	Instruction In General	12
3.	Reality	49
4.	Control Of Mind	99
	Worship	118
	The Path of Service (Sewa)	120
	The Path of Love and Devotion (Bhakti Marga)	127
	The Path of Yoga	136
	The Path of Knowledge (Jnana Marga)	146
	The Path of Silence	156
	Powers	158
	Samadhi, Realisation and Tapas	160
	Samadhi	161

Realisation 163

Tapas... 164

Essence of Teaching 165

5.   The Satguru (Reproduced from Guru Upanishad)...................... 168

Saga of Sri Sivabala Yogi 192

Glossary 291

Index 303

Preamble

1. Sri Sivabala Yogi was born on 24 Jan 1935 and shed his mortal body on 28 Mar 1994. His advent is a major event in the rich spiritual history of India and the world. His teachings are not yet widely known because, apart from initiating aspirants into the discipline of meditation, he gave no verbal instruction. Besides that, most of those who sought his company for spiritual growth were content with the initial teaching imparted at the time of initiation and did not display any serious intent to inquire after the Truth too deeply. Saints give instruction to their devotees which, if practised earnestly, helps them to attain Self Realisation. Neither money nor fame has any attraction for them. Teaching is always imparted in the matrix of prevailing times, requirements of aspirants and the divine mission ordained for them by the Lord. The divine knowledge given in Guru Upanishad was revealed in the above context.

2. Sri Sivabala Yogi's teaching was first revealed in the primary book, Guru Upanishad (though completed but not published yet) which is an exhaustive guide for aspirants of various grades and temperaments, who are curious to know the Truth. It contains divine knowledge of the highest quality, which is of special value for those seekers who want to pursue a spiritual quest seriously. Guru Upanishad sets out in great detail various aspects of the metaphysical nature of Reality and, more importantly, the means to attain It through control of mind achieved by personal effort and divine grace. A scriptural enquiry seeks knowledge that is not only abstruse but its esoteric nature is difficult for intellectual comprehension without purifying the mind through practice (sadhana) of a guru's instruction. Although Guru Upanishad is written in simple language, yet, it is not possible for an average reader with no more than rudimentary spiritual knowledge to appreciate the subtle nuances of its teaching without practical spiritual experience. The scope of Guru Upanishad is so vast that even advanced disciples do not need all its knowledge to progress spiritually. Its complete knowledge is primarily intended for highly evolved souls, who are close associates of the Guru, to further his mission in the future. Some aspirants, except for the very earnest ones, may, as a consequence, be put off by the elaborate nature of the Guru's instruction given in that

work. To spread the divine word to a larger audience, not too familiar with spiritual matters but are yet keen to learn its basic knowledge, Swamiji, as Sri Sivabala Yogi was called by devotees, had directed Gurprasad to prepare an easier to read version of Guru Upanishad after its completion. Laghu (means smaller or condensed version of) Guru Upanishad has been written with that end in view. This book is not a chapter wise condensation of the original work but comprises its essence for easier assimilation. And, yet, its sweep is broad enough to embrace all that a beginner needs to know. It has a twin purpose; one, to serve as guidebook for a deeper study of the Guru Upanishad; two, encourage people interested in pursuing a spiritual path to begin practice without which bookish knowledge is of little avail. Chapter 1 (with slight modifications), A Note and Contents from Guru Upanishad have been reproduced in full in the present work to give the genesis and broad overview of the teaching. Similarly, Chapter 34 (of Guru Upanishad) has been included as Chapter 5 (with slight modifications) to familiarise readers with Sri Sivabala Yogi's life story and divine mission.

3. This treatise follows the question and answer technique of the Guru Upanishad. The Guru's instruction, revealed in bhava samadhi, is given in the form of replies by Swamiji to questions asked by Gurprasad. The use of traditional words to convey certain ideas has been deliberately kept to the minimum to make instruction simple. They have been used only where their English equivalents are inadequate to convey their real sense or when some very commonly used ones that are generally understood.

24 Jan 2016   Gurprasad

A Note

(Reproduced from Guru Upanishad)

1. Sri Sivabala Yogi (24 Jan 1935 – 28 Mar 1994), better known as Sri Swamiji among his devotees, taught the path of Silence, a composite of all spiritual disciplines, that could, in effect, lead an aspirant to practise any path suitable to his or her nature. He was divinely ordained to do so after doing intense tapas (a special spiritual discipline) for twelve years (07 Aug 1949 – 07 Aug 1961). The essence of his teaching is that liberation is attained by making the mind silent through the practice of meditation on the self (atman dhyana), a variant of the path of Silence. Many saints teach in Silence but they usually explain their instruction, in words, to those who question them. Sri Swamiji's uniqueness was that he taught in absolute (i.e. without any verbal instruction) Silence and he was generally very reluctant to break It. His usual response to most queries was the advice to do meditation (to know the answers). Curiously, not many devotees asked him questions on spiritual matters. At times, though not very often, he would make pithy remarks to help aspirants in their spiritual growth. All doubts are resolved, on their own, when the mind learns to be still. Some aspirants got the answers to their problems this way. A few others obtained cryptic replies, from Sri Swamiji, when they sought to clear their doubts. But, the majority of devotees, due to spiritual immaturity, could not appreciate that verbal instruction cannot match the one imparted in the eloquence of total Silence. They would much rather hear the teaching in words. The work that follows was initiated to satisfy this desire. Apart from some answers given to specific questions raised by a few disciples, Sri Swamiji did not leave behind any codified teaching, which could satisfy the curiosity of the seekers of Truth. To do that, Sri Swamiji had directed Gurprasad to record his teaching in easy to understand language. It was revealed over a period of time, beginning in April 1977, and was reduced to writing from the summer of 1992 onwards. The teaching has now matured for wider dissemination.

2. Sri Swamiji's instruction is a comprehensive guide for all those who want to know the Reality. This work, almost encyclopedic in scope, covers all aspects of a spiritual quest from an aspirant's point of view. The divine wisdom revealed here has been gleaned from his power of Silence. It is suitable for aspirants of different temperaments and grades since it embraces, in its wide sweep, all the main doctrines on the nature of Reality as well as the major paths leading to It. A yogi who has completed tapas successfully is a perfect satguru, capable of guiding others on all paths and even creating new ones. Sri Sivabala Yogi belonged to this class. He was a living embodiment of the supreme state of absolute Silence, very rarely achieved in bodily form even by accomplished yogis.

3. The work is in the form of questions and answers. Sri Swamiji has given the answers and the questioner is Gurprasad. This has not been mentioned against each question and answer to avoid repetition. Questions and answers have been numbered serially for each chapter and letters Q and A have been used to indicate them.

4. Indian spiritual tradition uses many words, mainly of Sanskrit origin, to express certain ideas and tenets. The present generation is not too familiar with them. A few of these words have been used in this work and, when employed, their connotation in a particular context has been explained in the text. It is not essential to know them for a proper understanding of Sri Swamiji's teaching. However, a glossary of some commonly used words is given at the end of this work.

5. A brief life sketch of Sri Swamiji, along with a few questions on his life and divine mission, is given in the last chapter. Readers who are not familiar with his life story may like to read it first, though some of the answers would be better understood after going through the earlier portions. A reference made to Sri Swamiji in the text has been indicated by the words, the Guru; otherwise, the word, guru, has been used in a general sense.

07 Aug 2015   Gurprasad

TABLE OF CONTENTS OF GURU UPANISHAD

Chapter   **Subject**

PART I – Preliminary Instruction
A Note
1.   Introduction
2.   Teaching
3.   Guru
4.   Disciple-Devotee
5.   Practice
6.   Liberation and Bondage

Part II – Nature of Reality
7.   Reality
8.   Nature of Mind
9.   Nature of Creation
10.   Knowledge, Perception, Memory, Word and Creation
11.   Brahman and Ad Shakti (Divine Power)
12.   Omkar, Word and Name
13.   Atman (Self)
14.   Heart
15.   Love, Grace, Self-Effort, Free Will and Self-Surrender
16.   Karma
17.   A Pause

Part III – Control of Mind
18.   Self-Control
19.   Self-Discipline and Purification
20.   Self-Abidance and Subsidence
21.   Destruction of Mind
22.   Spiritual Experience and Progress
23.   The Path of Service
24.   Worship
25.   The Path of Love and Devotion

26.	The Path of Yoga
27.	The Path of Knowledge
28.	The Path of Silence
29.	Powers
30.	Samadhi
31.	Realisation
32.	Tapas
33.	Essence of Teaching
34.	The Satguru

Glossary

Index

LIST OF DIAGRAMS

Ser No	Title	Chapter
1.	Diagramatic Representation of Creation	9
2.	Diagramatic Layout of the Subtle Body	14
3.	Diagramatic Representation of the Subtle World	14
4.	Diagramatic Representation of a Chakra	14

Chapter 1

(Reproduced from Guru Upanishad)

Invocation

Salutations to the absolute Truth, the indescribable Reality that has manifested as the Guru for the sake of those who seek to know Its secrets. Blessed be they who seek the grace of the Guru, the embodiment of supreme Silence, the source of yogic power, pure love and divine knowledge. Praise be to the Lord who, out of boundless love and compassion, has revealed the divine word, given here, to save all struggling souls. Salutations to the eternal Guru, who incarnates in every age, to help those who take refuge in Him.

Introduction

Q1. What is the object of this work?

A1. Control of mind is the central theme of the Guru's teaching. The cause of human suffering lies in the mind; so does it's removal. Mind cannot be controlled through blind adherence to religious dogma. The only way to do it is to apply one's intelligence in making proper self-effort to earn divine grace. Scriptural knowledge and religious practices are only a means to that end. This work is devoted to the study of mind and the way to control it. It sets forth, in simple language, instruction, which, if followed, leads to the knowledge of absolute Reality. It does not seek to enter into any dispute with existing doctrines of a similar nature; rather, it complements them. It is meant to be a practical guide for those who seek the Truth through control of mind.

Q2. What is its scope?

A2. It synthesises various viewpoints on the nature of Reality and the many ways to attain it, in a holistic manner, by exercising control on the mind.

Q3. Does it subscribe to any of the previously known works of a similar nature or texts of various religions or sects?

A3. It accepts all such works as true, but, its interpretation of the Truth is its own.

1

Q4. What is its authority?

A4. The Guru's own experience of the Reality, which is characterised by the fathomless and unbreakable Silence.

Q5. Has a reference been made to teachings of other saints?

A5. It is based solely on the Guru's experience, although, at times, reference has been made to some viewpoints contained in other scriptures and of some sages for better understanding of the instruction given here. It does not contradict any of them. The Guru loves and respects all saints and scriptures from all countries in equal measure.

Q6. Is the Guru a follower of any saint or creed? Does the Guru wish to establish a sect of his own?

A6. The Guru is not a follower of any saint and does not subscribe to any sect or religion. He has gained direct experience of the Reality due to the grace of God, whom he regards as his Guru. He wishes to propagate the Truth, which does not admit of any denominational differences. The Lord has no favorite people or special place where He or She reveals Himself or Herself. Sects are set up by followers of gurus for their own selfish ends and not by the saints themselves who look at all creation with an equal eye. The Guru does not want to set up a new sect.

Q7. What is the necessity of having a new work when a large number of holy books already exist?

A7. The knowledge of Reality is eternal and has been revealed to mankind, by many sages, in all periods of history. Divine knowledge inheres in every individual soul, though it remains hidden due to mental impurities. It is known only in a state of Realisation. Thus, no one can claim any exclusive right to its revelation nor can anyone say that a teacher has copied the teachings of another saint. This knowledge, attained in Self Realisation, is absolute and is the same for everyone. However, its expression in words always varies because it is dependent on the temperament of the teacher as also of the student and is made to suit the circumstances prevailing at the time of revelation. The sacred teaching is made known in different languages, by divine dispensation, from time to time, to meet the requirements of devotees born in various parts of the world. Conditions change in every age and the Truth has to be re-interpreted to suit the prevailing level of spiritual progress of human beings. For example, most people find it difficult to follow older scriptures because of the archaic language used and the esoteric nature of their teachings. In this age of information technology, there is a plethora of godmen, priests and scholars who are propagating their own version of divine knowledge, often to make quick money and gain public recognition. Gurus are a dime a dozen these days. Their expositions are not backed by spiritual experience. Some of them offer quick fix solutions to attain nirvana (salvation). All that they have succeeded in doing is to cause confusion in the minds of ordinary people, by misinterpreting the scriptures in a narrow and sectarian manner. It has bred ill will, in some cases, for the followers of sects other than their own. All religions teach the same principles; only their modes of worship and rituals differ, which is exploited by evil minds for their interests. Spirituality these days is treated as a commercial proposition, with a promise, given to the ignorant, of a quick passage to heaven. There is darkness all around at present. and people in general are groping blindly to alleviate their unhappiness. The path of Truth and universal love has been forgotten. Selfishness is the ruling deity of the age and it has led to crass pursuit of sensual pleasure. Individuals and nations condone every kind of exploitation and injustice in the name of self-interest. People are nowhere near the mecca of happiness, despite having everything that they need in the world. There are some thinking individuals in this grim and dismal scenario who seek the light at the end of the tunnel. They want to get rid of their mental tension and search for peace and happiness. For them, this work offers a hope and it has been written in an idiom, which they can readily understand. It takes a non-sectarian and scientific approach to resolve the problems faced by modern day individuals. The higher purpose of this work is to set the record straight as far as the pursuit of a spiritual quest is concerned. After going through this work, a discerning reader can assess for himself or herself whether the pursuit of divine knowledge is as easy as it is made out to be by many people these days. There is nothing esoteric about the Reality except one's self-created doubts about It. It dwells in everyone's heart but to know that requires a prolonged practice of a spiritual discipline to control one's mind. There is no other way. It cannot be attained by reading or thinking or through magic formulae. The way to experience the Truth, which alone gives true happiness, is set forth in this work.

Q8. What are the special conditions of this age, which have been kept in view in the preparation of this work?
A8. The modern times are characterised by a tremendous scientific and technological progress, especially in the field of communications and the spread of information through electronic means, used by many to propagate half-baked scriptural knowledge. Consumerism and hedonism is a marked feature of modern life, especially in the better off sections of society. It has shaken the spiritual moorings of men and women everywhere. The upsurge of materialism is typified by a marked decline in the basic ethics taught by all religions. There is a mad rush to acquire more wealth. That none of it has brought any real happiness strikes very few (blessed) people. Material progress has been made possible by the present day system of education,

which encourages people to be empirical and accept new ideas after a thorough analysis in a rational manner. Although it has helped educated people to shed the prejudices and superstitions that were prevalent earlier but it has also bred a mind-set that regards the visible (i.e. worldly phenomenon) as true and everything beyond gross sensual experience as false. Thus, there is a curious mixture of openness and closeness in a modern mind: openness towards experimentation in the material sphere to broaden the frontiers of gross knowledge through research and development; closeness towards the world of .spirit because it is too subtle to be known by normal empirical methods. The latter thus remains outside the scope of scientific inquiry. Most religious bodies today have become business organisations; some are used as tools of political power. They lay stress on outward symbols and complex rituals at the cost of propagating the true teachings of their faiths. It has bred skepticism about the existence of God and the teachings of saints given in the scriptures. A majority of people today are unhappy and confused because material progress has not given them any real satisfaction. People are more selfish, callous, greedy and exploitative these days than ever before. There is a sharp moral degeneration, mainly due to the uncontrolled over indulgence in passions. Money is the new deity that is worshipped universally. These conditions are an ideal breeding ground for a plethora of hypocritical religious leaders and other assorted beings whose sole purpose is to fool gullible people. It would not be an exaggeration to say that there are more frauds in the spiritual sphere than any other field. Is it any wonder that spirituality has declined so steeply in this age?

Q9. In what way do these conditions affect the teachings given here?
A9. The modern mind accepts the primacy of rational thinking over mere faith. This has been kept in mind while enunciating the instructions given in this work. The Guru's teachings are based on reason, which any thinking person can understand, provided one has an open mind to examine fresh ideas. No one is asked to accept them because of blind faith. Any rational person would realise that one's desires expand faster than all the goods produced by factories. No matter how much progress science makes, it will never satiate human desires nor bring real, everlasting happiness which lies within and not without. The Guru wants to invite people with probing minds to embark on a journey with him to seek true happiness. Those who are ready to do so are advised to read this work without any prejudice or bias. It does not propagate any religious doctrine. It only shows the way to the ocean of infinite bliss in a rational manner.

Q10. Can a person experiment with the teachings?
A10. Most definitely. That is the primary purpose of the Guru's instruction. The sweetness of honey is known through its taste and not by merely talking about

it. Similarly, the Reality, too subtle for sensual perception, is to be experienced or realised and not just discussed intellectually. The essence of scientific temper, a marked feature of the modern mind, lies in its ability to accept or reject ideas after rational analysis and experimentation. The teachings in this work are open to a similar critical enquiry. No one is asked to accept the Guru's word by mere faith. Let a person accept or reject it after verification through practice because there is no other way to establish its veracity. Experimentation means that one must, first, intellectually imbibe the teaching through use of reason and then practise (abhayasa) it. If one does not gain anything during its course or at the end of it, one would be right to consider them as humbug. At the same time, to reject them without a proper enquiry would be an act of insincerity and hypocrisy.

Q11. Who all can read this work?
A11. All those who have failed to find true happiness in the world, for whatever reason, and seek to overcome their present condition can do so with profit, irrespective of their cultural, lingual, religious, sexual, caste and creedal differences. Many people, these days, find modern life too stressful; they suffer from worries and anxieties of various kinds. Even a little practice of what this work advocates would go a long way in making their lives more meaningful and happy. Those who want to solve the mystery of life and the world around them should study this work carefully. It is also suitable for those (rare ones) who seek divine knowledge for the sake of knowledge. A beginner and an advanced aspirant would find something relevant to their condition in this work; so would a lay reader.

Q12. Will the understanding and benefit be the same for every one?
A12. The benefit of studying this work will vary according to the level of individual spiritual maturity. So will its understanding, which is always subjective. Those who seek total freedom from the transitory nature of worldly pleasures will be benefited the most. Those who seek lower goals, like removal of worries, stress, strain, satisfaction of desires etc. will have a correspondingly lower degree of satisfaction. But, all those who read it, even once, will gain in one way or the other.

Q13. Is a full understanding of the work possible in one or two readings?
A13. Understanding is intellectual and spiritual; it starts with the former and ends in the latter. Spiritual understanding refers to the actual experience (i.e. taste of honey) of the thing (Reality) sought. Though given in simple language, a mere reading will give only a partial intellectual understanding because the subject falls outside the range of normal sensual experience. It must be emphasised here that the Truth is not a matter for mental speculation and

dry polemics indulged in by philosophers and scholars but something to be experienced directly within one's self. It is more vivid and real than anything seen or heard in the world. Since the teachings are an explanation of the Guru's indescribable spiritual experience, a fuller understanding is possible only for those who practice what is taught here. Divine knowledge is best imbibed in meditation. Perception and comprehension improve with practice (sadhana). A complete understanding comes with spiritual progress, resulting in Self Realisation. There is no other way.

Q14. What are the steps leading to complete understanding?
A14. First, the Truth must be heard from the teacher; second, it should be reflected upon; third, it should be practiced under the guidance of a guru; practice (abhayasa), when it matures, results in Self-Realisation.

Q15. Does this work encompass all the three steps?
A15. The first two steps are taken when the work is studied with sincerity; they form the basis for practice, which is done according to one's ability and maturity through the grace of a guru. Individual temperament and level of spiritual advancement determine the method to be adopted; an aspirant generally follows only one path out of the many given here. It is a matter that the guru explains directly to the individual concerned at the time of initiation.

Q16. Is belief in God essential to derive benefit from this book?
A16. No. Agnostics can read it with as much profit as believers, provided they have open minds and are prepared to practice the instruction. The aim of the teaching is to define various methods to control the mind. For that purpose, it is immaterial whether one accepts the existence of God or not. No one denies one's own self. Its knowledge is enough to achieve eternal bliss.

Q17. Does knowledge of other scriptures help in understanding this work?
A17. The essence of every scripture is the same. It is true of this work also. No previous knowledge of any scripture is required to understand the instruction given here. A study of this work will, in fact, help in having a better understanding of other scriptures.

Q18. Is anyone required to give up his or her present religious beliefs in order to follow the teachings given here?
A18. No. The essence of Guru's instruction is to control the mind. All religious practices are a means to that end. One should, therefore, follow the precepts and canons of one's faith, according to one's propensity, in a spirit of devotion and humility. The Guru regards them all as true paths leading to the attainment of Reality. Those who follow the instructions given here will

grasp better the real import of their religious beliefs. They can also follow their own local customs and traditions relating to worship, prayers, personal conduct and so on.

Q19. How is the work laid out?
A19. It is in three parts; part one contains preliminary instruction dealing with subjects of a general nature that have a bearing on a spiritual quest. Part two deals with theoretical aspects of the nature of Reality and non-reality from different viewpoints, culminating in a holistic overview to establish that none of them is antagonistic to each other. It sets out the proposition that is to be proved through spiritual experience only. The third part discusses various methods used to control the mind to attain Self-Realisation, i.e. the experience mentioned above. Each part is divided into a number of chapters with a suitable heading. The instruction in one chapter leads to the teaching in the next. The essence of teaching is given at the end of each chapter and, also, after discussing important points within it. The reader should try to imbibe and retain it in the mind. The language used is very simple and an attempt has been made to employ elementary logic to discuss some issues. Certain points have been explained with the help of analogies and similes.

Q20. How should this work be studied?
A20. Proper study serves the purpose of hearing and reflection. It should be studied with deliberation combined with contemplation and discrimination. Read only as much as one can easily absorb and have frequent pauses to reflect deeply on it. Contemplation implies that the instruction should become part of one's mental being. It is achieved by constantly dwelling on the subject matter that has been studied, and, then discriminating it, in the light of one's current knowledge. The use of one's intelligence to rationally analyse and accept the veracity of teaching is called discrimination. Practice (sadhana) follows the mental conviction given by contemplation. The result of one's reflection may be discussed with one's guru and other devotees to clarify one's mind. Best results are obtained when doubts that arise during hearing and reflection are cleared in a state of meditation as taught by the Guru. The second option is to discuss them with those devotees who, through practice, have attained some divine knowledge. Certain words and names traditionally used in Indian scriptures to explain various concepts have been mentioned in this work. They should not confuse readers; a discerning and wise student ought to remember that the Reality is nameless and wordless. Words are only an expression of the Inexpressible and one can assign any name to the Lord without affecting Its Truth. This work does not propound any teaching specific to some people or region or time. It is universal and beyond the bounds of time. It should be studied in that spirit. Readers are advised to study this work methodically

and systematically. A few general points are mentioned below for serious aspirants: -

(a) Make a study of this work a part of daily spiritual routine. It inculcates a sense of discipline in the mind; it is a basic step to spiritual development. Keep up the study even during advanced stages of practice.

(b) Read a few questions and their answers and ponder over them, using the faculty of discrimination. Think deeply of the subject matter with a concentrated mind. Re-study portions one finds hard to comprehend.

(c) Examine all answers critically and try to understand their essence. Use reason as the basis of rational analysis to draw useful deductions. It leads to a mental conviction of the truth of instruction. For example, Reality is said to have two apparently contrary aspects; it is difficult for an average mind to accept such a statement. However, this contradiction is resolved if one were to reflect deeply as discussed in Chapter 3 of this work. Comprehension improves if one is able to eject, from the mind, wrong beliefs currently entertained by an individual. Thus, acceptance of teaching follows rejection of unreal knowledge. A combination of steps (a) and (b) is known as contemplation done through discrimination. This process should be repeated till conviction arises.

(d) Try to get an overview of the subject matter, covered in a chapter, by imbibing its essence summed up at the end of it. Various aspects of a subject have been summed up separately. One should try to understand them and, if required, re-read the questions and answers leading to it.

(e) The scope of this work is quite vast and the knowledge that it reveals is comprehensive enough to cover all paths and viewpoints. It is meant for aspirants of different temperaments in various stages of spiritual growth. An earnest seeker, even an advanced one, needs to follow only one path to achieve his or her goal. Similarly, it is not essential to study all the theories on the nature of Reality to arrive at a basic understanding, which is enough to begin practice (sadhana). The knowledge, in all its complete details, enunciated here is required only by those who, after due authorisation, are expected to guide others. In the initial stages, a student should concentrate on those chapters that hold one's special interest. For instance, those who are inclined towards the path of yoga should study with greater care Chapter 4.

(f) Some portions of Chapters 3 and 4 of the work are likely to strike many readers as too abstruse. One should not feel discouraged by it because everyone, especially a beginner, does not require the knowledge revealed there. However, all serious aspirants are advised to have a working knowledge of the nature of maya, the way individual mind functions, specially the role of intelligence and will power, phenomenon of creation and the inadequacy of relative knowledge discussed in Chapter 3.

(g) Notwithstanding the above, the practice of a spiritual discipline is not contingent on study of this work. Aspirants are advised to begin practice and complement it with study. It will help in improved comprehension as well as in spiritual progress.

(h) Chapter 4 contains the crucial portion of the teaching. It serves two purposes; one, it indicates the general way to spiritual development for each path; two, some pitfalls that are likely to be encountered enroute. A study of the relevant (to one's chosen path) chapter should enable an aspirant to conduct practice more rationally and humbly, avoiding various obstacles.

Q21. The Guru's teaching has been expounded in the question and answer form. Why has this technique been followed?

A21. The Guru dwells in absolute Silence and It is broken only when a disciple has a genuine inquiry to make. The Guru has no desire to impart any verbal teaching because the power of Silence, which he gives to the devotees, is superior to it. However, many of them have prayed to him to give them some instruction to clarify their doubts. To fulfill their desire as well as the needs of the future, the Guru had asked Gurprasad, a keen seeker with a natural curiosity for knowledge, to record his teaching. He questioned the Guru on various aspects of Reality and spiritual life. A record of these conversations, carried out over an extended period, in the subtle plane, has been rearranged, subject wise, in the pages that follow. Instruction in a narrative form is generally too concise for easy assimilation. It leaves many points and doubts unanswered because it is too subjective. The question and answer method, on the other hand, gives comprehensive instruction from the point of view of a disciple who is inquisitive to gain a thorough knowledge of the subject from various viewpoints, leaving no doubts in the mind. Inquiry made after the Truth through questions is a technique followed by spiritually mature minds. It results in a more comprehensive examination of the Truth from various viewpoints. In this method, the subject is split into easy to understand segments and answers are given to specific doubts, which are likely to rise in the minds of all aspirants. It is a more direct method of teaching and, hence, easier to follow. Knowledge is best attained by an inquiring mind and, on that account, the technique of question and answer has been preferred over other methods.

Q22. Is there a repetition of any material in the work?

A22. Yes. Repetition in instruction is essential for its assimilation and examination from different angles. It leads to a more comprehensive coverage and, hence, better understanding. At places, some questions may appear to have been partially answered in the earlier discussions. Their repetition is due to the difference in the context in which they have been asked and, therefore, their answers may appear to vary. They investigate the subject from a fresh viewpoint. At places, a subject introduced in one chapter is covered more comprehensively in a later one. There are very few students who have the mental capacity to retain, in memory, most of what they read on an abstract theme, like the one covered in this work. Most answers are, therefore, comprehensive enough, to avoid cross checking with previous instruction. Hence some repetition is inevitable and necessary.

Q23. This work has been revealed in bhava samadhi. Would there have been a difference if the Guru had written it himself?
A23. None at all. The state of bhava samadhi has been briefly covered in Chapter 4. Suffice it to say here that it is a state of a highly introverted and purified mind, concentrated on itself (or, on the pure form of the object of one's worship); it is achieved through self-surrender, done out of love and devotion. It is the most intimate form of guru–disciple relationship. An aspirant feels the guru's subtle presence in the heart and is aware of it at all times. A revelation made in such a mind carries the stamp of authority of a guru. An aspirant normally understands the spoken word of a guru subjectively but the one revealed in bhava samadhi does not suffer from this defect because individual subjectivity is submerged in the guru's power. In bhava samadhi, one can converse with the guru more intimately than one can in the gross form; the guru's power works through such a disciple. Many of the world's great scriptures have been revealed in bhava samadhi. Know it for certain that this work, less the questions, is the word of the Guru.

Q24. Why were the teachings revealed in bhava samadhi?
A24. Because the Guru teaches in absolute Silence and he has no desire to break it. He does not acknowledge any other method of instruction. However, there is a large number of devotees who do not experience the Silence, immediately after initiation by the Guru, due to impurity of their minds. Many of them feel the necessity of verbal instruction to progress further. The Guru, out of love for such devotees, has revealed these teachings, in guru bhava (i.e. the relationship that exists between a guru and a mature disciple), so that they can do their duty to him, as he has done it for them.

Q25. What does the title `Guru-Upanishad' mean?
A25. The word upanishad, means to sit near a guru and listen to his or her divine teachings, on the Truth, in a mood of devotion. Revelations in bhava samadhi fall in this category of instruction. Amongst all forms of knowledge,

the upanishadic one alone leads to true freedom. It is the quintessence of Vedanta; it refers to divine knowledge that ends all types of relative knowledge. The title, in short, means the knowledge of Truth, revealed by the Guru, to a disciple.

Q26. What status does this work enjoy?
A26. It has the same status as other upanishads.

Q27. How does it differ from other upanishads?
A27. Most of the traditional upanishads were written in ancient times. In the absence of printing facilities, the language used in them was concise, cogent and pithy because they had to be transmitted through word of mouth from one generation to another. A sage would give their detailed and systematic exposition verbally to those who needed their knowledge. The upanishadic knowledge is abstract and many commentaries were written to explain it; even then most people found it difficult to imbibe its esoteric message. In due course, it became the preserve of erudite scholars who used it to establish their intellectual superiority over others, without in any way practising it. Although seers and sages have always taught and given primacy to this form of knowledge, yet very few of them codified it for the sake of clarity and ease of understanding. The Guru has revealed this work methodically to revive the quintessence of upanishadic knowledge suited to this age. It has been given in detail to avoid the pitfalls of misinterpretation.

Q28. Scriptures generally expound a particular doctrine. What viewpoint does this work subscribe to?
A28. The fundamental premise of this work is that the Silence felt in the void of one's heart is the only Reality. All else is a fancy entertained by the mind. The Truth is neither this nor that (e.g. dual or non-dual) mental concept. This knowledge arises on its own if the mind is controlled through self-effort and divine grace.

Chapter 2

Instruction In General

Q1. Modern life is very competitive and stressful and a majority of people do not know how to cope with it. Some of them have a vague notion that practice of a spiritual discipline can help them to live more peacefully. They have spiritual leanings but do not know how to fructify them. They visit temples etc., read scriptures, perform rituals and so on without making any substantive gains. How should they set about to embark on a spiritual journey? What is its nature? A1. The current age is characterised by rapid industrialization made possible by great advancements in research and development in every branch of science, especially in information technology that has made knowledge available to everyone at one's doorstep. It has led to globalisation of modern societies and breakdown of their traditional mores that were based on ethics and moral principles. People today are freer and less inhibited in wanting to satiate their passions. An average person, in the changed milieu, struggles hard to earn enough to keep up with the exponential growth in consumerism as well as an excessive indulgence in hedonism. Market economics encourage people to discard their conservative values of self-restraint by making them believe, through constant barrage of advertisements, that goal of human life is sensual gratification. The more one indulges in it, the happier one would be. Although many individual claim to give primacy to reason to solve their daily problems, yet it strikes very few, that the ephemeral nature of sensual pleasure can never satisfy anyone for long. Rather than find a way out of it most people slavishly follow the whims and fancies of their minds in the fond hope that they would discover a perennial source of happiness by doing so. They do not even pause to examine and analyse rationally the cause of their unhappiness nor why is it not possible to satiate all their desires. Some amongst them turn to religion, not so much to practise what the sages and seers have taught, but use it as a means to gratify their desires through divine intervention. A few of them have latent spiritual tendencies due to past karma but their notion of spiritual life is flawed. They believe that it is meant for killjoys who prefer to live in caves or torture their bodies by giving up all the so called good things of life. Then,

there are any number of god men and god women these days who promise
to take anyone to heaven in a matter of months if not in weeks, all of it for a
consideration of money. They put on holy garb and quote from scriptures to
entice the gullible to become their followers. In the context of above remarks,
an intelligent jiva (person) with a serious intent to begin a spiritual practice
should ponder on the following points. One, the happiness that a jiva seeks lies
within one's self and not without (i.e. in the external world). Two, no true guru
has ever advocated that an aspirant ought to leave his or her home and hearth
to pursue a spiritual discipline. One's home is as good a place to practise it as
any other. Three, merely being a good man or woman is not enough to earn the
reward of salvation. To indulge in the activities mentioned in the question as a
matter of routine to create an impression of being pious or to pray for the Lord's
intervention to solve a personal problem has very little to do with spiritual
growth. Four, a discerning jiva ought to realise that one's spiritual nature
cannot come to the fore by just doing meritorious acts (e.g. visit temples etc.).
Most people carry them out because they have been brought up to believe that
performance of rituals etc. would bring them all the happiness that they seek,
i.e., by fulfilling their material desires, hopes and wishes. Five, neither learning
nor good actions (as perceived by an individual; being good is a relative term)
nor cleverness of mind nor attending seminars etc. is of any help to a man or
woman who seeks divine solace. Six, anyone interested in a spiritual life should
introspect and reflect on the cause of one's unhappiness, which is primarily
due to non-satisfaction of innumerable desires. A jiva's chequered life is full
of pain and pleasure, mostly the former that is experienced due to either death
of a loved one or disease or loss in business etc. and the latter accrues from
sensual enjoyment gained through worldly objects (e.g. wife, husband, wealth,
property etc.). Even the rich and the powerful are unable to satiate all their
desires. The graph of happiness slides up and down on a daily basis. There is
nothing that is permanent in the world. Seven, a wise person should analyse
his or her present situation along the above lines and investigate how he or she
can find true and everlasting happiness. In this regard, he or she may consider
why is he or she happy in dreamless (or deep) sleep (one is always refreshed
and satisfied on waking up from it) as opposed to his or her experience in
either wakefulness or dream state, which is invariably a mix of pleasantness
and unpleasantness. A jiva is happy when the mind is at rest, as in deep sleep,
while it is not so when it is restless and agitated, as, for example in wakefulness.
The obvious conclusion is that mind free of thoughts (as in deep sleep) gives
it peace. Thus, self-analysis to discover the root cause of unhappiness as well
as to find ways to attain everlasting happiness is the starting point for most
people to begin a spiritual quest. There is no need at this stage to get involved
in larger metaphysical issues relating to nature of Reality, God, origin of life

and so on. Eight, a spiritual enquiry is defined as a search for absolute bliss within one's self and not without. To accomplish this goal, one needs to control the mind through self-effort and divine grace. Anyone who has a serious intent to launch a spiritual quest should seek a guru for guidance.

Q2. Does the above answer imply that only unhappy people take to spirituality? A2. No. The point being made is that no one can obtain perennial happiness from satisfaction of desires in the ever changing objective world. How can it be so when gratification of one desire gives birth to many more and not all of them can be satiated? The body is subject to disease, decay, old age and death; all of them cause grief and pain. Is there a man or a woman who claims that he or she has never suffered pain or unhappiness and would not like to experience bliss all the time? It is, however, generally true that those who are dissatisfied with their present condition (i.e. worldly life full of transitory pain and pleasure) take recourse to find means to overcome it. Many individuals take to spiritual life after undergoing a traumatic experience (e.g. death of a loved one). Those who are seemingly content with their current lives have neither the interest nor are they discerning enough to know that they are badly caught up in a quagmire (of ignorance) from which there is no escape and, as such, they have no incentive to change course.

Q3. What conclusions should one draw from the self-analysis mentioned above? A3. One should be able to deduce the following. A jiva's senses are actively involved in gaining ephemeral objective experience in wakefulness and dream state while they are dormant in deep sleep. The former gives a mixture of pain and pleasure whereas they are absent in the latter. Why is it so? Happiness accrues when the mind is dormant, as in dreamless sleep, but it is missing when it (i.e. the mind) is working, as in wakefulness and dreams. Thus, eternal happiness is attained only when the mind is made silent through conscious effort, unlike the state of deep sleep in which one is not aware of anything. This process is known as control of mind and it is the whole gist of divine wisdom, which the scriptures expound in great detail in various ways.

Q4. Is control of mind the sole means to be eternally happy? What role do religious practices associated with various sects and creeds have in it? A4. Control of mind is the only way to attain Self or God Realisation. A person who accomplishes it merges in a fathomless ocean of ineffable bliss and he or she is released from the endless vicious cycle of birth, death and re-birth. Mind is controlled through scientific application of one's intelligence over its vagaries, whims and fancies. Religious dogmas as practised by most people have little relevance to it because mental restraint is exercised through an internal process of introversion. External forms of worship, rituals, rites and other practices are beneficial to some extent when done out of devotion but are of little value if they are carried out mechanically.

Q5. How does spiritual practice differ from a religious one?
A5. Any effort done by the mind to know one's true nature (or the Self or God) is spiritual in nature. That is the essence of teaching of all gurus, saints, sages and prophets. An average follower of these holy beings does not practise their instruction, even when they are living, because it is not an easy process. He or she is taken in more by the outside world and often invents rituals and rites that are not authorised by his or her spiritual preceptor. It happens usually after the demise of the latter. Over a period of time, a set of dogmas, tenets, forms of worship and so on are created by the devotees of gurus etc. that are mostly at variance with the original teaching. A priestly class comes into being to enforce their compliance and, not unsurprisingly, there are enough gullible people who are ready to fall in line and be exploited. It is a play of politics, money and power. That is how most religions, as commonly perceived by the vast majority of people, have evolved. They miss the grain for the chaff. A wise student should adhere to the spiritual content of scriptural knowledge rather than follow religious doctrinarism.

Q6.How should an aspirant proceed after taking the first step (i.e. self-introspection)?
A6. One should seek sat sangha (company of a saint), which is an indispensable aid for anyone to grow spiritually and there is no better way to do so. Sat sangha should ideally be kept with a satguru (i.e. a divine incarnation in the guru aspect) and if that is not possible with at least a Self Realised person. An ordinary jiva is not discerning enough to know the greatness of such a man or a woman. One's karma (i.e. due to interconnection of previous lives) invariably leads one to such a holy being. In its absence, one should pray to the Lord sincerely to grant one the boon of sat sangha; an earnest entreaty made out of love and humility cannot but bear fruit. It is only with the greatest good fortune that one comes across a saint of that calibre. A wise seeker should avoid the company of self-styled gurus and godmen or god-women who are there to make money by having a large following. There are plenty of such frauds who have made spirituality into a business these days. One should also not be carried away by people who are adept at giving discourses but do not practise what they preach. It is better to associate with like-minded people, especially those who are engaged in serious practice (sadhana), till one discovers one's guru. Besides this, one should study scriptures to imbibe their knowledge through commentaries written on them by sages (as opposed to scholars) and autobiographies or biographies of sages and seers.

Q7. What benefit does a devotee get from sat sangha?
A7. What cannot be gained otherwise is obtained through sat sangha. The allusion is to divine grace without which an aspirant can neither begin his or her quest nor make effort to succeed in it. It is only through sat sangha that a devotee's search for a guru bears fruit. A satguru is the embodied form of the invisible and formless Lord (Ishwara) and who one can see and talk to. The powerful spiritual vibrations emanating from such a being are often enough to transform an aspirant's personality. The advantages of the company of a satguru are too numerous to be listed. What can be a greater reward than attaining Realisation through his or her grace? Know it for certain that association with a satguru is best of all aids and boons that an aspirant seeks. Sat sangha of others than a satguru is also beneficial but is not of the same grade. But, it does affect a person's mind and thoughts and impels one to take to a spiritual life.

Q8. What should one do in sat sangha?
A8. There are two aspects of sat sangha that a seeker must not ignore. One, to hear (sravana) about the Truth or God from a sage and two, to contemplate (mannana) on what one hears. These are the basic steps; one may question the saint to clarify one's doubts about various aspects of a spiritual enquiry including how one should set about it and what it involves. A guru's explanations about Reality and other related matters are usually of a general nature suited to the maturity levels of various seekers. After hearing, one should form a habit of contemplating on the words of wisdom, uttered by a sage, to imbibe its essence. There are some saints who do not talk much about spiritual matters. They do so to encourage students to begin practice (sadhana) at the earliest rather than indulge in mere talking. One can do that because practice gives the benefits of hearing and contemplation.

Q9. Should one accept a sage's word (or even scriptural knowledge) on faith or through rational analysis?
A9. Both attitudes are right; which one to adopt depends on individual mental proclivity. Most people seem to think that faith implies acceptance of a saint's teaching without considering it deeply. Real faith cannot develop without understanding the instruction because only then does it take firm root in the mind. One should, therefore, endeavour to grasp a seer's word to strengthen one's faith by querying him or her. Application of reason to critically examine the teaching is a good method provided it does not remain a mere intellectual exercise. How many persons are capable of considering an issue dispassionately and without prejudice to previously held views? Who has such knowledge that he or she can argue rationally with a saint? It needs to be borne in mind that a seer's knowledge is based on spiritual experience that an aspirant lacks. Thus, one cannot be too dogmatic about such matters. One should certainly use

intelligence to accept a guru's instruction but a beginner cannot carry it too far without sliding into intellectualism. Ideally, one should apply reason to imbibe a sage's word in a mental mode of humility and faith.

Q10. What is contemplation and how is it done? What is its importance?
A10. It is the inceptive form of meditation. It refers to one's ability to consider a guru's instruction (or scriptural knowledge) with a one pointed and concentrated mind. It means to reflect on an issue deeply (or to think about it in depth) not once but many times (maybe for days or months) till it is imbibed by the consciousness and becomes ingrained in it. The purpose of contemplation is to raise a strong and firm conviction in the mind about the veracity of the guru's teaching and the benefits that one derives from practising it. A jiva acts to fulfil a desire only if one is convinced of its beneficial effects. Thus, an aspirant is unlikely to begin serious practice unless he or she has a firm belief that he or she can be truly happy only if he or she follows the guru's instruction. To have such a potent conviction is not as easy as it may appear. A large number of devotees give up practice after some time because they lack it. A conviction arises only if one reflects on an issue with a discriminative mind, which, in its essence, refers to one's ability to reject wrong notions (picked up from listening to others or from reading) and eject them from the consciousness. It is only after one succeeds in doing so that one accepts the guru's teaching, which is then followed by the conviction mentioned above. It takes a long time to effect a mental change like that. Contemplation must be made into a habit by its constant practice, both before beginning the quest and afterwards till the goal (i.e. Realisation) is achieved. Only a contemplative person is capable of carrying out higher practices of any yogic discipline (e.g. meditation, remembrance of the Lord, self-enquiry etc.).

Q11. What is an aspirant's next step?
A11. One must then begin sadhana (practice) and it is the most crucial decision that one takes because spiritual growth is not possible without it. Neither study nor erudition nor even sat sangha (company of a saint) can substitute for it. An hour of earnest practice is better than a life time of learning.

Q12. What does practice imply and how is it conducted?
A12. Practice (sadhana) is the systematic and disciplined effort done regularly by an aspirant to put into effect the guru's teaching. It culminates in Realisation and must not be given up till that goal is achieved. One who indulges in practice is called an aspirant (sadhak) or seeker (of Truth).

Q13. What is the starting point of practice? When does it end?
A13. Sadhana begins only when a guru initiates an aspirant and in the process reveals the particular path or method that the latter should follow. Practice is

essential as long as a jiva's individuality (i.e. 'I'-sense), the root of the mind, is extant. It ceases only after the mind is destroyed; in other words, on attaining Realisation.

Q14. Can practice be done without a guru?
A14. No; a guru is a must for everyone.

Q15. Why is it essential to have a guru?
A15. It is the normal experience of all jivas that a new subject is learnt from a teacher who has acquired mastery over it. Even Einstein learnt physics from a professor. A spiritual journey takes one into an intangible and unknown territory crisscrossed with many apparently insurmountable and dangerous obstacles. How can an individual without any divine knowledge or power demolish them? The jungle of sensual experience created out of pride, jealousy, attachment, desire, greed, anger and so on is so vast as to be almost endless, besides being impenetrable without special guidance. A guru knows the way to go across it and has the spiritual power to take others with him or her.

Q16. Some modern day preachers of spirituality maintain that a guru is not required to attain Realisation. What merit do such views have?
A16. None whatsoever. It is a case of blind leading the blind. People who advocate views like the one mentioned in the question have no spiritual experience and are expounding knowledge that they neither understand nor practice. They do so only to make a fast buck and make a name for themselves in the world by acquiring a following. A serious aspirant should not concern himself or herself with them.

Q17. Who is fit to be a guru and what are his or her attributes?
A17. A guru should be able to remove the darkness of ignorance from an aspirant's mind and enlighten it with divine knowledge. A guru must have realised the true nature of his or her own Self or of Brahman (the ultimate Reality). A guru is an embodiment of divine qualities like love, discrimination, detachment, contentment, forgiveness, humility, grace, knowledge and so on. He or she must have the compassion to teach others. A guru occupies the foremost place in the hierarchical order of things (i.e. the visible phenomenon) created by the Lord.

Q18. Does a guru always appear in physical form? How does a devotee search for him or her?
A18. A guru may come in any form but he or she takes a human birth for most devotees. One may also have his or her vision (darshan) in the subtle body, usually in a dream or during prayers or while trying to meditate (without being initiated). A guru appears when an aspirant is ready to partake of divine grace.

One who seeks a guru must have an intense and strong desire (i.e. a constant longing) for spiritual guidance and solace. One must prepare oneself through regular prayer, worship and study (of scriptures) to fructify such a desire. It is not easy to come across a true guru and to do so is often a reward for deeply felt devotion. Those who are destined, due to past karma, to meet a guru do so at the appropriate time, provided they remain steadfast in their desire and devotion.

Q19. Do all Self Realised persons act as gurus?
A19. No. A guru is a special being authorised by God to save struggling souls. A guru must have the spiritual (i.e. tapas) power to be able to do so. Divine knowledge by itself is not enough; all Self Realised individuals have it but they do not have the power to grant salvation. Spiritual power of this type is acquired by gurus through the practice of an extremely hard form of a yogic discipline called tapas yoga. No ordinary aspirant can follow it and it is practiced only after attaining Realisation. Mastery over tapas yoga is acquired by divine incarnations and some ever free souls only.

Q20. Why does a guru need yogic (or tapas) power to guide aspirants?
A20. A jiva's (human being's) individuality (i.e. the 'I'-sense) is a creation of the omnipotent Lord. What power does one have to undo God's play (leela; the sensual world)? The Lord alone can reveal its mystery through Its divine grace. A jiva's mind looks outwards (to the world) to gratify its desires through sensual contact with external objects. An individual has been doing so for countless past lives, with the result that mental tendencies of extroversion have become so potent that one is powerless to exercise any meaningful control over one's self (or the mind). Extroversion of the mind is a primary cause of a jiva going through a cycle of temporary pain and pleasure. One cannot attain everlasting happiness or bliss until one is able to break mind's chronic habit of seeking happiness outside of itself. It can be done only if the mind learns to control itself by looking inwards to its point of origin. Guru's spiritual power helps an aspirant to introvert his or her mind, which he or she cannot do on his or her own. The guru gives this power to a devotee who then develops it through self-effort to attain Realisation. This point needs emphasis because a vast majority of people does not appreciate it; it is not mere knowledge, which one acquires through scriptures, that saves an individual but Realisation is attained only through divine grace (i.e. guru's yogic power).

Q21. How does a guru transfer his or her spiritual power to a seeker?
A21. It is done through initiation (deeksha). There are various methods of imparting it; the most common being through physical touch, as, for example, in the space between eyebrows (brikuti). It can be transmitted through any of the other senses; for instance, through sight or hearing (i.e. giving a divine

name or a mantra to a devotee for repetition). It may also be done in dreams or through a silent initiation in the mind. A guru may adopt any or all of the above ways to initiate a seeker. The power given is usually in seed form that requires self-effort by a devotee to germinate. Each aspirant gets the power according to individual capacity.

Q22. What does initiation signify? Is it carried out ceremoniously?
A22. It denotes a formal acceptance of a devotee by a guru, who then takes responsibility to guide one through his or her grace. A spiritual quest commences only after initiation. A guru gives instructions on what a devotee should do to control his or her mind. It is a particular form of teaching (unlike that given in scriptures, which is of a general nature, i.e., applicable to everyone) suited to the aspirant being initiated. It reveals the path to be followed and the method to do so. For example, a seeker is told how to meditate and on what aspect of God one should do so. It could be Its form, name, mantra or on one's self ('I'-ness) and so on. A guru may also lay down a minimum time for which practice should be done and may also give similar instruction on related matters. A devotee ought to clarify his or her doubts on various aspects of practice (e.g. diet, posture etc) at this stage. Teaching given during initiation, less points like timings, posture etc, should not be revealed to others, who may be imparted a different set of instructions. It is a form of self-restraint to do so. There may or may not be a formal ceremony to initiate aspirants. Each guru adopts a different method to do so. A point worth noting is that a guru does not reveal any secret method or mantra to control the mind. Various paths to do so are well known and described in scriptures. A real guru's initiation empowers them to be effective; for example, the divine name, Ram, has been in use since ancient times but a guru sanctifies it with his or her spiritual power when he or she initiates a seeker with it.

Q23. How should an aspirant approach a guru? Can the former test him or her before deciding to be initiated?
A23. A devotee should go to a guru with utmost humility and a sincere desire to learn from him or her. A true guru will never answer a vain question and an arrogant and a proud person is generally ignored by him or her. Can a droplet know the extent of a limitless ocean? It is height of conceit to imagine that an ignorant person can judge the spiritual greatness of a guru. Notwithstanding the above, an intelligent person can form a general opinion about a guru's attachment to money, relations, name in the world etc. Those who display such tendencies are not genuine gurus, even if they have evolved a little or have a few powers that often mesmerize gullible people lacking in discriminatory intelligence. A marked characteristic of a guru is to treat everyone, irrespective of race, colour, caste, creed etc. alike.

Q24. How does one know that one has come to the right guru?
A24. A guru is known only by his or her grace. Karmic connection (of the past) usually leads one to a guru who appeals to one instinctively. Usually, one feels peace and calm in the presence of a real guru or his or her words create a lasting impression on one's mind. After initiation, an aspirant should assess whether he or she has grown spiritually in terms of control on desires, mental tranquility and so on, provided he or she has followed the guru's instructions for practice in letter and spirit. Although exact subjective judgments on spiritual progress are invariably wrong, yet a beginner can get a rough idea of how one is doing on the above points after a practice of six months or so and even longer. One has obviously got into wrong hands if there is no real progress (in control of mind or senses) even after a year's or so practice.

Q25. What are the types of gurus?
A25. There are two primary categories; those anointed by the Lord and the self-appointed ones. The latter outnumber the former many times over and they are those who go by the name of god-men and god-women these days. Their distinctive mark is to put on a holy garb, give lectures, organise spiritual camps or retreats and generally make unfounded claims that they are reviving some ancient path long forgotten by ordinary people. Some of them have read a few scriptures while the others might have acquired a little spiritual knowledge or some psychic powers like predicting the future. None of them is able to conquer the ego. A few of them proclaim their divinity (i.e. 'I am God') and acquire a large following. They are out to dupe the gullible and the ignorant, of which there is a vast number. Know it for certain no one becomes a guru by mere talking about spiritual knowledge; one has to do intense penance (tapas) to attain that exalted status through grace of God. There is no other way. There are two further categories amongst the gurus ordained by the divine will. One, the satgurus or sadgurus; two, the ordinary gurus and they are both egoless. A satguru is an incarnation of Ishwara (God) who takes birth as a divine guru to save all those who take refuge in him or her. An ordinary guru is the embodied form of an ever free soul (a category of beings who are eternally liberated and have been created by the Lord to carry out specific divine tasks) or a god or a goddess (e.g. god Shiva, Vishnu, goddess Saraswati and so on). Although both satgurus and gurus do tapas (practice of a special yogic discipline) either in the subtle sphere or in this world, yet their spiritual power and the authority to grant salvation differs. A satguru has no limitation on his or her spiritual power and is the sole authority to give complete freedom to an aspirant. An ordinary guru enjoys limited power and can, at the most, grant a lower type of salvation, which, in effect, implies a sojourn for a limited period in one of the lokas or heavens (e.g. Brahma or Vishnu loka). A guru generally prepares devotees for their eventual liberation by a satguru. In practical terms, a satguru

is able to take a seeker to highest samadhi (sahaj nirvikalpa samadhi) resulting in Realisation whereas a guru is capable of guiding devotee to lower samadhi (savikalpa and bhava). Know it for certain that a satguru is a rare being and, although present in every age, is not found commonly. For instance, there have been only two saints (amongst the well-known names) of the satguru category in the last hundred years or so in India; they are Sri Ramakrishna and Sri Raman Maharishi. A satguru is referred to as a guru in normal parlance. This work regards only a satguru as being competent to teach and save struggling souls.

Q26. How does a guru teach?
A26. He or she may teach in absolute Silence in which there may be no verbal contact with a devotee. It is a rare form of instruction and only a satguru is capable of doing so. The other method is through speech or its combination with that of Silence, which again a satguru alone can do. A guru confines himself or herself to just one path while a satguru instructs on all disciplines and may even create a new yogic method to suit prevailing circumstances. A guru's words and actions are meant to teach others; one should be discriminative enough to learn from them.

Q27. How does a guru shower grace on a seeker?
A27. An aspirant meets a guru only by divine grace. It is in response to a heartfelt desire and earnest prayer that a guru guides a devotee to his or her abode. He or she gives instruction out of grace; same is the case with initiation. The all-knowing guru oversees every step that an aspirant takes during practice and does not fail to show the way till Realisation. One encounters many impediments in practice and the guru's grace removes them, often without even one's knowledge. Remember, a satguru's grace is omnipotent and infinite.

Q28. Does a guru test a devotee before and after initiation?
A28. A satguru does not deny grace to anyone for initiation. Gurus initiate people selectively because they have a limitation placed on their yogic powers; they can save only a fixed number or a certain class or grade of persons. All gurus test seekers for faith, devotion, steadfastness etc. before allowing them to progress during practice. It is for the benefit of devotees that their advancement is controlled by the guru. For, spiritual improvement is accompanied by release of spiritual energy that may cause problems unless one prepares for it adequately.

Q29. What should one expect from a guru?
A29. Nothing in the material sphere. Desires and cravings manifest due to an individual's ego, which one must control to restrain the mind. Ideally, therefore, one should not expect a guru to satiate one's worldly desires because to do so

would increase attachment to external phenomenon. It is, of course, easier said than done in the case of most devotees. They should learn to exercise control over their hopes and wishes. A guru may, on his or her own, fulfil some material desire of a devotee provided it would aid in one's spiritual growth. Again, it is best to practice desirelessly to make rapid strides in the spiritual sphere. Desire for experiences etc. must be curbed. Desire for liberation or salvation does not cause bondage and one may entertain it during practice but even that should be given up before it ends.

Q30. What attitude should a seeker adopt with a guru?
A30. The wise ones regard their gurus as their all in all. A satguru should be venerated and worshipped as the Lord in human form because there is no difference between them. An individual's conduct with other jivas is determined by the relationship that one has with them. For example, a man's behaviour with his mother differs from that with his wife. In the same way, devotees are advised to form a definite mental relationship with the guru who will then respond accordingly. It cements one's association with a guru and establishes a pattern of conduct through which one develops and manifests qualities like love, devotion and faith. The main relationships that one may assume are those between a child – parent (i.e. guru as a father or a mother or both) or of a benign master – servant or of two friends or of beloved – lover or of guru – disciple. The last two are difficult to form because they require very high degree of self-control and the ability to surrender oneself to the guru. They are suitable for very mature disciples. Friendship is between equals and an aspirant should not equate oneself with the guru. The best relationship for ordinary students is to regard the guru as a father or a mother or both and also as a loving master. They get the same benefits from them as more ripe seekers obtain from other relationships.

Q31. How is a guru served or worshipped? How often should one meet him or her after initiation?
A31. The best form of service or worship is to practice sincerely and diligently the guru's teaching. Also, to do sewa (service) to others, especially the needy, sick, poor etc because a satguru dwells in every heart. A mature disciple may not need to meet a guru again after initiation; for, he or she knows that the latter's real form inheres in the heart. A beginner should endeavour to keep a guru's company as much as possible according to circumstances. Physical association with satgurus is often not essential for those who practice regularly and earnestly.

Q32. Should a devotee emulate a guru?
A32. No; a guru is a unique being and his or her status in the divine scheme of things (i.e. the created order) is unattainable even by gods (e.g. Brahma)

etc. The trinity of gods (i.e. Brahma, Vishnu and Shiva) also gained their powers of creation, preservation and dissolution through the grace of a divine guru only. An aspirant should not, even by a gesture, try to copy or imitate a guru's conduct. One may attain union with the absolute Reality but never with the guru. Even the greatest saints keep their gurus on a special pedestal of reverence and veneration. A guru sets an example of selflessness and displays divine qualities like motiveless love, devotion, detachment etc. A seeker should endeavour to develop them to the maximum degree.

Q33. What should a devotee aspire for once practice begins under the guidance of a competent guru?
A33. Complete freedom from ignorance through control of individual mind is the only worth-while goal for the wise. Anything lower than that is not a state of permanent bliss and although one might obtain temporary relief (e.g. a sojourn in a heaven), yet it does not end the vicious cycle of pain and pleasure represented by repeated birth and death.

Q34. Why does the Guru Upanishad give attainment of eternal happiness as the primary aim rather than acquisition of divine knowledge, which is the most accepted view of sages?
A34. There is no dispute with what the seers say because real knowledge and true bliss are symbolic of the same state (of Realisation). Guru Upanishad gives prominence to absolute bliss as the ultimate goal because everyone seeks happiness, even in worldly life, whereas only a small number of persons aspire for knowledge, which is considered by most people to be dry and rather highbrow (and, hence, out of their reach). It is to make the final destination more acceptable to everyone that the Guru has set the above goal.

Q35. Ignorance is rather a vague concept for most readers to grasp. What, in specific terms, must an aspirant seek in practice?
A35. Non-knowledge of Reality is ignorance and, hence, every form of subjective and objective knowledge falls in this category. The mind itself is a product of ignorance (maya) and, hence, to destroy it implies the end of the latter. The mind's functioning is explained in the next Chapter but, for the time being, the palpable form of the mind is the bundle of thoughts that arise in it ceaselessly in rapid succession. The root of all of them is the 'I' thought or the feeling of 'I am' or 'I'-ness that everyone is familiar with. This feeling is never absent (not even in sleep) in an individual and is used to refer to oneself all the time. The 'I' is the point of origin of the mind or forms its centre and, hence, is the core of individual ignorance. Thus, to destroy ignorance implies the elimination of the 'I' feeling from the mind. That is the essence of control of mind and one should aspire for it in practice.

Q36. What happens if the 'I'-sense becomes extinct?
A36. The pure consciousness then shines as the absolute Reality and there is nothing beyond It. That is the state of true happiness (or bliss) and real knowledge. One who attains it is said to be liberated (from the bondage of the 'I' or ego sense) or free (from ignorance). Salvation is another name for the same state.

Q37. What is bondage?
A37. To be attached to one's self ('I'-ness), the body and the world is bondage. It binds a jiva to an endless chain of birth, death and re-birth to undergo a ceaseless experience of transitory pleasure and pain, mostly the latter. The 'I' or the ego sense is the primary bondage for a jiva. The individual consciousness is bound to its 'I'-ness and is liberated only after its disappearance (through effort and divine grace). The secondary form of bondage is the 'I''s attachment to the external world and the body that it creates for its pleasure. Bondage to the world and body (in that order) is destroyed prior to tackling the ego.

Q38. Who has created the 'I' sense and bondage?
A38. Ishwara (God) is the sole creator of all that exists. The ideas of 'I'-ness, liberation, bondage and the world inhere in the divine consciousness naturally. The Lord manifests them through Its supreme intelligence and will power.

Q39. Why has the Lord done so?
A39. It is a natural function that It cannot help but perform. Just as it is the sun's nature to give light, so also, it is God's to create the sensual phenomenon. Ishwara indulges in a never ending divine play (leela) involving creation, preservation and dissolution of the world, which is followed by re-creation again. The Lord has created ignorance as well as knowledge and liberation as also bondage. The 'I' sense, the body and the jiva have manifested by Its omnipotent will.

Q40. How can an individual undo (i.e. eliminate the 'I' or control the mind) what the omnipotent Lord has created?
A40. No jiva has the power to control the mind all by oneself. It can only be done through divine grace and, hence, the importance of a satguru who dispenses it to devotees.

Q41. If that be so, why should one make any effort to control the mind?
A41. Effort is essential because divine grace accrues through it only.

Q42. Many scriptures state that God is the sole doer and It acts through jivas. How can a devotee then exert to exercise restraint on the self ('I')?
A42. All problems end if one realises through spiritual experience that the Lord is all pervasive and nothing moves without Its will. Merely talking about it is

not good enough. One cannot find God as long as one's ego or the 'I'-sense is intact. The 'I' imagines that it is a separate and different entity from, not only other objects but from the Lord also. The 'I' of an individual impels one to act in both the material and spiritual spheres. Thus, it is in the nature of mind and, hence, of a jiva to do actions. Effort is required only to know through experience that God alone is. It is a high state of spiritual advancement in which one can see and feel the Lord's presence everywhere. Scriptures describe it for the benefits of devotees.

Q43. What is grace?
A43. It denotes divine pleasure and blessing. Just as a rich man distributes money when he is happy and pleased (with good fortune), so also does the Lord shower gifts on those It is pleased with for their love, devotion and remembrance. It may take the form of some material benefit but God draws close to Itself those It is most pleased with. This act of giving (by the Lord) and receiving (by a devotee) is known as divine grace. It is all pervasive and available to every object in equal measure, just as wind blowing across the ocean is to all sailing boats. But, only those sailors make use of it who set sails on their vessels and the rest stay stranded where they are. Similarly, a worldly person does not seek divine grace for spiritual upliftment but wants only material advancement that accrues as an effect of one's karma more than any other factor. An aspirant, on the other hand, prays for grace to have a vision of the Lord who is then pleased to guide him or her on the right path.

Q44. What is self-effort?
A44. It refers, in a general way, to any action done by the mind and the body to achieve a particular object. However, in the spiritual context, it alludes to the disciplined, regular and dedicated endeavour made over a long period of time, to realise one's Self (Atman). It is called sadhana (practice) when done under the guidance of a guru.

Q45. How is divine grace earned?
A45. Effort done rightly and sincerely to control the ego sense is the surest way to please the Lord. It finds special favour with It if one truly loves God and is fully devoted to serve It or Its creation. A simple and a humble person who remembers the Lord with devotion is indeed very blessed.

Q46. What is right effort?
A46. Effort must be done with dedication, earnestness and all one's energy to achieve one's goal, i.e., control of mind. It goes waste if that is forgotten. For instance, the time that one spends in reciting scriptures without understanding them or repeating a divine name without exercising restraint on the mind is of little spiritual benefit. To remember the Lord (i.e. through repetition of Its

name) while controlling the flow of extraneous thoughts is the right kind of effort.

Q47. Out of divine grace and effort, which is more important for spiritual growth?
A47. Divine grace is omnipotent and infinite in nature. There is nothing that it cannot do or undo. Self-effort (by an individual) is finite and capable of accomplishing limited goals only. There is, therefore, per se no comparison between the two. But, that is not the point at issue; what a devotee needs to understand is the link between the two and not what each can achieve. The Lord (or the guru) does not favour a person with grace capriciously. Why would the supremely intelligent Being give grace to one and deny it to the other? Grace accrues only when an individual makes the effort to know God. Thus, grace and effort are equally important for self-improvement. The more the effort, greater is the grace and vice versa. The wise ones know that grace is a quality of one's own mind, which manifests only when effort is made (by the mind) to arouse it from its latent state.

Q48. There are some people who maintain that Ishwara (God) would save them out of Its pleasure at some time in the future and they need not make any effort. Are they right to think so?
A48. Only the most ignorant entertain such absurd views. Those who say such things are weaklings incapable of escaping from the powerful net of maya (or the world). The Lord is pleased only with those who endeavour to earn Its grace; others would have to wait endlessly to be saved.

Q49. Is divine grace to control the mind available equally to men and women?
A49. Yes. Anyone who makes the proper effort receives grace according to its (i.e. effort's) quality and individual capacity. The Lord makes no distinction between male and female genders.

Q50. If that be so, why is there a general acceptance, even by some holy men, of the prevailing views, often ascribed to many sages of the past, that women cannot attain salvation on their own?
A50. All those who propagate such ideas are ignorant fools. Know it for certain that no true saint ever preaches against women or talks ill of them. Many of the words said to have the sanction of the seers of the past have been inserted in some scriptures by the priestly class and other interested parties to maintain their sway over society. Inferior status of women in the social order is a creation of men to suit their own self-importance and the prevailing circumstances. There is no divine sanction for it and it does not certainly affect a woman's capacity to grow spiritually.

Q51. There is a view that women become impure when they go through the monthly menstrual cycle. Is it valid?

A51. No; it has no effect on spiritual effort. The original injunction in such matters related to some women becoming irritable and listless during the menses. To avoid aggravation of their condition, they were advised then to avoid company (maybe for a day or so) and concentrate on the practice of discipline prescribed by a guru. The preachers and priests, ever ready to exploit the gullible, took advantage of such injunctions and imposed various restrictions on women during the above period (e.g. banned their entry to temples).

Q52. At what age can children take to spiritual life?

A52. Only when they can decide things for themselves. They should certainly not be forced into following a course of action that does not come naturally to them. They may develop aversion to it. An individual's karma impels him or her to launch a spiritual inquiry and it happens at the appropriate time. Children need proper education these days to get on in life. While doing that, a holy atmosphere at home would keep alive their latent spiritual tendencies for manifestation later on.

Q53. Is age a factor in beginning a spiritual quest? Can the sick do it? What about those who are illiterate or are not learned in scriptures?

A53. Old people (of any age) are as capable of making spiritual progress as others younger to them. The Lord is pleased with devotion more than any other attribute; those who have full faith in It are always saved. It should not be misconstrued to imply that effort is not required on their part. They can compensate for inability to do practice for many hours at a stretch (inhibited by age factor) by doing service (sewa) and being more devoted and having greater faith as well as developing other divine qualities like discrimination, contentment, humility etc. Those who are sick and diseased need to remember the Lord more than others because that is the surest way to alleviate their pain and worry. A guru would prescribe an appropriate path for them (i.e. suitable and easy to practice; for instance, repetition of a divine name). There is no bar on those who are not educated and lack scriptural knowledge to follow a spiritual path. Bookish or scriptural learning is not of any great help in pursuing a quest. In fact, it can act as a barrier because persons adept at it are invariably vain and carry such a heavy baggage of their own notions about spirituality that they are unable to shed it easily. Divine knowledge accrues on its own within a devotee's heart when he or she practices a guru's word.

Q54. Is there a bar on pursuing a spiritual discipline by various castes? Does race or creed make a difference?

A54. All created beings are equal in the eyes of the Lord. The sole way for It to judge individuals is the karma (mental and physical actions) that they do, specially its motive. The differences that one perceives amongst people is created by jivas themselves and one of the prime objects of practice is to remove them from one's mind. The grace of a satguru is available to all irrespective of their place of origin, race, creed, sex, language, looks etc. Everyone can follow a spiritual path with an equal chance of success.

Q55. Who all can launch a spiritual inquiry?
A55. All jivas should, especially in these stressful days of competitive modern living, but very few do it.

Q56. Why?
A56. They have no desire for it. One avoids doing an action for which there is no desire; for instance, a scholar devotes all his time to his research rather than divert his energy to become a great sportsman. Similarly, an average jiva is so deeply involved in the world that he or she does not think worth his or her while to change course. Even the interest of most people who talk about spirituality does not extend beyond solving some personal problem such as bereavement, loss in business, sickness etc. They revert to normal life after they find a temporary peace in the company of a saint. Only persons with a burning and an intense desire to find everlasting peace or God take to spiritual life seriously. Their number is small and they are indeed very blessed.

Q57. Is a deep desire the only factor to begin a spiritual life?
A57. No; it is the starting point. A jiva has innumerable desires but only those are gratified for which one strives. A desire gives birth to action if it is intense and one has the will power to execute it to its logical conclusion. A spiritual path is not meant for weaklings; only those who are mentally strong and are prepared to use their intelligence discriminatively can traverse it successfully.

Q58. Does one have to renounce the world to carryout sadhana (practice)?
A58. Yes and no. Renunciation is a mental act and not withdrawal into some mountain cave. The essence of spiritual enquiry is how to control the mind, which can be effected in one's home as successfully as anywhere else. Renunciation implies to detach the mind from the world and fix it on the Lord. The whole purpose of sadhana is to achieve that blessed state.

Q59. Does it imply that one should not do one's duty to the family? Who will look after children or earn money for their education etc.?
A59. The misgivings mentioned above are totally misplaced. It is a sin to neglect one's children, parents, family etc. Every jiva has a certain karma (e.g. earning wealth for the family) to perform in life, which cannot be averted. All that is

required is that it should be done in a detached manner, as a form of service. It is a very difficult ideal to accomplish but a guru's grace makes it possible through practice of his or her teaching. Spiritual practice can be carried out by anyone in the comfort of one's home irrespective of the profession being followed. A businessman has as good a chance to succeed in it as a soldier or a beauty queen or a scholar or a farmer or a worker etc. All that is required is to practice a guru's instruction faithfully and in the right spirit.

Q60. There are many taboos like eating meat, drinking liquor, indulging in sex etc. that are associated with spiritual life. Should a devotee give them up prior to commencing practice?
A60. No. An aspirant should continue with normal life style to which he or she is used to in the beginning of practice. There is no need to force oneself to give up anything because it causes aversion to practice. Moderate habits are a good aid for beginners and one may continue to satisfy basic bodily desires like sex in that spirit. The crucial point to understand is that desire for a thing or an object should disappear. Its forceful abnegation results in inner craving that is often difficult to control. Whatever has to be given up would happen on its own in practice (i.e. its desire would disappear).

Q61. What type of diet should one take during practice?
A61. A wholesome diet taken in moderate quantities is of great help in sadhana (practice). A satvic (suited for spiritual growth) diet based on milk, nuts, cereals, seasonal vegetables and fruits is good for aspirants because its subtle essences are in consonance with spiritual vibratory energy produced in the mind during practice. Salt, sugar, chilies, spices, onions, garlic etc. should be taken in small amounts only. One should avoid types of food that do not suit one's constitution. As a general rule, food that causes flatulence and is hard to digest, even after 4 – 6 hours, should not be taken. The importance of good diet increases as one progresses in spiritual life.

Q62. How much should one sleep?
A62. Neither too much nor too little. The requirement of sleep varies from individual to individual and depends on the work that one is engaged in. The body requires more rest (and a good diet) after hard physical labour. An aspirant must remain alert during waking hours, specially while engaged in practice. Laziness is a sign of lack of sleep or overeating or both of them. Even excessive sleep brings in lassitude.

Q63. What are the good timings for practice?
A63. The best time to practise is 2 – 3 hours before sunrise and at the time of sunset. The individual mind vibrates in consonance with the cosmic pranic (kinetic) energy that vibrates in the universe. It pulsates peacefully before the

sun rises and, hence, that time is suitable for practice; after that it becomes more agitated resulting in activity during the day. It begins to lose steam when the sun sets and one should take full advantage of it to do meditation then. It is easier to control the mind when the vibratory energy is undergoing a change. However, a beginner can sit for practice whenever it is convenient according to one's daily schedule. It is specially applicable to those who lead a busy working life these days.

Q64. Which is the best posture to adopt while doing meditation?
A64. One may sit down in any comfortable position that one finds relaxing and in which the body does not have to move too much, which should be kept as still as possible. Most people have lost the habit of sitting on the ground these days and it is hard for them to do so for practice. They may sit on a chair. Irrespective of the posture taken, one must try to keep the head, neck and chest straight in one line. One may even lie down for meditation as long as one can ward off sleep. Practice is best done with a relaxed mind and body.

Q65. Should an aspirant be meticulous in following the instruction on diet, sleep, posture etc.?
A65. All the points mentioned above, except for sat sangha (association with a saint), are minor aids to spiritual progress, specially for a beginner. One need not make a fetish about them because one can make reasonable progress without them. One often finds that some of the points mentioned above materialise on their own as one grows in spiritual life. Sat sangha is, of course, a major help and one cannot hope to move even an inch on a spiritual journey without it.

Q66. What are the types of aspirants who take up practice?
A66. They are categorised as satvic (high class; has purified and calm mind); rajasic (middling level with an active mind) and tamasic (lowest type; is mentally impure and lethargic). This classification is based on the development of divine qualities and how mature a seeker is to practise a guru's instruction seriously. A satvic mind is purified, to a large extent, of the dross of undesirable tendencies that leads to its loss of restraint. A satvic aspirant is motivated by divine qualities like love, devotion, discrimination, humility etc. and is fairly detached from the world. He or she is generally content and has very few desires. A devotee of that calibre has the best chance to control his or her mind and is capable of making good progress. One whose mind is highly purified and disciplined may even attain liberation provided one is prepared to put in real hard work with total devotion and full determination. A middling devotee is the worldly person with an extroverted mind (i.e. looking towards external objects to gratify desires, rather than inwards like a satvic mind). A person like that is outwardly religious, keen on rituals, visits holy places, reads scriptures

(quotes them often without understanding their essence) and is fond of showing off his or her (limited) knowledge. Those of them who take to a spiritual path practice it with enthusiasm initially, which often wanes later. However, rajasic devotees have a good chance to progress through service (sewa), which comes naturally to them. They can follow a discipline like that of remembrance of the Lord, which requires mental activity, quite successfully. A rajasic person needs to develop divine qualities, specially devotion and discrimination, to really purify his or her mind and be able to carry out advanced stages of any spiritual discipline. He or she has the potential to progress but must apply himself or herself very sincerely and earnestly. A tamasic person is mentally lazy and seldom uses intelligence to gain anything worthwhile. He or she has a dull mind with very little growth of divine qualities in it. He or she does not understand instruction even when it is explained to him or her. A devotee like that is best suited to do lower types of service like working in the kitchen (to serve a guru, other devotees etc), looking after the premises of a temple etc. He or she has a long way to go before starting a quest in right earnest. The above is a broad classification and it needs to be noted that no devotee is really of one type. Everyone has a mix of all the three types of minds mentioned above and one of them predominates at a time. It is only the ever free souls whose minds are highly purified and they remain so even in the travails of the world. They are the highest class of seekers. In general, the vast majority of seekers falls in the category of having a mixture of rajasic and tamasic tendencies with a heavy dose of the latter; their satvic content is very little. There are very few devotees in whom satvic attributes predominate.

Q67. How are the above categories distinguished in their approach to spiritual practice and its conduct? What is their broad percentage? Who amongst them is likely to begin a serious pursuit of a spiritual discipline?
A67. Out of a hundred devotees who seek a guru, ninety five percent would comprise the middling level (predominantly a mix of rajasic and tamasic tendencies). Two to three percent would be predominantly tamasic and the remainder falls in the satvic category. Persons who are satvic have become so due to past effort (i.e. done in previous lives). The above is a very broad way to classify devotees. Success in any spiritual endeavour is not time bound and it depends on one's devotion and determination to work hard to attain freedom from ignorance. For example, a rajasic person can outdo a devotee of satvic nature by sheer dint of perseverance because he or she would be bestowed with greater dose of divine grace. A beginner on a spiritual quest (mostly of rajasic nature) is characterized by having many doubts. He or she waivers quite a lot in deciding in how to set about practise. He or she would be more bothered about matters like diet, posture, giving up alcohol, sex and so on without realizing that none of them is an impediment to start the quest. Even if one is able to overcome

above doubts, there is every chance that one would be waylaid by religious bigotry, superstition, prejudice about one's caste, race, creed, gender and so on. A few are given to much talking without any corresponding action. Their practise ends even before it has begun. Some who decide to follow a spiritual path are likely to postpone it or do it lackadaisically on some pretext or another; like, where is the time for spiritual effort, I am a worldly person who has a family to support, a job to do, a party to attend, look after guests and so on. He or she is likely to bemoan his or her fate and blame everyone else including God for not being able to practise. That he or she is a weakling does not strike him or her. A few among this lot who do start practise give it up after some time. They develop fear of the unknown. Some (very few) will persist with their enquiring and make good progress. Tamasic aspirants have generally no doubts, due to lethargic minds; they are simple hearted and guileless. They are obedient but need constant prodding and guidance to do service selflessly. Their lack of understanding is their biggest obstacle. They can make good progress provided they stay in holy company (sat sangha). Devotees with satvic natures have the best chance to take up practice seriously but they also need to work hard with faith and sincerity. But many amongst them are erudite and learned and given to much thinking; they are clever in arguments and form their own notions about spiritual matters. Sometimes they even modify a guru's teaching as an assertion of their (bookish) knowledge. They are not likely to go far even if they begin practice. Irrespective of the above classification one of the most important factors that determines one's ability to begin the quest is to have an intense desire to seek freedom from a life of pain and pleasure (i.e. want perennial happiness). Everyone has an equal chance of success, no matter from where one begins the journey. The essential conditions to forge ahead are devotion and a strong will to work hard to begin practice and then sustain it. Divine grace accrues accordingly.

Q 68. How is will power strengthened?
A 68. Will is a function of intelligence; to use them both in a deliberate manner (e.g. in constant contemplation and then to act on the conviction gained) improves their efficacy. One must always learn to reflect on issues with a calm and a cool mind. Holy company (sat sangha) is a panacea for all ills that a devotee suffers from and so is it in the case of intelligence and will power. Its effect goes up manifold if practice is done sincerely through the grace of a guru.

Q 69. What is the duty of a devotee towards one's guru?
A69. To practise the guru's instruction sincerely and in right earnest is the best of all acts that a seeker can do. The guru has already conquered his or her ego and is desireless. There is nothing that a student can do for such an enlightened teacher who does not seek or need anything. By helping himself or herself to shed ignorance, a devotee aids the guru to accomplish his or her divine mission.

Q70. What should a seeker lay special stress on during practice?

A70. Practice cannot proceed on the right lines unless one develops divine attributes consciously and learns to apply them discriminatively. Mind is controlled through their application; their vibratory nature makes the consciousness peaceful and calm. At the same time, there are certain traits that agitate the mind; they must be given up because they are harmful and cause bondage, unlike their divine counterparts that bring freedom (from ignorance). Divine qualities are intrinsically more potent than the undesirable ones.

Q71. What are the divine qualities that an aspirant needs to nurture?

A71. There are many of them and, taken collectively, they indicate a person's suitability to pursue a spiritual inquiry in terms of individual mental strength. There is no yardstick to quantify how much of them one needs. Each attribute has an infinite spectrum of development and the more one has of it, the better it is. A devotee should always feel that he or she does not have these attributes in adequate measure and in that spirit he or she is likely to develop them more and progress faster. Some of the divine attributes are discussed in the succeeding paras:-

(a) **Love**. It is a mystic feeling of magnetic attraction that inheres in the mind to find its source. It is by its nature highly blissful, peaceful and tranquil. In the worldly sense, it manifests as attachment that binds individuals as relations, friends etc. Spiritually, it refers to the heart's pining and longing for union with the beloved Lord. Love arises due to a feeling of separateness caused by the ego, between a lover and the Beloved. It is like a gale when fully developed. The difference between worldly love (i.e. attachment) and its divine counterpart needs to be noted; the former causes bondage and the latter liberation. Of all the countless attributes that God has, divine love is the foremost and of all the powers that It has none can match it. Know it for certain that even the greatest yogis (those who master divine power) revere those who have love (for the Lord) in their hearts. Demons are powerless to act against them and gods worship them. Such is its extraordinary uniqueness. Every devotee should pay particular attention to develop love and it is not difficult because all human relationships are based on it. Love exists between parents and children, amongst friends, with relations and so on but it is selfish and motivated to please the ego. Divine love, on the other hand, is universal, selfless and a very potent means to conquer the ego. It manifests fully when a devotee's heart turns into an ocean of love that regards all objects, animate and inanimate, with equal love. It is not possible for an ordinary aspirant to love the invisible Lord. But, as a start, one should make an attempt to love others as much as one does one's own relations, friends etc. One should regard all created objects as being forms of the Lord (or one's guru) and love them accordingly. Being solicitous, caring, showing concern or serving others are signs of growth of love. Love developed along these lines grows into a giant tidal wave that rises up to engulf the Lord in its tight embrace. A feeling of divine love is self-purifying and its power subsumes every other thought in it, which results in mental concentration of the highest order. It is a prime quality without which no spiritual progress is possible, irrespective of the path that one follows.

(b) **Devotion**. It is closely related to the above attribute and denotes the single mindedness of a devotee with which he or she loves or pursues a spiritual goal. Love is sustained, even when it is unrequited, by deep devotion and so is steadfastness and dedication during practice. Devotion to the Lord or the guru impels one to begin a spiritual quest and later it ensures that one stays on course, despite setbacks caused by fear and doubt. Those who give up practice lack devotion and it is a serious weakness that many suffer from. Divine love does not mature unless one is truly devoted to the Lord. The practice of any path does not fructify without it. An aspirant encounters obstacles of various kinds during practice and they are over come through devotion. A guru invariably tests a seeker's devotion (and faith) before permitting one to advance further on the quest. The best way to develop devotion (and love) is to do so for its own sake; devotion for devotion's sake is the ideal of the wise.

(c) **Discrimination**. It is a quality of the utmost importance for serious aspirants. No substantive self-improvement is possible without it and its role in reaching the final goal becomes increasingly more crucial as one gets close to it. The destruction of the 'I', the last phase of the control of mind, cannot take place unless one has a very highly developed sense of discrimination. In very simple words, discrimination refers to sharpness of intelligence and its proper use to attain a desired object or end. Ordinary people use it to make worldly gains but aspirants employ it to give them up. Discrimination is a power of intelligence that makes a distinction between good and bad, false and true and Real and unreal. It is a form of rational analysis that leads to deductions based on reason. The essence of discrimination, however, lies in one's ability to reject (i.e. eject from the mind) what is false and accept (i.e. imbibe in the mind) what is true. Based on it, one then decides on a course of action, which is put into effect through will power. For instance, contemplation done on a guru's teaching through discrimination should reveal its veracity and lead to rejection of previously held false beliefs (about spirituality). The proper course of action thereafter is to begin practice, i.e., to put into effect the deductions made through the faculty of discrimination. One must use this power throughout practice to reject all forms of subjective and objective experiences. A majority of aspirants lack this attribute and even if they have it, use it rarely or fail to develop it properly. It is a major and serious weakness that detracts from the efficacy of practice.

(d) **Compassion**. It is another attribute that must be cultivated for self-improvement on a spiritual quest. To feel the pain of others (including animals, birds etc.) is compassion. It is closely related to the quality of love. Parents feel the pain of the children because they love them. The same is true for ones relations, friends, pets and so on. That is not real compassion, because it manifests more out of attachment than any other factor. One must know that the Lord experiences the same suffering that any creative being goes through because it does not regard any one apart from It. A true devotee should adopt the same attitude. It does not come easily because an ego centric person cannot look beyond oneself. This quality is best developed through practice (of the spiritual disciple); ones heart become stronger as the mind gets purified and then one begins to feel pain of others. To see someone suffer and not do anything about, is lack of compassion. One must do whatever possible to alleviate the pain of others. To serve others selflessly is an excellent means to develop compassion.

(e) **Detachment**. It is the opposite of attachment that afflicts all jivas. Everyone is attached through the senses to the external objective world. The so called love for one's family, children, friends etc. is no more than ego's attachment to them. People are attached to their homes, property, wealth etc. Then, there is attachment to one's body in all its three forms (physical, subtle and causal). To break sensual and mental contact with them is called detachment or renunciation or dispassion and to attain it is one of the primary purposes of practice. One of the important indicators of spiritual advancement is the degree of detachment that one develops in practice. The acme of detachment is reached when the 'I' sense ceases to be and it (i.e., the 'I'-sense) is not aligned with the actions that the body does.

(f) **Faith**. To have self-belief (i.e. to believe that one is capable of accomplishing a goal despite all odds) and have complete trust in the guru is called faith. One must have faith that the guru's teaching would lead to salvation and that he or she would save one from impediments enroute. At the same time, one must have a strong conviction that one's effort cannot but succeed. A wavering and an indecisive mind that continues to have doubts (often created by karmic failures) betrays lack of faith in one's self and the guru, which results in giving up practice.

(g) **Fearlessness**. Fear is a fundamental emotion and one of the most serious hurdles to control the mind. All jivas are beset by it in one form or the other; the most basic being the loss of one's individuality. Fear arises due to a sense of duality; as long as there is a feeling of another (object or jiva) fear in one form or the other persists. Only the Lord is fearless because It knows that there is nothing besides It. Many aspirants experience fear during practice for reasons that are not clear to them. A devotee must overcome such feelings through prayer and faith (in the guru). Fear is conquered only through divine grace during practice. One should adopt a deliberate mental attitude of fearlessness and carry on with practice with a firm conviction that the guru would not allow one to be harmed. It is a mental block that can be removed with effort.

(h) **Perseverance**. It is often not realised that practice demands a lot of hard work if one is serious about it. It is not a spare time indulgence. One must be regular and diligent in practice. There are many times that an aspirant feels like giving up practice for a variety of reasons; for example, a self-perceived lack of progress, ill health, bad luck in business etc. A wise student should not be deterred by such karmic factors that are of a temporary nature. One must press on regardless determinedly and not rest till the final experience is attained.

(i) **Open Mind**. Most people suffer from some prejudice or the other; many regard their religions as the best and others their gurus and deities the greatest. They think that practice of a spiritual discipline that their religious orders do not teach would make them unacceptable to their people. Some have their own notions of what spirituality is all about or how a guru ought to behave or what their scriptures teach and so one. Such views are a reflection of a closed and a narrow mind that fails to appreciate the real import of the universal and catholic teaching of all saints, which is misinterpreted by ignorant preachers and community leaders. It has very little relevance to religions as practiced by most people. A discriminative aspirant ought to keep his or her mind open to accept new ideas through rational analysis or better still through spiritual experience. At the same time, one must not have pre-conceived notions about a spiritual quest and, if held, one should be prepared to eject them after due deliberation. A biased and jaundiced mind is unlikely to effect much self-improvement.

(j) **Humility**. Practice should be carried out in a spirit of humility, which implies a strict check on one's ego. Conceited and vain persons are used to much talking and boasting but are hollow from within. Truly humble aspirants set about practice without making a show of it and are amenable to self-discipline and accept the guru's instruction more easily. Humility in its real sense manifests only on disappearance of the 'I' sense but one should cultivate it deliberately till that blessed moment comes. Jealously is an enemy of humility and must be curbed at all costs.

(k) **Contentment**. Mind's agitation is directly related to the desires that it entertains because its nature impels it to activity to gratify them. The mind becomes more restless when some of its cravings, hopes and wishes are not fulfilled; it is so because they are countless in number and forever on the increase. Contentment refers to a state of mind that is at peace with itself because it is desireless and does not seek anything that does not come on its own. No one can be happy till one is content with one's lot. Contentment comes only through progress in practice. It is of great help if a devotee endeavours to renounce false hopes and desires that it can never satiate.

Q72. How are the above attributes graded and developed?

A72. The overall state of mind determines the general level of qualities that an aspirant has. Mind is classified as satvic (purified), rajasic (middling level) and tamasic (impure); it is so according to the impact of maya's three attributes (gunas; satoguna, rajoguna and tamoguna) on the individual consciousness, which are discussed in the next Chapter. Both desirable and undesirable qualities are present in every mind; some of them are developed to varying degrees while the others remain dormant. Divine qualities grow in practice as the mind is purified. For instance, a satvic mind is imbued with divine attributes like devotion, detachment, faith etc. naturally, i.e., they grow on their own in a purified mind. Most worldly people have rajasic minds with a strong dose of impurities, which are characterised by a predominance of undesirable qualities like attachment, greed, pride etc. Devotion and other good attributes are not absent in them but they need to grow through practice done by the grace of a guru. Their embryonic (i.e. tamasic) form grows through its rajasic (middling level) and satvic (higher level) grades. Besides practice, sat sangha (holy company) is an excellent aid to nurture them. Another way is to be conscious of their importance and try to develop them through self-introspection deliberately.

Q73. What are the qualities that help a seeker grow the most spiritually during practice?

A73. Each attribute contributes to effecting control of mind and growth of one generally affects the others (i.e. qualities) also. Notwithstanding that, divine love is undoubtedly the prime quality to have. Those who have it are indeed truly blessed because its manifestation betokens divine grace as well as a high degree of mental purity. No one can develop love for the Lord without heartfelt devotion, which impels a jiva to seek It in the first place. No real progress on any path (including that of love) is possible without a well matured faculty of discrimination. Nor can one introvert the mind without detachment from the world. Generally, all other attributes develop on their own if one has a high level of the above traits. Devotion and discrimination is an ideal combination to possess and love germinates in a mind purified by them.

Q74. Discrimination is not an easy quality to develop; even most serious aspirants regard it as too esoteric and do not pay enough attention to apply it properly. How can they make up for it?

A74. The above observation is valid to a large extent but a serious seeker should certainly not consider it as too unique and beyond his or her ability to develop. In simple language, discrimination is no more than using one's head logically. Most people do it in their worldly affairs. All that is required is to apply it in the same manner during practice to control one's mind; learn to ignore thoughts, experiences, visions etc and concentrate on what the guru has instructed to do and discrimination will grow on its own. That is all there is to it. An aspirant should try to develop it as much as one can. Those who cannot ripen it to any great degree should compensate for it by being truly devoted to God (or the guru) and have love for It. They should carry out practice in a spirit of self-surrender. Know it for certain that a devotee imbued with divine love and a single minded devotion for the Lord and an abiding faith in Its grace is invariably saved even if his or her faculty of discrimination is not very highly developed.

Q75. What are the undesirable attributes that affect control of mind?

A75. These qualities cause restlessness in the mind and make it infirm and impel it to look outwards (i.e. the external objective world) to seek sensual gratification. Mind cannot be controlled as long as they exist. They are the chief cause of bondage to repeated birth and death, as also, of unhappiness. Divine traits grow only if they are given up. Some of them and their effects are discussed below:-

(a) **Attachment**. The 'I' sense of an individual creates the objective phenomenon for its pleasure and it has an almost unbreakable umbilical connection with the latter through the senses. It is termed as attachment, which is just another name for bondage. It is the primary cause of mental extroversion and one cannot introvert the mind (to its point of origin, i.e., 'I'-sense) till it is broken. Attachment develops over countless past lives, which chains the mind so badly to the world that it requires extraordinary effort and divine grace to sever it. All evil attributes stem from it. A jiva is attached more specifically to parents, children, husband, wife, friends, wealth, property, name, fame etc. Another form of attachment is to one's body, desires, cravings, hopes, wishes etc. The most serious of all is the feeling of 'I'-ness that binds the consciousness to it. Attachment to external objects is the chief cause of individual suffering, as also, of the cycle of birth, death and rebirth.

(b) **Desire**. The individual 'I' manifests in the consciousness to satisfy its inherent desires. They sustain it in a never ending chain of life after life. Desire is like an ever burning fire that keeps the mind on the boil (agitated) ceaselessly. Desire propels the mind towards outside objects, which then gets attached to them; sensual experience is the fuel that keeps the fire of desire burning all the time. It heats up the consciousness (or mind) in the form of turmoil, agitation and restlessness (i.e. the unceasing eruption of thoughts). The number of desires that a jiva has is infinite and the effort that one can do to satiate them is finite. All of them, cannot, therefore, be gratified, which causes mental tension, worry, anxiety and misery. Unfulfilled desires force the mind to seek more and more objective experience, which impels it to assume a body in every birth to satisfy them. Desire is the primary contributor to human bondage and the mind cannot be introverted till one learns to control it. Although all desires are bad, yet to long for liberation is non-binding and might in fact, sublimate them if it is really intense and long lasting. In the end, even that must be given up.

(c) **Doubt**. An individual is firmly convinced, due to past habit (formed in innumerable previous lives), that one is really the 'I' that associates itself with the body and the world. That is the fundamental doubt from which everyone suffers. The 'I' manifests only because the consciousness entertains a doubt about its true (absolute) nature, which arises due to ignorance (maya) inherent in it. It also sustains its existence. The objective knowledge that the mind gains through sensual contact is never complete due to doubt. A man wants to see a beautiful woman again and again because every time he looks at her a doubt creeps up in his mind that there is more to her than meets the eye. Doubt leads to mental indecision and restlessness, which results in lackadaisical action. A person afflicted with doubt moves about aimlessly, often in search of things that one is not sure of. The cycle of birth and death and, indeed ignorance, cannot end till doubt about one's real Self (Atman) does not disappear. Doubt, along with fear produces negative tendencies of the mind, as also impure thoughts.

(d) **Fear**. The 'I' of a jiva is inherently insecure due to an inbuilt fear that it would be caught out for its imaginary existence. The consequence is that it refuses to look at its own self, just like a scared child who closes his or her eyes in darkness. It does not investigate its real nature and looks outwards (to the world) as a defensive measure. An extroverted mind suffers from fear due to the sense of duality. It sees others as more powerful, richer, better looking, enjoying better luck and so on. Then, there is the insecurity caused by non-fulfilment of desires and of what the future holds. There is fear of death, ill health, loss of a loved one, failure etc. There is no one who does not fear something or the other. It numbs the mind and induces it to take irrational actions. It creates prejudice, superstition and impairs the mind's functioning. No one can traverse a spiritual path till one learns to tackle fear by detaching oneself from the world and, more particularly, to face boldly the prospect of losing one's identity ('I'- ness).

(e) **Pride**. It is an offshoot of the ego, which makes it to proclaim its supposed superiority over other jivas and objects. It is a false feeling that the 'I' manifests for its satisfaction and pleasure. Pride agitates the mind and often plunges it to depths of depression when it is hurt or causes anger and irritability if it is slighted or if its wishes are not gratified. Proud people seldom indulge in self-introspection to change course and rarely learn to control their minds. Pride may manifest even in practice if one develops some powers. Pride is the enemy of wisdom and does not allow the mind to break its connection with the world, which it wants to dominate.

(f) **Greed**. To crave for a worldly object incessantly and excessively is greed. It agitates the mind and is a manifestation of megalomania. Persons driven by it are unethical, exploitative and unmindful of other people. Greed is not only for wealth but it is inclusive of power to dominate others. Ambition stems from it, as also, from pride. Insane desire to hoard money and create property that one does not really need is another form of greed. A greedy person is unlikely to take to a spiritual life because he or she sees no material profit in it. Even if he or she does, it is usually to seek divine grace for more wealth. Can there be a greater proof of human ignorance than to ask for something that one leaves behind at death? All the millionaires and billionaires of the world earn no merit in the Lord's court unless they learn to share their earnings with others, specially the poor and the diseased.

(g) **Anger**. A sudden burst of an uncontrolled mind in turmoil is called anger. Its milder form is irritability of temper. Pride, jealousy and unsatiated desires bring about bouts of anger when the ego is badly bruised or hurt. An angry person acts irrationally, which one regrets later. No other factor causes restlessness in the mind as much as anger does. Even a small and gentle fit of anger agitates the mind for at least 3 – 4 hours at a subliminal level and, often, without one's awareness. One must learn to exercise self-control to curb a tendency to be angry.

(h) **Lethargy**. It refers to mental and physical listlessness that leads to a general disinclination to work and an attitude of always taking an easy way out. For instance, finding a ready excuse to skip or postpone practice to another time or day that seldom comes. Physical lack of vigour is restored through wholesome diet and exercise. The more serious problem is a mental habit of not using one's intelligence properly, primarily one's inability to be discriminative. Very few persons, even those considered intelligent in the worldly sense, use their will power to change the course of their thinking. This is an effect of mental lethargy. It is a major flaw from which practically everyone suffers, including most earnest aspirants. A majority of them are content with making small gains and do not attempt to go beyond them. Very few seekers are discerning enough to understand the real import of a guru's teaching because they do not apply their intelligence rightly.

(i) **Ill Health**. The seeds of all diseases lie in the harmful tendencies of the mind and their growth is hastened by stress, worry and fast living. Control of mind is highly beneficial for an anxiety free life. One cannot practise a spiritual discipline seriously for a long time if one does not keep good health. It is the duty of all devotees to look after themselves and avoid excesses of all kinds. The body needs regular exercise and wholesome food to maintain itself in a fit condition. One should not depend on divine intervention to cure a sickness or a disease. Although prayers do help, yet the most practical way is to get it treated from a competent doctor.

Q76. How does an individual save oneself from the above mentioned evil tendencies of the mind?
A76. They are not easy to restrain because the mind has got used to them through a long standing habit formed over innumerable past lives. Practice to control the mind through the grace of a guru is the only way out. Even then, it takes a long time before there is some improvement in exercising control over them. It is a slow and gradual process that culminates only when the 'I' (or the mind) is finally destroyed. It is always of great help if an aspirant knows his or her shortcomings and makes a conscious effort to get rid of them.

Q77. Out of the above, which attributes hamper the control of mind the most?
A77. All of them play a role in extroverting the mind and each has a bearing on the other. Qualities are not singled out for ejection from the mind which is

purified and brought under control as one whole mass of consciousness. An aspirant who pays particular attention to get rid of desire, attachment and pride is likely to make the most progress in restraining all of mind's evil tendencies.

Q78. What is self-surrender?
A78. To obliterate the sense of 'I' from the consciousness, which forms the root of the mind, by offering it to God (or the guru) is termed as self (I's) surrender. It is an act of submission to the divine will and cheerful acceptance of the enactment of one's karma as part of the cosmic play (leela) of the Lord. It is like handing over one's baggage to It to carry. God does so if a devotee sacrifices his or her 'I' for Its sake. Although most jivas claim that they live by God's will, yet, in reality, only a rare person actually acts in that spirit. People who simply talk and do not really feel Its presence do not know what self-surrender is. It betokens total dependence on the Lord, just like a baby's on the mother. One who surrenders one's self to God regards It as one's sole support and refuge. One then does not rely on self-effort, even for sustenance of the body and knows that every breath is taken only by Its grace.

Q79. What are the signs of self-surrender?
A79. Total surrender implies a state of Self Realisation. One who reaches it has no thought of the future nor of the past and is absolutely absorbed in the bliss of the Self (Atman).He or she knows that God is the sole doer of actions, whether good or bad. Neither victory nor defeat nor profit nor loss nor pleasure nor pain affect such a jiva (an individual). He or she has nothing to pray for nor a desire to fulfil nor does he or she seek anything in the world. One then carries out one's karma as service to the Lord and one sheds the body at the time of death as though one is discarding a dirty shirt. One who is successful in surrendering the self does not come back to the world of senses again.

Q80. How is self-surrender effected?
A80. Through sincere prayer, worship done with devotion and earnest practice of a guru's teaching. Divine love manifests only if one is prepared to sacrifice one's little self for the sake of the Beloved. It is a slow and a gradual process that matures with determined effort.

Q81. Self-surrender is obviously not easy to attain. What relevance does it have for a beginner who is following a spiritual discipline?
A81. Practice should be done in a spirit of self-surrender. A devotee must entreat the Lord (or the guru) for grace to show the way to shedding the ego and help and guidance in doing so. Pray to God that It alone can protect and save a jiva, who is really helpless. Pray for humility and request It earnestly to knock down pride. One should constantly beseech the Lord along the above lines desirelessly. Those who offer such prayers from the heart find the Lord

Itself making the effort to create a smooth passage to the Goal. But, one must not expect immediate results from praying just for a day or a week or a month or even a year. An entreaty like that must become a continuous refrain in the mind all the time till self-surrender is affected.

Q82. Is self-surrender not contradictory to the concept of free will? Is a jiva free to act according to choice or pleasure?

A82. Why does an individual make an effort to attain anything, spiritual or material, if one has no freedom to do so? Why should there be bondage in the first place? The 'I' of a jiva binds itself to the world because it has the freedom to look outwards (to the world). At the same time, it is free to stop doing so if it so wishes. God has created two basic paths for a human being; one, to be attached to the objective phenomenon and two, to be detached from it and It has given him or her a choice to decide (through intelligence) which way to tread. Consider it from another angle; a jiva is a finite form of the infinite Lord; this aspect would be discussed in the next chapter in more detail. If one accepts this viewpoint, the characteristics of the whole (God) must exist, albeit in a limited form, in a part (jiva). Thus, it cannot be denied that all jivas have the free will to do their karma as they please. Self-surrender is complete only if one is able to renounce external phenomenon. Its implication is that as long as the 'I' is intact, a jiva feels that he or she is the doer of actions. The Lord becomes the actor if the 'I'- sense is absent. However, the crucial point that an intelligent seeker ought to appreciate is that self-surrender is achieved through effort (an act of free will) and it is not some manna that falls on its own to save him or her.

Q83. How much freedom does an individual have? What is the difference between the divine will and that which the latter has?

A83. Lord's will is inscrutable, omnipotent, all pervasive and operates through countless objects in the entire creation. A jiva's will, on the other hand, is limited and its sphere of influence does not extend beyond a few objects. It functions to satisfy innumerable desires, which it cannot do fully because it is finite in nature, unlike the egoless God's omnipresent will. Individual will is limited by samaskaras and vasnas (mental impressions and latent tendencies; they are created by jivas' karma and are held in memory that impels the mind to function in a particular manner), which weaken it and also impair one's intelligence. A jiva can exercise his or her will within the constraints mentioned above. People who do not have strong wills fail to execute action with determination. A weak willed person is unlikely to investigate a spiritual inquiry and, even if he or she does, would give it up after a short while.

Q84. There are many types of devotees of differing temperaments and traits as described above? Who amongst them is likely to reach the end?

A84. An intelligent person who is simple, humble, sincere and determined to forge ahead despite impediments is sure to succeed. Realisation of Truth is assured for those who have highly developed divine qualities, especially of love, devotion, discriminative and detachment. These are the characteristics of a genuine seeker who is marked out from others by being fearless and having complete faith in one's guru; a person like that follows a guru's directions to the hilt and surrenders to the divine will readily. Know it for certain that divine grace accrues most to those who press on regardless of obstacles. Often, psychic powers develop after some progress in meditation. Then, there are feelings of extreme bliss and experiences of visions etc. Anyone who wants to destroy the mind must not get involved with them. An aspirant who has the above attributes is a rare being. He or she would assuredly be recipients of divine grace that enables him or her to attain realisation. No one who pursues a spiritual quest should believe that he or she is not the chosen one. To think otherwise would be an admission of mental weakness and defeat. No serious seeker should adopt an attitude like that.

Q85. What is the essence of teaching given in various scriptures? How should one study them?
A85. The knowledge given in all scriptures is of universal application. They differ only in the way they expound various view points and tenets to suit the spiritual level of a variety of devotees and, also, of prevailing times. That is why new scriptures are written in every age to express the same ideas but in a fresh idiom. There is no superior or inferior teaching; its relevancy is according to the spiritual maturity of a seeker. Scriptures must be studied carefully with deliberation and discrimination; mere recitation is of little value. One should try to understand the concepts that they elaborate rather than getting involved in their linguistics and then, more importantly, practice the teaching. The quintessence of all instruction is to control the mind; scriptures set forth various methods and paths to attain that supreme goal only.

Q86. Most scriptures sing the praises of the Lord's bounty, love, grace etc. for Its creation. Many people cannot reconcile this view with the suffering that they see around them. How is it, they say, that a benevolent and loving God allows misery and pain to be inflicted on His or Her children?
A86. The apparent contradiction of the scriptural teaching with real life lies in the lack of its understanding by the people who question it. A discerning and intelligent reader should keep the following points in mind on the issues raised in the question. First, one should endeavor to understand the instruction of saints and sages holistically. To quote a part of it and, that too, out of context would invariably cause confusion. The so called intellectuals do this all the time to prove a point. It is more a reflection of their ignorance rather than the

inconsistencies in divine teaching. Second, all scriptures state clearly that as one sows, so shall one reap. That, in nutshell, is the law of karma applicable to all jivas (human beings). The type of karma that one does and its effects (or fruits) are laid by the divine will. One is free to act according to one's will. Happiness or unhappiness accrues according to a jiva's actions. Why blame the Lord for what It has not done? Third, the argument of an ignorant person is that God should forgive and absolve a jiva of all the indulgences and wrongs that one commits. The Lord certainly does so provided one prays to It sincerely. But, a self-centered jiva is not prepared to do that. All that an individual wants is that one's every whim and fancy should be fulfilled by God and there should be neither punishment nor blame for one's actions. It is like arguing that every criminal should be forgiven or no one should not fall sick due to over eating. Can crime be controlled without punishment? Would anyone want to turn away from the world if excessive attachment to sensual gratification did not bring in some pain? Four, just as nations run according to certain laws, so does the created order of the Lord. There is room for clemency in the Lord's court as well as in the powers of a government. There is a proper way and procedure to obtain it. The divine justice is dispensed according the law of karma and those who want a reprieve from it should learn to control their minds and seek divine grace through prayer and worship. The loving God forgives every transgression of Its laws if one does that. But, those who criticise It out of ignorance and are not prepared to do anything about it are condemned to suffer from the same doubt life after life. Incidentally, people who claim that there is just one life that should be enjoyed fully through over indulgence in passions are like the blind man who denies the existence of the sun. Fifth, a spiritual quest can be launched by anyone who wants to know why jivas are unhappy, why is there birth and death, how has the world originated and so on. One's own mind provides all the answers if one were to learn to control it through the grace of a guru.

Q87. A mention was made earlier of ever free souls. Who are these exalted beings?
A87. It is a category of divine souls created by the Lord to carry out Its missions to help those who seek His or Her Grace. They are eternally free from ignorance and take birth in human form to give succor to all those who seek divine help. They usually accompany satgurus, yogis and avatars (divine incarnations) to further their missions. They can come to the world independently also to further their missions. They earn their spiritual power either in this or subtle world. Swami Vivekananda was one such being in recent history. Other examples from the past are St Peter, Vasistha and Mardana.

Q88. What are the guiding rules to carryout practice (sadhana)?
A88. An aspirant should pay particular attention to the following points:-

(a) Regular, diligent and sincere practice to be done in a spirit of self-surrender, humility and fearlessness.

(b) Learn to make the right kind of effort i.e. goal is destroy the mind.

(c) Seek holy company (sat sangha) and keep the mind open to imbibe its bliss.

(d) Develop divine qualities (e.g. love, devotion, discrimination etc.); neither progress nor liberation is possible without them.

(e) Evil attributes (e.g. attachment, pride etc.) must be controlled and ejected from the consciousness.

(f) Make contemplation of the guru's teaching a habit. The more one does so, the less it is.

(g) Never talk ill of saints. There is no sin worse than that.

(h) Pray to the Lord (or the guru) for divine grace and guidance.

(i) A beginner should learn to be moderate in matters of diet, sleep, sex etc.

(j) Remember, only the strong ones attain liberation. Do not ever give up practice irrespective of the odds that one faces in life. Those who do so are weaklings and are not fit to attain liberation.

Q89. Does metaphysical knowledge help in conducting practice?
A89. Divine knowledge that manifests within one's self with purification of mind during practice is the best. Similarly, the knowledge that a guru gives in the hearing stage is good and reliable. Intellectual knowledge acquired through self-study of scriptures and other books is highly subjective in nature. It is flawed and defective because it is an ignorant individual's mental perception of a sage's description of his or her spiritual experience, which occurs only when the mind is controlled. In other words, scriptural knowledge is based on spiritual experience (e.g. vision of God), which the mind cannot really comprehend without going through it. It is akin to the difference between merely talking about honey and actually tasting it. The above does not purport to decry the study of scriptures but has been stated only to highlight its pitfalls. Even scriptural knowledge must be obtained through sat sangha (company of those who are Self Realised). Although an aspirant does not need detailed and elaborate knowledge to carry out practice, yet it is of great help if one knows certain basic things. One can then do practice in the light of that knowledge. However, one need not wait for it before commencing practice. It is best to acquire this knowledge in the early stages of practice so that one takes full advantage of it.

Q90. What is that basic knowledge that aids an aspirant's spiritual growth during practice?

A90. A seeker ought to be clear of what the ultimate goal is; otherwise, one is likely to flounder enroute. A working knowledge of the way to get there and, also, of its nature is of great assistance to carry out practice. Some points relevant to the above issues are mentioned below and they are covered in more detail in the next two chapters:-

(a) The aim of practice is to control the mind and not to find the Reality. The latter is attained on its own if success is achieved in the former, which is also known as the state of liberation or Realisation.

(b) Know the nature of Reality. Although, It cannot be described in words, yet guru's instruction indicates what It is not?

(c) Understand the general character of maya (ignorance) and its effects.

(d) Have a broad knowledge of the genesis of creation.

(e) Acquire a functional knowledge of the working of individual mind, specially the role of intelligence and will power in controlling it.

(f) Try to comprehend that relative knowledge is unreliable, false and of no consequence.

(g) It is useful to know the broad contours of the spiritual discipline chosen for practice, specially the process involved in it to control the mind.

Some of the above aspects are covered in the next Chapter. Their explanation may strike some readers as esoteric and abstruse. They are advised not to bother much as practice of meditation or any other spiritual practice is not dependent on any deep grasp of theoretical facets of knowledge. One should learn to apply basic knowledge, learnt from a guru to bring about self-improvement; that is enough for beginners.

Chapter 3

Reality

Q1. What is the nature of Reality? How is it known?

A1. It is indescribable (in words), unknowable (by the mind) and inexpressible (to another). It is a state of fathomless and absolute Silence that is beyond speech and mental perception. The resultant obtained after the mind is controlled (i.e. destroyed) is Reality. It is the supreme goal that the wise seek. It is known through self-effort and divine grace.

Q2. Why cannot the mind know the Reality? What is Its connection with the former?

A2. The Reality is not an object of mental cognition. The mind can neither conceive of It nor think about It nor remember It nor concentrate on It (in order to know It). The Reality is totally and utterly beyond the mind and transcends any of the latter's states (i.e. wakefulness, dream and dreamless sleep). What relationship can the mind have with It? As for the Reality is concerned, It is not even aware that there is an entity known as the mind. Reality and mind are like light and darkness. Whatever connection there is between the two is only a fancy (of the mind). Mind is said to be a superimposition on the substratum of Reality for purposes of teaching only. The point to understand is that superimposition is possible only between two dissimilar things and not similar ones; the latter merge with each other when one is imposed on the other, as for example, water on water. A jiva realises the Self-effulgent nature of the Reality on its own if the superimposition of mind on It is removed through its control.

Q3. What does the word, Reality (or Truth or That), connote? What do the Self Realised say about It?

A3. It refers to a changeless state of being neither a subject (that perceives other objects) nor an object (of perception of some other entity). That state is of absolute consciousness or impersonal existence or absolute purity which alone is Real (true) as opposed to the constantly changing unreal world. It alone is;

the rest is false and non-existent except in fancy. Even those who have attained Reality are unable to convey any notion or idea about It to others because there is no object in the world that resembles it remotely or a word that gives even a hint or a suggestion of what It is like. They all talk about Its extraordinary uniqueness and advise others to experience It rather than know It through the mind. All that can be said is that neither birth nor death nor time nor space touch It. Reality is best described as being the middle of this or that (subject or object). Can the mind form a notion of what lies between the two?

Q4. Notwithstanding the above answers, all scriptures explain the nature of Reality. How have they done it?

A4. Scriptures and sages talk about the non-Reality and not the Reality in the sense discussed above. Reality has two aspects; one, absolute and unconditioned (nirguna) and second, relative and conditioned (saguna). The latter falls in the ambit of mental knowledge but not the former. Gurus explain the nature of relative form of Reality and not Its absolute counterpart. The former (i.e. conditioned Reality) undergoes constant change in time and space and, hence, is regarded as non-reality whereas the latter is immutable since It transcends time and space and is, therefore, considered as Real for purposes of teaching. Conditioned Reality is like the calm ocean in constant turmoil due to its waves. An entity to be known fully must stay the same all the time: otherwise, its knowledge is partial, as in the case of a wave that changes its form all the time.

Q5. What is the nature of saguna (relative form of) Reality?

A5. The saguna Reality, in its essence, refers to pure consciousness that is aware of itself as a subject (i.e. as a Being) that experiences Itself in the form of countless objects (e.g. world). Consciousness by itself (i.e. in absolute form) is unconditioned intelligence but it undergoes an apparent modification due to maya, a power that inheres in it naturally. Absolute Reality conditioned by maya is Its relative form and this apparent change takes place as a natural phenomenon. Similarly, absolute consciousness (of Reality) superimposed with maya is called the mind. In the conditioned Reality inhere countless qualities (e.g. love, attachment, greed etc.) that qualify It. The word, saguna, means with attributes (gunas) and they are inborn in the conditioned consciousness. An object is known only by its qualities; for instance, a rose is different from a wheat plant due to their diverse attributes. An idea or a thought is also a representation in energy form of the above qualities. Further, each attribute has a limitless potential for growth; for instance, love may be quantified from finite to infinity. Each finite object (e.g. human being, a tiger etc.) displays only some of the above mentioned qualities and that too in limited form; only the conditioned consciousness (of Reality or God) has them all with each one existing in an infinite spectrum. The visible phenomenon is created by intelligence and will power of the conditioned Reality (or Ishwara; God) from a combination of the above attributes by assigning names and shapes (nama and rupa) to various objects. The mind gains knowledge of objects through their qualities. One of the prime characteristics of saguna Reality is Its relativity from which arises sense of duality entertained by It; it implies the existence of two separate entities known as a subject and an object. A jiva is a subject that perceives objects (e.g. another man or women; a rose etc.) as apart from himself or herself. Similarly, God is the general subject and creation is a universal object of Its perception. The qualities of Reality are linked by the law of pair of opposites; for example, love and hate, cold and hot, male and female and so on. Their perception, and indeed of the objects formed from them, arises from their relation to each other. Neither heat nor cold, for instance, can be felt independently of each other because they are interconnected by the law of pair of opposites. The entire creation manifests from the attributes related to each other by the same law. Knowledge obtained by the mind and senses is similarly of relative nature. Relativity comes into being as an effect of apparent motion in the consciousness, which is induced by maya, unlike absolute Reality. In simple words, saguna aspect is typified by the constant activity of Its consciousness, which then brings the world about through it in the matrix of time and space. Another trait of saguna Reality is Its outward looking nature that results in loss of self-control. In short, saguna Reality refers to God and Its creation that is reflective of Its infinite qualities; knowledge gained by the mind and senses is of Its relative nature. One should know the nature of maya and the mind to acquire Its better understanding. These aspects are discussed in the subsequent parts of this Chapter.

Q6. What is nirguna (without attributes) Reality?
A6. What is not saguna is nirguna Reality. The word, nirguna, means without attributes. Objective form is created out of the qualities inherent in the consciousness through its activity, as explained above. Nirguna Reality is said to be inactive (motionless) and attribute-less and, hence, is considered to be beyond any form for purposes of teaching. In fact, it is none of these since they are mental notions. It is neither a subject nor an object and, hence, considered as non-dual. Maya has no effect on It and the mind cannot gain Its knowledge since It lies beyond its ken. It alone is. It cannot be described in anyway; just as one cannot put in words the experience of dreamless sleep to another in the same state, so also the Reality is so immersed in Its great Silence that one cannot fathom It. It is so unique that any connection that one tries to establish with It through sensual phenomenon falls in the realm of fantasy. It is the goal of the wise that they seek through control of mind.

Q7. It is said that there is a unity of nirguna (absolute) and saguna (relative) aspects of Reality. How is that established?

A7. There is just the Reality and all that exists apart from It is only a mental fancy as an effect of maya. How can there be oneness between existence and non-existence? Maya is an agent of illusion and all that is perceived in it is actually non-real, just like the water in a mirage. Reality alone is; there is nothing apart from It. The unity mentioned in the question implies that the single and only Reality has two aspects i.e. absolute and relative. This is accepted from the point of view of an aspirant immersed in duality and ignorance.

Q8. An illusion created by the mind has a basis in previous memory (of things seen and heard). How can the saguna Reality come into being without following a similar principle?

A8. The above observation is valid and its answer, in teaching, is that the illusion of creation arises from the absolute ideas (or absolute attributes) that are indistinguishable from the pure consciousness of the nirguna Reality. That the latter has such notions is only an assumption at present (i.e. in the state of ignorance in which the question has been raised) and can only be confirmed by being the Reality through actual experience. It is, however, logical enough for the intellect to resolve the apparent contradiction that seems to exist between the nirguna and saguna aspects of Reality.

Q9. Many words are used to connote the nirguna and saguna aspects of Reality. How should an aspirant make a distinction between them?

A9. Nirguna Reality is wordless, nameless and is, therefore, ineffable. However, a student needs to differentiate It from Its saguna counterpart for better understanding. For purposes of teaching only, words like truth, that, absolute, unconditioned, pure, transcendental, non-dual, real, true, formless, space-less, timeless etc. are appended to It. It must, however, be emphasised that all these words signify mental concepts and the Reality is none of these. It is neither formless nor non-dual nor for that matter anything else. These words only indicate what the saguna Reality is not. The latter is said to be infinite, limitless, conditioned, relative, and dual, with name and form, omnipotent, omniscient, omnipresent and so on. The objects of Its creation (e.g. a jiva) are described as limited, finite, transitory, subject to birth and death etc.

Q10. Reality is assigned many names in scriptures. What do they signify and how have they come about?

A10. Sages and seers have used many names for Reality over a period of time to indicate some of Its countless attributes, as also its many facets, which generally conform to a jiva's perception of how the world functions. The name,

Rama, for instance, represents the collective traits of a person called as such. All names and words that denote Reality have the same connotation and refer primarily to Its relative aspect. Although the absolute Reality is nameless and wordless, yet, for purposes of instruction, names and words employed for Its relative counterpart are used for It also. For instance, the term, God, is symbolic of the conditioned Reality but it may also be used for Its unconditioned aspect provided it is qualified as such, i.e., absolute God. Many scriptures do not make distinctions like these but a discriminative seeker ought to deduce them from the context in which various names and words are mentioned. Many names and words have also come to be associated with certain schools of thought from ancient times. For example, the word, Purusha, has a definite connotation in the Samkhya system but gurus and saints use it also even if they are not its adherents. Some of the commonly used words for the absolute Reality are Parbrahman (absolute Brahman), Brahman (God; in the absolute sense, the ultimate principle of pure existence), Truth, Self (Atman), That (Tat), absolute Knowledge (Jnana), absolute Love, Siva (the Pure One), absolute Consciousness and so on. There are countless names and words to describe various aspects of the relative nature of Reality. All of them resolve in a single Name (Nama) or Word (Shabda), which is their generic form. Absolute Name or Word denotes the unconditioned Reality. Omkar stands for Reality when conceived as a principle of sound that forms the basis of all ideas and knowledge. Rama refers to divine beauty and supreme auspiciousness. Reality is also referred to as Ishwara (God). Pure Mind, Ad Shakti (Divine or Primordial Power), Intelligence, Fearless, Silence, Satchitananda (Truth, Consciousness, Bliss), Consciousness, Awareness, Allah, Waheguru, Jehovah etc. from different viewpoints. A beginner is advised not to get involved in the semantics of the above names and words. One should just bear in mind that all of them allude to the Reality from various viewpoints.

Q11. Brahman (God) is said to have a divine power (ad shakti). Scriptures also talk about maya. How should a beginner understand the doctrine of divine power and concept of maya?
A11. An important facet of Reality is to conceive it as a power that creates the world as well as sustain it and then dissolve it. It empowers every object and controls its functioning. Maya is an integral part of this divine power and is not to be regarded as apart from it. The concept of Brahman and Its power (or Shiva Shakti) has the same connotation as a prime minister and his power, i.e., if God is conceived as a Being, as most people do, then It has power inherent in It. In reality, God and Its power are just two words to describe the same principle.

Q12. What is the nature of the divine power (ad shakti)?

A12. The conditioned Reality is conceived as a power in one of Its innumerable facets. It is not something distinct from It but Its consciousness itself exists as a power that is omnipotent, omniscient and omnipresent. It has two aspects, which are the effects of the pair of opposites existing naturally in the consciousness due to its relative nature, as discussed earlier. One is of wisdom, intelligence, will power, self-control, introversion etc. and the second is of ignorance, non-intelligence, un-control, extroversion etc. In normal parlance, the former is said to be the ad shakti and the latter as maya. A discriminative reader should, however, remember that ad shakti and maya are not two separate powers but the same principle that has two contrary aspects, i.e., positive and negative. The consciousness uses its perfect intelligence and will power to create the objective phenomenon by projecting it in maya. It exercises total control over its functioning in time and space through a cycle of creation, sustenance, dissolution and re-creation. Although the divine power is genderless, yet, for purposes of teaching and worship, its embodiment is usually represented in the feminine form and is given the general name, Devi. Goddesses like Saraswati, Lakshmi etc. are said to be Its finite forms. In the ad shakti inhere countless ideas and attributes that are employed by it consciously (i.e. by its intelligence) to create limitless number of objects. It determines the nature of each object and does not allow the latter to violate it. Divine power, if conceived as a self-existing thing by itself, is both the goal as well as the means to attain it, i.e., it has an absolute and relative form. Mind conforms to the latter aspect and the former is realised through its control. The discipline of Tantra generally follows this line of thinking. Many regard the ad shakti as an inseparable power of Brahman (God or conditioned Reality); in that case, it is a means to realise the latter. Amongst its innumerable qualities are love, compassion, graciousness and blissfulness.

Q13. How does the divine power exist in a jiva?
A13. It is an all pervasive power that is present in each cell and atom of not only the human body but also in all other animate and inanimate (e.g. air) objects. An atom's power manifests from the ad shakti. The latter's palpable form in an individual is the mind, whose chief characteristics are intelligence and will power. A jiva uses them to attain desired goals. It ought to be pointed out, however, that human intelligence and will power are limited forms of their divine counterparts. Although they have the potential for growth to almost any limit, yet they are always subservient to the omnipotent ad shakti's intelligence and will power; no jiva can, therefore, either violate the divine order or reach its infinite levels. Divine will is inscrutable and all-knowing and a jiva must learn to submit to it.

Q14. What relevance do the positive aspects (e.g. intelligence and will power) have for an aspirant?

A14. A jiva is caught up in ignorance because he or she fails to use his or her intelligence discriminatively. Even if he or she does so, it is invariably to gain worldly goals to gratify desires. Rare is a man or a woman who turns his or her mind towards God and then has the will power to pursue that quest relentlessly. Lack of application of intelligence or its wrongful use and an impoverished will power are major weaknesses and constraints that a majority of people suffer from. They are used for the least path of resistance, i.e., seek pleasure from worldly objects rather than look for its perennial source within their selves. The Lord has given human beings a choice, viz., either remain attached to the world and undergo pain or become detached from it and attain divine bliss. The cause of human suffering is not God, as most ignorant persons claim, but an individual being who does not use his or her intelligence properly to get rid of it. A spiritual pursuit is meant for those who are mentally strong enough to employ their will power and intelligence to control their minds. There is no other way for a man or a woman to escape from the powerful net of ignorance. Between the positive and negative (e.g. ignorance) facets of the divine power, the former is more potent and one can attain permanent happiness if one learns to use it intelligently for one's benefit.

Q15. In view of the preceding answer, what is the nature of maya?
A15. It is an invisible power that is inherent in the divine consciousness, just as heat is present in fire. Its nature cannot be determined exactly because no one has ever seen it. Whatever conclusions the wise ones have drawn about it are based on studying its effects (i.e. the objective world) in the light of knowledge attained in Realisation. It is assumed that its nature would conform to its effects since they cannot be different from their cause. Maya is known as ignorance in general (i.e. universal and all pervasive) that inheres in the Reality naturally. The latter is incomplete without it. Those who find this difficult to accept are told that maya has been created by God to indulge in Its sport (leela). Maya affects the consciousness in many ways. Its chief effects are to cause it to extrovert (i.e. look outside of itself) by inducing in it imaginary motion. The inactive absolute Reality is thus modified into Its active and relative form; in other words, maya acts as a cause of the creative phenomenon inclusive of its sustenance and dissolution. This process is set in motion due to temporary amnesia that the Reality suffers from as an effect of maya. It means that maya (ignorance) causes temporary forgetfulness in Brahman about Its real absolute nature. That is the state of Its relative form in which It begins to act as a creator, preserver and destroyer of the sensual phenomenon. The effects of Its forgetfulness create doubt and fear. Apparent motion in Its consciousness, caused by maya, makes the latter restless, which results in the manifestation of thoughts and imagination in it. Maya is a power of illusion that makes things appear what they are not. For instance, the formless and indivisible

Reality appears to be split into countless embodied objects; also, the non-dual (i.e. neither a subject nor an object) Brahman imagines that It is dual (i.e. a subject as well as an object). In the same way, the Reality begins to believe that Its immutable Self is the ephemeral individual 'I' subject to birth and death. Maya is a magical power that creates things out of nothing and enslaves the consciousness for as long as the latter is willing to submit to it. In short, maya causes delusions in the consciousness, which then indulges in a fantasy resulting in a fanciful play of creation and dissolution.

Q16. Maya must be supremely intelligent and powerful to affect the divine consciousness so badly?

A16. No; it is a power of non-intelligence or ignorance. Maya is regarded as a power in the sense that electricity is considered so; they are both made to function by intelligence that is not native to them. Maya is, therefore, incapable of creating anything on its own due to it being a principle of non-consciousness. It only creates an illusion of acting in Brahman who alone has the intelligence and will power to bring the objective phenomenon into being. It does so from the ideas (of creation) inherent in Its consciousness. Sensual perception is also by the consciousness only. The role of maya in the creative process is to reflect the consciousness in it, just as an image is seen in a mirror. The consciousness with all its ideas that inhere in it is projected in the mirror like surface of maya and the former then beholds its own image, split into innumerable objects, in the later. What it sees is the world of sensual phenomenon. An intelligent reader should note the following two points in the above teaching. Firstly, although maya induces the consciousness to look outwards to the images, yet it does not force it to do so, just as a mirror cannot compel a man to look into it. Secondly, what the consciousness observes in the reflecting surface of maya is not of its real (i.e. formless) self but its distorted form of a multiplicity of objects. Third, maya is only an incidental cause of creation that is brought into being by Brahman's intelligence and will power. Thus, a discriminative seeker should have no doubt that the problem lies in the consciousness (or the mind) and not in maya, which is only fulfilling its nature by projecting the former in it. The world is not perceived in deep sleep. Why? Because the consciousness has shut its eyes and, therefore, it does not see anything. Individual ignorance (an effect of maya) would end if one could do that deliberately and consciously in wakefulness. That is the whole purpose of following a spiritual discipline to control the mind, i.e., stop looking at the world or be detached from it through mental introversion.

Q17. How is it that the supremely intelligent Reality allows itself to be misled by maya to look outside of Itself to perceive the world?

A17. It can be explained in the following ways. Maya and the divine consciousness are intermixed with each other like water and milk. The former's effect on the latter, to adulterate it, is, therefore, natural. In the same way, maya makes the immobile consciousness believe that it is in apparent motion, which causes extroversion and forgetfulness. It is a temporary aberration that takes place naturally in the consciousness but it regains its true nature instantly through the use of its perfect intelligence. Another explanation is that the intelligent and omnipotent Brahman (God) indulges in Its divine sport (leela) of creation through maya knowingly and deliberately in a playful mood. Forgetfulness is only play acting on Its part. The truth, however, is that an illusion or fantasy does not follow any rules of logic. Is not a dream a disjointed affair?

Q18. The phenomenal world's reality is said to be dream like. Does it imply that it is non-real?
A18. The world is as one perceives it. A dreamer considers his or her dream to be true. Its true nature is discovered only on waking up. Similarly, the world appearance is real in ignorance but is unreal when perceived in the light of Realisation. Questions about the illusory nature of the objective phenomenon are often raised by students and are also discussed in scriptures. Aspirants, specially beginners, are advised to avoid rhetorical disputations and, further, they should base their knowledge on spiritual experience rather than intellectual knowledge. Cleverness of mind can prove or disprove any point of view. Whether the world is real or unreal is best decided by attaining divine knowledge through control of mind.

Q19. Maya's nature is also said to be characterised by its attributes and certain aspects. What are they and how do they affect the consciousness?
A19. A raw beginner is advised not to labour too much to understand the succeeding explanation. One can begin practice of a spiritual discipline without concerning too much about theoretical aspects. Maya's main facets are of veiling and projecting. Its veiling power (avarana) covers the consciousness like a translucent cloak. It creates an unreal sense of subjectivity (the 'I am' feeling) in the consciousness and thus gives birth to its relative and dualistic nature. The sense of duality manifests in two ways; in the general and particular sense. The general 'I' is symbolic of the whole of consciousness (or it stands for God as a general principle) and the particular 'I' signifies the individuality of an object, more specially of a jiva (i.e. a man or woman). A thing in general is to a particular what a whole is to a part. Maya's veil modifies the consciousness in general as well in particular. Further, the general and particular 'I' becomes aware (or perceives) objects in their ideation form (e.g. the idea of a horse is perceived in the causal or incipient stage of creation but the latter's form is not seen). The general 'I' (or God) is aware of all objects but a jiva (or the 'I'

in particular) perceives only a few of them. The veiling power thus limits the limitless (i.e. God) by modifying its consciousness into its individual aspect (i.e. as a jiva). To sum up, the veiling power induces a false sense of 'I'-ness in the consciousness and in this subjectivity inheres latent form of objects. The latter's embodied form is then seen on maya's mirror like surface due to the projecting power that impels the consciousness to cast its shadow on it. The multitude of forms and shapes (created out of ideas mentioned above) that the senses perceive as the world is thus a projection of the modified (by veiling power) consciousness (or the 'I'- sense) on the screen (or mirror like surface) of maya. In this process, motion that was latent, as an effect of veiling power, becomes more palpable. One should not imagine that maya is arranged in layers, i.e., one acting as a veil and the other as a screen to see the world appearance. Veiling and projecting powers are effects of maya's pervasiveness in the consciousness. In simple words, the thought of a rose that arises in a jiva's mind is due to the veiling power and the flower that the eyes see outside is its (i.e. thought's material form) is an effect of projecting power. Maya has three attributes that pervade its veiling and projecting powers; satoguna or satva (attribute of purity), rajoguna or rajas (quality of activity) and tamoguna or tamas (principle of inactivity). The consciousness (or mind) is affected by them due to maya's superimposition on it. Thus, the mind is described as being satvic (purified) or rajasic (active) or tamasic (lethargic). The modification of consciousness, as a subject (the 'I' feeling) and an object takes place through the above attributes in three forms, known as causal (karan), subtle (sookshma) and gross (asthoola). These words are used quite often in teaching and a beginner should try to grasp their connotations. The causal state of the subjective consciousness, for instance, refers to the latent or potential state of the 'I' feeling (or thought) in it, which arises as an effect of the veil of satoguna. The causal 'I', projected in satoguna, manifests as the causal body (of an object). The same consciousness when perceived through the veil of rajoguna and then reflected in it creates the subtle 'I' and subtle body respectively. This process is repeated further in tamoguna through which the gross 'I' and material (or physical body) comes into being. In other words, the effects of the three attributes on the consciousness is to make it function at three levels, i.e., causal, subtle and gross; their reflection in maya appears as the three bodies, i.e., causal, subtle and physical, of all objects, including that of human beings. An easier way to understand this phenomenon is to regard the causal state of the mind or the body as its dormant or potential form; the mind and its objects of perception assume their causal form in dreamless sleep. Objects seen in dreams are subtle in nature and so is the mind. Gross mind perceives physical objects through eyes, ears etc. The subjective and objective nature of any embodied form, including its attributes, is described as causal, subtle or gross. For example, the mind of a jiva is said to be either causal, subtle or gross and the same description fits his body; one may also describe love (or any other quality) as being satvic (highly developed), rajasic (of middling level) and tamasic (undeveloped). The consciousness is said to acquire its nature from the above attributes; satva makes it dormant, controlled, clear, full of light, calm, contracted or introverted, balanced and tranquil; subtlety, palpable motion, agitation, un-control, restlessness, turgidity, unevenness, activity and expansion or extroversion (of the consciousness) is caused by rajoguna; tamas creates in it a feeling of grossness, darkness, inactivity, impurity, inertia and lethargy. All those effects are present in the consciousness (or minds) of all jivas in varying degree except in those who control their minds completely. The colours, white, red and black, are associated with satva, rajas and tamas respectively. They are the basic colours and all others are formed from intermixing them in varying proportions. They are used by the consciousness to identify created objects. Finally, a discerning reader ought to remember that the manifestation of subjectivity in the consciousness as well as its projection in objective form is only a illusion. For, does not maya cause delusions and make things appear what they are not? Who suffers from such hallucinations? The consciousness; the difference between its general aspect (i.e. as God) and particular (i.e. as a man or woman) is that the former knows it to be unreal but the latter regards it as real.

Q20. It was stated above that maya is superimposed on the consciousness. What does superimposition imply?
A20. To place one thing on another is called superimposition. The consciousness is the substratum on which maya exists as an imposition. It is worth noting that superimposition succeeds only if the two things are of different natures; for example, water cannot be placed on water because their sameness mixes them and, hence, it is not possible to impose one on the other. Maya and consciousness cannot intermix because they are totally different from each other. Even the example quoted earlier, of maya and consciousness being like water and milk should be understood to be one of superimposition because they are two different substances with dissimilar properties. Their close contact affects them but they can be separated. Another point to keep in mind is that imposition produces a result that does not conform to their original principles; consciousness superimposed with maya creates a third entity, the world, which is neither of them. Maya affects the consciousness, as explained in the previous answer, because it is a superimposition and not due to its unity with it.

Q21. The purpose of a spiritual quest is said to be to shed ignorance. What is its tangible form that an aspirant ought to give up to know the Truth?

A21. Maya is ignorance in general (i.e. affects the whole of consciousness) as well as in particular (i.e. applicable to a part of consciousness or a jiva). To remove the former requires infinite effort done in infinite time by an infinite number of jivas, which is clearly an impossibility. Ignorance in general cannot, therefore, be shed from the consciousness in which it exists naturally. A seeker is required to give up only individual ignorance that affects him or her to attain Realisation. Maya's palpable form for an individual is the mind and the world; the latter is only a projection of the former. Control of mind, therefore, forms the crux of spiritual effort. Mind and its functioning is too tenuous to be tackled directly. The mind's tangible form, manifested by motion inherent in it, is the succession of an endless chain of thoughts. An aspirant should learn to control them, more specially, the 'I' thought, which is the root of them all. To do that, one must detach the mind from external phenomenon and fix it on the 'I' thought. The mind is controlled (or made motionless) if the latter is eliminated.

Q22. What is the nature of mind?

A22. The pure (or absolute) and motionless consciousness (i.e. unconditional Reality) that suffers from the effects of maya superimposed on it is called the mind. Maya makes the consciousness believe (wrongly) that it is in motion and that creates in it a sense of duality. This is reflected in mind's basic nature; that is, it is a subject (i.e. as an entity that perceives things) in which inhere all objects of sensual perception (i.e. world appearance inheres as an idea in the mind but is perceived outside by it as a reflection in maya). The subjective and objective nature of the mind is interlinked through the act of perception. The mind that feels that it sees a cat is its subjective form, which in teaching is known as the 'I am' or 'I' feeling (i.e. 'I see a cat'). The cat is an object that is formed out of its idea that inheres in the mind when it is projected on the mirror like surface of maya. The act of seeing the cat connects the subjective mind to its objective counterpart. This phenomenon is expressed as seer–seeing–seen or knower–knowing–known relationship in spiritual instruction. Another characteristic of the mind is its relativity, which implies that the knowledge it acquires is always dependent on its state determined by time, circumstances and the relationship between a subject and an object. For instance, a man's knowledge of the sun at dawn and midday is not the same. The mind is inherently a principle of intelligence, memory, will power and awareness of its subjective and objective forms. The mind is subject to powers of extroversion and introversion. It means that mind is outward looking if its motion is not restrained by intelligence but can be made to look inwards (to its point of origin) by controlling the latter (again through use of intelligence). The mind has two forms; general and particular. The mind in general refers to the whole of consciousness (i.e. God's mind) and is regarded as its universal or cosmic aspect that pervades all objects in creation. The mind in particular is of individual objects; for example, of a man or a woman. In the mind in general inhere limitless qualities or ideas and in that sense, it connotes the saguna (conditioned) Reality or Its relative consciousness. The mind in particular has only a finite number of attributes. A reader should note that the mind in particular is only a limited form of its general counterpart and, hence, potentially the same. Their relationship is like that of the sun and its reflection in a pitcher of water.

Q23. The word, consciousness (chit), is used very often in scriptures. What does it represent?

A23. Conceptually, mind and consciousness are interchangeable terms. Consciousness is regarded as a primeval thing in itself (i.e. as an independent principle); it is just another word for Reality or God in Its relative aspect. Consciousness stands for the power of awareness that is an effect of intelligence. Absolute consciousness is aware of only its Self and it is neither subjective nor objective in nature. Maya conditions it into its relative aspect; consciousness then gains awareness of its subjective nature, i.e., it has a feeling of being the 'I' (also described as 'I am' or 'I'- consciousness). That is the primary awareness that gives rise to its secondary or objective form, i.e., awareness of objects gained by the subjective consciousness through the senses. The subjective and objective awareness of the consciousness in general (or God's consciousness) is infinite, i.e., it is aware of all individual 'I''s and innumerable objects. A jiva's consciousness, which is a conditioned form of its general aspect, is aware of only itself (i.e. of one's own 'I'-ness) and a limited number of objects (perceived by one's senses). Awareness is qualified by alertness, vividness and vigilance. Alertness is the power of attention and speed with which the mind acquires subjective and objective knowledge or awareness. Vigilance prevents any interference in gaining such knowledge and vividness refers to the clarity with which it (i.e. knowledge) is obtained. In general, these qualities stand for the sharpness of the mind (i.e. its intelligence etc.), which is infinite and finite in its cosmic and particular forms respectively. They are also indicators of the self-control that the consciousness has over itself. The mind in general is fully concentrated, remembers everything and has supreme control whereas a jiva's mind does not have these traits in full measure and, hence, suffers from lack of self-control, is forgetful, subject to doubt and fear and so on. An intelligent aspirant should try to improve the quality of self-awareness (of his or her 'I'-ness) rather than objective awareness by keeping the mind alert, vivid and vigilant during practice.

Q24. It is said that the world appearance is a creation of the mind (or consciousness). How does it take place?

A24. The conditioning of the consciousness, by maya, is an act of divine will because the latter, being non-intelligent, is powerless to affect any change in the former because of its omnipotence. In other words, consciousness (or God) uses maya deliberately to effect a change in its absolute nature to indulge in its sport (of creation). This modification makes the consciousness (in general) aware of its infinite attributes. The divine intelligence then projects the consciousness on the screen of maya through its three attributes (gunas; satoguna, rajoguna and tamoguna). The result is the world appearance in three forms; causal (seen on the screen of satoguna), subtle (on rajoguna), material (on tamoguna). The objective phenomenon perceived in maya consists of an infinite number of universes with each of them having countless individual objects. A jiva (man or woman) is just one such object. All these objects are ordained to function in an orderly fashion by the divine will and intelligence. No object can violate the divine order. Human mind at individual level runs similarly but only as a part of the whole (i.e. of the consciousness in general) scheme of things. It means that a jiva's mind perceives only a small part of the whole (i.e. a limited number of objects) reflected in maya that envelopes it. This restriction arises because a jiva's subjectivity (i.e. 'I'-sense that perceives objects) is finite, unlike that of God, which is infinite.

Q25. What is the concept of God (Ishwara)?
A25. Most people find it too hard to understand that an abstract entity like the mind can be a creator, sustainer and destroyer (of the world). It is so because their ignorance does not allow them to conceive that material forms can emerge out of the disembodied consciousness. The idea of an Ishwara who is a personal being is given in teaching for those unable to comprehend that the mind (or consciousness) is the sole actor and repository of knowledge. An average jiva is more comfortable with the notion of a Supreme Being who is not only omnipotent, omnipresent and omniscience but also the creator, preserver and destroyer. It is easier for people to pray and worship an embodied God than get involved in the metaphysics of the mind. A personalised Ishwara (e.g. Sri Krishna, Sri Jesus) is only a finite form of Its disembodied aspect. An infinite God refers either to Its de-personalised cosmic form or to all the countless embodied objects of the past, present and future or to the consciousness in its disembodied aspect. For example, Sri Krishna's infiniteness alludes to his consciousness and not to his body that is subject to birth and death. Thus, it is better that one understands that Ishwara refers to a general principle of existence based on intelligence and that any of Its incarnations are only just one of Its innumerable forms. In that sense, disembodied Ishwara and mind in general have a similar connotation. In short, God is the embodied form of the saguna (i.e. with attributes) Reality in the general sense (i.e. not any particular incarnation but the whole of Reality) but, at the same time, by its very nature, it is also the absolute Reality.

Q26. What are Ishwara's qualities?

A26. They are limitless but they manifest according to God's divine will. Although Ishwara is the repository of all positive and negative attributes that appear according to the law of pair of opposites in the case of jivas, yet It does not permit undesirable traits to blemish Its being. It is so despite God's relative nature. Why it is so is explained as follows. A reader should note that a positive trait (e.g. love) is more potent than a negative one (e.g. hate). Self-control is a function of divine attributes whereas un-control is that of negative qualities. The divine qualities in the case of Ishwara are developed to an infinite level; because, firstly, by the nature of Its being, secondly, due to Its lack of ego and thirdly, on account of the utmost purity of Its consciousness. God has, therefore, a very unique form of self-control that does not allow undesirable attributes to manifest in It, despite their existence, just as germs, though present in the body, do not affect a strong and a healthy man. Ishwara is, therefore, always fully aware of Its true Self and acts in an utterly detached manner because It is egoless. It does not suffer from defects like doubt, fear, forgetfulness, dissipation of mental energy etc. Its chief divine qualities are love, devotion, discrimination, detachment, humility, contentment, forgiveness, graciousness etc. and they exist in It in infinite measure. God is a principle of pure intelligence and will power that are employed by It consciously to create the objective phenomenon in a limitless time and space matrix. It is also the supreme sustainer and destroyer. Ishwara is able to do all this because It is omnipotent, omnipresent and omniscient. There is no created object, including great gods like Brahma, that can match God in any way nor does it have the power to violate Its will. It is perfect in every respect. Maya is the Lord's handmaiden and does not affect It at all; it is Its own power that It uses according to Its pleasure.

Q27. God's (Brahman's) being-hood is an effect of the illusionary power of maya. Is It then not just an imaginary entity like any other object? If so, what benefit does one gain from praying to Brahman?

A27. Absolute Reality alone is; that is the supreme Truth but an ignorant jiva is not aware of It. He or she functions in the realm of duality, i.e., of a creator (God) and the created (e.g. man, woman, animals, plants etc.). If one accepts one's own being as true, then how can one consider Brahman as untrue? A dream is real for the dreamer but appears unreal on waking up. The dream world appearance has been created by the Lord through the incidence of maya for Its sport and, unlike a jiva, It knows it to be false. A jiva's dream existence cannot end without the grace of its creator, i.e., Brahman. The crucial point for an aspirant to understand is that God's omnipotent will is inviolable and no one can escape from maya's net without praying to the Lord, who alone has the power to grant liberation. A beginner should start with the premise that the objective phenomenon is real but end it by knowing through spiritual experience that it is unreal. Whether Brahman's existence is an illusion can be decided only in a state of Realisation.

Q28. Why is it said that Ishwara's end cannot be found? Is it possible for a jiva (human being) to become God?
A28. Can anyone ever count up infinity? The more one counts, more is yet to be counted. Similarly, there is no limit to God's disembodied being-hood or Its attributes. How can a finite jiva ever become the Infinite? If one could do that the Infinite would be reduced to finite, which is clearly a conceptual absurdity. No jiva can ever attain the status of Ishwara; to imagine otherwise betrays crass ignorance and megalomania of the worst type. A jiva is a finite being bound by the body and samaskaras (mental impressions) and vasnas (mental tendencies). How is it possible for such a person to be equated with the infinite consciousness (of God)? Even if an individual attains Realisation, he or she still functions in the ambit of his or her karma and not like Ishwara whose power pervades all objects in creation.

Q29. A jiva is said to be a reflected image of Brahman. How is it that the former is bound by maya while the latter is not?
A29. The relationship of God with a jiva is like that of a whole with a part. Although an individual is a reflected form of Brahman, yet the reflection is a partial one due to maya's attributes (satoguna, rajoguna, tamoguna). That a jiva is a part of a larger whole should be understood in this sense. An individual being is, therefore, a finite form of the infinite Lord and is incapable of displaying more than a few of the latter's qualities. The egoless Brahman is in total and complete control of Its consciousness whereas an egocentric individual has very little control over the mind. Negative qualities do not affect Brahman because of Its inherent self-restraint but they are the motivating factor for a jiva to act. It is a jiva's ego that binds one to maya through undesirable traits (e.g. attachment, greed etc.) and there is no way that one can attain freedom from it without learning to exercise control over one's mind.

Q30. The words, 'I Am' and 'I am' are used frequently in Guru Upanishad. What do they signify?
A30. An object's existence or subjectivity is centered in its 'I'-ness. For instance, a jiva knows, in wakefulness, that he or she exists because he or she is aware of his or her 'I'-ness. But in deep sleep, he or she is not aware of anything because the 'I'-sense is missing. The above words are used, in teaching, to indicate the being-hood of an object, which is the most primary of all ideas that the conditioned (i.e. by maya) consciousness entertains. The 'I Am' refers to the absolute and immutable Reality, more specifically to Its Self (Atman), on the assumption that the latter's existence is centered in the former, as it is in the case

of jivas. Reality, of course, does not entertain any such notion but there is no other way to symbolize it in teaching. The 'I Am' is conditioned into 'I am' by the veiling power of maya. The 'I am' feeling in general alludes to Brahman's being-hood; its further modification, in maya, signifies a jiva's individuality, i.e., the 'I' that all individuals identify themselves with. The 'I am' feeling in God denotes the centre point of Its infinite consciousness (or mind in general) and, for a jiva, it refers to the point of origin of individual mind. Words like 'I am' or 'I' or 'I'- consciousness or mind have the same general connotation. Ego is also a form of the 'I' but it signifies pride, vanity and selfishness. The use of the 'I' to denote a person's being-hood is thus preferred over the word, ego, to indicate the same essence. The 'I am-ness' of Ishwara or a jiva is only feeling that arises in the consciousness in the inceptive stages of the creative process to make It or an individual aware of its identity. The expression of this feeling in words (e.g. 'I am') manifests much later when jivas begin to identify themselves with their gross bodies. Jivas use words of various languages to express it.

Q31. How does the mind of a jiva (human being) come into being?
A31. Individual mind is a modified form of the cosmic mind. The latter is a general principle of relative consciousness that pervades the entire creation and it comes into being as an effect of maya, more specifically its veiling power, superimposition on the absolute consciousness. The genesis of the mind in general lies in the motion (an effect of rajoguna) that keeps the consciousness in a state of seeming activity, which acts as a cause for further modification of the consciousness. The individual mind evolves as an effect of the latter; this manifestation (of a jiva's mind) occurs because the idea of jiva-hood (individuality of an object) exists in the consciousness. It is the same mind (in general) that becomes particularised in a jiva; in other words, the motion that runs through the universal mind pervades the individual mind as well but at a much lower scale. A jiva's mind lacks the omnipotence, omnipresence and omniscience of its cosmic counterpart on account of two factors; one, its finite nature and two, inherence of samaskaras (mental impressions of past karma) and vasnas (mental tendencies formed from previous karma that give rise to desires) that pollute it and thus impair its capacity. The mind in general is like a limitless ocean and a single wave in it is akin to the individual mind. Just as an ocean has infinite number of waves so does the cosmic mind run through countless objects of creation. The distinctiveness of individual mind of each object is characterised by its samaskaras and vasnas, just as there are big and small waves in the ocean.

Q32. What is the nature of individual mind?
A32. Mind is a subtle and intangible entity that gives a jiva subjective and objective awareness (or knowledge). It is just another name for the consciousness

that imagines itself to be a particular person (e.g. 'I am Rama'). The palpable form of the mind is the endless chain of thoughts that erupt in it. An average mind is always in turmoil and its restlessness forces it to look outwards (to the world) rather than inwards (to the point of its origin). A normal worldly person has very little control over an extroverted mind; practically, everyone succumbs to its whims and fancies in search of (transitory) pleasure through satisfaction of desires. These are its negative aspects, which are countered by its positive facets. Amongst the latter is the mind's potential ability to exercise control over itself by looking inwards (to its source) to seek perennial happiness. The mind is capable of introverting (to its point of origin) provided one makes the desired effort to break the bonds of attachment to the external world. That very few people attempt to do so is a sign of mental weakness and not due to any divine scheme. The centre point of the mind is the source of its energy and also forms the genesis of the 'I' sense of an individual. Although everyone uses the 'I' to refer to himself or herself, yet it is not experienced tangibly because it is a latent feeling. The 'I' (or 'I am') feeling is regarded in teaching as the fulcrum (or the centre or point of origin) of the mind. The latter acts at the 'I''s behest and for its pleasure. The mind (or consciousness) functions (for the sake of the 'I') in three modes; as intelligence (buddhi), memory (smriti) and roving mind (manas or mann). All the above components (including the 'I') are collectively known as anthakarna, the inner or invisible organ of perception; although a jiva, for example, feels that his or her eyes behold an object, yet they (i.e. eyes) are only an extension of the consciousness, which alone is capable of seeing or perceiving an object. The mind gains objective knowledge to satiate 'I''s desires through the roving mind (called so because it keeps jumping from one object or a thought to another all the time) when the senses, which are its integral parts, come in contact with external objects. The knowledge gained thus by the roving mind including senses is discriminated by intelligence to determine whether a desire of the 'I' has been gratified or not. The 'I' experiences happiness (or pleasure) or unhappiness (or pain) accordingly. The memory's function is to keep a record of all that the roving mind, senses and intelligence do including whether the 'I' feels happy or unhappy. The above phenomenon is illustrated with an example. A desire arises in a man's mind (or in his 'I'- consciousness) to read a novel. To fructify it, a thought manifests in the roving mind (it is that part of the consciousness in which thoughts erupt) to pick up the book from a shelf. The man does so by looking for it and then begins reading. Intelligence plays a dual role in the above phenomenon; one, it allows the roving mind including the senses and the hands to search for and collect the book. It could control this desire and disallow any action to take place. Two, as one reads the novel, the intelligence decides if it is a pleasant or an unpleasant experience, which is then actually felt by the 'I'. All the above acts are imprinted in memory for future reference automatically and without any effort. There are countless such experiences in a day and they are all recorded in memory. These mental impressions are known as samaskaras. A discerning reader should note the role that intelligence plays in the working of the mind. Along with the discriminative faculty, it has the will power to restrain any activity of the roving mind and senses. This innate ability is used to control the mind during practice (sadhana).

Q33. How does the mind gain subjective knowledge (i.e. of the 'I' of a jiva)?
A33. The feeling of 'I' (i.e. the 'I' that everyone uses to refer to one's self) exists as a powerful latent vibration (or pulsation or current) in the consciousness. It is the primary and the first thought that the individual consciousness entertains but it is not experienced as such for two reasons. First, on the 'I' thought are superimposed countless other thoughts (samaskaras) that impel the consciousness to extrovert (to the external world) on account of their impure nature; second, an individual identifies one's self ('I') with the gross body and, hence, cannot feel the subtle 'I'-pulsation. The 'I' – current is felt only if samaskaric soot that covers it is removed. Also, one ought to dissociate the 'I' from the body by discarding the notion, 'I am the body', that is deeply embedded in one's mind. For that, a jiva must indulge in practice to control and purify the mind. The 'I' is experienced only after the mind is purified sufficiently (i.e. mind becomes causal) and it takes place in lower samadhi (savikalpa or bhava). To attain knowledge of the 'I' forms the immediate goal of practice, which is then followed by the effort to destroy it (in higher or nirvikalpa samadhi).

Q34. Kindly explain by an analogy the relationship of the 'I' with other components of the mind.
A34. The 'I' is like the president of a republic, in whose name the government (i.e. the mind) functions. Intelligence is its all-powerful prime minister who actually runs it and controls its (i.e. government's) functions. The roving mind (manas) is a wayward and corrupt finance minister who is constantly engaged in emptying the treasury (i.e. mind's energy) in league with his revenue officers, i.e., the five senses (of sight, hearing, smell, taste and touch) and five organs of action (hands, feet, mouth, genitals, parts of the body used for excretion of waste material). The senses are used to earn false wealth (i.e. objective experience), which is stored as counterfeit currency (i.e. the samaskaras) in memory. All that a jiva earns through this money is a life full of pain, misery and disease mixed with an occasional dose of transitory pleasure. This is the state of an uncontrolled and extroverted mind (of an average jiva) who does not use his or her intelligence properly, i.e., to restrain the roving mind and the senses. Only fools allow this state of affairs to continue for long.

Q35. What is a thought?

A35. Thoughts constitute the tangible nature of the mind. The latter is like a limitless ocean and its waves form the thoughts that arise in it. A thought is a vibration (vritti) of kinetic energy felt by the individual consciousness. A wave rises before falling down and so does a thought; it manifests and then disappears to be succeeded by another thought. A thought is a manifestation of one of the almost countless samaskaras (impressions of past deeds) that exist in the consciousness and in it inheres subjective or objective knowledge or awareness. Thoughts erupt in the mind only when it is in motion as in the waking and dream states but they are absent if the consciousness is either at complete rest (as in Realisation) or becomes dormant (as in deep sleep). The primordial thought is the omnipotent 'I am' feeling of Ishwara and it is the primary vibration (in the consciousness) of kinetic energy. All other thoughts, infinite in number, are inherent in it in latent form. The Lord creates the objective world, through the incidence of maya, by using this thought energy. For example, the thought, 'I am the world' entertained by Ishwara's consciousness materializes instantly in the form perceived by senses. The divine intelligence and will power make this possible. Similarly, our universe created by Brahma has its genesis in the thought energy in his consciousness, i.e., the universe is conceived by Brahma prior to its projection in maya, which is then perceived by the senses. Ishwara is able to create the world appearance from thought energy because Its consciousness is pure and under Its complete control. A jiva is unable to do so due to mental impurities and dissipation of thought energy caused by lack of self-restraint. The basic thought that a jiva has is of his or her individuality, i.e., of 'I'-ness. All one's desires, hopes, wishes and emotions as well as their fulfilment and experience exist as thoughts only but they are superimposed on the 'I' thought. Thus, every form of objective knowledge or experience begins with the awareness of the 'I'; for example, 'I see a horse', 'I am happy', 'I want to eat' and so on. No thought can arise without being related to the 'I'. All thoughts are offshoots of the 'I' as experienced in wakefulness but submerge in it in deep sleep (i.e. thoughts do not erupt in it because the 'I' thought becomes dormant). The subjective 'I' thought is the primary bondage that a jiva is caught up in; all other thoughts constitute secondary bondage. The latter is removed prior to tackling the former. Liberation is attained only if the 'I' thought is destroyed.

Q36. Why do thoughts arise in a haphazard manner in the mind?

A36. Thoughts manifest from samaskaras (mental impressions of past karma), recorded in memory, at the time their seeds are ready to sprout. Some thoughts lead to action to reap the harvest (or reward and punishment) of karma done previously. Many other thoughts fall in the realm of fantasy and day dreaming, which are signs of an uncontrolled mind given to its whims and fancies. There is no particular pattern in which thoughts arise; the mind may jump from one thought to another without any apparent connection between them. A man may think of his wife one moment and then without any effort entertain a thought of the moon. This is a common experience of all jivas lacking in self-control. It is possible to establish a certain method in the eruption of thoughts if one can concentrate the mind. For example, a man who is deeply engrossed in the contemplation of his beloved continues to think about her, to the exclusion of other thoughts, as long as his concentration (on her) stays intact. Intrusion of extraneous thoughts depends on the degree and quality of mental concentration. Thoughts arise in the consciousness according to the strength of their samaskaras (mental impressions) at the time they are recorded. A thought that is repeated often enough is more potent than the one to which little attention is paid. For example, a mother who thinks more often of her daughter (due to attachment) than her husband creates a more potent mental impression (in memory) of the former than of the latter. The samaskaras of the attachment to the daughter will manifest earlier in the mind of the mother than of the husband. An uncontrolled mind keeps a record of its activity haphazardly because its functioning lacks any method. A computer displays only what its memory contains, even if its record is defective; similarly, thoughts arises in a jiva's mind according to the strength of its samaskaras and the way they were recorded in the first place.

Q37. What are samaskaras (mental impressions) and vasnas (mental tendencies)?
A37. Samaskaras are the mental impressions imprinted in memory of a jiva's mind and they are created by the subjective and objective knowledge gained by the senses as also by the actions of the body. All that an individual has ever desired, hoped, sought, done and experienced (e.g. happiness, pleasure, pain, despair etc.) in any state of the consciousness (i.e. wakefulness, dream and deep sleep) during every second of one's existence (including innumerable past lives) is recorded in one's memory as samaskaras. They exist in a latent form in memory of a jiva and their number is almost infinite. They manifest as thoughts at the appropriate time, according to their strength and suitability to give fruit, which may extend to any length; for instance, a samaskaras of an action done a thousand years back may manifest in one's present life. An average jiva's samaskaras are pollutants and are the chief cause of mental impurities because they germinate from undesirable traits like attachment, greed, pride, selfishness, jealousy etc. Even the so called good actions (e.g. giving in charity, looking after old people etc.), though highly commendable, fall in the above category because they are done to please the ego (i.e. to gain name and fame in the world). A spiritual discipline aims to remove samaskaric impurities ingrained deeply in the 'I'-consciousness; the 'I'-current is experienced only if the mind is purified of its samaskaric dross. A set of samaskaras of a similar

nature, which may come into being over many lives, creates latent tendencies in the mind to impel it to function in a certain way. For example, a man wants to become rich and devotes most of his life in that effort to succeed; his mind is mostly engaged in devising ways to earn wealth and this constant refrain creates samaskaras that are more potent than his other mental impressions (e.g. of love for his wife). These samaskaras condition the mind to think more often of wealth than other things and their addition in every life make them even more potent. It creates a powerful mental latent tendency that impels one to think and act to become rich. Such tendencies are termed as vasnas and from them are formed an individual's traits, character, habits, desires, hopes, cravings, wishes etc. They force a jiva to act in a way to fulfill them and to become their victim is a sign of lack of self-control. A person is greedy or a show off or prone to anger or proud due to vasnas. Often, one does not even know why one acts in the way one does; the cause lies in the deep rooted vasnas and those who have no control over their minds act at their behest. Their manifestation depends on the time when a jiva is ready to do karma dictated by them and reap its fruit in terms of pleasure or pain. They determine a person's moods, which are subject to constant change. A jiva in an angry mood does karma in an irrational manner, which brings pain, as opposed to one who acts in a mood of calmness that results in pleasure. In simple words, vasnas make the mind think along habitual lines and are being formed every day. For example, reading a newspaper in the morning is a manifestation of a mental habit (vasna) formed over a period of time. Most vasnas are formed over many previous lives and have very deep roots in the consciousness. They require really hard labour done over a long period of time, to be destroyed. Vasnas are a major cause of a jiva's attachment to the world and no genuine spiritual progress is possible without controlling them. They are restrained on their own if the mind is purified and controlled through the practice of a spiritual discipline. Vasnas are either desirable (e.g. of love, compassion) or undesirable (e.g. of jealousy, pride); both must be given up to attain liberation. In brief, a person's nature is primarily determined by one's vasnas, specially the desires one entertains.

Q38. How is the mind as well as its samaskaras and vasnas classified? What are its states?
A38. The veil of maya on the consciousness consists of three layers, which conform to its three gunas (attributes; satva, rajas and tamas). The consciousness is conditioned by maya's three qualities into three different forms as satvic, rajasic and tamasic. A jiva's (person's) mind is said to be either satvic or purified (i.e. influenced by satva) or rajasic or active (predominated by qualities of rajas) or tamasic or lethargic (under the impact of tamas). Every jiva's mind evolves through these stages during its extroversion and involutes through them during introversion. A satvic mind is calm, peaceful, purified and tranquil. It

is the most suited to carry out spiritual practices of a higher order and attain liberation. Rajasic mind is characterised by restlessness, activity and surfeit of desires; all the workaholics of the world have a predominance of rajas in their minds. A rajasic jiva is basically a worldly active person. Tamasic mind is non-inquisitive, lethargic, indifferent and dull. This is a broad classification. Every mind is a mix of all three types with one or the other guna (satva rajas, tamas) being more prominent than others and this predominance keeps changing with time according to one's samaskaras and vasnas. An average jiva's mind is mostly rajasic with a heavy dose of tamas in it; its satvic component is very little. Those who pursue a spiritual path seriously for a long time (maybe many lives) have predominantly satvic minds. The minds of ever free souls are always satvic, even if they display some rajasic or tamasic tendencies. Another way to typify the mind is to relate it to the predominance of various gunas during its functioning in the three states of consciousness; it is satvic or causal in deep sleep, rajasic or subtle in dream state and tamasic or gross in wakefulness. The mind's extroversion as an effect of motion in it, begins from the satvic veil and it is then described as causal (i.e. latent or dormant or in seed form). Rajasic veil makes the mind subtle (i.e. there is a spatial difference between the 'I' and objects as perceived in dreams). Tamasic mind is gross that perceives material objects. The difference between subtle and gross mind is the degree of restlessness that pervades it, the latter being in greater turmoil. Thoughts are latent in causal mind, agitated in its subtle counterpart and very forceful in the tamasic one. A satvic mind conserves its energy whereas a tamasic one dissipates it the most. A jiva's samaskaras and vasnas are classified similarly and their state conforms to that of the mind; for instance, a satvic mind's samaskaras and vasnas are of the same nature (i.e. they are purified). Individual mind's states are described under two conditions; firstly, of an average jiva engaged in worldly activities and secondly, of an aspirant who practices a spiritual discipline. Intelligence functions best in wakefulness and one is able to exercise some control over one's self; it malfunctions in dreams (they manifest from previously recorded samaskaras and in response to some deeply felt vasnas) and, for that reason, they are always disjointed affairs. All components of the mind ('I'-sense, intelligence, memory, roving mind and senses) become dormant in deep sleep and, hence, it is a state of non-experience (of one's subjectivity as well as of the objective world). The mind is at rest during dreamless sleep and on that account one feels happy and refreshed on waking up. The change over from one state to another is determined by a jiva's samaskaras. Wakefulness is the state of the gross mind, dream of a subtle mind and deep sleep of a causal mind. A discerning reader should note that in neither dream nor deep sleep states does an individual exercise any control over the mind. This is sought to be set right during effort to control the mind. Practice (sadhana) of a spiritual discipline is done in wakefulness by the gross mind; the purpose is to make it subtle and causal in a conscious manner so that one can control it, unlike their counterparts in dream and dreamless states of an average mind over which one has no control. Gross mind becomes subtle after it is purified to a certain level and an aspirant sees visions etc. in this state. Although it is akin to the normal dream state, yet the vital difference is that the mind is under greater control, thoughts lose some of their energy and desires do not bother a seeker as much as they did earlier. This state is, therefore, described as wakeful sleep (or dream) state. A similar difference arises in the causal state of the mind for aspirants. Deep sleep of an average person is a state of causal mind that is not aware of anything. A devotee, on the other hand, purifies his or her mind to the causal (i.e. purified) level consciously by exercising great control over it. He or she then has very few desires and thoughts become latent in the mind. He or she is fully aware of his or her individuality (i.e. his or her 'I'-ness) in that state and, hence, it is referred to as wakeful deep sleep. Ishwara's (or cosmic) mind, whether in its causal, subtle or gross form, is always in a wakeful state, which is state of enlightenment and full self-control. A jiva, on the other hand, suffers from samaskaric impurities, unlike Ishwara, which must be removed before attaining the wakeful state (of the subtle and causal mind). An aspirant begins practice with gross mind and passes through its subtle and causal forms after purifying it. This process is called introversion of the mind. There is yet one more state of the mind; the transitory or intermediate stage, i.e., the state between wakefulness and sleep (or vice versa) and between dream and deep sleep (or vice versa). It denotes a restful state of the mind, as noticed in half sleep or half wakefulness before either going to sleep or on waking up. The same phenomenon is noticed during the effort to control the mind when one becomes aware of gaps between thoughts. The mind gives the impression of being motionless then and reveals divine knowledge, besides being very blissful.

Q39. The mind is said to be the creator of the objective world. What is the relationship of the subject ('I'-sense) with the object? How does it evolve?
A39. In the 'I' inhere countless ideas (or thoughts) pertaining to objects. The 'I'- consciousness imagines that it is this or that object; for example, 'I am a rose' or 'I am a horse' and so on. That thought materialises in a bodily form, which consists of a causal, subtle and gross body, when it is projected in maya's three attributes (satva, rajas and tamas). Thus, what the senses perceive outside is a projection of the 'I' itself and an object, as such, is not different from its subject though it appears to be otherwise due to ignorance. The spatial separation that exists between the 'I' and objects of its creation (in subtle and physical forms) is an effect of maya, which is eliminated only when the mind is controlled and detached from the external phenomenon. A fully introverted mind rests on its 'I'-ness and all objects are withdrawn into it through practice

of a spiritual discipline. The evolution described earlier is only for purposes of teaching. The truth is that a subject and an object are inseparable and their existence is interdependent. They both come into being together at the same time and disappear similarly, as happens in deep sleep when neither a subject nor an object exists.

Q40. What are the qualities of a jiva and how are they classified? How are they developed?

A40. Every object of creation is a manifestation of the divine consciousness that entertains the 'I' thought. For example, the consciousness that imagines that 'I am a jiva' appears (in maya) in human form and the same consciousness manifests as a cat when it thinks 'I am a cat'. Although their principle (i.e. consciousness) is the same, yet all objects appear to be different because of their attributes. Further, each object displays similar qualities in a general way, though individual variations exist due to samaskaric difference. All jivas, for instance, have the same attributes but the degree of their manifestation varies from one individual to another. Although all mothers love their children, yet the attachment is different in each case. A jiva's qualities stem from the ego (or 'I') sense. Broadly, they are craving (kama), anger (krodha), greed (lobha), attachment (moha) and pride (ahankara). Craving refers to the ego's desire for pleasure through objective experience. It includes lust, gluttony, desire for wealth and fame etc. It is the main driving force for a jiva's karma. An unfulfilled desire leads, at times, to a sudden violent turbulence in the mind that is hard to control; it is termed as anger. Its latent form is irritability and it is also the cause of jealousy and hate etc. An angry mind is irrational and cannot be controlled. To give way excessively and repeatedly to craving is greed and to be bound to pleasure obtained from it is attachment. Pride is the feeling of superiority, over other objects, that the ego entertains, which thinks no end of itself and dreams of grandeur and power. All the above traits are inter-dependent and from them arise many other attributes like intolerance, impatience etc. A jiva's qualities develop from the effects (samaskaras) created by one's daily objective experience, which are either pleasurable or painful. A sensual experience that gives pleasure creates a desire for its repetition. Most people find sexual act highly satisfying and they want to repeat it as often as possible. This creates feelings of lust and attachment between two partners. Aversion and dislike manifests in the mind when either one or both partners find the sexual act unsatisfying (or its effects are painful). A jiva's traits are formed when similar type of experiences are repeated often enough. They create latent mental tendencies (or habits; vasnas) that impel an individual to display certain attributes. Individual qualities are either satvic or rajasic or tamasic. Satvic attributes manifest in a purified mind only and they are divine in nature; unselfish love, devotion (for God), discrimination (i.e. ability to separate falsehood from truth) and detachment from the world are some of them. Rajasic traits arise in an active mind engaged in satiation of worldly desires; they include anger, lust, attachment, greed and pride. Tamasic attributes are a sign of mind's indifference (due to its lethargy) to fulfil certain desires; to be callous, unsympathetic, unconcerned etc. are signs of an undeveloped (tamasic) mind.

Q41. What are divine qualities and how are they distinguished from their non-divine counterparts? Do they inhere in a jiva? What is their importance and how are they developed?

A41. Divine qualities are those that manifest in an ego-less mind like that of Ishwara and their growth is an index of self-control. They bring calmness to the mind and are universal in their application. For example, God's loves the entire creation equally unlike a jiva whose love is finite and limited (to some objects only). Non-divine attributes are undesirable and they arise in an uncontrolled and agitated mind impelled into activity by the ego to satisfy its desires. Some of them have been discussed in the previous answer. Individual mind is the finite form of the infinite mind of Ishwara. Divine qualities inhere in it in a latent and finite form and a jiva can develop them through practice of a spiritual discipline by purifying the mind. One cannot develop them to an infinite level because individual mind is finite and remains so even with spiritual growth. Know it for certain that no spiritual progress is possible unless one cultivates divine qualities consciously through practice and, at the same time, shedding their undesirable counterparts.

Q42. What is the nature of pleasure (sukha) and pain (dukha)?

A42. They are the effects of objective (or sensual) experience of an individual's effort to satisfy desires. The ego feels happy and pleased when its desires are fulfilled and, if they are not, it experiences unhappiness and pain. A jiva's desires are limitless and obviously no one can ever satiate them fully. An individual's life is mixture of pain and pleasure, mostly the former because it is not possible to extinguish (through normal means) the fire that desire starts in the mind. Ever increasing number of desires is the fuel that keeps the fire burning all the time. Temporary pleasure that one feels by gratifying a desire carries within it the seeds of pain. An investor is pleased when he makes millions of rupees as profit in the stock market but is also immediately worried about its loss in the future. Pleasure and pain are the effects produced as per the law of pair of opposites in which two apparently contradictory qualities are related. Thus, there is a relationship between happiness and unhappiness, love and hate and so on. A quality manifests only if its opposite is absent (i.e. dormant). Thus, pleasure is experienced in the absence of pain and vice versa. A befuddled jiva is bound by the idea of seeking pleasure (through sensual experience) but ends up suffering pain because he or she does not understand its nature (i.e. it is temporary and brings pain in its wake). Perennial happiness is attained only when one gives up pleasure and pain through control of mind (i.e. by realising one's real Self).

Q43. What are the powers of the mind?
A43. The mind in general (i.e. of Ishwara) has limitless powers because it is ego-less, pure and fully concentrated on itself. An average jiva's mind is its finite form and has limited powers of perception due to its samaskaric impurities. Besides that, the ego is a limitation in itself. Individual mind is purified through practice of a spiritual discipline, which also conserves its energy and makes it more concentrated. A purified (i.e. subtle) mind's range of perception (e.g. of seeing and hearing in a state of meditation) increases considerably, which gives objective knowledge of greater clarity, besides that of things not normally cogitated by the senses. An average jiva's perception of subtle objects (as in dreams) is like seeing them through fog whereas a purified mind perceives them as on a sunny day. This phenomenon gives rise to manifestation of certain paranormal powers (called riddhis and siddhis) of the mind. It is a common occurrence during practice. The crucial point that a serious aspirant ought to appreciate is that such powers are a major hurdle to spiritual advancement. Anyone who gets involved with them cannot grow spiritually and those who misuse them are inviting divine retribution. All powers of the mind are of a temporary nature and one is back to square one once they are exhausted. A wise student should avoid them like the plague.

Q44. What is knowledge and its types? What is its source? What is its importance for an aspirant and how is it acquired?
A44. Knowledge is the perception or recognition of a subject or an object by knowing its characteristics. For example, to know that a tiger has stripes, four legs and is carnivorous is its knowledge. The divine consciousness uses its inherent knowledge to create the world appearance and its myriad objects. Knowledge is gained in the light that exists naturally in the consciousness. The veil of samaskaras partially blocks the divine light from enlightening the individual mind and, hence, the knowledge of objects that a jiva attains is incomplete and defective. Objective knowledge is acquired by the consciousness, which is used for a variety of purposes; electricity, television, cars etc. have come into being through it only. Knowledge is not attained in darkness, as, for example, in deep sleep; hence, only wakeful consciousness is capable of gaining it. The darkness of ignorance (i.e. lack of knowledge of one's real nature) pervades the mind of an average jiva and the only way to overcome it is through the light of divine knowledge imparted by a competent guru or, in a general sense, by the knowledge contained in various scriptures, provided it is put into effect through

practice. An earnest aspirant must understand the nature of knowledge in order to employ it in controlling the mind. One cannot make substantive spiritual progress without it. Knowledge is of two types; absolute and relative. Absolute knowledge is the thing in itself and it is just another word for the Reality. It is neither gained (by anyone) nor is it lost and it requires no proof of its existence. It is known only by transcending or destroying the mind and is, therefore, indescribable in words. Relative knowledge is the knowledge that the mind acquires of its subjective and objective nature. The triad of knower (subject; seer), knowing (seeing) and the known (object; seen) is a must to gain relative knowledge. It requires proof of its existence either through direct sensual perception (e.g. seeing a cat) or by inference (e.g. to deduce that a friend has arrived when he blows the horn of his car) or through memory (i.e. an inference drawn of intangible knowledge from a study of visible phenomenon; as, for example, the discovery of law of gravity). The source of relative knowledge is the divine consciousness of infinite Ishwara. Absolute knowledge has no origin and is its own causeless cause. It is very important that an earnest aspirant learns to appreciate the inadequacy and unreality of relative knowledge in order to grow spiritually. It is a common failing amongst most students to disregard this crucial aspect of spiritual training. Know it for certain that one matures spiritually only if one learns to reject all types of relative knowledge as false. It is a habit that one should form in the very early stage of practice (sadhana).

Q45. What is the type of knowledge that the individual mind gains?
A45. Mind attains subjective and objective knowledge of three grades. A causal (or satvic) mind acquires knowledge of the causal (or latent) 'I' and of objects in their ideation (or thought or latent form). The subjective 'I' and the objects are not spatially separated in this type of knowledge, which is of the highest class. It gives knowledge of the inner core of objects (i.e. their essence). The 'I'-current (or vibration in the consciousness) is experienced only by a causal mind, which implies that the samaskaric dross superimposed on it has been purified to a great extent. A rajasic or subtle mind is partly purified and the subjective knowledge that it gains is of the 'I' that associates itself with the subtle body (of a jiva). Simply put, it refers to the knowledge that the subtle body gains (as in visions or dreams), just like the physical body does of the phenomenal world. Objective knowledge that the subtle mind attains is of the subtle body of objects. The 'I' is separated spatially from objects in this form of knowledge and, hence, it is partial and inadequate. The difference between causal and subtle knowledge is that the former is full whereas the latter is incomplete. For instance, the idea of a cat inherent in divine consciousness contains in it the knowledge of all cats whereas the subtle knowledge that one acquires (during meditation) is of the cat that the mind perceives (as a vision), which by its nature must remain limited. The same criterion is applicable to gross knowledge that

the gross mind gains. The subjective knowledge of the gross or tamasic mind is affected by the 'I''s alignment with the physical body. It means that the mind acquires knowledge for the sake of the body (i.e. to satiate its desires), which the 'I' imagines itself to be. In other words, the embodied 'I' is the subject and it gains knowledge of object through gross senses. Knowledge of this type is only of the outer covering of objects (i.e. not its essence). For instance, physical senses perceive only the gross knowledge of a rose but not of its inner (i.e. subtle and causal) form. All types of knowledge mentioned above is gained by senses (e.g. eyes, ears etc) in their physical or subtle or causal forms.

Q46. What is the nature of relative knowledge?
A46. Subjective (i.e. of one's own self) and objective knowledge that the mind gains is relative in nature because it is attained through a relationship, i.e., between a subject (the 'I'- sense or an individual) and an object. Subjective knowledge refers to the knowledge of the mind and its genesis, the 'I' of a jiva, its characteristics (e.g. propensity to extrovert or its inherent power of introversion), nature of desire, doubt, fear etc. and how they affect its functioning and so on. Subjective knowledge is regarded as relative because its perception varies according to circumstances; for example, an average jiva mistakes his or her 'I' with the physical body in wakefulness, subtle body in dream state and is not aware of it in deep sleep. Also, one knows oneself as apart from others because of the relationship that one has with them. For example, a father and his son are two different beings. Objective knowledge is of the attributes of objects that the 'I' (or the mind) acquires to satisfy its desires to derive pleasure (temporarily). Although everyone uses the 'I' to identify oneself with the body in normal parlance, yet its knowledge is obtained only by a purified and an introverted mind in a state of lower samadhi (savikalpa and bhava). This knowledge is gained in relation to the 'I' of Ishwara and other jivas. To know that a rose is a beautiful flower and gives joy to one's aesthetic sense is objective knowledge. Relative knowledge forms the basis of action by Ishwara (i.e. to create, sustain and dissolve) and an individual. This type of knowledge is attained by the consciousness in motion; that is, vibrating 'I'-consciousness (or mind) gains knowledge of objects in which inheres kinetic energy and, obviously, the act of knowing takes place in the same state. An average jiva is not aware of this motion because the mind is habituated to it for a very long time. It should not be difficult to appreciate that the knowledge gained by the consciousness in a state of flux (i.e. when the knower is in motion and so is the known and act of knowing) cannot be but partial and incomplete. Normal objective perception is akin to what a man, in a moving train, sees of a beautiful woman in another train running in the opposite direction. A fleeting glimpse like that ensures that a subject does not stay long enough in contact with an object to gain its full knowledge. It is true even if the contact is repeated

very often. For instance, a mother may claim that she knows her child fully because of their long stay together but even that knowledge is inadequate due to the constantly changing moods (of the mother) and growth (of the child). An angry husband perceives his wife differently than when he is in a calm state of mind. Similarly, doubt, fear, stress, worry etc. affect a subject's ability to gain knowledge of others. A man sees a rope in darkness and imagines it to be a snake due to fear. It is not only objective knowledge that is partial in normal perception but it is so even in the case of its subjective counterpart. A man is self-assured and confident when he is calm but begins to doubt his ability in a state of dejection. The quality of subjective and objective knowledge is determined by the mind's level of purity. The fragrance of jasmine in normal perception is not a patch on that experienced in meditation, i.e., in a state of mental purity and concentration, which reduces the spatial difference between the 'I' and jasmine which smells many times more. An object is apprehended not as it is but as one imagines it to be. It is like the sunlight that appears to assume the colour of one's blinkers. Objects are perceived differently during day and night as well as by one's viewpoint that is determined by one's vasnas and samaskaras. No two persons cogitate the same object similarly. For instance, a table seen by two jivas from different vantage points gives them varied perceptions. One of them may pay more attention to the quality of wood while the other considers the carving of the legs more appealing. Individual perception is subject to even greater difference in apprehending and expressing intangibles knowledge like emotions, feelings, notions. For instance, there is no standard yardstick to measure love that is described as great or little. Another striking feature of relative knowledge is that it is determined by the relationship that one (i.e. a subject) has with an object. A man is a boss in the office, father to his daughter, friend of another businessman and so on. In each case he perceives them in that particular relationship and knows only that aspect of theirs. Similarly, an employee regards his employer in a different light than his own subordinate. A jiva responds to another individual only in the relationship that exists between them. A man's conduct with his wife is not the same as with his mother. Relative knowledge is also affected by time and space. A woman is passionate about her lover in young age but is not so in old age. A tree appears to be small when seen from a distance but becomes big if one is close to it. The same object is often a cause of happiness and unhappiness at the same time. A young girl is a source of joy to her parents but makes her competitors in a beauty contest envious. Further, every jiva has his or her own notion of beauty, honour, greatness, ugliness and so on. No two persons are likely to agree on such matters. This is true of scientific knowledge also; discovery made by one physicist is disputed by another. An analysis of relative knowledge carried out on the above lines leads only to one inevitable conclusion; that is, it is unreliable, partial, inadequate and undependable to give permanent happiness to anyone because it is subject to constant change. A wise student ought to realise that knowledge which manifests in the consciousness (or mind) as an effect of maya cannot but be false and illusory. It is, in fact, knowledge of ignorance and wisdom lies in giving it up.

Q47. What is ignorance?

A47. Non-knowledge (or non-awareness) of the Self (Atman; a person's real nature) is ignorance. It is an effect of the pervasion of maya in the divine consciousness. How should one regard the awareness of one's self and the world? Subjective and objective knowledge arises in the consciousness as an effect of maya; in other words, it manifests in a state of ignorance (i.e. in Self forgetfulness or non-awareness of the Self) and, hence, it cannot be regarded as real. All that the mind and senses perceive is thus a manifested or palpable form of ignorance, which is another name for the relative nature of consciousness (or knowledge). Ignorance is either general or particular; the former pervades the whole of consciousness and the latter only a part of it (e.g. a jiva). Ishwara (God) is not affected by ignorance due to Its supreme intelligence and total self-control. Ishwara has not made any effort to be so since It is like that naturally. A jiva lacks self-control because of defective intelligence and extroversion of mind. One forgets the Self in that state and one is, therefore, subject to individual (or particular) ignorance. In spiritual effort to attain salvation, an aspirant is required to destroy only individual ignorance. Its general counterpart is a power of Ishwara, which must prevail according to Its will to indulge in the divine drama of creation.

Q48. Why is a jiva's relative knowledge of an object regarded as incomplete?

A48. This type of knowledge is known in a position of relativity between a subject and an object, i.e., the relationship and viewpoint that the former adopts with the latter. For example, a daughter knows her father but is not aware how all the other daughters regard their fathers, not only of the present but also of the past and future as well. An object's full knowledge can be attained only if all the countless subjects of the past, present and future were to get together and arrive at a definite conclusion about the nature of an object. It is obviously not possible to do so. The problem is compounded further if one takes into account the ever changing nature of a subject and an object. Similarly, a hill viewed from one vantage-point looks to be different than seen from another angle. Further, the hill's beauty varies according to the time of day and night when it is seen. It is possible to gain complete knowledge of the hill only if all the possible viewers (of the past, present and future) were to look at it from all possible viewpoints at all possible times; it is clearly an impossibility. Similarly, there can never be consensus on notions like beauty, honour, freedom and so on. Only Ishwara's knowledge (of any type) is complete because It is an embodiment of principle of infinity, i.e., It pervades every atom of existence, time, space etc. A jiva is a finite being and, hence, one can never obtain full knowledge of any object.

Q49. Does not an aspirant aim to acquire infinite knowledge during practice? A49. No; infinite knowledge can be attained in infinite time only. How can a finite jiva hope to do that? Besides that, what purpose does the acquisition of false (i.e. infinite relative knowledge) knowledge serve? A wise student's aim is to gain absolute knowledge by giving up its relative counterpart.

Q50. How does relative knowledge manifest?
A50. Relative knowledge is based on the principle of pair of opposites. It implies that two attributes of opposing natures are intrinsically interlinked naturally in their ideation forms and they are known only in relationship to each other. Examples of the qualities in pairs of opposites are male and female, light and darkness, pleasure and pain, love and hate, attachment and detachment, heat and cold and so on. An attribute is known only in relationship to its contrary form; pleasure, for instance, is experienced in the absence of pain only and both of them cannot be felt at the same time. The relationship between attributes of contrary natures is self-existing in their ideas held in the divine consciousness and Ishwara creates the objective world from them. All objects, for instance, have male and female traits but their predominance in each of them varies. Although female characteristic predominate in women, yet they are not totally absent in males. This is true of all objects. This relativity arises due to the wave like motion in the consciousness. The ascendant wave of consciousness manifests the positive aspect of an attribute and its negative counterpart appears when it (i.e. consciousness) descends. A positive thought of love indicates an upward movement of the consciousness whereas that of hate of its downward counterpart. The rapid succession of positive and negative thoughts occurs due to this natural phenomenon of an agitated mind. It is an effect of maya's nature, which is to make a thing appear what it is not. Light inheres in darkness (latent form) and vice versa; so does love and hate and vice versa and so on. One of them manifests at a time according to circumstances, as, for instance, light during daytime and darkness at night, though both are present in each other. The above phenomenon is applicable to subjective knowledge also. The 'I' of an individual exists in relationship to other jivas; the ideas of 'you', 'he', 'her' etc. are present (in latent form) in the 'I' itself but they become apparent when the consciousness is embodied in maya. Thus, duality (i.e. 'I' and 'you' being two different jivas) cannot disappear as long as the 'I' remains extant.

Q51. What is the basis of the law of pair of opposites? Why is it said that there is no finality in relative knowledge?

A51. The Lord has created the above law to manifest diversity and multiplicity of objects, emotions, feelings, thoughts etc. The interconnection of two opposing attributes also establishes their common origin in the consciousness that is apparently broken by maya. It is play acting of Ishwara through the incidence of maya. Sensual perception of different objects would not have been possible but for the above law as also the motion that propels them to activity. To be aware of only one thing all the time implies that the consciousness is motionless, which is contrary to normal experience. For instance, no one feels hot all the time; invariably, sensations of heat and cold alternate with each other in time. Sensual perception of heat takes place when its sensation, felt by the sense of touch, is compared by intelligence with that (i.e. sensation) of cold. It is possible for intelligence to do so because there is an innate relationship between the ideas of heat and cold held in individual memory. In the theory of relativity, as manifested in the pair of opposites, a quality grows at the expense of its opposite attribute but none of them can ever reach zero level. Thus, relative love develops in place of hate but the latter cannot be totally eliminated as long as the mind remains extant. Both these qualities have an infinite level of quantification and their limit can never be found. The level of their manifestation in various objects extends in a limitless spectrum. It is applicable to all attributes of Ishwara. A wise student should deduce, from the above discussion that the aim of spiritual practice is not to develop relative love to an infinite level but to give it up totally. That is the way to wisdom (or Realisation).

Q52. What is the nature of divine knowledge? How does it differ from its normal objective counterpart?

A52. The word, divine, is used for Ishwara (God) and those of Its attributes that bring to an end the relativity of knowledge (or ignorance). Divine knowledge is the desirable and superior form of relative knowledge, which is used to destroy the mind and its undesirable traits (e.g. pride, attachment, greed etc.). It is the knowledge that a guru imparts to a seeker during the initiation and hearing stages of spiritual instruction as well as that contained in scriptures. Unlike normal subjective and objective knowledge, it is reliable because it is revealed by saints, sages and seers who have attained the Reality through it. Divine knowledge is regarded as relative because its expression in words is understood differently by various types of aspirants and others (who hear it) according to their own mental states. Moreover, a mere intellectual comprehension of this form of knowledge is not enough. It must be proved through spiritual experience, which again varies from one individual to another. The reference here is not to the attainment of Reality but to the experience that one has during various stages of the control of mind. Although acquiring divine knowledge by an aspirant from a guru, is a mental act (i.e. by a highly purified mind), yet even that must be given up to attain the supreme state of Realisation.

Q53. What is the nature of perception? What purpose does it serve?

A53. Perception is the act of knowing the known (i.e. an object) by the knower (i.e. a subject or individual self). To know one's own self ('I'-feeling) is a subjective form of perception. Objective perception arises through sensual contact (with objects) and the knowledge gained thus is presented by the roving mind (manas) to the intellect for discrimination (i.e. to determine its pleasant or unpleasant effects), which is then fed to the 'I' that feels happy or unhappy depending on whether its desire is gratified or not. The record of this entire process is kept by individual memory. Subjective perception (i.e. of the 'I') is attained by a purified and causal mind that is able to concentrate on the 'I'-pulsation (aham sphurana) and which forms its (i.e. mind's) core (or source). Objective perception is of three types; gross (i.e. of material objects), subtle (i.e. of objects seen in dreams or visions or of ideas held in memory) and causal (i.e. of objects and ideas in latent form) gained in samadhi. There are two primary ways in which perception arises; one, through direct sensual contact (e.g. a rose seen by the eyes); two, indirect contact in which the existence of an object is inferred by analysing the sensual data with that stored in memory. For instance, a girl in her study room knows what her mother is cooking from the aroma that she gets from the kitchen. The girl has arrived at an inference, which is an indirect form of perception, of what is being cooked by comparing the smells of food being cooked to what she had eaten previously and whose record is held in her memory. The mind indulges in objective perception to gratify its innumerable desires. A lustful man, for example, is impelled to seek the company of a woman and yet his desire remains unsatisfied, which acts as an impetus to look for more women (i.e. to indulge in repeated objective experience). An aspirant ought to endeavour (to attain subjective perception (i.e. of one's 'I') so that he or she can destroy it (or the mind).

Q54. How does creation evolve from relative knowledge?

A54. The limitless attributes (guna) of Ishwara (God) are held in Its divine consciousness in the form of ideas. An idea contains in it the general or particular form of subjective or objective knowledge pertaining to an object. For example, the divine consciousness entertains a notion that 'I am a tiger'. It is one of the innumerable attributes (of Ishwara) in which inheres the knowledge that a tiger has four legs, two eyes, stripes etc. The divine will creates all tigers that we see from this idea (or knowledge). Similarly, there is an idea that the earth has five continents having mountains, jungles, rivers, deserts etc. and they are surrounded by vast oceans. The planet that we live on manifests from this knowledge. An idea in the divine consciousness exists in the form of a pure thought which is like a single wave of vibratory energy in an infinite ocean (i.e. the divine consciousness). A thought (or an idea) is said to be causal, subtle or gross when perceived under the impact of maya's satvaguna, rajoguna and tamoguna respectively. This gives rise to creation in three forms; causal (satvic), subtle (rajasic) and tamasic (gross material). In the same way, each object has three bodies; a tiger, for instance, has physical, subtle and causal body to conform to an idea of three types. An object cannot exist without a subject; the latter is, in fact, the cause of the former. All ideas in the divine consciousness, therefore, begin with the 'I' (i.e. the subject). Ishwara does not entertain notions like, 'that is a rose' or 'this is a tiger' (i.e. a rose or a tiger is apart from It) but imagines that 'I am a rose' or 'I am a tiger' (i.e. It has assumed the form of a rose or a tiger), which implies that It is both the subject and the object; in other words, the divine consciousness is the 'I' that itself turns into a rose or a tiger.

Q55. How does the objective world perceived by the senses manifest?
A55. The world appearance is a reflection of Ishwara (or saguna Reality or relative consciousness) in the mirror like surface of maya. Another explanation is that it is very much like seeing images on a cinema screen projected by maya (i.e. by its projecting power). The 'I' (or 'I am') feeling of Ishwara manifests due to the veil of maya and so do the individual 'I''s of myriad objects (e.g. 'I am a jiva', 'I am a tiger' etc.). These feelings exist in the form of ideas whose projection in the three gunas (attributes of satva, rajas and tamas) of maya is then perceived by the senses as the world of name and form (i.e. nama and rupa; objects having definite names and shapes; for example, an animal named tiger has four legs, stripes etc.). Although the individual 'I' (of any object; for example, of a jiva) is a reflection of the general 'I' (of Ishwara; both feelings exist in the same consciousness) yet the former regards itself as being independent and separate from the latter due to ignorance and forgetfulness. A jiva, for instance, does not consider oneself as being an image of Ishwara but imagines that one has a unique identity, apart from other objects. Individualisation of consciousness (e.g. of jivas, animals, trees etc.) comes into being in this manner. Ishwara knows that the infinite creation is Its own form and is aware of it at all times. But an individual jiva lacks this knowledge due to a self-imposed limitation (of one's 'I'-ness) that arises from forgetfulness of one's real nature, which restricts one's awareness to a finite number of objects. An individual's sensual perception is thus confined to a small number of objects. Forgetfulness that a human mind suffers from is an effect of maya. God is not affected by it because of its total self-control.

Q56. What role does the divine intelligence and will play in creating the world appearance?

A56. Maya is like an insentient reflecting surface that projects myriad images of Ishwara in it. The nature of maya being what it is, Ishwara's countless images would have been reflected and then re-reflected again so many times in it so as to cause an utter confusion in viewing them. The divine intelligence and will power does not allow such a chaos to prevail. Ishwara's will imposes a certain order in which Its projection in maya takes place so that the creative process appears to be like a well-directed and executed film. In other words, the objective phenomenon perceived by the senses is organised by the divine intelligence to run in an orderly fashion according to a certain definite scheme (or natural order) of things. For instance, the sun rises in the east on our planet because Ishwara has willed it so and maya, despite its nature to cause illusions, is incapable of changing it. The obvious conclusion from the above is that divine intelligence and will is the co-efficient (i.e. it causes the creation or wills it into being) and material (i.e. objects are made out of constituents that are inseparable part of the divine consciousness) cause of the objective phenomenon. Maya is only an incidental cause in which objects appear so that senses can perceive them.

Q57. What is the divine scheme of things or the natural order (of things) mentioned above?

A57. The divine intelligence of Ishwara conceives of the limitless creation in Its causal mind prior to its manifestation in maya. It is arranged in a certain definite pattern and it functions according to a laid down scheme (or order) based on rational laws and principles ordained by It. The natural order is like the constitution of a country and the laws enacted under its authority to govern a state. The basic divine scheme is that the objective phenomenon undergoes three phases; creation, preservation and dissolution (followed by recreation). The entire creation is divided into innumerable universes with each one of them having its own individual creator, preserver and destroyer. They are known as Brahma, Vishnu and Shiva respectively in the Indian spiritual tradition. A universe is further split into a vast number of worlds, each one different from the other and having its own forms of life. The number of worlds in our universe and the types of life that exist in them is so vast and varied that a human mind cannot even conceive of them. The trinity of gods (Brahma, etc.) lays down its own natural order for each universe to carry out their respective functions but it cannot violate Ishwara's divine scheme. Social groups and individuals work out their own set of rules, customs, codes of conduct etc. to ensure that they can all live in harmony with each other. Every object in the Lord's natural order has certain laid down attributes and traits and they function according to them. No object can transgress its divinely ordained nature; for, that is the divine law. For example, Brahma cannot cease from creating nor does it have the power to dissolve a universe, which only Shiva can do. No blemish is attached to an object if it acts according to its nature. A demon cannot be blamed for acting the way it does because that is its innate character, just as fire is not at fault when it burns a body. The natural order that affects our material world is revealed through scientific research and enquiry; as, for example, was done by Newton when he discovered the law of gravitation. The laws that govern the subtle world or those that affect the spiritual growth of individuals are revealed by sages, saints and seers. Scriptural knowledge is an example of that.

Q58. What is the divine scheme for jivas?
A58. Jivas (human beings) alone, amongst the myriad objects of creation, have been blessed by the Lord with discriminative intelligence. Its proper use allows an individual freedom of choice (i.e. free will) to act in various ways. There are two basic paths that a jiva can follow in the divine scheme of things. The first is of an uncontrolled mind, which implies that an individual acts with the sense of 'I' (i.e. the 'I am the doer' feeling) to satisfy one's incessant desires through sensual gratification. A jiva on this path succumbs to every whim and fancy of the mind and binds oneself to the objective world to reap the fruit of one's karma through a cycle of repeated birth and death. It is the way of the ignorant that is beset with pain, sorrow and occasional pleasure. The second path is of the wise who seek divine knowledge through control of mind. Those who tread it are blessed by the Lord with complete freedom from ignorance, misery, birth and death. Their reward is absolute happiness of knowing their true natures. An individual has the choice to follow either of the above paths and reap its fruit accordingly.

Q59. What are the various views on the evolution of creation discussed in Guru-Upanishad?
A59. There are two basic ways by which teachers explain how the creation comes into being. First, the doctrine of sudden creation (drishti srishti), which says that creation and its seer (i.e. God) exist simultaneously and there is no evolution (of creation) as such. All that exists (in the entire cosmos) now or was there earlier or will be experienced in the future has always existed and will continue to be so in times to come. The entire creation came into being the moment its seer, Ishwara, became aware of Itself (i.e. in the nascent reflection, of the divine consciousness, in satvaguna of maya). As long as the seer (i.e. Ishwara) exists, so will the creation; if a subject exists, so must the object. The relationship between the seer and seen (creation) is akin to that of a dreamer and a dream. Both of them come into being together and vanish at the same time. In other words, a jiva's awareness of one's self ('I'-ness) is an essential condition to see the dream and the moment it disappears, as in deep (dreamless) sleep, so does the latter. This phenomenon is repeated in the highest samadhi (the super sensuous state of consciousness) in which the mind (or more

specifically an aspirant's 'I'- ness) is destroyed. One then does not perceive the creation. The second viewpoint is that Ishwara creates Brahma who after doing tapas (a special yogic discipline) manifests the universe we live in. He evolves the objective world from his mind over a period of time gradually. It is then preserved by Vishnu for a certain length of time (running into countless billions of years) and is finally dissolved (not completely destroyed; only made dormant) by Shiva. It is then re-created after some time by a new Brahma. There is no finality in the teaching on creation because it is given according to spiritual maturity of aspirants. Out of the two tenets mentioned above, the former is the more mature viewpoint. But, the really wise seekers know, through spiritual experience gained in highest (or sahaj) samadhi, that creation is really non-existent because it is not perceived in the state of Realisation. What does not exist there cannot be anything but untrue. The objective world of sensual experience comes into being as an effect of maya (ignorance) on the divine consciousness. It is a fantasy entertained by the mind, just as a rope appears to be a snake in darkness. A thing that manifests due to ignorance cannot be but unreal and false. The truth is that Reality alone is, there was never any creation nor is it there now nor will it be in the future.

Q60. Who are Brahma, Vishnu and Shiva? What is their nature and what do they represent?
A60. Most spiritually immature people cannot appreciate that the divine drama of creation, preservation and dissolution is a play of the consciousness in combination with maya. They are so obsessed with the notions of name and form (nama and rupa; means objects having names and shapes to distinguish them from each other) that they cannot imagine that the intangible consciousness can be a creator (of objects having a form). It is not possible for them to conceive of an amorphous Ishwara (God). Teachers then go down to their level and explain that God can assume a definite form for the sake of devotees. The embodied form of Ishwara is then said to be the supreme creator of limitless number of universes. Just as the number of universes is infinite, so is the count of their creators, preservers and destroyers. Each universe is considered to have its own creator, preserver and destroyer. Brahma, Vishnu and Shiva are the embodiment of the powers of creation, preservation and dissolution respectively of our universe. It is worthwhile to note that this trinity represents only a fraction of the infinite power of Ishwara. For example, the Lord creates innumerable universes, whereas Brahma manifests just one of them. Further, unlike God, the trinity signifies just one aspect of the supreme power for each of its members; Brahma, for instance, stands only for the creative force and not powers of preservation and dissolution. Brahma, Vishnu and Shiva are, therefore, regarded as gods with limited power. None of them has any particular form. They assume a body as the mind of a devotee conceives of them. Each

of these gods does tapas (a special yogic path to acquire divine power) to perform its functions. Out of them all, Shiva's tapas is the most potent because dissolution of the universe (pralay) can take place only if it can overcome the combined power of Brahma (i.e. the power of creation) and Vishnu (i.e. the power of preservation). A discerning student should note the following points concerning the trinity of gods. First, these gods, although fully Realised, are products of ignorance and, in fact, they perpetuate it. Second, creation manifests when Brahma extroverts the mind in general while Vishnu preserves it by sustaining mental extroversion; Shiva does not destroy mind's outgoing nature but merely makes it dormant (i.e. the mind introverts to its latent form during the dissolution of the universe) so that a new creation can manifest again. Third, the trinity cannot grant liberation to jivas (human being) because it is contrary to its assigned role in the divine scheme of things. It is, however, authorised to accept worship to give boons, impart partial knowledge that can take one to lower samadhi and grant a limited type of salvation (i.e. a temporary reprieve from the cycle of birth and death gained through a sojourn in one of regions or loka where the trinity dwells). Fourth, the trinity is an embodiment of the general principles of creation, preservation and dissolution, which is really genderless. However, to make teaching simpler and easier to follow, Brahma, Vishnu and Shiva are depicted as males. But, their worship is incomplete unless done conjointly with their female counterparts (or consorts), Saraswati, Lakshmi and Parvati respectively. The latter are regarded as limited forms of the Devi. Brahma etc. are just names to signify ideas of creation etc. Many other religious traditions assign different names to express similar notions.

Q61. What is the concept of the Devi? How does it differ from that of Ishwara? Why is the trinity of gods (i.e. Brahma etc.) depicted to have a female counterpart (i.e. Saraswati etc.)?

A61. Jivas (persons) of a worldly nature cannot conceive of the divine consciousness as being above the idea of male or female sex. It is contrary to their sensual experience, which invariably makes a distinction between objects based on their gender. To teach such ignorant people, sages depict Ishwara as male and the Devi as female. This differentiation is totally notional and has no basis in the Reality, for which both these words are used. Ishwara and the Devi refer to the embodiment of the divine consciousness in two gender forms. The consciousness assumes a male or female form to satisfy the vasna (inborn desires) of individual devotees. It does so to conform to a jiva's normal experience of seeing people in both genders. An embodied form is a manifestation of some of the divine attributes (gunas). Brahma and Saraswati, for instance, represent the powers of creation and wisdom respectively, amongst many other attributes. Although Ishwara and the Devi symbolize the divine consciousness in general, yet their embodiment as males and females make them finite and limited. Another point worth noting is that spiritual instruction is based on the concepts of nirguna (absolute and non-dual) and saguna (relative and dual) Reality. In that context, Ishwara, the male principle is regarded as nirguna and the female principle, the Devi, as the saguna. It implies that the Devi is considered as the power (shakti) of the inactive Ishwara, which creates, preserves and dissolves the objective phenomenon. A similar logic is applied to the manifestation of the trinity and its consorts. A discriminative reader should try to understand that various concepts and doctrines on Reality and creation are merely points in teaching to answer the doubts of students of diverse temperaments and different levels of spiritual growth. The knowledge imparted in this manner is relative and there cannot, therefore, be any finality in it. The state of one's own mind, at a particular stage of one's spiritual improvement, determines its veracity. What a beginner regards as true appears to be unreal to an advanced disciple. Such is the nature of knowledge that the mind acquires.

Q62. What do the tenets of time (kal) and space (akasha) connote?
A62. Time and space are self-existing ideas in the divine consciousness and a major cause of individual bondage. The conditioning of consciousness in maya takes place in time and space. Ishwara alone remains unaffected by them. The divine drama of the Lord (i.e. creation, preservation and dissolution) is enacted in their matrix as part of the natural order of things. The divine will has created the notion of time to make the cosmic play subservient to it. Time ensures that no object of creation, from Brahma to a blade of grass, becomes eternal. It stands for the principle of transience that is applicable to the entire created phenomenon. All objects (e.g. a universe, a jiva, a mountain) are subject to birth, death, decay, dissolution, disease, old age and so on because time puts a limit on their being-hood. Time is an attribute of Ishwara who uses it to turn the infinite creation into its finite form (e.g. a jiva). In the creative process, it is the most potent of all divine qualities; even Brahma, Vishnu and Shiva are subject to its reign and power. That is why phenomenal world is preserved for some time before it is dissolved for re-creation. It is equally applicable to individual objects; a jiva is born in time and lives in it for a while before being consumed by it. Human beings are bound by time; for example, there is time for lunch, sleep, office and a host of other activities. It can appear in an embodied form and its sight is dreadful and hideous to look at. It controls agents (i.e. gods etc.) of death, disease, destruction etc. It is a primary agent of ignorance and the mind cannot be subdued without vanquishing it. Time entices jivas into it tight embrace by making false promises of fulfilling their desires, expectations, and wishes; that is why, an individual hopes that an unsatiated desire today would be gratified tomorrow and if not then, maybe in the future. Time thus ensures that no one can break out of its vicious grip. It is relative in nature and in its notion inheres the ideas of past, present and future. A moment of present

becomes a moment of the past in a moment of the future. Time has created days, nights, seasons, years, hours etc. It is the ruler of a human being's fate and a nation's destiny. It is considered so because the effort to achieve anything matures within its ambit; for example, civilisations rise and fall in time as do the fortunes of individuals. Time is measured according to one's estimate of it. There is no standard yardstick for it due to its relativity. What we consider to be year here may be regarded as hundred years in another world or just a few minutes in yet another planet. Indian spiritual tradition has divided time into various cycles (yuga) to delineate the predominance of some characteristics that affect human life in so far as spiritual growth is concerned. Briefly that are called satya yuga (age of truth), treta yuga (third age), dwapar yuga (second age) and kaliyuga (age of darkness; current time cycle). Division into four ages is based on the analogy of truth having four legs to stand on in the satya yuga and it is reduced to one leg in kali yuga. People are most selfish in the current age and least in the satya yuga. In the other two cycles human beings are more selfish in dwapar yuga than treta yuga. Human life is longest in satya yuga and least in kali yuga (maximum of about 100 years). Taking these factors into account, sages have prescribed certain spiritual paths that are more suitable for practice in each age. But, Self-Realization is equally difficult in all of them. Similarly, there are variations in the solar and lunar calendars. Different objects have their own estimation of time; a day of Brahma's life is equal to many millions of years for human beings. The absolute divine power (ad shakti) that is concentrated on its space-less centre expands outwards due to a divine impulse and its reflection in maya is perceived as space by the senses. Space is not empty nothingness but is filled with vibratory energy (its sound form is called Omkar) that is released during the expansion. The same energy appears as ether (akasha; the subtlest of all basic elements) after its further modification by the divine will. Space is a form of extroverted consciousness and limitless creation emerges out of its energy. The separation that exists between a subject and an object or amongst objects is caused by space. A jiva, for instance, does not feel the presence of the Lord due to spatial separation from Him or Her. An aspirant has to reduce this gap, through control of mind, to attain samadhi (i.e. the last stage of practice in which 'I' is destroyed). Measurement of space, like time, is relative in nature and is according to one's estimate of it. What is vast and big for one set of objects may appear to be small and tiny to other forms of creation.

Q63. What is the nature of creation perceived by the senses? What are individual objects made of?

A63. Evolution of creation takes place in three phases; reflection of the consciousness in satva is called its causal (karna) body and the latter seen in rajas and tamas appears as the subtle (sookshma or linga sarira) body and gross (asthoola sarira) body respectively. The embodiment of the subjective (i.e. 'I') consciousness in causal, subtle and gross forms is its objective counterpart. It means that the projection of the 'I' consciousness in maya's three attributes, satva, rajas and tamas, results in the appearance of the world of sensual perception. For example, Ishwara's reflected image in satva is called its causal body; in rajas and tamas as Its subtle and gross (or physical) body. All the countless universes and their individual objects appear in these three forms. A jiva goes through the wakeful state in the physical body; dreams are perceived by the subtle body and dreamless sleep is experienced by the causal body. The difference between these bodies is notional; the same entity (i.e. consciousness) appears to have diverse forms due to maya's attributes. Thus, the mind of a jiva and his or her body are the same in their essence. Each individual has his or her own samaskaras and vasnas (mental impression and latent tendencies) and they are imbedded on his or her consciousness (i.e. mind). No two jivas look alike because their samaskaras are different and their reflection in maya appears in the form of myriad types of bodies. The body (causal, subtle and gross) is composed of the basic elements (ether, air, fire, water and earth) and prana. The divine intelligence determines the proportion of each element in the constitution of various types of bodies. For example, a stone has a much greater proportion of the earth element than, say, a mango that has more of the water element in it. Human body is constituted of approximately eighty five percent of earth and water and five percent each of ether, air and fire.

Q64. How are the basic elements characterised? What does the word, prana, imply? How do the senses (eyes, ears etc.) manifest?
A64. Prana is the yogic word for motion. The inactive (nirguna) consciousness become active (saguna) due to prana. Motion in the consciousness is unreal since it is an effect of maya (i.e. due to its rajoguna) but it regards it as real due to forgetfulness (or ignorance; again an effect of maya). Prana is also said to be the life force. It implies that it gives life to an object; a stone is lifeless because prana is latent in it. A dead human body is prana-less, unlike a living one. The divine will uses motion energy (prana) to mix the basic elements in a certain fixed proportion to manifest a particular type of body. The elements in the descending order of subtlety and power are ether (akasha), air (pawan), fire (agni), water (jal) and earth (prithvi). They exist in the divine consciousness in ideation form and assume their tangible forms during its reflections in the attributes (satva, rajas and tamas) of maya. The neutrino form of each element is called tanmatra; it is so infinitesimally small as to be beyond sensual perception. Tanmatras have a causal, subtle and gross form; in the latter aspect, they are like the atoms that go to constitute the physical elements. Each basic element is composed of tanmatras and they are the building blocks of various objects. Every object is constituted from a combination of tanmatras of all basic elements. A stone, for

instance, is made up from a mixture of the tanmatras of all elements but it is predominantly earth based with very little content of water, fire, air and ether, which remain in dormant form and so does prana. A bird's body, on the other hand, is composed primarily of earth, water and air tanmatras; the presence of very small quantities of ether and fire provide it with limited intelligence and metabolic energy respectively. It has life because prana is in active mode in it. The basic elements have certain innate characteristics; ether produces sound and the sense of hearing manifests from it. In the same way, air is responsible for the sense of touch, fire is associated with heat and light, out of which the sense of seeing comes into being, the sense of taste and smell manifest from water and earth respectively. A jiva, for example, hears because of the presence of tanmatras of ether in the body, which are activated by prana. Ether is also associated with intelligence and purity; air with happiness and bliss; fire with metabolism; water and earth with growth and materiality respectively. Tanmatras of various objects are mixed by the divine will according to their attributes superimposed with their samaskaras and vasnas. Objects are recognised due to the colours that they acquire when their tanmatric composition is reflected in satvaguna, rajoguna and tamoguna of maya. White is the colour of satva; red and black of rajas and tamas respectively. Myriad other colours are formed from their varied combination in different proportions.

Q65. Scriptures talk of the five sheaths of the body. What do they connote?
A65. The absolute Self (Atman) is said to be covered by the above sheaths, which appear as the body perceived in maya. It implies that the imperishable supreme Atman (or Reality) dwells within the body that has five different forms. An easier way to understand this phenomenon is to consider the sheaths as part of the causal, subtle and gross body. The five sheaths are annamaya kosa (physical sheath), pranamaya kosa (subtle sheath), manomaya kosa (mental sheath), vijnanamaya kosa (intellect sheath) and anandamaya kosa (bliss sheath). The physical sheath refers to the gross body; a combination of subtle, mental and intellect sheaths comprise the subtle body while the bliss sheath alludes to the causal body. The physical body is sustained by food; the subtle body is characterised by the presence of prana, roving mind including senses and intelligence as well as will power. The causal body's primary experience is of bliss (or happiness, as felt in deep sleep) with accrues only when the mind is controlled. Beginners are advised not to labour too much to understand such esoteric points.

Q66. Kindly illustrate the relationship between the three types of bodies (causal, subtle and gross) and their genesis from the mind by a simile for ease of understanding?

A66. The body (of a jiva) is a modification of the individual mind including its samaskaras when it is reflected in maya. The seed of a tree is its causal body and the power of growth that inheres in it is the causal mind. The germination of the seed into a new shoot is the tree's subtle body and the power that impels it to grow further the subtle mind (i.e. it is only a modified form of the causal mind). The fully grown tree is the equivalent of the physical body that attains its shape due to the gross mind (the power that matures the sprout into the tree). The seed that gives birth to the tree strikes roots deep in the ground and, hence, is invisible. In the same way, causal mind and body are not perceived in normal experience because they remain embedded in an extroverted consciousness. The sprout ripens into the tree (i.e. they are indistinguishable) and so does the subtle mind and body into their gross counterparts. To see the subtle and causal body, one must purify the gross mind to its subtle and causal aspects. It implies that one should remove the illusionary appearance of the trunk of the tree of ignorance to perceive the sprout of the subtle body and then do the same to the latter to experience the causal body. A point worth noting is that all trees of the same species (e.g. mangoes) do not attain the same height or girth nor do they give fruits that are exactly similar in taste. This is so on account of samaskaric differences; similarly, although jivas have the same general characteristics, yet there are individual variations due to one's samaskaras.

Q67. What do the doctrine of Omkar, word and name stand for?

A67. Objects that senses perceive are formed from their ideas and, hence, are not different from them. An artist conceives of a picture before painting it. The conception is formed from ideas, words and names. For example, a painter has a general idea of a scene that he wants to depict. He gives a concrete shape to that idea through words (shabda) and names (nama). He wants to paint a mountain for which he first thinks of the word for it (i.e. the mountain) and then plans to show a river (again conceived as a word) named Ganga. A reader should note the interconnection that exists between an idea, word and name in the mind. How does a painter become aware of the idea of a mountain? He does so because it exists in his mind as a thought. The difference between an un-manifest idea and a thought (i.e. a palpable form of an idea) is akin to the experience of a jiva in deep sleep and wakefulness. There are no thoughts in dreamless sleep and yet they exist; they are not perceived because they are dormant and, hence, they are like the un-manifest ideas that are extant in the consciousness in general (i.e. in its nascent causal stage of evolution). A jiva on waking up perceives the latent ideas in the form of thoughts. A thought is the manifested form of an idea and a jiva acquires its awareness due to its sound vibrations. A thought arises in the consciousness due to the vibratory nature of prana (motion). The highly elusive and intangible divine consciousness itself manifests as mystic sound, as a natural effect of its inherent prana; in other words, motion in the consciousness produces a vibratory sound in it, which is indistinguishable from it. Every thought, including the basic 'I' thought, exists as a sound vibration. That principle of sound or consciousness conceived as sound is called Omkar; its dormant (satvic) form becomes subtle (rajasic) and then gross (tamasic). It is audible in these forms, depending on the level of spiritual development. The shortened form of Omkar, called Om (pronounced as Aum), is symbolic of the basic sound produced in the body of a jiva and is representative of all the possible sounds that exist in the universe. Human speech begins in the vocal cords, which are part of the larynx, and then it passes through the area between the tongue and palate, ultimately culminating in the lips. There is no other way that words can be articulated in speech to express ideas. The word, AUM, when spoken begins with the letter A and its sound is produced in the larynx (i.e. it cannot be articulated in any other way; neither in the palate area nor by the lips). The letter, U, is pronounced in the area between the tongue and the palate while the sound of M can be made only by closing the lips. A, in effect, signifies the genesis of sound (of any type), U its middle and M its end; in other words, AUM stands for the entire spectrum, infinite in its scope, in which sounds of myriad types manifest. It is thus a symbol of the basic sound from which countless varieties of sounds are produced (or the entire range of sounds heard in the universe resolves into this primary sound). AUM also represents the trinity of Brahma, Vishnu and Shiva when its letters are considered singly. Brahma as the creator is signified by A and Shiva, as the destroyer, by M while the interval between them (i.e. preservative phase that falls between creation and dissolution), symbolised by Vishnu, is signified by U. The word, AUM, stands for Ishwara (i.e. when considered as a single word and not as separate letters) or is said to be Its mystic symbol. The sound of Omkar is self-existing and is divine in nature. It is called anhad shabda (unstruck sound) to distinguish it from the sound that is normally heard by jivas when two of its agents come together; as, for example, the sound produced by clapping of hands or air striking the vocal cords. All spoken words and names are made from sound vibrations (of Omkar). They give expression to ideas held in the divine consciousness; for example, Ishwara becomes aware of the inchoate idea of creation when words pertaining to it are formed in Its consciousness. This takes place to give a concrete shape to God's intent to create. The creative process begins when It imagines a universe (a word) with countless worlds (i.e. more words) having an infinite number of objects (even more words). Ishwara conceives the creation in word form but It assigns them names or even qualifying words to distinguish one object from another. As a general rule, words (in any language) are used for inanimate objects (e.g. moon, earth) or to express feelings (e.g. of love), ideas (e.g. Reality's absolute and relative aspects) and so on while names are used to distinguish animate objects from one and another (e.g. Rama); some inanimate objects are also given name (e.g. Mt Everest). Words and names have a general and a particular form; for instance, universe is a general word for all the innumerable stars, suns, moons, planets etc. that exist in it whereas its particular counterpart distinguishes one planet from another (e.g. earth from mars). Similarly, a name in general is applicable to all the objects in a species (e.g. mango is a general name for all its varieties) while its particular form is used to differentiate one variety from another (e.g. dusheri is different from langda mango). All particular words and names resolve into their general forms (e.g. all varieties of mangoes are signified by the word, mango). In the same way, all words and names originate from one word or one name. That single word is Omkar because its sound vibrations go to constitute all possible words. All names (of various animate and inanimate objects) resolve into one name. In that sense, name has the same connotation as Ishwara. A man and his name cannot be separated. For instance, one cannot conceive of Rama without his name. Similarly, Ishwara and Its name are inseparable. A reader should remember that Omkar, word and name (in general form) have the same connotation as Ishwara and are used in spiritual instruction to emphasis the non-corporeal nature of even the saguna (i.e. created) form of Reality. Same words can be used for the absolute Reality. Absolute Omkar, word or name refers to the transcendental Truth (or Reality). In a general sense, Omkar and word refer to the disembodied Ishwara (or consciousness) in the form of sound and knowledge (i.e. word is the repository of all knowledge since it is symbolic of all the words that express ideas of tangible and intangible subjects; for example, of astronomy and philosophy). A name in general (e.g. Rama) alludes to Ishwara as an infinite Being in general, while in particular (e.g. Sri Krishna, Gobind) refers to person named as Sri Krishna.

Q68. Kindly give the gist of the theory of karma. Does a jiva (human being) have freedom to act?
A68. A jiva is a microcosmic image of the macrocosmic Ishwara. The latter's infinite attributes become finite in the former. The Lord has total freedom to act while an individual has limited free will. The finiteness of a jiva manifests due to the 'I'-sense (or individual mind) superimposed with one's samaskaras and vasnas (mental impressions and latent tendencies or desires). This restricted freedom forms the cornerstone of the doctrine of karma. Any mental or physical action done with the 'I'-sense (i.e. carried out with a feeling 'I am doing this or that act') to satisfy a desire, which leaves an impression (samaskaras) in the consciousness (or in memory) is called karma. It is akin to planting seeds (i.e. samaskaras) in the soil of consciousness that are bound to germinate in due course; some earlier (e.g. present life) and some later (e.g. future lives). It is important to note that the memory of a jiva records one's motive as well as the

act that stems from it. Even the raising of a hand or eruption of an innocuous thought creates its samaskaras and there are countless such acts in a day. Karma (i.e. action done with the 'I'-sense) creates bondage because the samaskaras that one creates in the process of performing it must bear fruit sometime (maybe in future lives). The theory of karma is based on cause and effect; that is, as one sows, so shall one reap. A jiva's karma of past lives creates an immeasurable samaskaric burden that impels one to be entangled in a web of repeated birth and death in order to expiate it (or reap its fruit). It is an endless and vicious cycle because an individual keeps adding to one's fathomless samaskaric burden in every life. A jiva assumes a body (or is born) to reap the fruit of karma done previously. An individual is what one's karma is; it determines a person's nature, character, personality, age, shape of the body (i.e. height, weight etc.) place and family of birth and so on. The karma that leads to one's embodiment and what one is potentially destined to do in current life is called prarabdha karma. It is only a very small portion of the vast storehouse of almost infinite karma of past lives. The past karma (of previous lives) that has yet to bear fruit (or has still to be worked out by assuming a bodily form) is known as sanchit karma. The actions that one has to do in future lives is kiryamna or agami karma and it is added to sanchit karma for expiation in the future. Karma done with 'I' can be categorized as either good or bad; its fruit is pleasure or pain respectively. Both types cause bondage. Bad karma refers to those actions that cause pain to others, including by speech. Such actions are bound to cause pain to others, including by speech. They are bound to cause pain to their doer and result re-birth in hell, lower species of life (e.g. snakes) and so on. It is only when one has expiated one's bad karma that one is reborn as a human being again, which is a rare gift in the divine scheme. A karma done according to the moral law (i.e. dharma; based on truth, righteousness, duty etc.) is rewarded with happiness (i.e. a life of prosperity, sojourn in heaven after death, re-birth in good families etc.); but, it does not give the reward of salvation which is acquired only by giving up idea of I-ness i.e. 'I am doing this or that'. The pre-destination of karma relates to the formation of vasnas (mental tendencies and desires) that impel a jiva to act in a certain way. But, it does not bind an individual to act only in watertight manner; for, there are options available to do every type of karma. A jiva should use his or her intelligence and free will to choose the best option. One feels thirsty at a particular time according to one's karma but one has a choice to satisfy it through many options. For instance, thirst can be quenched by drinking coke, tap water or tea. The future consequences of one's actions would be according to what one takes to satisfy one's thirst. Those who think that they are bound by fate (i.e. to act in a pre-determined way) are mentally weak and lacking in discriminative intelligence. The law of karma is based on the freedom to act. Destiny is created by a jiva;

what prevents him or her to alter it? Most people are playthings of fate but those who make the right effort can change it. No jiva, wise or ignorant, can give up karma because it is against the divine will's natural order. That being so, what is the best way to act? To do one's karma desirelessly and unselfishly (i.e. without the feeling 'I am the doer') is the way of the wise. Its reward is much higher than mere worldly pleasure; it leads to divine bliss and liberation. Best of all karma is to remember the Lord and develop divine qualities like love and compassion etc.

Q69. What is the concept of divine play (leela)?
A69. It is one way of explaining the nature of the creator and its creation. A jiva's actions are motivated by the ego (or 'I'-sense) to gratify its desires. What is it that impels the Lord to create the phenomenal world? It is ego-less and desireless and, hence, one cannot ascribe any motive to it. It is in this context that God is said to indulge in a sport only to fulfil Its nature. A small child's ego sense is undeveloped and yet he or she is playing all the time. He or she makes a house of wooden blocks and then brings it down without any apparent reason because he or she has no motive in doing so. Ishwara is said to be a creator like that. It is important to remember that in the divine drama (leela), the Lord is the producer, script writer, director, the stage, hero, villain, supporting cast, the audience, the theatre and so on. All that is visible and invisible is the form of the Lord only. There is nothing apart from It. The one Lord appears to be many (objects) because of Its own divine will that manifests the world appearance in maya. That is Its leela.

Q70. What do the doctrines of dualism (dwaita), qualified monotheism (visistadvaita) and non-dual (advaita) stand for?
A70. Duality implies the existence two separate entities; subject and object or Ishwara and jiva or creator and creation. Both are apart from each other and have different characteristics. Adherents of this view try to please God through worship, prayers, rites, rituals etc. and hope to get salvation. Qualified monism states that Ishwara has infinite attributes and a finite number out of them is used by It to create myriad objects as perceived by senses. In its essence, the doctrine of monotheism states that there is only one God who appears to assume many (i.e. infinite) forms. In other words, the subject is the object also but with a different name and shape. It lays emphasis that an object (e.g. a jiva) is a limited form of the subject (i.e. Ishwara) and that the former's limitation arises because it is a reflection of the latter in maya (or its cause is ignorance). An intelligent student should appreciate that the tenets of monism accepts duality in a latent form; for, it does not advocate the destruction of the subject ('I' sense of a jiva or the mind). If that be so, the object must continue to exist because its end is conterminous with the former. Belief in monism

implies that an aspirant perceives God to exist in every object. Non dualism (advaita means not two; neither a subject nor an object) refers to the state of consciousness that is neither subjective nor objective. It is the state of the absolute and pure consciousness, unlike its relative form, which entertains the feeling of being a subject (the 'I am' feeling of Ishwara and jivas) as well as an object. Advaita points to the nirguna (absolute) Reality while the other two viewpoints relate to Its saguna (relative) aspect. The above doctrines are often associated with certain sages and seers to imply that they advocate three ways to attain liberation. This is a mistake made by people who are learned in scriptures (i.e. scholars) but lack any spiritual experience. The best way to have a true understanding of the above concepts is to relate them to the spiritual development of an aspirant. Every seeker begins the quest from duality (i.e. a jiva's current state of ignorance) and passes through qualified monism (in which an aspirant experiences his or her subjectivity, i.e., 'I' sense or has vision of God) to end in non-dualism (i.e. destruction of the 'I'-sense or mind or ignorance). In other words, duality is experienced in the stages up to manolaya (subsidence of mind), qualified monism in lower samadhi and non-dualism in the highest samadhi. A saint who lays emphasis on qualified monism, for example, is doing it merely for the benefit of his or her devotees who are not yet ready to attain the highest state (of advaita). By no means should it be construed to imply that he or she is denying the truth of non-dual Reality.

Q71. What is the essence of teaching, in this Chapter, that a lay render ought to remember?

A71. A beginner need not have detailed knowledge of some aspects of Reality discussed in this Chapter. It will help him or her if basic understanding of some of the points, mentioned below, is acquired:-

(a) Reality is called by many names; for example, God, Brahman, Truth, That, Word, Name, Ram and so on. One should keep in mind that It has two aspects; absolute (nirguna i.e. without attributes) and relative (saguna i.e. with attributes). The former is the goal that the wise seek through control of mind whereas the latter is the visible phenomenon perceived by the senses.

(b) The individual mind originates from the 'I' feeling that the consciousness entertains. In it inheres intelligence, memory and roving mind. The latter keeps flitting from one thought or an object (through senses like eyes, hearing, smell etc.) to another. The aim in spiritual effort is to control the flow of thoughts and purify memory. That is done by using intelligence and will power which exercises overall control on the mind. Everyone associates one's self with this feeling; it is not merely a point of academic teaching but is actually experienced as a vibration in the consciousness in advanced stages of practice (i.e. in lower samadhi).This feeling is then eliminated from the consciousness which results in destruction of the individual mind. That blessed state is known as Realisation.

(c) Maya is an invisible power that envelops the Reality. It is like a reflecting surface of a mirror but its chief characteristic is that the images seen in it do not conform to the object being reflected. It causes distortions; for example, formless appears to have form. Thus, the absolute Reality (i.e. formless and attributeless) appears as the phenomenal world of form having attributes. Maya is, hence, called a power that causes illusions and ignorance. Individual mind is befuddled by it.

(d) Students do not often pay attention to appreciate the utter unreliability of relative knowledge. Simply put, it is the knowledge gained by the mind that perceives various objects in relationship to itself. For example, a man's perception of his daughter is different from her husband's because of their varied relationships. Relative knowledge is incomplete and varies with time and circumstances. A wise aspirant should learn to reject such knowledge as false.

(e) Karma (performance of actions or deeds) done with the 'I' sense (e.g. 'I' am eating) causes bondage and results in repeated birth, death and rebirth. It is applicable to both good and bad karma. The best way to perform one's karma is to do it selflessly (i.e. without the sense of I-ness). That alone leads to liberation.

Chapter 4

Control Of Mind

Q1. The Guru's teaching relates essentially to control of mind. What relevance does the previous instruction have with it?

A1. Theoretical knowledge forms the foundation on which an aspirant builds the superstructure of practice (to realise the Truth). Contemplation on it done discriminatively and seriously convinces a sincere seeker that the only way to find real and everlasting happiness is to practise what a guru teaches. Mere reading of scriptures is of no consequence. It must, however, be noted that knowledge given in various scriptures and in Guru Upanishad has not been revealed through mental speculation. It is based entirely on spiritual experience that results in union with the Reality. Similarly, an intelligent student should verify the knowledge revealed in the preceding pages through one's own spiritual growth and enlightenment. It would then no longer remain in the domain of theory; rather, it would form the basis of truthful living (i.e. to live in the world after being firmly established in the Truth).The teaching that follows is broad-based enough to cover all the main disciplines whose practise leads to Self-Realisation; beginners are advised to confine their initial reading to the path of their interest.

Q2. What does the control of mind imply?

A2. The palpable form of the mind is the incessant flow of thoughts that all jivas are aware of. To control the mind means to stop their eruption. The origin of the individual mind lies in the feeling of 'I' that every jiva entertains (e.g. 'I am Rama'). The 'I' exists as the primordial and basic thought on which are imposed countless other thoughts. The 'I' thought exists as a vibration in the consciousness and samaskaras (mental impressions) are created when it impels the mind into activity to gratify its desires. These samaskaras are superimposed on the 'I' in the form of latent thoughts and they manifest at the appropriate time (i.e. one becomes aware of a thought only when it is time for it to appear in the consciousness). The 'I's desires propel the superimposed thoughts to manifest at the appropriate time. To control the mind, the superimposed (or secondary) thought are made dormant first and then the primary (i.e. 'I') thought is destroyed. Thoughts arise in the mind due to the inherent motion in the consciousness. They are restrained only if the mind is stilled into non-activity. Thus, the control of mind implies the total absence of motion and thoughts (i.e. primary 'I' thought as well as secondary thoughts) in it. Further, the sense of duality (i.e. the consciousness imagines that it is a subject as well an object; it is an effect of the 'I' thought) is destroyed if the 'I' disappears. Similarly, the experience of monism (i.e. after duality ends, one becomes aware of the subject being the object) must be overcome to attain the final stage of practice (i.e. Realisation). What is left there-afterwards is the absolute and non-dual consciousness (or Reality), the state of unconditioned bliss (or knowledge) that an aspirant sets out to achieve. The conclusion from this is that the mind must be destroyed completely to realise the Self (Atman). In the context of the above teaching, an intelligent reader should note that one is able to make the mind immobile because motion that gives birth to thoughts in it is unreal. The implication is that the consciousness does not actually move at all; it is only a false feeling of motion that it entertains as an effect of maya, just as a man goes to Delhi in a dream. Thus, the mind itself is an unreal entity. There was no way that the mind could be controlled if the motion in it was real.

Q3. What is the nature of an average mind? How does it affect its control?
A3.

(a) A normal jiva's mind is characterised by restlessness and extroversion (i.e. its habit of looking outwards to the world to satisfy its desires). An individual's attachment to the external phenomenon is so strong that one is unable to exercise any control over the whims and fancies of the mind.

(b) An average mind lacks any real power of concentration and its functioning is affected by doubt and fear. These factors make the mind weak, which is reflected in individual intelligence failing to exercise proper control over it.

(c) The mind's activity is motivated by desire, anger, greed, attachment, jealousy, pride etc.

(d) Notwithstanding the above, the mind has certain inherent strengths that very few people generally care to nurture. The most crucial amongst them is the power of intelligence and will power to exercise self-control. The power to control the mind through application of intelligence is called yoga shakti, which is an index of the power of concentration that an individual has. It can be developed, through self-effort and divine grace, to a high level, enough to annihilate the mind.

(e) The mind has the power to look inwards (i.e. towards the point of its origin or the 'I' sense); it is called introversion. It is effected through self-effort by using one's intelligence to control the roving mind (manas) and senses. Attachment to the world must be given up to effect mental introversion.

(f) Divine qualities like love, devotion, discrimination, detachment, contentment, humility, faith etc. are inherently present in every mind. They are developed through guru's grace and self-effort. The mind is controlled by their intelligent application and they are also used to destroy negative attributes like attachment, pride, desire etc.

(g) In short, the mind is the disease (i.e. cause of ignorance) as well as the cure (i.e. has the power to destroy ignorance).

Q4. How is the mind controlled?

A4. Mind is controlled by the mind only by using its positive aspects, brought out in the previous answer, through application of intelligence and will power. The implication is that one must make the requisite and right effort to do so. Divine or guru's grace is an absolute must to succeed in it. One should, however, realise that even grace dwells in the mind only and it plays its part if effort is made. Those who depend on fate or are looking for magical mantras or indulge in rituals and other similar activities to attain instant salvation are bound to fail. Control of mind requires hard work; neither learning nor erudition nor cleverness (of mind) is of any avail in doing so.

Q5. How is the attainment of absolute Reality related to the control of mind? What is the special effort required to know It? What should a seeker aspire to achieve in a spiritual quest?

A5. Reality transcends the power of the mind and, hence, It is not an object that it can gain. Mind can acquire only relative knowledge and not its absolute counterpart. Reality is an inactive principle of consciousness and is not even aware of the mind's activity. In a spiritual quest, effort is required to control the mind and not to know the Reality. That ought to be the aim of a wise student. Truth is realised on Its own if the mind is controlled (i.e. destroyed).

Q6. When is the mind considered to be under full control?

A6. Only when the 'I', from which the mind originates, is destroyed and there is total stillness in the consciousness in all the three states (i.e. wakefulness, dream and dreamless sleep). Any stage before that is of partial self-control. A fully controlled mind has the same connotation as the pure, thoughtless, motionless and absolute Consciousness.

Q7. Why is divine grace so essential to control the mind?

A7. A jiva's 'I' sense manifests due to Brahma's tapas shakti (spiritual power gained through severe penance) and is, in fact, held in its place by the same power (i.e. in Brahma's consciousness). What power does a jiva have to undo what the creator has done? Only a satguru's (i.e. God in human form as a guru) omnipotent divine grace has the power to destroy the bondage of ignorance manifested by Brahma.

Q8. What are the various steps in control of mind?
A8. Mind is an intangible entity and it is difficult to lay down any straitjacketed stages through which it passes to restrain itself. Steps given below are for purposes of teaching to make it simpler for comprehension:-

(a) **Self-Discipline**. An aspirant must be self-disciplined to succeed in practice (sadhana). It is a primary requirement that effort must be done in a disciplined and systematic manner; without it, one cannot sustain one's sadhana for long. Most beginners give up practice after some time or at best practise lackadaisically because they are not disciplined. An average mind is so used to looking outwards (i.e. towards the external objects to satisfy its desires) that it finds it very hard to break this habit; but, it is not possible to introvert the mind without doing so. This requires deliberate effort that must often be carried out in the beginning even if one is not inclined to indulge in it. A beginner invariably finds many reasons for being irregular in practice (e.g. to attend a party, looking after guests etc.). Self-discipline implies that a seeker follows a laid done routine of sadhana despite all the temptations to violate it. It is a form of training the mind to give up its harmful habits (i.e. indulge in its whims and fancies to satisfy its desires but in the bargain increases the bondage of ignorance) and cultivate desirable ones (i.e. follow a strict routine that includes practice of the guru's teaching). Initially, one has to force oneself to practice for the prescribed (by the guru) time and adhere to his or her other instructions. Even a little regularity in sadhana goes a long way to channelize and concentrate mental energy to look inwards (or introvert) rather than dissipate it on useless worldly pursuits. Similarly, one should make it a habit to contemplate the guru's teaching with a discriminative mind from the earliest stages of one's practice. Its benefits are immense. Besides laying down a regimen for practice, a serious student should evolve a code of conduct consisting of dos and don'ts for strict adherence. It is a self-imposed guide consisting of ethical rules that governs one's social behaviour. It is a major aid to develop self-control. For example, it is always tempting to lie to make profit rather than follow the path of truth. But, every time one is able to resist doing so, one gains in mental strength. One can include any number of points in the code that one can conveniently follow; amongst them, one should lay emphasis on development of divine qualities (e.g. love, devotion, discrimination, contentment, humility) and avoid causing injury to others (i.e. through speech, thought, deed), covetousness, speaking ill of others, pride, anger, and so on. An aspirant who is able to discipline his or her mind by giving up undesirable habits and inculcating desirable ones is well set for serious practice to control the mind. A beginner should also set apart some time for sat sangha (holy company) and doing sewa (selfless service).

(b) **Self-Purification**. The feeling of 'I' pollutes the individual consciousness and it is made worse by the superimposition of countless samaskaras and vasnas (mental impressions and latent tendencies) of past karma. Self-purification refers to the process of cleansing one's mind of the samaskaric dross as a first step and then removing the 'I' from the consciousness. That would leave the consciousness in a totally pure form. Samaskaras and vasnas are held in memory; hence, their destruction is said to purify it. In a sense, the whole of an aspirant's sadhana is devoted to purification of mind only. An individual mind is never totally impure because it has always elements of purity in it. The degree of impurity varies from jiva to jiva (i.e. according to one's samaskaras). Ishwara's mind is infinitely pure, a state which no jiva can attain because it would require infinite time to do so. All that an aspirant needs to do is to purify the mind to a certain level so that the 'I' vibration is experienced for it to be annihilated. The best way to purify the mind is to practise sincerely the guru's instruction. Selfless service (sewa), self-discipline, remembrance of the Lord and sat sangha (company of a liberated sage) are excellent means to achieve the same end. Pranayama (control of prana through breathing exercises) is also an approved method of mental purification but it should be practised only on the directions of a yogi who has mastered its technique. There are very few yogis (in fact, they are very rare) of that calibre in this age. Pranayama done incorrectly, specially retention of breath beyond one's capacity, often does more harm than good. Purification of the mind requires earnest effort carried out for a long time and it is a slow and gradual process. The mind is cleansed a little bit every time one practices (the guru's teaching). The mind must become one pointed before one can carry out any serious practice. One pointedness refers to the concentration of mental energy in point form that is sharp enough to introvert on its source (the 'I'-consciousness) through the maze of samaskaric filth. The mind attains this state through its purification. To sum up, an impure mind cannot be introverted; only its purified counterpart is capable of experiencing the 'I' before exterminating it.

(c) **Self-Abidance**. A moderately disciplined and purified mind that is able to dwell on a subtle object (e.g. embodied form of Ishwara, divine name, word, mantra, a thought) for a certain length of time (i.e. at least an hour) is said to be in a state of abidance. It denotes a middling level of mental introversion in which a seeker is able to detach himself or herself from external objects but attachment to their internal counterparts is still intact. Only a one pointed mind is able to reach and sustain this state. Abidance gives a certain degree of peace and tranquility of mind; one sees visions of many types (e.g. of gods, goddesses, saints, light etc.), hear divine sounds and have many other spiritual experiences in it. Most indiscriminative aspirants are usually befuddled by such experience and fail to progress further. An intelligent student should realise that although abidance indicates spiritual development, yet one is only half way through on the journey. One must reject every experience as false to proceed further. All that abidance signifies is that an extroverted mind's dissipating energy (in the outflow of thoughts) has been arrested and it has achieved concentration of a middling level (i.e. it is focused on the mind's subtle centre) due to practice (sadhana) of the guru's instruction. The onset of this state is indicated by the thoughts becoming subtle (i.e. less forceful and lacking in intensity), as compared to their gross forms which cause turmoil in the mind. Abidance of mind signifies its partial and a fair level of control; the 'I' still has its desires to gratify, though they may be reduced somewhat.

(d) **Self-Subsidence (Manolaya)**. It is the state of a dormant mind, much like what it is in deep sleep but with a very crucial difference: dreamless sleep is an effect of mental dullness whereas manolaya is characterised by a high level of alertness of the mind. A jiva is neither aware of one's self nor of the world in deep sleep. In manolaya, however, the objective world is pulled back into the 'I'-consciousness due to mental introversion but there is no palpable experience of the 'I'-vibration because the causal sense of duality (i.e. objects do not fully merge in the 'I' but are in intimate contact with it) is still existent. Initially, manolaya appears like dull sleep but it attains alertness with practice. One is then asleep to the world (i.e. sensual experience of objects appears to be absent) but awake within (i.e. awareness of one's self and objects in causal or dormant form). That state is called yoga nidra (yogic sleep). Self-subsidence is a state of causal 'I' in which the latter withdraws its projection (seen as objects reflected in maya) within itself. Thoughts in causal form are present in manolaya. The 'I' and objects are spatially separated in self-abidance but this is reduced to almost zero (i.e. objects are not totally withdrawn in the 'I') in manolaya. The mind continues to gain objective knowledge in manolaya but in causal form. Mental agitation assumes its causal character, which then gives feelings of bliss, peace and calmness. Manolaya indicates a fairly high degree of self-control but it is important to note that the causal ego sense and, hence, the mind, is still extant. There is no permanency in it and samaskaras (i.e. thoughts) sprout again during non-practising hours. In short, self-subsidence is characterised by concentration of the mind on the periphery of its centre (i.e. on the 'I'-sense), which many immature aspirants regard as the equivalent of attaining liberation.

(e) **Destruction of Mind (Manonash)**. The process of self-control is completed only when the mind is destroyed. It refers to the disappearance of the 'I', the source of the mind from the consciousness, which then attains its pure and absolute state. The feeling of duality (i.e. of the consciousness being a subject and an object) ends when the mind ceases to be. A seeker who sets out on a spiritual journey aims to destroy individual ignorance (represented by subjective and objective knowledge gained by the mind) and that goal is achieved in manonash. It requires very great effort done with pure devotion and a highly developed sense of discrimination to succeed in the last phase of self-control. As one makes progress in the final phase of the quest, one realises the crucial and all important role that divine (or guru's) grace plays in destroying ignorance. Manonash is attempted and executed only after an aspirant reaches the samadhi stage (a state of a very highly purified and concentrated mind in which the 'I' is destroyed). It is a slow and gradual process but its end comes suddenly. Basically, manonash is carried out in two steps; first, experience the 'I'-current and second, isolate it from its general aspect in order to exterminate it. The latter requires a little explanation; the individual 'I' is an offshoot of its general counterpart (i.e. a jiva is a finite form of the infinite God or Ishwara), which it can never know fully. A finite entity (i.e. an aspirant) can never fully know an infinite one because it would require infinite time. That is clearly an impossibility for a seeker. The aim in manonash is, therefore, not to get involved with knowing more and more about Ishwara and possibly acquire greater powers but to keep the individual self apart from the general 'I' (or Ishwara) and destroy it through guru's grace. That is the right and proper method to overcome ignorance but it is perpetuated if one continues to gain more relative knowledge. The 'I' is destroyed through practice of any of the paths taught by a guru. The essential element in all of them is to use the power of discrimination to isolate the 'I' and then burn it by concentrating on it. The resultant is the state of Self Realisation that is characterised by absolute knowledge, unconditioned purity, introversion and unalloyed bliss.

Q9. What are the salient features, in the above teaching, that a student keen on spiritual development ought to keep in mind?
A9.

(a) The stages, discussed above, describe in a general way how an aspirant evolves spiritually. Self-discipline and purification are the basic states that cannot be quantified. The mind passes through them from the beginning of the quest to its end when they attain their highest levels. For example, self-abidance is a state of mental discipline and purification only. Each of the above states is a natural progression of the preceding one and difficult to demarcate. Notwithstanding the above, the samadhi state in which the mind is finally destroyed is very unique and its attainment, besides being a quantum jump, in spiritual advancement, is identifiable as a distinct stage. A discriminative student with a very alert mind may also be able to know when one reaches the manolaya state. But, most aspirants are likely to confuse it with some earlier phases of practice (e.g. abidance) because of the similarities of some indicators common to them (e.g. falling asleep in practice).

(b) Aspirants are fond of making judgements on how much they have progressed spiritually. All such subjective assessments are invariably biased and, hence, wrong. They can make one proud and vain because mind creates delusions of self-improvement in order to sustain its existence.

(c) A seeker must make a conscious effort to develop divine qualities like love, devotion, discrimination, detachment, humility etc. They purify the mind as well as calm it. Spiritual progress is made through their intelligent application in practice. They ripen on their own as an aspirant steps forward from one stage to another.

(d) Similarly, there should be a deliberate attempt to eject undesirable qualities (e.g. pride, jealously, attachment, greed etc.) from the consciousness. One cannot advance spiritually without being able to do so. Growth of divine attributes would reduce their harmful influence because they cause agitation in the mind. The mind can neither be disciplined nor purified nor controlled unless undesirable traits are removed from it.

(e) Doubt and fear keep nibbling at the mind throughout one's sadhana (practice). They are a major obstacle for a seeker's spiritual growth.

One must have faith in the guru as well as in one's own ability to traverse the path of spirituality.

(f) Thoughts are not controlled individually nor is the mind purified in parts. As one progresses through various steps, mentioned above, the gross mind turns subtle and then causal. It means that tamasic (impure and lethargic) mental tendencies are replaced by their predominantly rajasic (active and moderately purified) counterparts. With further practice, the same mind is transformed into its satvic (highly purified and calm) character. A similar phenomenon occurs in the case of gross thoughts, which become subtle and then causal. The implication is that thoughts, in various forms (i.e. subtle and causal) persist throughout practice, even till its end when the 'I', which is itself a thought, is finally rooted out from the consciousness. Their control refers to the force, rapidity and intensity with which they arise in the mind. A gross mind is very restless because thoughts that erupt in it cause turmoil due to their potency and ceaseless succession. They are not so powerful in their subtle form and lose much of their energy when they become causal and, hence, they are so peaceful. An aspirant's vasnas (latent tendencies of the mind that impel it to function in a certain way; desires) undergo a similar change with spiritual advancement.

(g) Thoughts arise in the mind due to its inherent motion and their control restrains the latter as well.

(h) The power of self-control is inherent in the mind and it is called yoga shakti. It refers to the power of mental concentration. The spiritual growth of a seeker is dependent on how well one is able to develop yoga shakti. Thoughts and motion are controlled on their own if one is capable of concentrating the mind on, say, an object for a certain length of time.

Q10. What is a spiritual experience? How does it differ from its normal sensual counterpart?

A10. A spiritual and ordinary experience is gained by the mind in two different states. The former is of an introverted, purified and concentrated mind whereas the latter is of its extroverted, gross and uncontrolled counterpart. Spiritual experiences usually take place when one practices a spiritual discipline during any stage described in Answer 8. They may take place in dreams also. A normal sensual experience is of material (or gross) objects (i.e. of their external surface) gained by an extroverted mind. It takes place in wakefulness. A spiritual experience, on the other hand, is of an introverted mind and it gives knowledge of the internal (i.e. subtle and causal) nature of objects. Unlike an ordinary experience, its ultimate aim is to feel the 'I' vibration sans its attachment to a subtle or a causal body. A spiritual experience is of a mystic nature; that means, it lies beyond the ken of normal sensual cognition. The mystic part of an experience, for instance, is illustrated by the smell of a rose; although it is pleasant even in normal sensual perception, yet the fragrance smelt spiritually is extraordinarily powerful and utterly unique. Another difference is the effect that both types produce on the mind. A spiritual experience brings joy and bliss and it leaves a deep imprint on the mind; an ordinary one produces either transitory pleasure or pain and its impression does not last very long. For example, an aspirant may hear sounds of thunder during meditation, which is a very pleasant experience whereas the same sound heard ordinarily may frighten a person. Both types of experiences are undergone to satisfy vasnas (latent desires). Spiritual experiences begin when the mind is purified to its subtle form; they are objective in nature because the 'I' identifies itself with the subtle body and subtle phenomenon. Subtle eyes see visions or subtle ears hear sounds and so on. An advanced spiritual experience is of a causal mind; its real form is subjective (i.e. to feel the 'I' in samadhi state), yet one may attain objective knowledge also through it because the latent sense of duality (i.e. existence of a subject and an object) persists almost till the end of one's practice. A spiritual as well as a normal sensual experience is of the effects produced by the basic elements. Sound inheres in akasha (ether), touch, light and heat, taste and smell are effects, respectively, of pawan (air), agni (fire), jal (water) and prithvi (earth). Thus, sounds that one hears, for example, in meditation or otherwise are the by-products of ether; similarly, the experience of touch (i.e. the sense of closeness or intimacy between two objects), seeing, tasting and smelling manifests from the basic elements. Every sensual perception, spiritual or otherwise, is predominated by one sense but the others are not absent. Light, for instance, has in it traces, in dormant form, of sound, touch, heat, taste and smell. They are activated as the mind is purified; for instance, a vision of light or one's ishta deva (object of worship) seen in samadhi encompasses in it all the joy and happiness that one would feel from hearing divine sounds, pleasurable sensations produced by touching another object, tasting the food of gods and smelling heavenly fragrances. The exhilaration that the mind feels, during practice (sadhana), from the aggregation of the effects of all the basic elements is called divine bliss. In the earlier stages of practice, divine bliss of a lower quality is produced from the effects of a combination of one or two or more elements.

Q11. What are the various types of spiritual experiences that an aspirant has during different stages of practice?
A11. In general, spiritual experiences that one gains in practice, in all phases, are of a similar nature. For instance, one may see a vision of one's guru in the abidance stage as well as in lower samadhi. Although the experience is the same, yet its impact on the mind and the knowledge that it reveals is different.

An experience of lower samadhi gives more knowledge, is far more blissful and its effect lasts for a longer time as compared to a similar experience in abidance stage. The difference between the above experiences, despite their similarity, arises due to following factors. Firstly, the level of mental purity is far greater in lower samadhi than in the abidance state; secondly, spatial separation of objects from the 'I' is reduced in samadhi and, thirdly, a spiritual experience in advanced stages of mental introversion, as in samadhi, tends to be an aggregate of the effects of all basic elements. As a rough guide, following are some of the experiences that seekers have during practice:-

(a) Feelings of bliss, calmness and peace.
(b) Seeing visions of one's ishta deva (object of worship) and guru. In addition, one may see images of saints, gods, goddesses and other celestial beings.
(c) Visions of light of varied hues and luminosity.
(d) Hearing of divine sounds (e.g. of devotional singing, musical instruments, blowing of couch shells etc.). They are all derivatives of the supreme sound of Omkar that is heard in samadhi.
(e) Perceiving ambrosial tastes and smells.

Q12. What should one do on attaining the above experiences? Do all aspirants have same experience or go through all the above mentioned ones?
A12. All experiences are of a temporary nature. They appear and disappear on their own. A wise student should pay no attention to them because involvement with them delays and hampers one's spiritual growth. They are all creations of the mind to satisfy latent vasnas (desires) and, hence, part of general ignorance. One should make it a habit to reject them as false from the beginning of the quest. No two individuals have the same experience because of the samaskaric differences in their mental makeup. However, this is not applicable to the final experience (of Realisation), which is the same for everyone blessed enough to attain it. Besides the feelings of peace etc., seekers usually have experiences of only one type mentioned above.

Q13. Do experiences described above indicate spiritual progress? Which of them is its good indicator?
A13. Seeing of ordinary visions etc. is not a sign of any great self-improvement. Although their experience does indicate a certain degree of mental purity, yet it is also a sign that desire (vasnas) to see etc. has not been curbed. However, to see a vision of God (in the form of one's guru or ishta deva) portends progress but the real form of the Lord is seen only at the end of lower samadhi. That is an excellent sign. Any of Its visions in the earlier stages is usually of pictures seen on calendars etc. To hear the sound of Omkar is also a good sign. It

must be emphasised that it is not essential to see visions etc. to judge spiritual advancement. Many aspirants may have no such experience. However, the best indicator of spiritual growth is to make the mind peaceful, tranquil and calm; it betokens control on mental motion, which is the cause of agitation due to eruption of thoughts. It would also be reflected in development of divine qualities like love etc. and curbing of harmful attributes (e.g. desires, anger, attachment etc.).

Q14. How is spiritual progress defined? What are its signs?

A14. Although the ultimate destination (i.e. destruction of mind) is well delineated, yet a spiritual journey to it traverses over an unknown territory without any real dimensions and, hence, advancement on it is intangible and difficult to qualify. There are no clearly defined signposts enroute to indicate how far one has travelled. Nor is the length of the journey standard for everyone; it can be long or short depending on one's mental strength, quality of effort, development of divine qualities and guru's grace. Certainly, no seeker should try to judge for himself or herself how much distance he or she has covered; all such subjective assessments (usually based on bookish knowledge) are invariably self-congratulatory, delusory and wrong. Although there are individual variations, yet some general indicators of spiritual growth are mentioned below as a rough guide:-

(a) Know it for certain that progress is inbuilt in self-effort (to practice a guru's instruction). Every time one practices sincerely, some advance is made without even one's awareness.

(b) Spiritual development is an internal process (i.e. related to mental purity and introversion) and one should not look for any external signs. This is specially applicable to beginners who tend to regard fulfilment of some worldly wish as its indicator.

(c) Those who practise for minimal time (i.e. one hour or so daily) should not expect miraculous results. It would take a long time for such persons to know that they have progressed.

(d) It is not possible to determine progress on a daily basis. But, if one critically examines oneself after a gap of few, say six months, one would notice a change in one's attitude to the world, towards family, friends and so on. The mind would be more peaceful and desireless troublesome.

(e) There are always ups and downs, almost till the end, in practically every student's spiritual development despite regular practice. It is due to one's vasnas (mental tendencies) that have very deep roots in the conscious. It should not dishearten a student; determined practice ensures steady progress despite the above phenomenon.

(f) It is a good sign of progress if one perseveres with practice even if there is no apparent improvement.

(g) Spiritual growth is also indicated by reduction in desires, development of divine qualities (e.g. love, contentment, humility, detachment etc.), control over harmful attributes (e.g. pride, attachment, greed, anger etc.), ability to face adversity with equanimity and not being affected by prejudice based on religion, caste, race, community, gender etc.

(h) An aspirant is assuredly doing well if he or she notices the following points. One, the mind becomes more calm and peaceful as compared to what it was prior to commencement of practice or any other fixed time frame. Two, loss of power in thoughts; they do not arise with same vehemence and force as they did earlier. It is a good sign to be aware of gaps between eruptions of thoughts. Three, tenderness of heart to feel the pain of others. Four, a feeling of lightness in the body and consciousness.

(i) One may be able to attain some degree of mental restraint during the actual practice of meditation. The real test of progress is how much impact it has on the mind during non-practising hours.

(j) Development of divine qualities must be reflected in one's conduct; otherwise, be certain that there is only peripheral improvement.

(k) Finally, control over one's self ('I'-ness) determines how far has one journeyed to the final destination. Often, during practice, immature aspirants conclude that the 'I' thought has disappeared (e.g. in manolaya and lower samadhi). One must be very alert and discriminative not be taken in by false clues.

(l) The points brought out above are at best rough indicators of the progress made to control the mind. They manifest on their own during various stages of practice (i.e. must not be induced to appear); not only that, a portent that signifies progress in one state is also applicable to another. For instance, one becomes aware of impoverishment of thoughts during the abidance phase of practice but that is only its beginning. Thoughts really lose their power and intensity in samadhi stage and, therefore, it is very likely that an indiscriminative aspirant would arrive at a subjective judgement of being in that state (i.e. in samadhi) on just making the mind abide in itself. The best course for a wise seeker, therefore, is to practise sincerely and in a spirit of self-surrender and leave everything to divine grace to take one forward.

Q15. Destruction of the mind is a lengthy process and is rightly considered the goal for an aspirant. Should one set for oneself an intermediate aim to be attained during practice?

A15. Yes; one may do so. Initial object of practice is to experience the 'I'-current; it can be destroyed only after that. That happens in lower samadhi (savikalpa and bhava) and all states of control of mind prior to it are only a preparation to attain it. Seekers of devotional natures often pine for a vision of God; that should be the object of their practice to begin with. A word of caution here. A devotee beholds vision of God in many embodied forms; for example, one can see Sri Krishna during various phases of practice (i.e. in meditation). His form may be different every time one has his vision because it appears from memory of the pictures, made by artists that one has seen previously. The real form of Sri Krishna would manifest only in lower samadhi and that too in its concluding stage. Those who set for themselves the goal of having a vision of God should, therefore, be very discriminative to know how to achieve it.

Q16. Prevailing times being what they are, how should a beginner generally go about following a spiritual quest? How should he or she learn to do sadhana (practice) and ensure steady progress?
A16.

(a) Spiritual leanings are formed over many lives and to give them a meaningful direction (i.e. through practice) is part of a jiva's karma. By and large, there are two categories of people who take to spiritual life in a serious manner. First, those who find something missing in life or are unhappy about it despite their apparent success, wealth, family etc. Usually, persons of this type are those who have developed spiritual tendencies during past lives. Second, many turn spiritual because of some traumatic experience, suffering, bereavement etc. It must, of course, be pointed out that not many amongst the above actually try to find an answer to their problems. They think a little about them and read some books and let the matters rest as they are. Their spiritual tendencies are obviously not potent enough to impel them to take more concrete steps; nor do they have the mental strength to get out of the rut of mundane life. A few of them are prepared to do a little more than just moan about their fate. They look for guidance from those more knowledgeable than them and many of them land up in the laps of assorted godmen and godwomen. A vast majority of the latter consists of frauds but some amongst them have a little spiritual power and do genuine social service. That is the most that can be said about them; they have neither controlled their egos nor are they what they claim to be (e.g. some even claim to be incarnations of God). It is only a very small number of the people, described above, who have an intense desire to solve the riddle of life and find out the cause of their unhappiness and dissatisfaction. They are prepared to search for a solution through serious introspection and reflection aided by prayer and discriminative study of scriptures. With that knowledge and sincere intent, they look for a real guru who is not only a Realised soul but also has a divinely ordained power to save them. Gurus of this calibre are very rare and it is only with the greatest blessing that one can meet them. A spiritual quest begins only after being initiated into practice of a particular discipline (or path) by a guru of this type. The above is a very brief description of the general state of spirituality these days and the points mentioned in succeeding paragraphs are addressed to earnest devotees who take to practice not as a pastime but want to achieve something really substantive.

(b) After hearing instruction from a guru (or by study of scriptures) one must learn to contemplate on it. That is the best way to imbibe it and be mentally convinced that it is worthwhile to put it into effect. Practice cannot be sustained without such a conviction. It is of help if a neophyte is generally aware of the working of an individual mind and nature of maya, creation and relative knowledge.

(c) Be clear of the aim of practice, i.e., destruction of mind (or ignorance) and pursue it relentlessly, sincerely and determinedly. Remember, absolute Reality is not an object of the mind; It is attained on its own if the latter is annihilated.

(d) One should remember that senses (i.e. seeing, hearing etc.) are the projection of the mind. They are a cause of a person's attachment to the external world. Their control is as important as the control of thoughts. Though meditation is of great help, yet one must try to divert one's attention away from sensual experience throughout the day (i.e. during the non practising hours) to the divine Lord. One can best do that by repeating a divine name as much as one can.

(e) Time spent in making the effort (e.g. repeating a divine name) is as important as its quality. For example, as merely saying 'Ram, Ram' for one hour is not beneficial as concentrating the mind on the sound produced in repetition of 'Ram, Ram' whilst paying no attention to intervening thoughts.

(f) It needs to be stressed that mind is controlled by the mind only through hard self-exertion; don't have faith in some self-styled guru who promises otherwise. Self-effort (to control the mind) and divine grace are both essential to progress in spiritual life. Their relationship is of cause and effect; grace inheres in effort and vice versa.

(g) Remember, there are no short cuts to attain liberation from ignorance. It takes a long time to succeed in doing on. Progress on it is often slow and there are moments when one gets frustrated due to its apparent lack. One must press on regardless because spiritual growth is inbuilt in effort. There is no obstacle that a guru's grace does not remove instantly. It requires dedicated hard work and only gullible people expect miracles to substitute for it.

(h) Follow a certain routine in daily life. Apart from earning an honest livelihood, one should spare some time for introspection and reflection. Practise the guru's instruction (or meditation) earnestly for at least one hour. If that is not possible, do it for a shorter period to begin with and try to reach that goal as soon as one can. Practice beyond one hour is desirable and a beginner should try to extend that time as much as it is possible to do so.

(i) A beginner should not be squeamish about posture, diet, sex etc. Begin practice sincerely and all such matters would resolve on their own. It is preferable to do sadhana at the same spot and time every day. Always pray to the guru or ishta deva (object of worship) before commencing practice. Follow guru's advice in the performance of religious rituals and rites; gurus of the highest class rarely insist on them because they are not essential for spiritual growth.

(j) Pay particular attention to cultivation of divine qualities, specially of love, devotion and discrimination and annihilation of undesirable attributes like pride, jealously, attachment, greed etc. Growth of divine attributes is an index of spiritual advancement and is applicable to all paths.

(k) Every jiva goes through ups and downs in life to reap the fruits of one's past karma. Most people who begin a spiritual quest entertain hopes that their karmic problems and painful experiences would disappear as a result. A serious student should realise that, although an individual can improve one's karma by exercising one's intelligence, as brought out in Answer 68 of Chapter 3, yet that should not be one's goal of practice. Following points are relevant in this regard. Firstly, the aim of practice is to control the mind and in the process get rid of the notion of karma (i.e. discard the 'I am doer' feeling). Secondly, it is inevitable that the body suffers the consequences of past deeds. That is the divine law. It is applicable to the wise as well as the ignorant. For instance, even a great yogi like Jesus Christ went through the torture of crucifixion. Thirdly, the feeling, 'I have prayed so much and practised hard and yet I suffer', that many a beginner has causes confusion and doubts in one's mind about the efficacy of practice. It may even become a hurdle in making spiritual progress. It is important that devotees do not link spiritual development with karma.

(l) Do not seek or induce or imagine spiritual experiences. They are a play of mind and are of no consequence in knowing the Truth. In fact, they are a hindrance and one should learn to ignore and reject them as false from the earliest stages of practice. This is applicable even to the feelings of bliss.

(m) Meditation should be carried out with an alert mind. Sleep often supervenes during practice. It is important to keep the consciousness vigilant in order to prevent it from falling asleep. Serious seekers would notice that a certain dullness pervades the mind during meditation. This persists even in manolaya (self-subsidence) and early stages of samadhi. It is also because consciousness thinks, 'I am the body', which is primarily tamasic (lethargic) in nature. The effect of this notion is that the mind is under heavy influence of tamas. One can overcome this debility by regular and constant practise to make the mind sharp and electrically alert.

(n) Psychic powers often manifest on their own during sadhana. Getting involved with them is to invite divine wrath and eternal damnation. There is no bigger obstacle to spiritual growth than using them, even on the pretext of doing service or good to others.

(o) No matter which path one follows, always repeat a divine name during non- practising hours and do selfless service to others. It increases the efficacy of every path and hastens the process of mental purification.

(p) The best way to practise is in a spirit of self-surrender and without any desire, i.e., neither for knowledge nor for bliss nor to make progress and definitely not to attain any powers.

(q) Finally, practice, practice and practice till the goal is reached. Be determined to succeed and have full faith in the guru and in one's own self. Always have a feeling that one is not doing enough. There is no way that one would not attain Reality with an attitude like that.

Q17. What are the primary methods to control the mind or the paths that lead to it?

A17. Traditionally, sages have devised certain disciplines for purposes of teaching. Their delineation is based on two primary factors; first, varied temperaments of aspirants and two, on certain attributes of the mind. A reader ought to note some points in this regard. One, division into various paths is more for ease of imparting instruction than separating them into watertight compartments. All paths are the same in their essence and aim to achieve the same end, i.e., control of mind. They differ only in laying emphasis on certain points. Two, there are four basic temperaments that jivas (persons) usually display, which are derived from the predominant traits of their natures; they are, active (karmic), devotional, intellectual and scientific. A person of an active nature is a workaholic and, though, sincere and dedicated, yet is not habituated to thinking much. Love and self-surrender come easily to a person of devotional nature. An intellectual jiva is an introvert, has a discriminative mind and likes to acquire knowledge while the one with scientific temperament has a practical bent of mind, which likes to experiment with teaching (i.e. is prepared to practise with an open mind to determine its veracity) rather than read too much about it in order to determine its veracity. Three, each path lays stress on a certain trait of the mind, without ignoring its other characteristics, and then exploits it to gain control over it. Based on the above discussion, the primary paths or disciplines generally advocated are as follows:-

(a) **The Path of Service**. To do one's karma in a selfless and unattached manner forms the core of teaching on this path. It is an excellent means to purify the mind and should be practised by everyone either in combination with other discipline or as an independent path. It is followed mostly by persons of extroverted natures who love to work.

(b) **The Path of Love and Devotion**. It aims to control the mind through remembrance of the Lord done with love and devotion. It is suitable for those who are ready to submit to the Lord's will in a spirit of self-surrender and out of love for Him or Her.

(c) **The Path of Yoga**. It lays emphasis on meditation done on an object to conserve mind's out flowing energy as well as to purify it. People of scientific temperaments find its practice very useful. The mind is destroyed through the development of power of concentration (yoga shakti) by following this discipline.

(d) **The Path of Knowledge**. Those who have intellectual bent of mind are attracted to this path. Its primary purpose is to locate the source of ignorance (or the point of origin of mind, i.e., the 'I'-sense) and then discover its unreal nature. It seeks to gain absolute knowledge and not its relative counterpart, i.e., it rejects relative knowledge as false and unreal.

(e) **The Path of Silence**. It uses the power of Silence earned by a satguru through the practice of a special yogic discipline called tapas yoga to silence the mind of a devotee. It can be followed as a path by itself or in combination with others, usually the latter. All aspirants are capable of practising it in the second aspect.

(f) **Worship**. It is not a discipline by itself but is practised in combination with any of the above paths. It is specially useful for beginners and consists of prayers, various modes of worship, rites, and rituals and so on.

Q18. It was stated earlier that in each age (yuga) some paths are more effective than others. What is the most suitable discipline for the current age?

A18. Control of mind is the goal in every age; i.e. liberation is achieved only by destroying the mind. All paths are practised in every yuga (age) but some are more effective in an epoch due to two factors. One, length of human life and two, degree of selfishness. The current age (kaliyuga) is characterised by extreme selfishness. It is made worse by shorter life spans (approximately 100 years at the most). Environmental factors such as pollution are a cause of multiplicity of diseases. Rituals are less effective in kaliyuga because to bear fruit they must be carried out over prolonged periods. Their efficacy is more in other yugas because human beings live longer in them. The path of love and devotion is suitable for every age but more so in current yuga because quick results can be obtained through self-surrender, love and devotion. Other paths can also be practised in kaliyuga but temperamentally there are fewer people who can do so now than in the earlier ages.

Q 19. What are the major points that have a general application on the practise of above disciplines?
A19. Points mentioned below are relevant for aspirants, irrespective of the paths that they pursue:-

(a) A spiritual discipline is practised to control the mind, which in its essence implies to locate its point of origin and then to destroy it. The palpable form of the mind is the conglomeration of thoughts that rise and fall in it ceaselessly. The base of all such thoughts is the 'I' thought, which, is the source of the mind. The practice of any path results, firstly, in restraining the outflow of thought energy and its concentration on the 'I' and, secondly, in finding the latter and then destroying it. Mind is not considered to be under full control till the 'I' exists. The resultant thereafter is the indescribable state of Realisation.

(b) The mind must be disciplined and purified to a certain level before one can hope to make substantive progress. That is the initial stage of practice of any discipline. Its middle state is marked by greater self-discipline and mental purification; it (i.e. middle stage of practice) begins with abidance of mind and concludes with its subsidence (manolaya). The last or final phase of practice is of destruction of mind. In it, the mind attains its highest levels of purification and discipline in a state of samadhi. The mind's existence ends only when one is able to gain the highest samadhi (i.e. sahaj samadhi; the state of absolute consciousness).

(c) Mind is controlled only through an efficacious use of the power of discrimination and other divine qualities by one's intelligence. The latter holds the reins of roving mind (manas) and senses and restrains their movement through its will power.

(d) The power of concentration (yoga shakti) must be developed fully to control the mind.

(e) All paths accept duality (i.e. existence of a subject and an object) in the beginning of practice but end up by proclaiming its falsehood and accepting non- dual (i.e. neither a subject nor an object) Reality as the sole Truth. The middle of practice is characterised by monotheism, i.e., an object appears to be the same as a subject or objects are perceived as images of God.

(f) Although gurus usually teach only one path, yet those of the highest class (i.e. satgurus) can initiate aspirants on any discipline. A guru selects a path for a devotee according to one's temperament. However, what comes naturally and easily to an aspirant is the path suited to him or her.

Worship

Q 20. What is worship and its significance?

A 20. A mental act done out of love and devotion, which reminds one of God to earn Its grace is worship. It must be done with a concentrated mind to be fully effective. There are some forms of formal worship (e.g. performance of rituals) in which the body also plays a part. It is a lower form of worship and is useful only if done with love and devotion. Worship is a means to express one's faith and love for the Lord or one's ishta deva (chosen deity of worship). It does not by itself control the mind but is an important aid for beginners to develop divine attributes of love, devotion, compassion, faith, self-surrender, humility etc. An average person's idea of worship relates to formal prayers, rituals, rites etc. but he or she misses out on its deeper significance, which is to remember the Lord with love all the time.

Q21. What are the objects of worship?

A21. God is the sole object of worship for a devotee. It may be worshipped in Its disembodied form (i.e. through remembrance of Its name) or in the embodied form of any of Its divine incarnations. Lower than the above is worship of Brahma, Vishnu and Shiva along with their consorts and other gods and goddesses. Its benefits are much lower than those given by worship of the Lord. Then, there are objects like rivers, animals, trees, basic elements consisting of fire, water etc., diagrams (used in tantra) and so on, which are often used for worship by worldly minded people not given to much thinking.

Q22. What are the forms of worship? Is it essential to be initiated by a guru to derive benefit for it?

A22. Worship done under the directions of a guru is always more effective. However, gurus initiate devotees for the main disciplines, discussed earlier, and there is no need to do so separately for worship. The latter should be carried out in addition to the practice of a chosen path. There are three kinds of worship;

superior (satvic), middling (rajasic) and inferior (tamasic). Satvic worship is to put into effect a guru's teaching, i.e., practise earnestly any of the paths, mentioned earlier, after being initiated by a guru. In other words, to control the mind is the best and highest form of worship. Rajasic worship comprises bodily actions (karma) done with love and devotion; it implies that in addition to mental activity the body also plays a part in doing it. It is a formal type of worship with which most people are familiar and it is performed daily in temples, churches and other holy places associated with various religions, sects etc. according to their own traditions evolved over a long period. Much of worship of this type is laid down by the priestly class and religious leaders who have very little knowledge of spiritual teaching of saints. It consists of prayers, charitable acts, feeding the pilgrims and the poor, visits to holy places, performance of laid down rituals etc. The third form of worship is of animals, trees, stones, rivers, diagrams to appease deities of a lower grade etc. It is indulged in by ignorant people with dull minds who cannot comprehend instruction of a guru. It is the lowest class of worship and has very little significance for those who want to control their minds.

Q23. What are the fruits of worship of various types?
A23. Fruit of any action is according to one's motive and the quality of effort put in. Most people perform worship to fulfill a wish or a desire. If done sincerely and humbly, some minor desires may be gratified by doing worship; however, it needs to be remembered that satiation of desires is dependent more on one's karma than any other factor. Mechanical performance of worship (i.e. in which love and devotion for a deity is missing) is practically of no use. The rewards of practising a guru's teaching sincerely are the highest in not so much as gratification of worldly desires as of having a vision of the Lord. What else does one need if one can attain that?

Q24. What are the ritualistic forms of worship? What purpose do they serve?
A24. A ritual is an action done formally in a laid down manner at certain fixed timings to offer prayers to God or gods, goddesses and other deities. It can be a simple affair or an elaborate one depending on the purpose for which it is performed. Non-stop recitation of scriptures, bathing in holy tanks, ceremonial worship of idols, images, and symbols through lights, flowers and other materials, parikrama (to go around a deity or a holy place), rites like havans and yagnas, ringing of bells and so one are some examples of rituals. They exist in some form or the other in all religious traditions of the world. A ritual should be done out of love and devotion for the deity being worshipped to seek its blessings. But, that is not the way most people indulge in ritualism. They do it out of a religious duty, taught traditionally in families, in a routine and mechanical manner on certain auspicious days or occasions or times in order to earn some merit or supposedly wash off sins or gratify a wish. Rituals like these

are usually done by priests with very little participation from those for whose sake they are performed. A ritual carried out like that has practically no value; what benefit can it give if one is mentally not involved sincerely in worship? Another point worth noting is that sages and seers (rishis and munis) in ancient times used to prescribe simple rituals for those of their devotees who were not yet ready to practise higher forms of spiritual disciplines (e.g. meditation, self-enquiry). It was meant to be a preparatory stage for spiritual development by inducing a certain degree of devotion in them. It would also start the process of mental discipline and purification, specially when it was combined with doing service (sewa). However, the priestly class over a long period of time, modified the above rituals into an intricate maze to exploit gullible and ignorant people to make a living out of it. The result is that an ordinary person is a slave to performance of rituals; he or she neither understands that a rite is just another form of karma nor that the spiritual power lies in the saint who devices a ritual and not in the act itself. A rite done under the direction of a guru bears fruit but its result is always uncertain if a priest performs it in a routine manner. In general, the benefit of a ritual is according to one's karma and one should expect no miracles from it. A discriminative aspirant should realise that the purpose of ritual is to express one's love and devotion for a deity but in their absence it achieves very little.

Q25. Is performance of rituals a must for aspirants? Is there any particular rite that aids in spiritual advancement?
A25. No; one may or may not indulge in doing them. As a general rule, there is neither special merit in performance of rituals and rites nor a benefit in abstaining from doing so. It all depends on an aspirant's spiritual maturity, mental proclivity and guru's direction, if any. Those who feel their necessity should continue to carry them out while the others may skip them. Those beginners who feel that they would benefit from their performance should do them with devotion. The mind turns away from them on its own as one makes spiritual progress. One may indulge in ritualistic worship according to the traditions of one's religion, creed, sect etc. or any other form of worship that appeals to one's self. A simple rite done with devotion and love is more effective than a complex one in which these qualities are missing. One gets the benefits of all rituals by practise of the discipline prescribed by a guru. Repetition of a divine name to remember the Lord has the same effect.

The Path of Service (Sewa)

Q26. The path of service is highly lauded by all saints and scriptures. It has been termed as the basic discipline in Guru Upanishad. Why is it so? What, in brief, is its essence?

A26. Action is intrinsic to the body as long it exists and there is no way that a jiva (an individual) can avoid doing one's karma. That being so, there are two courses open to an individual; to act with the ego-sense or without it. An action done with the 'I'-sense (e.g. 'I love her', 'I hit him', 'he is my son') causes bondage to the chain of birth and death and rebirth. The evil qualities of attachment, greed, pride, anger etc. act as a catalyst for such actions. Satiation of one desire leads to the birth of many more and they cannot all be gratified, which brings about pain, misery and unhappiness. The second method is to do one's karma without the involvement of ego. It means that a jiva performs the same actions that he or she is destined to according to his or her prarabdha (present life's) karma but without a feeling that he or she doing it. In the examples quoted above, it would imply that the 'I' in the statements, 'I love her' or 'I hit him', is missing. A jiva does not, as indeed one cannot, give up action but carries it out without a sense of participation. That forms the crux of the path of service and is the way of the wise, unlike the path of the ignorant, i.e. to act selfishly. Thus, the essence of true service lies in carrying out one's karma without the motivation of satisfying one's desires or seeking a fruit for one's efforts. Most people work to attain name and fame in the world to please their egos. Even charitable deeds are proclaimed to the society through advertisements in newspapers and television. That is not the way of the wise who seek release from life of pain and misery. All gurus, sages and seers lay special stress on doing service for the following reasons. First, if one accepts that action is inevitable for an embodied being, which no jiva can deny, then why not do it in a manner that reduces the bondage of ignorance, eventually leading to salvation? It is regarded as the basic path for this reason. Second, an individual must be temperamentally suited and inclined to pursue paths like yoga, love and devotion, knowledge etc. There is no such requirement for the path of service since everyone has to go through one's karma. Third, service is an excellent means to discipline and purify the mind, two vital requirements for carrying out advanced practice of any discipline. Fourth, there is no better way to develop divine qualities of love, devotion, compassion, contentment, humility, forgiveness and so on than to practise this path. Most people including aspirants talk about the importance of these attributes but rarely put them to practice for whatever reason. Service gives an opportunity to everyone to display that one has indeed made divine attributes as part of one's nature. Fifth, the Lord is pleased most with those who do selfless service to others because it benefits a large number of objects (i.e. people, animal, birds etc.) created by It. Divine grace overlooks the shortcomings of those devotees who do service. In fact, more people attain salvation through this path than any other.

Q27. Is there any substance in the belief of some people that service purifies the mind somewhat but its practice does not result in complete liberation? Must it always be followed in combination with other paths or can it be practised by itself?

A27. There is no validity in the assertion that service cannot lead to freedom from ignorance. All those who make such statements do so without any divine knowledge that is gained only in spiritual experience rather than study of scriptures. Why would saints and seers extol this path if it was designed by the divine will to give half ripe fruit? Why would the gurus and sages set a personal example of selfless service to their devotees if it could not lead to salvation? Know it for certain that desireless service is one of the primary and most effective means to know the Truth. It is the supreme prayer and superior to any ritualistic form of worship. Arjuna is a well-known example from past history of a devotee who attained the Reality through motiveless action. There are many others like Saint Peter, Ali, Baba Buddha, Swami Vivekananda and so on who served their gurus selflessly. The path of service can be followed independently or in combination with others. In the former case, a devotee usually lacks the mental inclination for any serious introspection and contemplation to even have a conviction to follow a discipline to control the mind. Action comes to him or her naturally and easily and the Lord has ordained that he or she can attain everything if it is done in a spirit of self-surrender and service to Him or Her. Majority of the devotees fall in this category. However, they get better results if they repeat a divine name (i.e. of God) in addition to doing sewa (service). The efficacy of any path (e.g. of love, yoga, knowledge) increases manifold if it is practised in combination with that of selfless service. That is why gurus advise all their devotees to indulge in service.

Q28. Who should a devotee serve?

A28. The highest ideal is to do service for the sake of service only. There is no particular object that one has in mind to serve but to carryout one's karma without any feeling of doing it; it means that the 'I am a doer' feeling that a jiva entertains is absent. Most devotees find it hard to serve in this manner. They should regard the Lord or their guru or ishta deva (object of worship) as the being they want to do service to. They should surrender all their actions and fruits attained from them to the Lord (or the guru or ishta deva). They should consider every deed that they do as a sacrifice for the sake of God. Even this is not easy to follow because the Lord is invisible and unknown. How can one serve an intangible entity? This problem is overcome if one regards the embodied form of one's guru or ishta deva as that of God. Further, one should imagine (to begin with) that all created objects are the manifested forms of the Lord (or one's guru or ishta deva) and one is serving Him or Her through them. That is the best way to serve and carry out one's karma.

Q29. The 'I' and its vasnas (desires) are the basis of action. Is it feasible to act without the 'I'?

A29. Yes; all saints and sages continue to act in the world after they attain Realisation (i.e. the state of consciousness in which the 'I' does not exist). Many like Sri Rama, Sri Krishna and Guru Gobind Singh have fought wars in this state. There is no awareness of the 'I' in deep sleep and yet a person turns from one side to another without any thought process involved in it. The karma of a jiva is programmed similarly to unfold whether the 'I' is involved in it or not. The supreme Lord is egoless and yet It creates infinite number of worlds and their myriad objects without any sense of 'I am the creator'. An individual should aspire to carry out one's karma in the same manner, which would ultimately lead to the supreme goal of Realisation.

Q30. The fundamental premise in the practice of a spiritual discipline is to control thoughts or the mind. Is it possible to do so through service?

A30. Yes; all thoughts stem from the primary 'I' thought. The purpose of doing service is to submerge or surrender the 'I' to the object for whose sake it is being done (God or guru or ishta deva). A devotee believes that the Lord dwells in every object and he or she regards service to another jiva only as a means to offer one's self ('I') to It. This process of self-surrender purifies the mind and controls it. One who wants to serve others should try to have no feeling or thought, 'I am doing service'; rather, one should think of Him or Her as being served in another's body. Service done in this manner weakens the intensity and energy of thoughts in the initial stages of practice (i.e. during the first three phases of control of mind; discipline, purification and abidance); in the next state (i.e. manolaya) thoughts become dormant and in the last phase (i.e. manonash) they are withdrawn into the primary 'I' thought, which is then destroyed through divine grace and self-effort (i.e. to do service). The implication is that one must continue to serve selflessly till the mind exists. It requires no emphasis that the above process is not an easy one. It requires a rare combination of compassion, devotion, love, perseverance and determination to sustain this practice over a long period of time (i.e. maybe many lives) to achieve success.

Q31. Are there various grades of service?

A31. Although it is possible to classify service as being satvic (high), rajasic (middling) and tamasic (low), yet to do so is to give an impression that the fruits of carrying out one type are superior to others. It would imply that doing some form of karma would lead to salvation while others might not give the same results. For example, one may imagine that an erudite person who writes a commentary on a scripture in a spirit of service (to the Lord) has a greater chance of attaining liberation than a mere cook who feeds pilgrims with the same mental attitude. To be a scholar or a cook is a matter of one's karma and though, to the ignorant, the former appears higher and the latter lower, yet, the truth is that both have an equal opportunity to go through their karma selflessly. The important point to understand is that how one acts, as opposed to the action itself (which is to some extent pre-determined due to past karma), is what brings freedom to an individual. Thus, the cook who serves others in a spirit of self-surrender and love is a more likely candidate for salvation than a great scholar who flouts his or her learning to boost his or her ego (i.e. gain name and fame in the world). To do one's karma, in whatever station one is placed in life (e.g. housewife, actor, prime minister, beauty queen, farmer, soldier, priest etc.), in a selfless manner is, therefore, the best form of service.

Q32. Most people think that doing service refers to serving in holy places or looking after the saints, the poor, the sick, the old, the needy etc. and indulging in charitable work. What is the validity of this view in the context of the previous answer?

A32. To serve the kind of people or indulge in activities mentioned in the question are certainly very meritorious acts and those who do them, are specially blessed by the Lord, as long as it is not done to gain name and fame. But, to narrow the concept of service just to them would imply that those who do not get an opportunity to serve people of the above type cannot do sewa (service) at all. It should be appreciated that karma of many persons is involved when individuals render service to others. For instance, it must be part of a devotee's karma to do personal service to a saint and, equally, it should be within the latter's karma to accept it. Not all devotees of a guru get a chance to stay in his or her company all the time. How would a soldier serve the poor or the sick when his karma keeps him occupied in a war? Similarly, what about the needy, the sick and the old? Should they serve no one? How can a destitute person contribute money for charity? Thus, doing service should not be confined to just a few of its types; its notion should rather extend to include all its forms, which would imply that everyone should carry out his or her karma desirelessly and without any motive. It is a loftier ideal to achieve and it gives everyone a chance to purify the mind and to advance spiritually.

Q33. How should one begin on the path of service? What mental attitude should one adopt to follow it?

A33. Service is best done through the grace (i.e. initiation) of a guru. A little self-analysis and introspection would reveal that one's lot cannot be better than what it is due to one's past karma. One has taken birth in a certain rich or poor family, has many or very few friends, is well employed or not at all, enjoys good or poor health and so on as a consequence of the merits (punya) and demerits (pappa) earned in previous lives. The seed of the tree that bears fruit now (i.e.

present life) was a planted a long time back and the clock cannot be reversed. One should realise that in whatever position or status one is placed now is the result of one's own past effort and there is no one else to be blamed for it (least of all, God). If that be so, what should a jiva do? Should one give way to despair and indulge in self-pity or cease making further effort to improve the state of affairs? Only weak willed and mentally deficient people take recourse to attitudes like these. Intelligent persons endeavour to find a way out of the karmic quagmire they find themselves in. They hear a guru's instruction and ponder over it deeply to reach a conclusion that the way to real happiness lies in detaching themselves from the fruits of karma rather than making a futile effort to give it up altogether. For, who has the power to stop acting? Who can violate the divine will that has ordained that the body must work till its death? It does not mean that one should not attempt to make worldly progress. One must continue to do so within the constraints of one's karma and the various choices that one has to carry it out. Do that by all means but do not get attached to its fruits. One should try to give up desire for acting but not the action itself. It should be of no concern to a wise jiva (person) whether performance of karma brings pleasure or pain, success or failure, profit or loss etc. An action done with a motive to gain wealth, name, fame etc. might bring temporary joy if one is successful but there is an equal chance that it might result in pain in case of failure. But, a desireless and motiveless action that does not seek anything brings everlasting happiness. That is the best way to do one's karma and one should constantly endeavour to act in this spirit. One need not and should not announce to the world that one is indulging in sewa (service). Whatever one wants to do must remain a covenant with one's own self. A devotee on this path should pay particular attention to the following points:-

(a) Use work as a means to surrender one's self ('I'-ness) to the Lord. To do so, one should perform one's karma as a duty enjoined by the Lord in Its divine drama (leela), much like an actor who has a bit role in it. Offer the work and its effects (i.e. fruits) to the Lord as a means to sacrifice the 'I'-sense (i.e. the devotee gives away the fruit of one's labour to God, keeping nothing for oneself). It purifies the mind and brings it under control. To act in this spirit is the best of all yagnas (rites) and rituals.

(b) Service is carried out successfully by those who have an all pervasive love (i.e. for God and Its creation) in their hearts. Other equally important qualities to have are humility, compassion, contentment and detachment (i.e. the ability to divorce karma from its effects; in other words, be not attached to the fruits of one's actions).

(c) Remember, serving others does not imply that one neglects one's children, family etc. One must do one's duty to them; serve them just as one serves others by thinking that the same Lord dwells in their hearts as He or She does in other people. Let a mother prepare a meal for her children by imagining that she is going to feed the indwelling Lord in them. It is a very effective way to overcome one's attachment.

(d) Doing service should bring joy to one's heart. It is not meant to be a forced labour that pleases some unseen master. The indwelling Atman (Self) feels happy when one acts for Its sake.

Q34. What are the signs that one is progressing well on this path? Are there any particular experiences that one has while doing service?

A34. Spiritual experiences accrue according to one's nature and has no great relevance to the discipline being practised. Progress is indicated by the degree of joy that work gives (e.g. feeling of happiness itself becomes divine bliss in advanced states of one's practice), being calm and cool under adverse circumstances, remaining cheerful even if criticised by those one is serving, regarding one's wealth as a burden and ceasing to plan for the future (i.e. it betokens self-surrender to God).

Q35. What are the main characteristics of a person pursuing this path?

A35. In general, people who carryout sewa (service) are simple hearted and guileless. They have great faith in their guru and do the latter's bidding cheerfully. They have a firm conviction that whatever happens, good or bad, is as per the divine will and to accept it without remonstration under all circumstances is the best course of action. They are not depressed easily and make it a point to cheer up those who need help. They do sewa (service) for sewa's sake and do not seek any rewards (e.g. publicity in newspapers and visual media). They regard themselves as the servants of the Lord.

Q36. What are the major impediments to success while doing service? How are they overcome?

A36. The beginning stage of one's quest is rather difficult because an average person cannot really discern the difference between selfless and selfish service. One imagines that donating money for charity and good causes or visiting the sick etc. is all there is to sewa. There is certainly merit in doing so but it misses the crucial element that is so essential to advance spiritually. Sewa (service) is done to curb one's ego and not to inflate it, as is likely to happen if one wants to be proclaimed a karma yogi in one's social circles. A beginner must constantly remind himself or herself that sewa is only a means to control the mind and be on guard to nip the ego from manifesting. It is not as easy as it might appear because most people are unable to distinguish between what is being done to please the ego or to check it. One must be very discriminative in such matters.

All hurdles are destroyed by the guru's grace, which is best earned through self-surrender to the Lord. Also develop divine qualities like compassion, love, humility, contentment, faith etc. and get rid of their undesirable counterpart like pride, attachment, jealousy, greed etc. Always remember the Lord by repeating Its divine name; optimum results are achieved if sewa is done in addition to the practise of another discipline like meditation.

Q37. What is the essence of teaching on the path of service?
A37. The divine will has ordained that selfless service done with love, compassion and self-surrender in the current age (kaliyuga) reduces an aspirant's effort, to attain salvation, by half. There is, therefore, special merit in learning to act without any motive, desire or expectation to receive its fruit. No jiva (individual) can avoid or give up doing one's karma. It is in that sense that it is regarded as the fundamental discipline that everyone must follow. Why not then carry it out in the spirit of service to the Lord who dwells in every heart? Always act without the 'I''s involvement or a feeling, 'I am the doer'. Selfish actions strengthen a jiva's bondage of ignorance whereas unselfish ones remove it totally. They purify the mind and lead to its control. A seeker's spiritual progress becomes faster if one carries out sewa (service) in addition to the practice of some other path.

The Path of Love and Devotion (Bhakti Marga)

Q38. What are the characteristic features of this path and what is it based on?
A38. The mind's impurities in the form of samaskaras and vasnas (mental impressions and latent tendencies created by past karma) dwell in its memory. They are the cause of mental extroversion that makes an individual forget one's true (i.e. divine) nature. Many undesirable attributes like attachment, pride, greed, jealousy etc. manifest in the mind due to them. The path of love is based on the mind's inherent nature to remember things. An average jiva's mind is characterised by remembrance as well as forgetfulness; when one thing is remembered the other is forgotten; as, for instance, there is no thought of her husband in a mother's mind when she remembers her son (i.e. she forgets the husband). A jiva's mind is constantly fluctuating between remembrance and forgetfulness. The path of devotion aims to prolong the period of remembrance to an almost infinite level and in doing so make it (i.e. remembrance) as thing in itself (i.e. reach its absolute state). In this process, an aspirant is detached from (i.e. forgets) the world and one's self ('I'-ness). Remembrance, in the relative sense, requires an object to dwell on. Worldly objects create bondage when they are remembered; a mother becomes attached to her children due to constant remembrance. The memory of a divine object (e.g. God or Its incarnations, holy sages etc.), on the other hand, purifies and introverts the mind due to its

inherent sanctifying qualities. The crucial element in remembrance is that it must be done with love, devotion and concentration. Thus, this path is distinguished from others by the emphasis that it lays on a focused (i.e. on God) mind's ability to control itself through its own activity to remember the Lord out of love and devotion.

Q39. Why is this path called as that of love and devotion if remembrance is its primary feature? What is the inter se connection between them?
A39. Objects are remembered only when there is love for them. A mother does not remember others' children as much as she does her own. Know it for certain that love is the crucial element that plays a predominant and conducive part on this path. Those who have divine love in their hearts need nothing else because the Lord is the quintessence of love and the absolute Reality is its unconditioned form. Devotion is the steadfastness with which a devotee loves God unwaveringly. Remembrance of the Lord is an expression of love and to do so unreservedly without a break is a measure of devotion. Thus, effort to remember the Lord bears fruit only if it is done with love and devotion; it remains barren otherwise.

Q40. Objects are also remembered due to jealousy, hate, greed, attachment etc. Are their effects the same as remembrance done with love as the motivating factor?
A40. No; each quality has a different effect on the mind. Anger cannot produce the same effect on it as love does. Broadly, attributes are classified as desirable or divine and undesirable or evil. The former comprise unselfish love, devotion, compassion, discrimination, contentment, detachment etc. while those mentioned in the question are those that fall in the latter category. Divine qualities calm and purify the mind but their non-divine counterparts agitate it. Amongst the desirable attributes, love is the most potent in its effect on the mind and, hence, its prime importance to control the mind needs no emphasis. Remembrance done as an effect of evil qualities invariably causes turmoil in the mind and is, therefore, the very antithesis of what is required to be done in a spiritual quest. Undesirable attributes extrovert the mind whereas their divine counterparts introvert it. In any case, does anyone endeavour specially to remember unpleasant people?

Q41. What is the nature of remembrance (smaran) as related to the path of love and devotion?
A41. To recall or recollect a previously stored samaskaras (mental impression) or knowledge in the mind (or memory) is called remembrance and it is a natural function of the consciousness. It gives subjective and objective awareness; in other words, a jiva becomes aware of his or her self, due to a deeply ingrained

memory of the 'I'-sense. Objective awareness arises similarly; a mother is aware of her daughter only when she remembers her. A thing that is absent in memory is non-existent. Remembrance is primarily subjective in nature; it means that a jiva's awareness of his or her self ('I'-ness) precedes that of other objects. Its implication in the context of the practice of this path is that, although, a devotee needs an object of remembrance, yet, it must ultimately lead to the experience of the 'I', whose destruction is sine qua non for attaining liberation. Remembrance, in the spiritual context, is an act of willful application of intelligence to recall something that already exists in memory. It requires that mind must be focused and concentrated on the object that it wants to recall. It is everyone's experience that one has to concentrate the mind to remember something that one has forgotten. A jiva is not aware of the Lord or one's true nature due to forgetfulness caused by mental extroversion. The mind must concentrate or introvert to remember either of them. A jiva has the power to recollect anything one wants to with appropriate effort. One partakes the qualities of whatever one remembers; to remember the Lord is to immerse one's self in the ocean of Its bliss and to do the same to the world is to derive pain and misery of repeated birth and death.

Q42. What are the objects of remembrance in the practise of this path?

A42. Ishwara (God) is the only object that one ought to remember because It alone has the power to grant liberation from ignorance. It is the source of all knowledge, bliss and divine qualities. All gods and goddesses are Its finite forms and, hence, have limited power (i.e. only some divine attributes manifest in them). God is, however, an intangible principle of consciousness and difficult to conceive of by most devotees. It takes birth as a guru (e.g. Guru Nanak and Sri Raman Maharishi) or an avtara (incarnation) like Sri Krishna to help those who seek Its grace. To remember saints of this calibre confers the same benefit as in the case of Ishwara. Worship of gods and goddesses like Brahma, Vishnu, Shiva, Saraswati, Lakshmi and Parvati and a host of others is also useful, up to a point, in the pursuit of a spiritual quest. However, none of them has been empowered by God to grant total freedom from the bondage of repeated birth and death.

Q43. What are the divine qualities, besides love and devotion that a devotee ought to have to succeed on this path? How are they nurtured to grow? Who is competent to practise it?

A43. The path of love is best practised by those who develop a mental altitude of self-surrender to the Lord (or one's guru). They regard It as their sole support and rely on It totally for everything. It is not easy to practise in this spirit unless a devotee has genuine love (for God), devotion, faith, detachment, humility, contentment and discrimination. All these attributes inhere in every jiva's mind to some degree or the other and they can be developed to any limit with appropriate effort. The way to do so is to be aware of their absence to the required level and then make deliberate attempt to nurture them. It is possible to act in this manner provided one uses one's sense of discrimination to reject evil qualities during the course of one's daily chores. It must, however, be stressed that most aspirants, on any path but specially this one, do not have a properly developed sense of discrimination. It becomes apparent during sadhana (practice) when devotees are satisfied with minor gains (e.g. feelings of little peace or seeing visions etc.) and are unable to proceed beyond them. It is a serious hurdle on this path and one must endeavour to specially develop discrimination in addition to other attributes. There is no better way to ensure their growth than regular and sustained practice of the guru's teaching. They mature on their own if the mind is purified, introverted and controlled through remembrance of the Lord because it (the mind) acquires Its attributes in the process. This path can be practised by anyone who desires to have a vision of God and attain permanent happiness. Unlike disciplines like yoga and knowledge which emphasise restraint on mental activity from their inceptive stages, this path tries to sublimate it through remembrance of the Lord. Most people find it easier to pursue it because they are already used to indulge the mind in some form of activity or the other. All that is required is that the mind should change its focus of activity from the world to God.

Q44. How does a devotee set about on this path?

A44. A beginner has generally only a vague idea of the nature of the Lord. He or she has some faith in It but is not sure whether It is formless or with form or where It dwells or how to find It. He or she is not inclined to delve deep into scriptural knowledge by contemplating on it. Whatever little he or she knows is based on books written by scholars who themselves have no spiritual experience, the only true source of divine knowledge. A person like that tries to practise scriptural teaching as he or she understands it but his or her gains are not commensurate with the effort put in nor are they up to the desired level. An individual in that confused state requires guidance and it is advisable that he or she should seek the grace of a guru. Know it for certain that no substantive or serious spiritual progress is possible without the latter. Most devotees meet a guru according to a karmic connection of past lives. They should pray to God with humility and sincerity to guide them to a guru. The Lord responds to all such supplications with promptitude if an aspirant's desire to meet a guru is very intense. An individual's spiritual quest starts only after one hears about the Lord from a guru, contemplate on the latter's word, clarify one's doubts and then takes an initiation from him or her. In the course of initiation, a guru generally gives an aspirant a divine name (of the Lord) or a mantra to repeat for a certain length of time. One should then do a regular practice of the Guru's instruction.

Q45. What is the relevance of the doctrine of name (nama) to this path?

A45. A name is a word ascribed to an object to distinguish it from another similar or dissimilar objects. Words are usually used to make distinctions in the general sense; for instance, men and women, birds and animals etc. A name particularises a general word into a specific object; for example, a man called Rama is an individual different from say John, in his personality, traits and character. A parrot is unlike a hawk and each of their species is categorised further by assigning them different words or names. An object is known only by its name that stands for its attributes. Objects are recalled in memory only through their names; a father, for example, remembers his daughter only by her name. The same object may have more than one name; the man, Rama, may have many pet names, which may refer to his specific qualities (e.g. Jumbo alludes to his size). Just as objects are known by their names, so is the Lord known by Its divine name only. God has innumerable names because Its qualities are infinite. Sages and seers have assigned names to Ishwara according to some of Its functions as perceived by human beings; for example, It is called Gobind as a protector of the world. Names like these exist in all languages in every country. There are countless objects having a limitless number of names. All of them resolve into one name; or, all of them originate from one source and that is called the name. Name is thus a word used for all generic names in all languages of past, present and future. Just as Ishwara has created the world and its myriad objects, so have all the names (of objects) manifested from the single name. The Name has, therefore, the same connotation as God (i.e. a name is not different from the object specified by it). Name is either relative or absolute; this distinction has the same connotation as saguna (relative; God) or nirguna (absolute) Reality. The doctrine of name is specially relevant to the path of love because the Lord can only be remembered by Its name. Even an idol or a picture made to remind one of God must have a name. Although a divine name uttered by a lay person is highly beneficial, yet an aspirant who sets out to control his or her mind should repeat only a name (or a mantra) given by a guru because it is specially sanctified by the latter.

Q46. What is a mantra?

A46. A mantra is sacred syllable that may constitute a word or a part of it or a combination of many words arranged in a certain order used in spiritual effort to purify and control the mind. A mantra (or a name or a word) is made up of sound vibrations and its energy sublimates the mind to its subtle and causal aspects. It must be remembered that consciousness of an average jiva suffers from extroversion due to its kinetic energy imparted to it by one's samaskaras (mental impressions) and vasnas (latent desires). A mantra's vibrations, created when it is repeated, have the power to introvert the mind. The supreme mantra is Omkar because all possible sounds that go to form words and names emanate from it. Besides that, it is symbolic of God in sound form and the Lord is said to be made up of power of mantra (i.e. of Omkar). There are many types of mantras used for specific purposes. Some of them are recorded in various scriptures. Their most effective use is when they are blessed by gurus. Satgurus have the power to create new mantras. For a devotee, a mantra that seeks the Lord's grace through Its praise or salutation is the best. No serious aspirant should repeat mantras to gain psychic powers as they can only take one astray.

Q47. How is remembrance of God carried out through Its name or a mantra?
Q47. The name or mantra given by a guru is uttered repeatedly with a concentrated mind to express a devotee's love and devotion for the Lord. The mind's attention is focused on the sound (of the name) produced by the repetition, called japa, to the exclusion of other thoughts. Immature devotees often fail to appreciate that the real aim of japa is to control the mind (i.e. thoughts) and a mere mechanical repetition of the name with a wandering mind serves little or no purpose. Japa must be done in a disciplined manner for a certain specified time laid down by the guru. The power of self-control (yoga shakti; the power that controls the mind) develops gradually, through japa, over a period of time, which ensures one's spiritual growth. An aspirant should understand what the name or a mantra stands for and try to imbibe the divine qualities of the saint or the deity to which it (i.e. name or mantra) pertains. Japa is more effective if one does not try to imagine the form of the saint or deity being remembered. It diverts the mind from repetition and creates an unnecessary attachment to an imaginary form that one has given up in the end. Why should then one start this practice at all? Japa is done in three ways; loudly, softly and mentally according to an aspirant's capability. Loud japa is suitable for raw beginners; it is inaudible to others but not to oneself. Lips and the tongue move in soft japa to create an almost inaudible sound. Mental japa is done in the silence of the mind (i.e. mental motion is restrained in it due to concentration) in which the tongue, held firmly in the palate, is not allowed to move. Silent japa is the best and one should aim to practise it in that form as early in one's quest as one is capable of doing so. Japa is also classified as gross, subtle and causal according to the state of one's mind. A devotee begins japa with an extroverted (i.e. gross) mind but as it introverts (due to spiritual progress) repetition is carried out by its subtle and causal forms. Initially, an aspirant has to make effort to do japa but after some sustained practice one notices that it (i.e. japa) resonates on its own (i.e. japa begins as soon as one concentrates the mind on it). It is due to the power of samaskaras of the divine name created in memory during japa. Once one reaches that stage, one should continue with the repetition of the name rather than merely listen to the japa. The later disappears on its own if one listens to it with attention. A stage further than this is when an under-current of the japa is formed in the mind.

In it, a devotee is conscious of the vibration of the name or the mantra without being aware of the words that go to make it. One should then concentrate on the under-current to regain awareness of the words of the mantra or name again. At times one may lose awareness of the mantra or name due to mental dullness or sleep. One should begin to repeat the name or mantra as soon as one becomes aware that the japa (repetition) is missing. The phenomenon of a devotee falling asleep or of being not aware of the name (or the mantra) occurs in the early stages of japa also. The solution lies in doing japa with mental alertness and, in case it is lost, to begin repeating the name or mantra as soon as one overcomes the feeling of sleep. The method outlined above is the basic one; it may be modified on the instructions of a guru but not otherwise. For example, japa may also be done in conformity with the acts of inhalation and exhalation or by concentrating the mind on the brikuti (the space between the eyebrows) or any other spot. One should try to repeat the name or mantra as fast as possible. One may not be able to do so in the beginning. However, it becomes possible with improvement in the level of mental purity and alertness.

Q48. How much time should an aspirant devote to japa and how long should one carry on doing it?
A48. Japa ceases on its own when the mind is fully controlled (i.e. destroyed) and one should, therefore, persist with it till that blessed stage. Ideally, a devotee should repeat the name or mantra all the time. A beginner cannot obviously do that. A guru usually lays down the minimum time for which japa must be done. A beginner should start with at least an hour and gradually extend it according to one's capacity.

Q49. Ritualistic forms of worship are usually associated with the path of love and devotion. Should an aspirant indulge in them?
A49. Anyone who repeats the divine name of the Lord with sincerity and out of love and devotion need not perform any ritual. Japa gives the benefit of all rites. However, those who are addicted to rituals or feel their necessity may continue to carry them out.

Q50. Is it possible to attain the non-dual (nirguna) Reality through remembrance of the Lord (i.e. effort made in the sphere of duality)? In this context, what does para bhakti (devotion to formless Reality) imply?
A50. The absolute Reality is nameless and wordless and transcends the power of the mind. How can the mind remember It? It is often forgotten by most people that the aim of japa is to control the mind and not find the Reality. The non-dual Reality is attained on its own if the mind is destroyed. One can do that by repeating the divine name with a fully concentrated mind, i.e. by excluding all thoughts from the consciousness except that of the name. The guru's power

that inheres in the name helps a devotee by, firstly, isolating the 'I' thought and then eliminating it. Para bhakti does not mean that one should try to remember the absolute Reality. It implies that one should do japa of those names (e.g. Omkar, Rama) of the Lord which refer to Its disembodied form (i.e. the all-pervasive consciousness that is formless). Japa of this type is highly beneficial because it eliminates the need of a form to be remembered. A devotee has to give up attachment to name and form (nama and rupa) to succeed in sadhana (practice). Para bhakti begins on the premise that form does not exist.

Q51. How does japa help in controlling the mind during its various stages? What are the obstacles that one encounters and how are they overcome?
A51. The name or a mantra given by a guru is sanctified and suffused with the latter's spiritual power. Its repetition (japa) produces samaskaras that are pure in nature and their imprint in memory cleanses it of its impure samaskaras (of past karma). The mind purified in this manner introverts on its own towards its point of origin (i.e. the 'I'-vibration), which, in its essence, is the crux of this discipline. The other factors that are crucial to the practice of japa are that it must be done with love, devotion, faith, discrimination and use of other divine qualities as well as mental concentration. Extraneous thoughts must not be allowed to interfere with japa. A devotee is likely to experience bliss (of various kinds), see visions, and hear sounds etc. during the course of one's sadhana (practice). To get involved with them (including the feelings of peace, calmness, divine joy etc.) is to halt one's spiritual progress. One should be strong enough to use the power of discrimination to reject all experiences, however lofty and elevating they might appear to be, as creations of mind and, hence, false. Even the wondrous vision of God, seen in the last stages of samadhi, must be regarded as unreal. Real progress is made by those who have such a discriminative attitude during practice. Besides that, one must always pray to the guru for grace and guidance, which are always forthcoming for a sincere devotee, specially the one who does sadhana in a spirit of self-surrender, motivated by love for the Lord. There is no hurdle that guru's grace does not remove in a trice. A devotee should aim to control the mind in two major stages; first, experience the 'I'-current (i.e. source of the mind) or have a vision of God and second, destroy the 'I'. The 'I' feeling is experienced as a vibration in the consciousness on its own when the mind has been purified to sufficient degree. The mind passes through the steps of self-discipline, self-purification, self-abidance and self-subsidence (manolaya) during the effort made to find the 'I', which is then destroyed in samadhi. Sadhana (self-effort) is done to discipline and purify the mind and it is a process that continues till the end (i.e. destruction of mind). States of abidance, subsidence (manolaya) and samadhi (in which the mind is destroyed) are indices of discipline and purification only. Mind is said to be fairly disciplined if a devotee is able to

practise japa for the minimum prescribed time (usually an hour) on a regular and sustained basis without a break. Loss of intensity of desires and to be a little detached from loved ones indicates the nascent state of mental purification. Abidance stage is reached when the mind is purified further due to regular practice, which extends to 4 – 6 hours. One should then be able to do japa for at least one hour without interruption from extraneous thoughts. Manolaya requires practice exceeding 6 – 8 hours and the mind becomes dormant (or causal) in it. One should resist falling asleep then by keeping the mind very alert. The undercurrent of japa, mentioned in Answer 47, is formed at this stage. The mind is destroyed in samadhi; the 'I'-current (or vision of God) is experienced in lower (savikalpa and bhava) samadhi, which is then annihilated in its higher (nirvikalpa) form by the guru's power that inheres in the name of mantra. The resultant is the state of Realisation. Practice of samadhi should be carried out for at least 12 hours plus to destroy the mind. Timings mentioned above need not be continuous; one can interpose periods of rest depending on one's mental and physical capacity.

Q52. What are the general points that would help a devotee during practice (sadhana)? What are the signs of progress on this path?
A52.

(a) Fear of the Lord generally precedes the birth of divine love. It is good to have a feeling of divine fear in the beginning because it helps one to follow the guru's instruction more faithfully. The Lord does not frighten anyone; fear is intrinsic to individual consciousness imbued with a sense of duality. Fear of violating the divine law makes a devotee carry out good karma with highly beneficial consequences, just as a law abiding citizen lives in peace and without worry.

(b) Establish a relationship with the guru, as brought out in Answer 30 of Chapter 2.

(c) Kirtan (devotional singing) is an excellent aid to create a mood of love and quieten the mind. A devotee should make it a regular habit to either sing oneself or hear it as part of one's daily routine.

(d) Practice of this discipline should be done in the spirit of self-surrender to achieve good results. Regard the Lord and guru as one's sole refuge and support.

(e) Develop divine qualities, specially those of love, devotion and discrimination. It is difficult to love an unseen God, with whom one cannot communicate. But, one can make a beginning with loving Its creation and serving it selflessly. The Lord is always most pleased with those who are devoted to It. One should press on regardless with practice with all one's energy. Its rewards are beyond one's imagination.

Learn to regard every spiritual experience as false and reject it through the power of discrimination. It is the best way to progress.

(f) A beginner should devote some time daily to sat-sangha (company of the holy beings). There is no better aid to spiritual progress.

(g) Some indicators of spiritual growth are feelings of peace, detachment from the world, lessening of desires, extension of love to embrace people beyond one's family and friends, a tender heart that feels the pain of others, a feeling of separateness from God that causes an intense pain in the heart that longs to have a sight of the Beloved and so on.

(h) Finally, remember love and self-surrender are the beginning, middle and end of this path. Its uniqueness is that the Lord comes to a devotee (i.e. love draws It to a devotee), unlike other disciplines in which aspirants have to travel to It.

The Path of Yoga

Q53. Yoga is a very commonly used word. What does it really mean in the spiritual context?

A53. Yoga literally means union. In practice, the word refers to the effort made to attain unity or oneness between the jivatman (individual soul) and the Paramatma (the Supreme Self or the Reality) through control of mind. Quintessentially, yoga is a discipline or a method adopted by an individual to control the mind, the only way one attains unity with the Reality (or attain Realisation). As a general term, yoga embraces all paths and disciplines practised by an individual for spiritual development. It must, however, be qualified with another word to indicate the specific path that a seeker traverses. Thus, jnana yoga means that knowledge is the means to attain union with the Reality. The other primary disciplines are of bhakti (path of love and devotion), karma (path of selfless action) and of yoga. The last is a path by itself in which meditation plays the central role. Meditation can be done on a number of objects and its particular form is indicated by qualifying it (i.e. object) on which the mind concentrates; for example; atman dhyana yoga (union through meditation on the self), ashtanga yoga (union through eight steps delineated by Patanjali), hatha yoga (union through meditation on chakras or centres of consciousness, asnas or physical postures, pranayama or science of breath) and so on. Yoga, as a spiritual discipline, is thus a general word that embraces all paths that lead to union with the Supreme Being on account of meditation (power of concentration) being central to them in one form or the other. The most superior form of yoga is tapas yoga. It is a special discipline that is practised only by the divine incarnations. One who completes it successfully is called a yogi, though the term is also applied to those who attain Realisation through the practice of path of yoga outlined above.

Q54. Guru Upanishad devotes a complete chapter on a discussion on the Heart? What relevance does it have with the path of yoga? What is its essence for an average reader?

A54. An aspirant without any previous knowledge of the subject might find the subsequent answer as too involved and complicated. He or she is advised to begin meditation; it is not essential to have theoretical knowledge of the subject for that purpose. The Heart and Its derivatives (or reflections in maya), called chakras (centres of consciousness located in the subtle body and mind), serve as objects of meditation in certain well known disciplines like tantra and hatha yoga. There are many misconceptions that most people, including the adherents of the above paths, entertain about them. An attempt has been made in Guru Upanishad to bring out the complex nature of this subject. Simply put, Heart is just another word for the supreme Reality when It is conceived as being the centre of an embodied individual's existence. The Heart is the spaceless centre on which the absolute ad shakti (divine power) is concentrated with an unbreakable unity. The Heart is in this absolute and transcendent (i.e. beyond senses) state due to the power of yoga (or concentration) that inheres in It naturally. The relative form of the Heart comes into existence due to maya's presence in It. The absolute Heart, inconceivable by the mind, is an infinitesimally small pointless point of un-manifested divine power. The same power (of pure consciousness) seems to expand or extrovert, due to maya, and it is then called the mind, in general as well as in particular. The Heart is said to be located in the body below the right nipple and an aspirant feels Its presence in the samadhi (super-conscious state) state. Its localisation in the body is accepted only from the point of view of an aspirant habituated to regard it (i.e. the body) as one's real self ('I'). The truth, however, is that everything exists within the Heart and not without. The following points, highlighted here, have been dealt with in greater detail in the Chapter alluded to in the question. First, the power of concentration (or yoga) inheres naturally in every individual mind and is called the yoga shakti. An extroverted mind is introverted (or controlled) through its application and an aspirant must develop it, through self-effort and guru's grace, to succeed in sadhana (practice) irrespective of the path being followed. Yoga shakti's sublimated and cosmic form is known as tapas shakti, which is used by satgurus to grant liberation to its seekers. Second, the relative Heart, in a tiny point form, shines like a jewel made up of unimaginably brilliant white light. It is like an incandescent flame that emits yogic heat (brahman agni) and light (jyoti). It is called the flame of yoga and knowledge. Yogic heat, an effect of the power of concentration, is used by the divine will for metabolic purposes for creation at cosmic and individual levels. The divine light, again an effect of concentration, represents the unitary nature of relative knowledge in its inceptive form (i.e. each of the infinite number of attributes of the Reality is like a ray of radiant light but at this stage they coalesce as the flame). Three, the manifestation of the relative Heart or the divine flame is the equivalent of the conditioned states of Atman or Brahman or Ishwara, Omkar or divine name or word or knowledge. Its experience is similar to having a vision of God or hearing the sound of Omkar or of the feeling of 'I', 'I'. Four, serial projection of the Heart in maya manifests as the creation in general (i.e. at cosmic level) and in particular (i.e. as individual objects), in their causal, subtle and gross forms. The causal creation exists around the Heart, subtle creation is in the chakras (centres of consciousness that exist in the subtle body) and the latter's reflection is the material world that jivas perceive through their senses. Whatever exists without (i.e. material world perceived by senses) exists within (i.e. inside the body) also. For example, snow clad Himalayas, are only a reflection of similar hills in the subtle world; both are used by yogis to do serious tapas (penance) in gross and subtle bodies respectively. Five, much is often made of chakras in the popular version of spirituality. In fact, they are nothing more than the state of one's subtle mind, denoting its different grades of subtlety and power. The knowledge given in most books about them is of an elementary type. There are thousands of chakras in the body and not merely six or seven as it is assumed by most people. Know it for certain that liberation is attained only when the mind is absorbed in the Heart (i.e. the seat of causal consciousness) and not when it reaches the sahasrara chakra, located in the head, as is commonly assumed and propagated. Similarly, there is an unnecessary stress on the awakening of kundalini shakti, the serpentine yogic power, which is again nothing more than the empowerment of the subtle mind by its own inherent power. The same power must be sublimated to its causal form, known as atmanic shakti, before the mind enters the Heart. Kundalini that lies dormant in an average mind is aroused best by following a guru's instruction to practise any of the paths. Ideally, its arousal must not cause any disturbance in the mind nor should it affect the body violently. Sixth, the science of prana (the yogic word for motion) is an intricate and complex subject. A serious aspirant should understand that prana is controlled on its own if one practices any of the spiritual disciplines. One need not do hard exercises of breath control (pranayama) for this purpose. The current popularity of pranayama, mainly due to practitioners of tantra and hatha yoga, has more to do with its effect on good health and gaining of some minor powers without any real spiritual benefits. A serious practice of pranayama is best avoided because it is very time consuming; those who cannot resist the temptation are advised to learn it from a competent yogi (a rare being in this age) rather than charlatans. Seven, the Chapter concludes by stressing that although meditation on chakras, as advocated by tantra, hatha yoga and some other schools, is an accepted and well recognised discipline for attaining liberation, yet it is not suitable for this age (kaliyuga). It has many pitfalls; it is very time consuming, arduous and offers many allurements like the manifestation of paranormal powers that are often the cause for an individual's damnation. Finally, an average student does not need detailed knowledge of this subject to begin practice, which accrues on its own as one goes on the path. For example, experience of seeing a chakra is far superior to anything written about it.

Q55. What does the path of yoga deal with? What does it aim to achieve and how does it go about it?
A55. The path of yoga, as a discipline by itself, is primarily concerned with the control of individualised ad shakti (divine power). The consciousness is infused with divine power, which affects it in two ways; if uncontrolled, it leads to mental extroversion; second, the mind is introverted by restraining it. Ad shakti empowers the mind with intelligence and will power to counter the effects of extroversion (or lack of self-control). The yogic discipline tries to introvert the mind by arresting the outflow of divine power through its concentration on an object by willful exercise of intelligence. The essence of teaching on the path of yoga is that the divine power, which has lost its unitary state, as an effect of maya, be brought back to its original and true state, i.e., of its absolute oneness, through mental concentration. In simpler words, the practice of this path aims to control an extroverted mind through yoga shakti (the power of mental concentration) by introverting it on its source (i.e. the 'I' thought) and then destroying the latter. Yoga shakti exists in every mind in varying degrees determined by the variations in individual samaskaras. The practice of any spiritual discipline develops this power. One of its effects is to produce brahman agni (yogic heat) in the mind, which purifies it by burning its impurities. The mind sinks (or introverts) to its point of origin (the 'I'-sense) on its own when it is cleansed of its dross. The 'I' is then exterminated by concentrating on it. The method of intelligent application of yoga shakti (power of concentration) to control the mind is called meditation, which is the chief characteristic of this path.

Q56. What does concentration of the mind imply?
A56. To focus the mind's energy on a point, which maybe an object with or without form or a thought (e.g. of a divine name) or the 'I' sense, is called its concentration. It is not as easy as it might appear to those who have never tried to practise it. For, it implies that, apart from the object of concentration, there must be no other thought in the mind. Its aim is to stop the dissipation of mental energy by breaking sensual contact with external and internal (e.g. visions) objects.

Q57. What is meditation (dhyana) and how is it done? How does it differ from concentration?

A57. A prolonged act of concentration is known as meditation. The former's inceptive stage may last a few seconds; in the later stages, it progresses from beginning to middle and advanced states from roughly one hour to three or four hours and ten or twelve and above hours respectively. Meditation requires an object to concentrate on. It is a complete discipline in itself; for, not does it only purify the mind, it puts it through all the steps required to control it, i.e., discipline, abidance, subsidence and destruction. Meditation is employed in one form or the other in all yogic disciplines; for example, the essence of japa (repetition of the divine name) is to meditate on the name; similarly, self-enquiry on the path of knowledge is carried out by a meditative or concentrated mind. It is everyone's experience that mind is perpetually restless and it jumps from one thought to another incessantly. One cannot retain even a pleasant thought (e.g. of one's child) for any length of time. In meditation, an aspirant brings the mind back to its object of concentration every time it is waylaid by a new thought. This repeated act of keeping the mind focused on an object forms the crux of meditation for a beginner. It is possible to do so only if one is able to, in the first place, break contact with external objects and ignore the eruption of extraneous thoughts. Another point to remember is that meditation aims to make mind inactive (motionless), unlike japa that is dependent on its activity. Meditation must be done intelligently (that is done by using the power of discrimination to keep the mind concentrated on the chosen object) despite the flow of thoughts. The latter keep erupting even in advanced stages of practice. One must persevere despite all odds using one's will power. Gradually, thoughts lose their intensity and mind begins to introvert (to its source, i.e., 'I' sense) as it gets purified. Process of purification takes effect due to yogic heat (brahman agni) generated by mental concentration. Intelligence is employed to restrain the motion (in the mind) to put a brake on the functioning of the roving mind (manas) and senses. Regular practice of meditation develops yoga shakti (power of mental concentration), which in turn improves its quality and in the end makes the mind completely motionless (i.e. it is controlled fully). Meditation is also a means to acquire subjective and objective knowledge in its subtle and causal forms. It does so by sharpening intelligence which is then able to penetrate through the outer core (i.e. physical body or sheath) of objects to their subtle and causal bodies. Similarly, the 'I' reveals its knowledge when one meditates on it. Objective and subjective knowledge accrues in the mind as a result of the divine light that shines in it due to its proximity to the yogic flame.

Q58. What are the objects of meditation on this path and how does an aspirant select one of them for practice (sadhana)?

A58. One should meditate on an object assigned by a guru because it is sanctified by him or her. An average mind's natural tendency is to think or see only external objects having a material form. Keeping this in mind, gurus usually ask beginners to meditate on the embodied form of the Lord who is the sole object that one seeks. Though the divine consciousness (i.e. disembodied Ishwara) is formless and imperceptible to the senses, yet it assumes a form for the sake of devotees who pray to it sincerely. That is how Ishwara (God) incarnates in human form as a satguru or a yogi or an avtara (divine incarnations) etc. Their embodied forms while they are living serve as objects of meditation; after their departure from this world, their idols, images etc. can serve the same purpose. Beginners may also use pictures, idols etc. of various gods and goddesses. It needs to be stressed that meditation on an object with a form, specially idols etc., is suitable only for those incapable of doing so in its higher forms. One can get addicted to a form, which is the exact opposite of what the mind is supposed to do; that is to detach itself from the world of name and form. It should be resorted to only by raw beginners. One can also meditate, in the initial stages, on the act of breathing (may be combined with other forms of meditation) or any object that one finds appealing; for example, a vision, candle, flower etc. Meditation on various chakras (centres of subtle consciousness in the body), as advocated by tantra and hatha yoga schools, may be done provided one is able to avoid its pitfalls. It is better to concentrate on the brikuti (the psychic centre located in the space between the eyebrows) and upwards rather than on lower chakras. The purpose of meditation, after the initial stages (i.e. once the mind has been disciplined and purified somewhat) is to locate the 'I' so that it can be destroyed. As one progresses, one should switch the object of meditation from the embodied form to the subjective 'I'. The latter is the primary object of meditation, unlike those mentioned earlier, which are secondary in nature. Atman dhyana (meditation on the self or the 'I') is the best of all types of meditation because it aims to concentrate the mind on the point of its origin (i.e. the 'I'-sense), which is the source of individual ignorance.

Q59. How should an aspirant meditate on an object with form?
A59. One should follow a guru's instruction in letter and spirit to derive maximum benefit. As a general rule, the object should always be considered as being held within the centre of mind and not without (i.e. in the external space). The senses of sight and hearing should be concentrated on it. Beginners invariably use physical force to concentrate the mind. That is incorrect; the body and mind must stay relaxed while meditating on an object, which should not be allowed to slip away from the consciousness (or one should not lose its awareness). The mind must remain alert at all times during practice; it is important to learn to do so right from the start because mental dullness

invariably leads to sleep. Eruption of thoughts is the primary source of mental diversion during meditation. Constant flow of thoughts is inevitable and one should not get upset that one cannot control the mind. It takes a very, very long time to do so and very strenuous practice is required for it. A wise student should press on regardless. One should bring the mind back to the object every time it strays away from it. A constant struggle to keep the mind concentrated makes it strong, develops yoga shakti and disciplines and purifies it to a certain degree so that it becomes one pointed. That is generally the stage of abidance (of the mind) and once it subsides (in the mind) with more practice, it is advisable to meditate on the self (atman dhyana).

Q60. What is atman dhyana (meditation on the self) and how is it practised? What are the various stages in practice?
A60. The mind originates from the 'I' (the feeling of selfhood caused in the consciousness by motion), which is the source of individual ignorance. To control the mind fully means to destroy the 'I'. To do so, one must first locate it or feel its presence as a highly surcharged current (or a vibration) in the consciousness. One experiences it only in lower samadhi, i.e., the state of mind in which an aspirant is able to subside all thoughts in the consciousness except that of the 'I' thought. It requires very hard practice to be able to do so. One method of indulging in it has been described in the previous answer. The other way is to begin the quest with atman dhyana. It is possible to practise it only if one has the grace of a satguru, i.e., through his or her initiation. A satguru's spiritual (or tapas) power is so potent that it enables even a beginner to practise atman dhyana. An average jiva's attachment to the body is so great that he or she confuses the 'I' with it. The 'I' of a jiva is too tenuous and indistinct a feeling, due to the samaskaric dross that covers the consciousness, to be experienced without any practice. Notwithstanding this, atman dhyana advocates that an aspirant concentrates the mind on its centre, which signifies the point of origin of the 'I' thought (or the mind). All thoughts have their genesis here, i.e., they are offshoots of the 'I' thought. For instance, every thought or form of perception begins with 'I', as in 'I see a horse' or 'I am happy', even if the 'I' is not experienced directly. The feeling of 'I' is so deeply and powerfully ingrained in the consciousness that a jiva identifies with it naturally and without its actual experience. How does an aspirant determine the mind's centre in the practice of atman dhyana? Some of the ways to do so are as follows. First, the mind is concentrated on its centre on its own when one meditates on a divine name or form; it is applicable even if there is no object (e.g. embodied form) on which one meditates. Second, observation of one's thoughts with a view to trace their trajectory leads to the mind's centre. It is possible to do so only if the mind is highly purified and has attained a high degree of one pointedness. Third, one may assume a centre from which

the thoughts originate. An average aspirant's attachment to the body does not allow him or her to practise this method. Fourth, an easier method that everyone can follow is to concentrate on certain parts of the gross body that conform to the reflections of the Heart; as, for example, the various chakras (centres of consciousness) in the subtle body. The disadvantages of concentrating on the lower chakras have been highlighted. It is better to begin meditation with concentration on the brikuti (the space between the eyebrows) that conforms to the tri-junction of nadis or channels through which spiritual energy flows in the subtle body. The brikuti (or any other part of the body) then becomes the assumed centre of the mind because it is a reflection of the Heart from which it (mind) originates. An aspirant needs to keep the following points in mind while doing atman dhyana with the help of brikuti (or any other bodily part). One, brikuti is merely an aid to concentrate the mind since a jiva is so used to regarding the body as his or her self. The aim is not to awaken the kundalini or activate any chakra but to control the mind. Two, the guru's initiatory power dwells in the mind's centre (i.e. in the brikuti) and it draws an aspirant's consciousness to it during meditation. Three, an aspirant should gaze at the brikuti (even when eyes are closed) and imagine the power of hearing to be located there. Four, keep the mind concentrated on the brikuti, without using force, while ignoring thoughts as they erupt. Four, effort made along the above lines would steady and calm the mind after some practice. The first sign that mind is being disciplined and purified, to some degree, is when an aspirant feels a little detached from the world, specially from one's family and friends. Fifth, thoughts lose their potency and intensity as one progresses further. It indicates that the mind has been stilled somewhat (i.e. it is not as restless or subject to motion as it was earlier) and it is well on the way to introversion (to its centre). The mind then becomes one pointed and that is the stage of abidance. A little more hard practice would reveal gaps between thoughts. One should then concentrate on them. The mind then subsides in itself (i.e. state of manolaya; thoughts become dormant in it). The next stage in practice is to attain samadhi in which the 'I' current is perceived and then destroyed through meditation on it. That ends one's practice in Self Realisation. Sixth, although the process of atman dhyana begins on the brikuti, yet it is completed only when the mind is withdrawn completely into the Heart. Samadhi state is attained only if the individual consciousness is totally indrawn to It. Readers desirous of knowing more about the subject are advised to study Answers 104-106 of Chapter 5.

Q61. Many aspirants experience 'currents' during meditation. What is their nature?
A61. The absolute consciousness is conditioned into its relative form by prana (motion), which manifests in it as an effect of maya. Individualisation of the relative consciousness, brought about by a jiva's samaskaras and vasnas (mental impressions and latent tendencies) constitutes the mind of a human being. A

primary characteristic of the mind is that it is in constant wave like motion. An average jiva is not aware of it for two reasons; first, the mind is so used to it that a person pays no attention to it; second, rarely does one look inwards to examine how the mind functions. The currents, mentioned in the question, are a sublimated and more potent form of this kinetic energy. They are experienced when the mind is brought under control by the practice of a spiritual discipline. Vibratory energy of the mind gains power when it is conserved in practice (sadhana), which is then felt acutely by the purified consciousness. Currents are called so because they are similar in nature to their electrical counterparts. They are of three types; causal, subtle and gross. Causal currents are felt by a highly purified mind in manolaya (subsidence of mind) and samadhi. Although the mind attains its latent (causal) form in those states, yet their impact on the consciousness is very potent, which can last for a long time, may be even for months. Subtle currents are experienced during the abidance stage by a subtle mind. They are not as powerful as the causal ones and their experience is generally not prolonged. Gross currents are felt by beginners in the initial stages of their practice as a result of sudden release of vibratory mental energy. They are fleeting in nature and are usually felt in the lower parts of the body or in the arms. Causal and subtle currents are experienced in the areas of the Heart and head respectively. The arousal of kundalini shakti (the subtle power that dwells in the subtle mind and body) may also manifest in the form of currents. They may even be violent at times, specially if the ascent of kundalini is not well controlled. The tapas power that a guru gives at the time of initiation is also experienced in the form of currents. It is a sign of grace that portends spiritual growth. In general, experience of currents is a good indicator of one's progress, specially if they are felt in the head or the Heart. Violent currents of kundalini are best avoided. An aspirant should seek a guru's grace for that purpose. Currents help in purifying nadies (channels for flow of kundalini in the subtle body), improve health and remove obstacles that impede a student's spiritual development. To sum up, beginners ought to remember that the manifestation of currents is quite a normal phenomenon during practice and there is no need to be unduly concerned about them.

Q62. What are the divine qualities that are essential in the practise of meditation? How are they developed?
A62. Attributes of love, devotion, discrimination, detachment etc. play a vital role in the progress of an aspirant. Meditation should be done in mental mode of self-surrender, like any other discipline. Those who are highly discriminative achieve the best results in meditation. Qualities are developed on their own in practice with some deliberate effort to do so. The mind partakes the qualities of the object on which it meditates.

Q63. What are the obstacles that one faces on the path of yoga? How are they overcome? Who is competent to follow this discipline?

A63. A reader ought to remember that the yogic discipline deals primarily with restraining the divine power (ad shakti) at an individual level and it is not easy to do so because it is like controlling a flood, i.e., divine energy activated in practice can be unruly if one does not know how to slow down its march in the chakras. Para-normal powers often develop on their own during the practice of this path; as, for example, in the course of meditation on various chakras. There are very few aspirants who are spiritually mature enough to resist the temptation to misuse them for boosting their egos. For this reason, most seekers are unable to go beyond the rudimentary stages of this path. An aspirant must be mentally strong to follow the yogic discipline. There must be single minded devotion to control the mind and fight its evil tendencies. The path of yoga offers two choices, much like what a nuclear scientist encounters; that is to either develop nuclear power for peaceful or destructive purposes. The really wise seekers use divine power's positive nature to control the mind whereas the foolish ones employ its negative aspects (i.e. misuse of psychic powers) to drown themselves. Some of the other obstacles that one generally faces in the practice of meditation are lack of mental alertness, indulgence in reverie, accidental or premature arousal of kundalini without adequate mental preparation, to entertain notions like 'I am God' and so on. Hurdles of every kind are overcome through faith in the guru, divine grace, self-surrender, humility, regular practice and, above all, use of one's head (i.e. discriminative power).

Q64. What are the indicators of spiritual progress on the path of yoga?

A64. The real test of progress is an aspirant's ability to hold an object of meditation in one's consciousness (or be aware of it) without interference from extraneous thoughts for progressively longer time with an alert and concentrated mind. It is reflected in detachment from external phenomenon, reduction in the intensity of desires, mental calmness and manifestation of divine qualities. A beginner who persists with meditation, despite apparent lack of spiritual growth, is doing well.

Q65. What is the essence of teaching on the path of yoga?

A65. The term, yoga, is comprehensive enough to embrace many independent disciplines. What distinguishes this path from others is its emphasis on meditation as the primary method to attain total freedom from ignorance. Meditation requires an object to concentrate on, which maybe the Lord's embodied form or one's own self ('I'-ness) or the chakras (centres of consciousness) in the subtle body. Out of them all, meditation on the self (atman dhyana) is the safest and the best. The object (of meditation) is given by the guru. Meditation produces brahman agni (yogic fire) that purifies the mind of its samaskaric pollutants, eventually leading to its destruction. Success in meditation is dependent on two factors; development of yoga shakti (the power of mental concentration) and growth of divine qualities. One must pay special attention to nurture them.

The Path of Knowledge (Jnana Marga)

Q66. What, in brief, is the essence of this path? How does one begin practice on it?

A66. It employs knowledge as a means to control the mind. What, in effect, it seeks to realise, not merely intellectually but through experience gained in practice (sadhana), that relative knowledge is false and unreal. Relative knowledge comprises subjective (i.e. of the 'I') and objective knowledge and it is acquired by the mind. A student in a confused state of mind approaches a guru to seek enlightenment. The guru explains the basic teaching; that the knowledge attained by the mind is unreliable and, hence, not worth acquiring; further, the falsehood of subjective and objective knowledge can be established only if one knows who gains such knowledge. The guru asks the student to think over this proposition before proceeding further. The obvious conclusion that anyone would draw is that 'I' acquires such knowledge. The guru then tells him or her to find out who that 'I' is. That, in a nutshell, is the basis on which one traverses on this path. Most students are unlikely to accept this simple proposition easily. They would ask questions and doubts from the guru. The latter advises them to contemplate on his or her instruction with a rational and critical mind. Contemplation should be done with a discriminative mind to imbibe the guru's teaching and be convinced that its practice would lead to liberation. An aspirant's ability to use the power of discrimination with reason as the basis of self-analysis (i.e. to find the 'I' through the guru's instruction) forms the cornerstone of this path. Unlike other disciplines, the path of knowledge lays great stress on searching for the 'I' (the source of ignorance) as its primary and sole goal right from the beginning of one's practice. It does so by first rejecting all that is not the 'I', i.e., the objective knowledge gained in one's daily experience (one is not conscious of the 'I' in day to day objective experience). This process of rejection is called 'neti, neti' ('not this', 'not this') implying that every type of sensual experience is false and the mind need not dwell on it. If done successfully, a discriminative mind sheds the baggage of objective knowledge and is then able to experience the 'I' pulsation. A seeker then compares the knowledge of his or her 'I' with what the guru has taught him or her about the real 'I' (Atman; the absolute Self that is changeless and unknowable by mind). After a further self-analysis, the student arrives at a conclusion that the 'I'-experience that he or she undergoes is also false and using the same method (of 'not this', 'not this') rejects the 'I' as unreal through the power of discrimination. What is left there afterwards is the supreme Atman whose experience is indescribable. That is the state of absolute knowledge or of Self Realisation.

Q67. The path of knowledge is generally considered a difficult one. Why? Who is competent to follow it? What are qualities required to practice it?
A67. The difficulty in practising a spiritual discipline lies not so much in what it advocates but in the competency of aspirants based on their temperamental differences. The aim of jnana marga is to find the 'I' and then destroy it. That is precisely what the other paths teach but they adopt different approaches to achieve it. One must have a highly developed sense of discrimination, hunger for divine knowledge and an ability to rationally examine every issue clinically. Most aspirants lack these attributes because of mental lethargy. It is indeed a difficult path for them. But, there cannot be a more simple discipline than jnana marga for those whose nature makes them suitable to follow it. This path is practised best by those who are inquisitive by nature, have calm minds capable of self-introspection, whose intelligence is sharp enough to discriminate subtle nuances of a guru's teaching and one's own spiritual experience and have sufficiently developed divine qualities (e.g. devotion, detachment, humility, faith etc.). It is a path of self-reliance, implying that a seeker accepts the premise that there is nothing apart his or her own self that exists and there is no external factor that can help him or her to achieve the goal. That is why persons who are addicted to rituals and prayers and have faith in pre-determined destiny and so on are generally unable to practice it successfully. In short, jnana marga is highly suitable for those who are mentally strong and have great faith, but not pride, in themselves.

Q68. It has been said above that knowledge is used to control the mind. What is its nature?
A68. The knowledge that a guru imparts to a seeker is the sole means to control the mind. It is divine in nature, which has the power to destroy subjective and objective knowledge. Although scriptures and books contain the knowledge that a guru imparts, yet his or her words are sanctified to leave an imprint on a student's mind. All that the latter is required to do is contemplate on it, as described above, and begin practice. Knowledge is of no avail if it is not used to gain the desired end. Many people know how electricity is generated but only few engineers employ this knowledge to generate electricity for everyday use. Similarly, intellectual knowledge of the scriptures is of no use if it is not put into effect. Although this knowledge is relative in nature, yet it is reliable because, firstly, it is based on guru's experience of the Truth and, secondly, it leads one to the goal. However, even this type of knowledge must be discarded before one reaches the end.

Q69. The goal that an aspirant seeks on this path is to know the Atman (Self). Why is the latter preferred to words like Reality, Brahman etc.?

A69. Atman (Self) has two aspects; absolute and relative. It refers to the individual 'I' in the latter sense. The path of knowledge seeks to know the falsehood of an individual's 'I'-sense. The absolute Atman (Self) is not an object of the mind and hence, it can never find it. But if the non-existence of the individual 'I' is established (i.e. by destroying the mind), the absolute Self is known on its own. Each school of teaching emphasises certain aspects to highlight its suitability for students to follow it based on their natures. Those who practise jnana marga give primacy to reason and rationalism to control their minds. All other paths begin within the ambit of duality and then gradually proceed to attain the non-dual Truth. But, a seeker on this path begins the quest with the intellectual premise that non-dual Reality (i.e. It is neither a subject nor an object) alone is true and all else is false (or non-existent). There is then no scope in such a scheme of instruction to discuss whether God exists or not or what the nature of Reality is. Rather than indulge in talking about such doctrinal points whose validity or otherwise can be debated endlessly, a disciple on this path is advised to find out the existence of his or her own self. No one denies one's own existence even if it is confused with the body. Everyone is aware of his or her self (or 'I'-ness) at all times. All that one is required to do on jnana marga is to search for one's 'I' and discover it for what it is, i.e., it is non-real or non-existent. What is left then is the real Self (Atman), which stands for the ultimate Existence that is absolute and unconditioned in nature. Just as a jiva has his or her self, it is assumed in teaching that the absolute Brahman (or Reality) has Its Self. It is done to conform to a seeker's current state (i.e. of ignorance) that perceives things in dual terms. A jiva is not different from his or her self and so is Brahman the same as Its Self. Thus, to know the Self is to know Brahman, the ultimate principle of existence. Realisation of Self is given prominence in the teaching on jnana marga for these reasons but it does not mean that other words like Reality, Brahman, Truth etc., which represent their absolute forms, are not used.

Q70. The teaching on the path of knowledge is often said to be summed up in the four great maxims (maha vakas); 'I Am Brahman' (Aham Brahmasmi), 'That Thou are' (Tat Tuam Asi), 'Absolute Knowledge is Brahman' (Prajnanam Brahman) and 'This Self is Brahman' (Ayam Atman Brahman). What do they signify?

A70. The above sayings contain the essence of upanishadic or vedantic teaching (refers to the knowledge that ends relative knowledge). The words 'I Am' stand for the absolute Atman (Self) and Brahman for the ultimate Reality. 'I Am' and 'Brahman' do not denote different principles or facets of the supreme Truth but are merely two words that signify Its unitary and indivisible nature. One ought to make a distinction between the statements, 'I Am Brahman' and 'I am Brahman'. The latter alludes to the relative form (saguna) of Reality and Its absolute nature is realised only by transcending it (i.e. by rejecting the notion of relativity). 'I am' represents the 'I'-ness of Ishwara and a jiva. It is the creator of duality, i.e., there is a creator (God or Ishwara) and the created (a jiva). From a dualistic point of view, a jiva can never be equated with God. How can the created (i.e. a part) equal the creator (i.e. the whole)? It is, therefore, a false and blasphemous feeling that many immature aspirants entertain during their quest. It is only by giving it up that one realises the truth of 'I Am Brahman'. Incidentally, Ishwara has no feeling that 'I am Brahman (God)', because of Its supreme self-control and it is mentioned in teaching to make it simpler for students to imbibe it; just as a jiva has a sense of individuality, so also has, it is assumed, Ishwara. Under the influence of duality, a student even on this path feels that he or she ought to seek Brahman. That is, his or her 'I' should become Brahman (God). It is an impossibility because a finite thing (i.e. 'I' of a jiva) can never turn into an infinite entity (God). To do so would require infinite time and which jiva can live that long? Thus, say the wise, give up 'I am a jiva' and 'I am Brahman' notions and know that 'I Am Brahman'. The real import of the latter is that a seeker should not carry his or her convictions, based on duality, into the realm of non-duality. In other words, an aspirant who experiences the Self (Atman), after destroying the 'I am' feeling, should know that It is the Brahman that he or she had sought in the beginning of practice (sadhana). Just as the 'I' (jivatman) of the individual is not different from him or her, so also Brahman and Its ('I') (Atman) is the same. The other sayings have a similar connotation. In 'That Thou are', That stands for the impersonal Reality and Thou for the Self (Atman), and establishes their existential identity. 'Absolute knowledge is Brahman' means that the knowledge, absolute in nature, that one gains, after destruction of the mind, is the Brahman that one seeks. There is no difference between the supreme Brahman and Its absolute knowledge. One attains this state only after giving up relative knowledge (i.e. subjective and objective knowledge) that a student acquires in sensual and spiritual experience. 'This Self (Atman) is Brahman' has the same significance as the maxim, 'I Am Brahman'.

Q71. The objective world is often said to be mirage or dreamlike by teachers of jnana marga. There is also a simile given of a rope being mistaken for a snake. What do the above analogies purport to convey?

A71. The analogies mentioned in the question contain the kernel of divine wisdom that forms the theoretical basis of teaching on jnana marga. A student should try to understand their import through constant contemplation, and, once convinced, begin practice; contemplation should continue even after commencing practice. Just as water in a mirage is only an illusory appearance and, in fact, nonexistent, so is the world perceived by the senses. To seek happiness in the latter is like quenching one's thirst from the water in a mirage. Wisdom lies in realising the nature of the created phenomenon and detaching one's mind from it completely to realise the Truth. A dreamer regards a dream as real till he or she wakes up to know its unreality. Similarly, an ignorant person (i.e. the dreamer) considers his or her sensual experience (i.e. the dream) as true in a state of ignorance (akin to sleep in which a dream is perceived) but on Self Realisation perceives it to be false (like the dream). This simile explains how the world is perceived in a state of duality (i.e. of ignorance) and non-duality (i.e. of wisdom). The analogy of a rope and a snake is given to highlight how false perception of a non-existent and an illusory entity arises as a superimposition on a real thing. Further, it aims to show how the perceiver of the above phenomenon suffers unnecessarily by regarding a delusion as true. A man sees a rope in darkness and erroneously regards it as a snake due to similarities in their shape. A reader should note the following points in this analogy. First, a non-existent snake appears as a superimposition on the rope. In the same way, the phenomenal world is an illusion that has arisen on the substratum of the absolute Reality. Second, the delusion of seeing a rope as a snake manifests only in partial darkness (the rope is seen as a rope in conditions of light). Similarly, the Reality is perceived as the world due to maya (or ignorance) which cannot totally eclipse the brilliance of the ever shining Atman (Self). Third, only the seer (person) of the unreal snake is affected by it due to non-knowledge of the rope (i.e. the Self). The seer is rooted to the spot due to fright that paralyses him or her from acting. The perception of the snake, the fear that it generates and inability to do anything about it are the direct result of the seer's mind's malfunctioning (i.e. mental turmoil makes him or her forget that there is a rope where snake is seen). An ignorant jiva's (a human being's) perception of the world is exactly the same. He or she has forgotten the Reality and sees the world instead of It. The fault lies in his or her mind, which causes him or her to suffer from doubt (about the nature of the observed phenomenon) and fear (caused by the sense of duality). The cause of a jiva's misery and unhappiness lies in one's mind that perceives one's self (i.e. the 'I' or the seer) and the world as real when, in reality, they are unreal (just like the snake). Fourth, how can one correct one's mistake (of perceiving the world and one's self as real)? All that the man who cogitates a snake in a rope has to do is to switch on a light and to discover his or her error. An ignorant person ought to do the same to get rid of the wrong perception (i.e. the 'I' and the world are real).

Q72. If the world appearance is indeed mirage like or akin to the illusion of a snake perceived instead of a rope, what means does a student employ to correct his or her mistake?

A72. All that one has to do is to enlighten one's mind by acquiring divine knowledge from a guru (equivalent to switching on a light mentioned in the previous answer). The false perception of the world will disappear then. A seeker keen to know the Truth should learn to control his or her mind, the creator of the sensual phenomenon; if the perceiver (mind) disappears, so will the perceived (world). A student on this path should be convinced, after hearing the guru's instruction, about the creative power of an extroverted mind to indulge in sensual gratification to satiate the incessant desires of its own progenitor, i.e., the individual 'I' (jivatman). The only way to stop mind's activity is to introvert it by detaching it from external phenomenon (gross, subtle and causal) and search for the 'I' (or enquire after it), the root cause of false perception, and then destroy it. Introversion would be easy but for the hurdles that it encounters enroute, viz., the samaskaric dross that prevents the mind from finding the 'I'. Thus, to discover the 'I' and then realise its unreality, one should first cleanse the mind of its impurities, i.e., samaskaras and vasnas (desires). The path of knowledge advocates the use of vichara for this purpose.

Q73. What does vichara (exercise of discriminative power) mean and how is it carried out?
A73. Vichara refers to the employment of one's intelligence and will power in a discriminative and rational manner to know the Self. It must not be construed as a mere dry intellectual exercise. It is a spiritual effort made by the intellect, due to a guru's grace, to halt the restlessness (or motion; manifested in eruption of thoughts) of the mind. As brought out earlier, the path of knowledge lays great stress on the use of discrimination and reason to control the mind. Vichara has different connotations at various levels of spiritual development; for a beginner, it refers to the ability to separate the desirable from the undesirable (e.g. what is better? Spiritual or worldly life?). For an aspirant who starts practice with a serious intent, it implies the use of discrimination to eject the desire for objective experience from the mind and to an advanced disciple, it is a means to enquire after or search for the individual 'I' to discover its unreality. Contemplation and meditation done with a discerning mind is also a form of vichara. In simple words, a student who reflects on a guru's teaching, begins practice to find the 'I' by rejecting all forms of sensual experience as false and then gives it up (i.e. the 'I') is doing vichara. Following points are worth noting in the above exercise. First, vichara is always done with a concentrated and one pointed mind. Some seekers may need to practise meditation, on the advice of a guru, to achieve the above state. Second, intelligence is used to discern the difference between what would take a seeker to the goal (i.e. liberation) and what would keep him or her in bondage. To know or accept that guru's teaching is the right way to freedom as opposed to giving in to the whims of the mind is a proper use of intelligence. In the same category

falls the conviction that indulgence in sensual gratification for the sake of 'I''s desires cannot free a jiva from ignorance. Third, after determining what would lead to liberation, an aspirant should have the will power to put into practice the guru's teaching to attain it. For example, if a student is convinced that objective experience is harmful, he or she should be strong enough to keep the mind and senses under control, i.e. reject sensual experience as false and do not allow the mind to indulge in it. Fourth, vichara is an activity of the mind and, hence, the supreme Self (Atman) is beyond Its scope. The latter is known on its own if the 'I' is found to be unreal. Fifth, vichara is a means to acquire divine knowledge (imparted by a guru), which is used to reject subjective and objective knowledge as false. Sixth, it is practised by posing questions to the guru or one's own self, and seeking the right answers through discrimination. For example, one may enquire, 'why am I unhappy'; 'why is the world phenomenon subject to constant change; 'how has the mind originated'. This technique is adopted to acquire divine knowledge, which then must be put into effect through practice.

Q74. What is the difference between vichara and power of discrimination (viveka shakti)? How is discrimination carried out in practice? What do the words, real (sat) and unreal (asat) and accept and reject, imply in the above instruction?

A74. Discrimination is a power of intelligence that denotes its sharpness to distinguish between desirable and undesirable activities of the mind. For instance, to investigate the nature of the 'I' with a focused mind is beneficial but to indulge in reverie is harmful. The second aspect of sharpness is the mental ability to cut through the veil of samaskaras and vasnas (mental impressions and deep rooted mental tendencies), which obstruct a seeker from knowing the unreality of the 'I'. A very highly discriminative mind is like a knife that passes through the butter of samaskaras to discover that the 'I' is an illusory entity that comes into being as an effect of maya. Discrimination of this quality requires utmost alertness, concentration and one pointedness of the mind. As an illustration, an aspirant's enquiry to know the 'I' is bound to be waylaid during practice by thoughts of objective experience (e.g. of one's child). Sharpness of intelligence implies, firstly, that he or she does not allow the mind to dwell on it at all and he or she does so by pulling it away (from the thought of the child) or totally ignoring it, secondly, continue the search for the 'I' despite interruptions by intervening thoughts. To employ discrimination in a systematic, disciplined and sustained manner is called vichara. The word, real, is used to denote the principle of immutability, absoluteness, truth and existence; unreal is its opposite, viz., subject to change, relativity, falsehood (or illusory) and non-existence. Acceptance means that the mind imbibes discriminated instruction (of the guru) or knowledge (gained through spiritual experience) that would lead to the goal. Rejection refers to the mind's ability to empty itself of the baggage of objective and subjective experience, including its samaskaras and the vasnas that impel it. The mind (including memory) is purified and introverted due to it. It needs to be stressed that essence of discrimination lies in not merely distinguishing real and unreal but in mind's ability to reject and eject from the consciousness all that is undesirable.

Q75. Students on the path of knowledge are advised to discriminate between the Real and unreal, which is often compared to separating water from milk. What do these statements imply? How is the power of discrimination developed?
A75. Maya (or ignorance) is so closely intertwined with the Reality (even as a superimposition) that it is very hard to separate the two, just as it is difficult to take water out of milk. There is a heavenly bird, called hans or swan, in the subtle world that has the power to suck water from milk. This analogy is given to stress that it is not possible to reject false subjective and objective knowledge from the consciousness unless one's ability to discriminate is as sharp as that of a swan. A seeker's mind must be laser sharp to be able to discern the difference between Truth and falsehood. This power is developed through regular practice and guru's grace. Reality transcends the mind and, hence, a seeker should not imagine that there are two entities that are to be discriminated. What the statement means is to reject the unreal (i.e. subjective and objective knowledge) through discrimination and what is left afterwards is the Real.

Q76. What is self-enquiry (atman vichara)? How is it conducted?
A76. The process adopted to enquire after the self (individual 'I'; not the Self) in order to find it or locate its source is called self-enquiry. It forms the crux of the path of knowledge and aims to know that the individual 'I' (atman; not the Atman or Self), the root cause of ignorance, is an illusory effect of maya on the divine consciousness. In other words, to find through the practice of vichara, as explained above, that the 'I' is, in fact, an unreal and non-existent entity. Just as the rope appears to be a snake and is regarded as real in darkness, so also the absolute Self is mistakenly perceived by a jiva(a person) as his or her 'I' in the darkness of maya (ignorance). Self-enquiry is practised to enlighten the mind with divine knowledge; the stars are not seen in the brilliance of sunlight and, in the same way, the 'I' is not perceived in the absolute radiance of divine light. The way to find the 'I' is to search for it or enquire after it deep within one's self (or mind). It is done with a one pointed mind that is totally concentrated on the search, in much the same way as one would look for a misplaced gold ring whose location one has temporarily forgotten. For a forgetful jiva (an individual who has no memory of the Self) self-enquiry is a means to purify one's memory (of its samaskaric filth). Self-enquiry is conducted by asking a simple question to oneself, 'who am I'. It is not to be repeated as a mantra but

constant contemplation on it is meant to attune the mind to find the 'I' with all its energy. Everyone's obvious response to the query, 'who am I' would be, 'I am the body'. One should examine this critically. To confuse the 'I' with the body would imply that the same body should be reborn after one's death. This is contrary to spiritual knowledge and testimony of sages that 'I' assumes a new body after its death. Similarly, a dead body has no consciousness of the 'I'. The implication is that the connection between 'I' and the body is a very tenuous one and in fact, is neither permanent nor unbreakable. Obviously, the highly elusive 'I', which is a thought current cannot be the body. It is a wrong notion and needs to be rejected. A student would, during the course of the inquiry, get many false clues every time he or she reflects on 'who am I'. Another wrong notion that an individual entertains is 'I am the doer (of actions)'. It must be discarded to experience the 'I'. It is done by vichara of the objective experience and renouncing it as unreal. Detachment from sensual experience conditions the mind to know the 'I'. Thus, rejection of objective knowledge forms the first part of self-enquiry. A jiva is attached to the body and external world to satisfy the 'I''s desires by indulging in sensual or objective experience for its sake. One should enquire the cause of this attachment and how it brings in its wake temporary pleasure or pain. A critical examination would reveal that mind's propensity to seek sensual gratification is the primary cause of its attachment to the world. Similarly, one should rationally analyse one's daily experience to determine its nature and effects; i.e., happiness or unhappiness. Of what use is an experience that does not bring permanent happiness, the real goal one seeks. It should convince any discriminate person that sensual experience is not worth having. One should make a beginning by giving up painful experiences and, later, renounce even those that bring pleasure. Vichara done along the above lines reduces the hold 'I am the body' and 'I am the doer' ideas on the consciousness, which makes it easier to know the 'I'.

Q77. What is overall scheme of spiritual development on this path in the light of preceding instruction?
A77. Following points are worth noting:-

(a) Jnana marga's primary concern is to know that the individual 'I' is an unreal entity. This is done through mental introversion to the source of the mind, i.e., the 'I' thought. The method adopted is through vichara, i.e., use of discriminative intelligence in a rational manner to reject all that is false. The technique of vichara is to question one's self to find answers to the cause of one's unhappiness and to find out who suffers.

(b) The path is practised in two basic steps; first, to detach the mind from objective experience, which forms the discipline and purification stages of the control of mind. It ends when the mind becomes one pointed, i.e., it abides constantly on the mental current to search for the 'I'. Second, in the phase known as self-enquiry, a student tries to locate and experience the 'I' current by constantly seeking an answer to the question, 'who am I'. A seeker who is able to introvert the mind from the abidance stage by rejecting subtle phenomenon and experience (including of peace and bliss) attains manolaya (subsidence of mind). Vichara done in manolaya (i.e.by constantly seeking an answer to the query, 'who am I') takes an aspirant to the samadhi stage, in which the 'I' is experienced for the first time and then done away with (through vichara) in the radiance of the flame of knowledge by the grace of a guru. A seeker who attains this state is known as jnani (or brahman jnani; knower of absolute Brahman) and he or she realises the true Self.

(c) Success on this path is possible only if one's divine qualities, specially of discrimination, are highly developed.

Q78. What are the signs of spiritual progress and the experiences that a student has on this path?
A78. In general, those who practise jnana marga are not enamoured of seeing visions etc. nor of gaining occult powers. They are satisfied with calmness of the mind, which they must renounce to progress. Mental peacefulness itself turns into the supreme Silence of the Self if it is given up. Intelligence becomes sharp as one advances on this path. Growth of detachment, devotion and reduction of desires are the other signs of progress.

Q79. What are the chief obstacles to progress on this path and how are they overcome?
A79. Most students who want to follow the path of knowledge are fond of reading scriptures and asking questions to gain knowledge. Some cannot go beyond this intellectual exercise due to lack of will power. They are prisoners of their intellects. Many of them develop vanity because they think others are not their intellectual equals. Some find the path too dry and abstract and give it up after a little practice. They do so because their power of discrimination is not well developed. Impediments on this path are best tackled through determined practice, guru's grace including his or her sat sangha (keeping his or her company) and development of divine qualities, specially of discrimination and humility.

Q80. What is the essence of teaching in jnana marga?
A80. The divine knowledge that a guru imparts to a seeker is used as a tool to destroy the false subjective and objective knowledge. The basic premise of this discipline is that the knowledge that a jiva gains through the mind, of the world or of one's own self, is unreal and illusory. How has this delusion arisen?

Maya or ignorance is its cause and its effects must be removed from the mind to know the Truth. The root of individual ignorance lies deeply embedded in a jiva's mind, i.e. in the feeling of 'I'-ness. A jiva's problems would end if he or she could find the 'I' and discover its unreality. This is done through control of mind by practising vichara; which, in its essence, means to reject, with a laser sharp intelligence all that is unreal, i.e., the triad of a seer, seeing and seen (or the 'I', the experience it or the mind has and the objective world) by constantly dwelling on the query, 'who am 'I'.' What is left after that is the real Self and that state is known as Its Realisation.

The Path of Silence

Q81. What is the nature of Silence?
A81. Readers who do not have much spiritual knowledge are likely to find explanations that follow as esoteric and obtuse. They are advised not to dwell too much on the teachings given below. Motion (prana) in the divine consciousness, caused by maya, creates disturbance in it, which manifests as thoughts, a form of sound energy. The same consciousness becomes totally silent when its motion is controlled (i.e. Realisation attained after destruction of mind) and that state cannot be described in words because it transcends the mind. For want of a better expression, it is said to be a state of Silence; just as the silence felt in deep sleep cannot be communicated to another, so also the Silence must be experienced and not talked about. The Silence lies in the experience of Realisation of the Self, which has two aspects (must be noted that these are not two different states); first, in which pure memory exists and the, second, in which it is absent. The latter is an utterly unique state and its difference from the former is that its experience in the embodied form is vouchsafed only to the divine incarnations. A reader should not confuse the above explanation to imply that Self Realisation is of two types. Anyone who attains It has the knowledge of the memory-less state of absolute Silence but continues to perform one's prarabdha (present life's) karma as an effect of the general memory (of Ishwara). The divine incarnations, in human form, carry out their prarabdha karma without even this memory. This point is not likely to be appreciated by a general reader without spiritual experience. The absolute Silence, mentioned above, assumes Its relative form as an effect of maya. What it really means is that the individual mind functions as a superimposition on the Silence and It dwells deep within every object. The mind's extroversion and activity makes one unaware of It. It is experienced if the mind introverts and becomes completely motionless (i.e. thought free).

Q82. What is the path of silence?

A82. The divine consciousness is said to be pervaded by utter Silence due to the unbreakable power of concentration that inheres in it naturally. This power is so potent that it reduces the consciousness to a spatial naught. It then transcends the effects of maya. It is the same power that was described earlier as yoga shakti (the power of self-control), applicable to an individual. Its quintessential and macro form is called tapas shakti. The latter is earned by divine incarnations only through the practice of a special discipline, called tapas yoga. Tapas shakti when transmitted to an aspirant (i.e. through initiation by a satguru) makes the latter's mind silent, in the same way as it reduce the divine consciousness to a naught. The effort that a seeker is required to make is only to be aware of it and it would do the rest, i.e., it introverts the mind and dissolves all thoughts, doubts, undesirable qualities in it. Divine attributes grow on their own as its effect. It makes the mind totally silent (or motionless) and leads to complete self-control (i.e. absorbs the 'I' in it). The power of Silence sucks (or introverts) the mind into a spiritual black hole from which it cannot escape (i.e. it is destroyed). Best results are achieved by those who surrender unconditionally to the guru's tapas power. There are two ways to practise the discipline of silence; first, as a path by itself and, second, in combination with other paths. The former is its classic form and was taught by the celebrated guru, Dakshnimurthy, to some sages at the beginning of time (i.e. the current cycle of creation). There was no exchange of words between the guru and disciples; the former divined the latter's desire for liberation, initiated them in silence and they practised in silence to attain Self Realisation. Just as a lighted candle melts on its own, so do the mind's impurities burn away automatically when the power of Silence is transplanted in it by a satguru. This path can be followed only by highly competent seekers, usually the ever free souls. The second method is to combine this path with the practice of other disciplines and then every devotee can follow it. An aspirant is initiated into any of the paths described earlier but the guru also gives the power of Silence (or tapas) along with it. For example, a devotee maybe asked to repeat a divine name, which is blessed with the power of Silence. The mind is pulled inwards or is introverted by tapas shakti as one does japa (repetition) of the name. It makes the repetition far more effective than it would have been otherwise. In this method, an aspirant endeavours to control the mind by introverting it towards its centre (the point of its origin of the 'I' sense); that effort gets a fillip from the guru's power that dwells there (i.e. in the centre), which acts like a powerful magnet to draw the mind there. Tapas shakti makes it easier for an aspirant to effect self-control. Effects of this power on paths of knowledge, yoga and service are similar. The path of Silence, in any of the above forms, helps a devotee in all stages of the control of mind, i.e., discipline, purification, abidance, subsidence and destruction. It removes all kinds of obstacles to one's progress and the divine knowledge that it manifests (in silent form) destroys fear, doubt, pride, attachment and so on. As a general rule, those who practice this path are vouchsafed the experience of mental calmness, peacefulness and blissfulness. They are usually saved from the menace of manifestation of occult powers and visions etc., which often waylay immature devotees.

Q83. Who is a competent teacher and a student on this path?

A83. A satguru (i.e. a divine incarnation) alone is empowered to teach it because he or she is the only one capable of practising tapas yoga from which accrues the power of Silence. This path, in both its variants discussed above, is highly suited for those who are capable of surrendering their selves to their gurus (or God). This is possible only if one has highly developed divine qualities like love, devotion, discrimination, faith, dispassion, humility, earnestness etc. It should not, however, deter a sincere devotee from practising it because divine attributes grow on their own if one follows this path. Tapas shakti works best for those who have perseverance to press on regardless with practice and are determined to succeed.

Powers

Q84. Paranormal powers mesmerize most people who are apt to regard their manifestation as a sign of divinity. The acquisition of powers has been severely condemned in Guru Upanishad. Why?

A84. Hypnotic influence that psychic powers have over people is indicative of their ignorance. Know it for certain that those who seek powers and then display them, even for carrying out so called service to others (e.g. curing of diseases), are only doing so to satisfy their egos. Ignorant people proclaim them as saints but that is a fallacy because powers manifest in the mind to damn an individual eternally and from which there is no easy escape. The use of powers is against the divine scheme of things and anyone presumptuous enough to do so is sure to invite the Lord's wrath and punishment. Their manifestation is a major obstacle to attain liberation because there are very few aspirants who are mature enough to shun them. All genuine seekers are warned not to fall prey to them because they are more dangerous than cancer. Fools seek powers and bigger fools use them to gain a name and fame in the world.

Q85. Notwithstanding the above caveat, miracles, apparently caused by employment of psychic powers, are associated with practically every well-known saint. How is it they use them?

A85. It is a misconception that holy sages make use of powers to satisfy the desires of those who entreat them. A saint who uses powers does not deserve that name. The truth is that gurus and yogis bless those who pray to them to solve their problems. The grace that inheres in a guru is divine in nature and it transcends all powers. A word uttered by him or her has the sanction of the omnipotent Lord, which is invariably fulfilled. But, it must not be confused with occult powers that the so called godmen display. A saint's utterance is part of his or her prarabdha karma empowered by the tapas shakti (the power earned in practice of tapas yoga), which grants a devotee's sincere prayer. Equally, it must be part of a devotee's karma to be blessed by a sage and have his or her prayer answered because wishes of everyone are not fulfilled. For example, Jesus Christ did not restore the eyesight of everyone who approached him. It must, however, be remembered that a guru's blessing does not ever go waste; at times, fulfilment of a desire can harm an individual but in every case of non-satiation (due to karmic hurdles) a person is able to bear the disappointment with equanimity.

Q86. What is the nature of occult powers and how are they acquired?
A86. An average mind has a certain range of perception that is limited by the senses, impure memory (e.g. one does not remember one's past lives) and impaired intelligence that allows free rein to the roving mind (i.e. does not control it fully to gain better cognition). The mind is purified by the practice of a spiritual discipline, which increases its range of perception. The power of concentration improves with spiritual growth with the result that intelligence is able to perceive things better. Memory is the repository of samaskaras (mental impressions) of the past, present and future. But, an average jiva remembers events of the recent past only (i.e. of this life) but when it is purified, one may be able to recall happenings of past life or see what is likely to take place in future. Similarly, normal senses perceive objects up to a certain range only. For example, gross eyes are able to see up to a few hundred metres but their subtle counterpart (i.e. in the subtle body) can observe them at a much longer distance. Other subtle senses have the same superior quality of cognition. Thus, a spiritually advanced person can use his or her subtle senses to perceive things in a much larger framework of time and space. There is, therefore, nothing really miraculous about the so called powers and they manifest on their own in purified minds. Another aspect worth noting in this regard is the role of prana (or motion) to control the mind. Mind's purification and introversion implies that one is able to arrest and even stop the flow of prana in it. The objective phenomenon appears spatially separated from the 'I' because prana moves the former away from the latter due to lack of control over it in a normal mind. However, objects come close to the 'I' when prana is restrained due to practice of a spiritual path, which improves objective perception. Prana is also used by divine intelligence to create infinite variety of objects by mixing the tanmatras (causal form of neutrinos) of basic elements (e.g. air, water etc.) that inhere in the consciousness. The atomic structure of these objects, in their causal, subtle and gross forms, can be changed through control of prana, effected by the practice of a spiritual discipline. Thus, control of mind (or prana) has two

effects that manifest as powers; improved subjective and objective perception and the ability to change the atomic structure of objects. There are two types of powers; higher (siddhis) and lower (riddhis). The former manifest in a causal mind (in manolaya or subsidence of mind and samadhi stages) and are effects of prana on ether element. Lower powers appear in a subtle and gross mind that has been purified through control of prana and the latter's effects on air, fire, water and earth elements. No jiva can acquire more than a few powers; only Ishwara (God) is omnipotent. Higher powers are gained through spiritual practice only; lower ones, besides practice of a spiritual discipline, can also be acquired through boons (e.g. by gods and goddesses etc.), repetition of mantras and performance of some rituals. Most godmen who display powers (riddhis) these days attain them through low grade mantras and they are all of a minor nature. It is also worth noting that the present age (kaliyuga) is not suitable for acquisition of powers, specially the higher ones, because most of them require very long practice.

Q87. What should a devotee do if powers manifest during the course of practice (sadhana)?

A87. Powers appear to satisfy an individual's latent vasnas (deep rooted desires). One should pray to the guru to keep them under his or her control, as and when they manifest. One should not trust one's self in such matters because their allure is so tempting that anyone but the very mature seeker is able to resist them. The best way is to do sadhana in a spirit of self-surrender to the guru. No true guru would then allow powers to develop in the mind.

Samadhi, Realisation and Tapas

Q88. Swamiji often used to say that the above subjects are rather complex. An average aspirant would find it difficult to comprehend their nature without adequate spiritual experience. Could you please impart some basic knowledge on the above subjects.

A88. People, even the so called learned ones, often talk glibly about the above themes without understanding them properly. Instruction on the above subjects can be fully comprehended or appreciated only if either one has, preferably, attained the spiritual states, mentioned above, or, at least, advanced sufficiently in one's spiritual quest to get a general idea about them. Consider that in general, out of a hundred sincere seekers, probably one to three are likely to reach the samadhi stage and that, too, its lower form. Amongst those who attain samadhi, it is a considered a great blessing if one or two percent make it to Realisation, a state that can in no way be described in words. As for tapas, it is a yogic discipline practised only by divine incarnations and some higher type of ever free souls. What benefit would a beginner get by merely reading about such matters? Can a student of class one understand the theory of relativity? It is for these reasons that the Guru advises aspirants to confine their reading to their level of spiritual growth. Otherwise, there is a real danger of developing wrong notions about them. However, a very general idea about the above subjects is given below.

Samadhi

Q89. What does the state of samadhi indicate?

A89. It is the concluding stage of an aspirant's practice and all that precedes it is only a preparation to attain it. The thoughts of objective phenomenon become dormant in the consciousness in manolaya (the state before samadhi; subsidence of mind) but they do not merge in the basic 'I' thought, even though they are in its close proximity. The objective consciousness (or thoughts of objective phenomenon) are withdrawn into the 'I'- consciousness in samadhi. It is yet another step of progress in introversion of a very highly purified, disciplined and one pointed mind. It requires prolonged dedicated effort marked by a very high degree of devotion, detachment and discrimination. Guru's grace plays an important part in attaining samadhi. One must be mentally and physically strong enough to bear its impact because, besides generating powerful spiritual energy in the form of currents, the body should be prepared for kumbhak (i.e. retention of breath; acts of inhalation and exhalation become increasing slow, almost to be non-existent, as one progresses in samadhi). It is thus not an easy state to attain and yet everyone must aspire for it because liberation is not possible without it. Unlike earlier states of mind, samadhi signifies permanence of self-control and from which there is no slide backwards. The mind is very peaceful, calm and blissful in samadhi because its motion becomes latent, just like the thoughts that it gives birth to. In very simple words, samadhi stage is reached only when the mind becomes causal. In it, the 'I' thought (or pulsation; vibration) is experienced as a powerful current for the first time; the next step is to destroy the 'I'. What is left after that is the supreme absolute Self. One who achieves Its Realisation is also said to be in sahaj samadhi (i.e. one's real and natural state). Thus, the word, samadhi, indicates a state of a highly controlled causal mind as well as the state of an embodied seeker's pure consciousness.

Q90. What are the types of samadhi?

A90. Although samadhi is traditionally considered to be of varied categories, yet it is better to regard it as the same state having different stages. It is so because samadhi is indicative of the experience of causal 'I'-consciousness and how the 'I' is made to disappear from it, leaving the consciousness in its pure and absolute form. A wise aspirant's aim throughout his or her practice is to experience the 'I' current and then destroy it. Samadhi begins when the 'I' is experienced as a pulsation or vibration (aham sphurana) in the consciousness and ends after its destruction to realize the Truth. For ease of understanding, three steps in its evolution are called lower samadhi, higher samadhi and highest samadhi. The 'I'-current is localised in the consciousness in lower samadhi and experienced as a powerful pulsation. It indicates a highly purified mind's concentration and introversion on its own centre. Its traditional name is savikalpa samadhi, which signifies the existence of subjectivity (i.e. 'I' thought) of consciousness that is still capable of gaining knowledge (i.e. latent objective knowledge exists in the 'I'-sense; a subject and object must cohere). Its other form is called bhava samadhi. Bhava refers to a state of ripened love that manifests in the mind due to deep devotion and self-surrender to one's object of worship (ishta deva). Bhava samadhi is a state of a mind that has purified itself to a great extent and wants to immerse itself totally in the love of one's ishta deva (i.e. one's chosen object of worship). One is able to communicate, on a subtle plane, with the holy being whose bhava (love) one has in the heart. Both forms of lower samadhi are similar in nature and indicate a high degree of self-control. A devotee attains either of them according to one's temperament and the path being pursued. Higher samadhi, known as nirvikalpa (without thoughts, i.e., 'I' thought) samadhi, is the state in which 'I' is destroyed finally. It is the most difficult part of one's practice and only the blessed few, marked by highly developed divine qualities, reach it. It requires very strenuous prolonged practice, which ends in the sudden death of the 'I'. The state after that is known as the highest samadhi or sahaj nirvikalpa samadhi. The word, sahaj, indicates the natural and real state of one's existence; it also means a state of permanence. It is the state of effortlessness because the 'I', the agent of individual effort, is absent in it. It is also called the Fourth State (Turiya), i.e., a state of consciousness beyond wakefulness, sleep and deep sleep. The Self is realised in the Fourth State. There is yet another form of samadhi known as maha (great) samadhi. It is applicable only to the divine incarnations who follow the discipline of tapas yoga; its other name is Beyond The Fourth State (Turiyatitta). It is a state of absolute Silence, discussed earlier, in which purified memory ceases to be.

Q91. What is the overall experience of samadhi?
A91. The experience of lower and higher samadhi is one of extreme bliss, manifestation of divine knowledge and appearance of extraordinary powers. Most aspirants are befuddled by such experiences and are unable to reach the end because they cannot resist indulging in them. Many develop even the blasphemous notion, 'I am God' and damn themselves in the process. Know it for certain that experiences of the above kind are a play of the 'I' to prolong its unreal existence. They must be rejected as totally false because they represent ignorance. Only then can one attain Self Realisation.

Realisation

Q92. What is Realisation?

A92. How can a state beyond the mind be described? It has no word that can even give a remote idea about it. The explanation that follows is only to satisfy, however imperfectly, a genuine seeker's curiosity. To be the Real (or Truth or Self or Brahman or Reality) is said to be the state of Realisation (Sakshatkara). It should be noted that It is a state of Being and not becoming Real etc. It is not something new that a jiva attains. It exists on its own and what the mind does, as an effect of maya, takes place on Its substratum without affecting It. A jiva forgets It due to maya (ignorance) and one becomes That automatically if the mind is destroyed. Realisation transcends any mental notion or idea and, hence, It is said to be indescribable. For purposes of teaching only, It is called a state of absolute and unconditioned knowledge, love, divine power, bliss etc. Those who become Realised while still living are known as jiwan muktas (liberated while living). It must, however, be stated that jiwan muktas in this age (kaliyuga) are usually only the ever free souls; others become so only at death (vidhea mukta) because an ordinary aspirant can rarely bear the impact of the process of Realisation due to bodily and mental impurities. All those who attain absolute knowledge of the Atman (Self) or Brahman are called atman or brahman jnanis (knowers of Atman or Brahman).

Q93. How is a brahman jnani or a Self Realised soul recognised?

A93. No ordinary person or even an advanced adept has the spiritual acumen to know about the state of a brahman jnani (one established in absolute Knowledge). How can the mind establish what transcends its power? The Self Realised are recognised only by the Self Realised. Others know of them through their grace and that too only that much what they reveal i.e., according to the capability of those who seek their company. One should be wary of the self-proclaimed brahman jnanis. Know it for certain that they are frauds.

Q94. Do the jiwan muktas (liberated while living) have some special karma to perform? How do they act? What are their attributes?

A94. Jiwan muktas are found in all walks of life and their actions are dictated by their prarabdha (present life's) karma, just like other jivas. They carry out their karma spontaneously and without thinking of their consequences. For, to them victory or defeat, profit or loss, praise or dispraise etc. are the same. They regard the visible phenomena as the Lord's leela (sport) and they do their part in it without being involved, though the ignorant ascribe motives to their actions. People come across them as kings, ministers, scholars, school teachers, illiterate farmers, shopkeepers, house wives, bankers, soldiers and so on. There is no limit to where they are found. A jiwan mukta is the epitome of divine qualities, specially of love, compassion, dispassion, contentment and humility. They display attributes according to their prarabdha karma, i.e. a soldier, for example, would be motivated, in the eyes of a casual observer, by the qualities that his profession demands.

Q95. What is lower salvation?
A95. It absolves a devotee from rebirth for a certain time frame. It is gained by those who have extreme love and devotion for their gurus or ishta devas (objects of worship). The implication is that a devotee establishes such a strong attachment with one's ishta deva that one's subtle body is reborn, after death in this world, in the region (loka) where the former dwells. One may stay there in holy company as per the merit earned in spiritual practice done in physical body. It may extend to many yugas (epochs) or just a few years. But, their rebirth in human body is certain unless they continue practice in the subtle world to reach liberation state. It is usually attained by those who render selfless sewa (service) to a saint or a god or a goddess out of love and devotion or have reached at least the lower samadhi stage.

Tapas

Q96. What are the essential points that a neophyte ought to know about tapas?
A96. In a general sense, tapas (tapasya or tap; penance) refers to the practice of any spiritual discipline to control the mind through its purification. The mind's impurities are cleansed by the yogic heat (brahman agni) that is produced when it (i.e. the mind) is concentrated. Tap (heat) is a by-product of yoga shakti (the power of self-control or concentration). Be that as it may, the subject of tapas described here pertains to a special yogic discipline (it is an extremely severe practice; the most supreme yogic discipline of all) that is practised only by divine incarnations who take human birth to carry out a divine mission. For instance, to impart spiritual instruction to those who seek it and grant them liberation (from ignorance) or to uphold virtue and restore balance in the divine order of things when evil upsets it. The former are known as satgurus (i.e. form of the eternal guru, God) and latter as avtaras (or divine incarnations who appear as kings, statesmen, soldiers etc.). They are called maha (great) yogis, which implies that they have successfully succeeded in the practice of tapas yoga. Jesus Christ, Sri Shankra, Guru Nanak and Sri Raman Maharishi are examples of yogis who appeared in the world as satgurus and Sri Rama, Sri Krishna and Guru Gobind Singh as avtaras. Why do the maha yogis have to practise tapas yoga? It is to acquire tapas shakti to save people from the cycle of birth and death. What is tapas shakti? It is the spiritual power that a yogi gains through practice of tapas yoga, which is the cosmic (or general) form of yoga shakti (the power of self-control used by an aspirant) and it inheres only

in Ishwara (God). A guru transmits tapas shakti, at the time of initiation, to a seeker who uses it to control his or her mind (i.e. it becomes yoga shakti for that individual). Why is tapas shakti essential to control the mind? The created phenomenon comes into being through the tapas power of Brahma, which is sustained by the tapas power of Vishnu and dissolved by that of Shiva. In other words, the trinity of gods did severe tapas at the beginning of time to carry out the functions of creation, preservation and dissolution. Creation perceived by the senses has come into being through extroversion of divine consciousness effected by Brahma's power. A jiva exists as a thought form in the highly energised (by tapas power) and extroverted consciousness of Brahma. How can a mere jiva (human being) escape from the clutches of the creator? The only way to get out of it (i.e. from ignorance created by Brahma, sustained by Vishnu and dissolved temporarily by Shiva) is through some superior power and that is the tapas shakti of omnipotent Ishwara (Supreme Being). In other words, yogis acquire tapas shakti to counter the power of the trinity of gods. That is why it is said that only God or Its incarnations can grant liberation and no god or goddess is authorised by the divine will to do so. How is tapas yoga practised? Some important points in this context are as follows. One, it is practised only by those who have already attained Self Realisation. Two, a divine guru (i.e. God or Its incarnations) is a must to initiate a disciple in this discipline. Three, its practice involves facing the four cardinal directions to subdue the power of the trinity. North is associated with Brahma, east with Vishnu and west with Shiva. The southern direction is considered to be the seat of the Devi (God in the female gender) or of Ishwara. Tapas is carried out through the latter's blessing. Four, conduct of tapas facing north, east and west is extremely arduous and there are almost insurmountable obstacles, specially in the west, to be overcome. Five, no ordinary jiva can survive its severe ordeal. Yogis go through this very difficult penance due to their highly purified minds and bodies whose tamasic (impure) content is less than normal jivas. Six, tapas may be done either in gross body in this world (i.e. after birth) or in the subtle body prior to one's birth. In the latter case one may need to do no serious practise to attain tapas shakti (to carry out one's divine mission) because it is inborn in one's consciousness. The above is a very brief account of an extraordinary discipline that requires utmost determination and strength and very highly developed divine qualities to achieve success. The next chapter elaborates, in some detail, the method followed by the Guru in practice of tapas yoga.

Essence of Teaching

Q97. What, in a few words, is the overview of teaching given in this work?
A97. The absolute Reality alone is. There is nothing, absolutely nothing, besides It. All that the senses perceive is an unreal appearance created by the

divine will through the incidence of maya (ignorance) for its sport. It arises on the substratum of Reality, which is not affected by It. Although the above proposition is easy to state, yet it is difficult to realise, i.e., its mere intellectual understanding is of little consequence unless it is proved through spiritual experience. The way to do so is to control the mind, which implies to still its motion completely and obliterate vestiges of all thoughts. The 'I' thought is the root of the mind (or of ignorance) and its destruction completes the process of self-control, which in its earlier stages passes through the phases of discipline, purification, abidance and subsidence. The mind is controlled through self-effort and divine (or guru's) grace. There is no other way. The above is the gist of teaching, not only of the Guru but of all sages, seers, saints, prophets and scriptures. The latter have used different ways to explain it and devised various paths (e.g. of knowledge, love and devotion, yoga, service) to put it into practice. Readers are advised to remember the following points:-

(a) It is of crucial importance to keep in mind that a spiritual quest is pursued through practice of teaching and not merely reading about it. For a serious aspirant, one's mantra should be Practice, Practice, and more Practice.

(b) Read carefully how one treads on one's chosen path, which has been described earlier in this Chapter, to get a fair idea of how to set about one's quest. One may also study Answers 101-113 of Chapter 5 to have further elaboration of practical aspects of training one's mind to attain the Goal.

(c) Most beginners are generally bound by religious dogma and prejudices of sect, caste, race, community, language etc. They must learn to shed them because they are all man-made and have no divine sanction. Reflect for a moment, what connection do the above have with controlling one's mind? What relevance has so called fate with stilling the mind?

(d) Mind is controlled by the mind only through hard, disciplined and sustained practice (sadhana). The sooner one begins it, the better it is. Don't postpone it to tomorrow or even the next minute. Be certain that those who do it will never start it. It is more beneficial than mere reading (scriptures etc.). The more one studies, the more doubts one has. Doubts are clarified only in the stillness of mind. Do not indulge in futile discussions and disputations about doctrinal points like the reality or otherwise of the world. One can prove anything with cleverness of mind.

(e) A guru's grace is essential to succeed in sadhana. One should follow his or her advice to practise any spiritual discipline. In addition, make a habit of contemplation, repeating a divine name and doing service (sewa).

(f) Acquire working knowledge of the nature of maya, creation, individual mind and how it functions and the inadequacy of relative knowledge to satisfy a jiva's desires are aids in spiritual growth.

(g) Develop divine qualities like love, devotion, compassion, discrimination, dispassion, contentment, humility etc. and get rid of undesirable attributes like pride, attachment, greed, jealousy, anger, desire etc. The latter agitate the mind and former calm and control it.

(h) Of all the qualities, love, devotion and discrimination are the best. One can never have enough of them.

(i) Of all the modes to control the mind, to do so in a spirit of self-surrender and without any desire is the best.

(j) Of all the activities of the mind, to remember the Lord with love is the best.

(k) Of all the methods to control the mind, to use one's intelligence in a discriminative manner is the best.

(l) Of all the ways to do one's karma, to act selflessly is the best.

(m) Keep trying till the goal of Self Realisation is attained. Do not be waylaid by doubts and fear. Those who are determined to succeed will assuredly do so. Press on regardless because a true guru would remove all obstacles and hindrances.

(n) Finally, one should have faith in oneself and in one's guru. The Guru saves all those who practise sincerely and would never forsake those who take refuge in the Lord.

Chapter 5

The Satguru

(Reproduced from Guru Upanishad)

Adivarpupetta, a hamlet approximately 25 km from the railhead of the coastal town of Kakinada, on the Bay of Bengal, in Andhra Pradesh, is hardly likely to merit a mention on any map. There is nothing that sets it apart from scores of villages in this area of the East Godavari district, which is well known as the rice bowl of the state (paddy is harvested three times in a year), thanks to its extensive irrigation network that takes off from the dam across the nearby Godavari River. There are a number of well to do farmers in the district but the vast majority of its people are landless, poor and illiterate. Although there has been some development lately, yet the lot of an average person has improved only marginally in the last half a century. The rigid caste structure does not allow its impoverished people to break loose from their traditional occupations. Of the time (1935) that this little piece is concerned with, Adivarpupetta's inhabitants were mostly weavers, just as they still are, with a sprinkling of a few land owners. Sri Sivabala Yogi's advent in Adivarpupetta (in 1935) has some curious features or rather their lack that might seem a bit odd to those who usually associate some supernatural events with the coming of Divine incarnations. But, the divine will is inscrutable and it is not bound by any logical connection that one may form with lives of great sages of the past. Consider the following. Neither Sri Sivabala Yogi's family nor any of the other villagers had any marked spiritual leanings nor were they overtly religious. Adivarpupetta had no temple, the nearest being a hoary historical shrine, devoted to Shiva and Parvati, in Darkshram, a small town connected to it by a two kilometres or so of a dirt track (in 1935), which has now been made into a tarmac road. It is an ancient tradition that the yogis normally prefer to practise tapas yoga (a particularly hard yogic discipline; considered the king of all yogic practices; also, refer to a brief description of Tapas in Chapter 4) in cooler climates (such as Himalayas) but Adivarpupetta's oppressive heat and sultry climate, practically throughout the year, except for a short winter, is hardly suited for the practice of such a severe discipline. The tiny village had, in 1935, no more than 200 inhabitants of the Devanga community. For shelter, they had thatched huts arranged on either side of a kaccha (earthen) street. There were very few brick built houses. The village was (and still is) set amidst paddy fields (rice is the staple diet of the people) with high bunds separating them to facilitate watering around the year. It makes the humidity worse than what it would have been otherwise. The area is interspersed with coconut and palmyra groves. There was no electricity then, which led to life in the village coming to a standstill after sunset. Bed time was early for children and so was it for tales to be told by the elders. It was common for peasants and weavers to begin work by sunrise before it got really hot. Like everywhere else in rural India of that time, people were simple, mostly illiterate and had no great expectations from life. They shared each other's joys, sorrows and tears and faced adversity with stoicism that is so characteristic of people inured to hardship and strong belief in fate.

Sri Sivabala Yogi took birth, in a family of weavers, on 24 January 1935. His parents, Sri Alakka Bheemanna and Srimati Parvathamma, named him Sathyaraju. He was the youngest of four children, an elder brother and two sisters. Sri Bheemanna had married Sri Parvathamma, from the same village, with the consent of his first wife, Srimati Shravanamma, who was childless. The latter made a request, when Sathyaraju was about two years old, that she be allowed to bring him up as her son and his parents accepted it readily. Sri Bheemanna passed away in 1937 and that left the family in dire straits, which forced both the widows to move to their parental homes; Srimati Parvathamma to her father's house in Adivarpupetta and Srimati Shravanamma to her village about 20 kilometres away. Sathyaraju, being too young, lived with his mother but went to stay with his step mother when he was five years old. He missed his mother and was back with her after six months. Later, Sathyaraju returned to the step mother's village twice; once, when he was eight years and second in 1947 but on both occasions his stay was cut short to a few months because he found the atmosphere in her house uncongenial. Thus, he spent his entire childhood in Adivarpupetta, in his maternal grandfather's small brick built house that had a well of its own in the backyard.

Sathyaraju had a happy childhood despite the family's impoverished state and the imperative need for him to work strenuously for the family's livelihood. Though no more than eight years old, he would be at the looms from early morning to 10 a.m. when he would go to the village primary school. He was good at weaving cloth with his nimble fingers. It was only in the evenings that he had some time to spend with his friends. He was physically strong for his age and was fond of games the boys of the village played. He was a natural leader of his playmates because of his ability to outplay them in all sports. He was a good student and keen to study but unfortunately the family's poverty prevented him from going beyond class two. Sathyaraju thus had practically no formal education; apart from Telegu, his mother tongue, he did not acquire knowledge of any other subject. Sathyaraju was particularly close to his mother and maternal grandfather and, later, always spoke about them with deep love to his devotees. His maternal grandfather, Sri Goli Sathyam, was a remarkable person, who despite the poverty, never swerved from the straight path. He was Sathyaraju's earliest mentor and taught him the virtues of self-respect, honesty, uprightness and fearlessness. He learnt from him that one need not compromise one's moral values, just because one is poor. It was under the influence of his grandfather and loving care of his mother that Sathyaraju developed a strong will, a habit of independent thinking and a firm resolve to always adhere to the truth, no matter what the consequences.

07 August 1949 – Sri Sivabala Yogi was initiated in tapas
near the grove on the top left of this picture

There was nothing remarkable about Sathyaraju's childhood that would mark him out to be a great yogi in later years. Apart from an occasional visit to the Shiva temple at Draksharam, he did not exhibit any sign that he had spiritual leanings. Sathyaraju's life was like any other ordinary boy's in the village. The struggle to overcome endemic poverty was the enduring feature in the lives of the majority of the people in the village. Sathyaraju's family was equally affected by it but he was determined to alleviate it by his hard work. Like all energetic boys of his age, he was fond of games and pranks. In later years, he would always admit, with a grin, that he was a naughty boy who was ever ready for a fight. Needless to add, he invariably emerged as a winner. No one dared to bully Sathyaraju, as he was certain to get a befitting reply because of his physical and mental strength. This was another characteristic of his, which remained with him throughout his life. Sri Sivabala Yogi always impressed on his devotees to remain firm and steadfast when faced with any adverse and unpleasant situation.

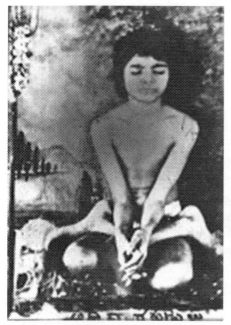

1949 – At age 14 after four
months of tapas

Bodhi Tree under which Sri
Sivabala Yogi sat for tapas for a
few months (since uprooted)

Sathyaraju was only fourteen and some months old when a divinely inspired event changed forever the course of his destiny. The transformation was as unexpected as it was sudden. It was 7th of August 1949, a Sunday, and it was like any other day in the humdrum routine of the village life. Being an off day from school, young boys were free to indulge in fun and frolic. Along with a few friends, Sathyaraju played, near the village school, a game of marbles, of which he was very fond, till about 2 o'clock in the afternoon. Rather than wait for lunch, which was not ready, he was persuaded by a friend to go for a swim in the Godavari Canal, a small water channel really, that runs on the outskirts of Adivarpupetta. On the way, Sathyaraju played another game of marbles, which he won, as he was doing since the morning. A few boys joined Sathyaraju and his friend for the planned swim. Enroute to the canal, the boys sauntered around the nearby fields. It was about 3 o'clock when they neared a palmyra grove, a couple of hundred metres away from the canal, and noticed three palmyra fruits falling from one of the trees. Some of the boys rushed to gather the fruit and brought them to Sathyaraju for distribution amongst the twelve of them. Laughing and joking, the group of friends then reached the canal bank. As Sathyaraju was preparing to eat his share, his body began shaking for no apparent reason. All of a sudden, Sathyaraju saw a brilliant flash of light emerging from the fruit in his hands and he heard the sound of Omkar emanating from it. As wave after wave of the blissful sound hit him, he was struck by wonder at its novelty, due to lack of previous knowledge of such matters. The trembling of the body ceased soon afterwards but he was perplexed further when he found that he had a black shivalingam (a stone symbol of Shiva), eighteen inches or so in height, in his hands instead of the fruit. This was not the end of his mystification because immediately after that emerged, from the shivalingam, an exceedingly beautiful Divine form of a yogi, made of luminous light. The yogi was over seven feet tall and had matted hair tied in a knot on his head. He had a commanding and awe inspiring presence. In his bewildered state, Sathyaraju thought that he was a member of the Jangam Devar, a sect of holy men devoted to Shiva, commonly found in the area. Later, towards the close of his tapas, he discovered the true identity of the yogi; it was Ishwara (God) in the form of Sri Shankar Bhagwan who had appeared that day as his Divine guru and guided him throughout the tapas and subsequent to its completion also. The Divine Being asked Sathyaraju (in Telugu) to sit in padamasana, a traditional yogic posture adopted for meditation for long periods. Sri Shankar Bhagwan taught Sathyaraju how to adopt it when the latter expressed his ignorance about it. Thereafter, the yogi touched the brikuti (space between the eyebrows) of Sathyaraju, who immediately went into samadhi, oblivious of the vision that he had just seen as also of his friends. The divine Guru thus initiated Sathyaraju into tapas yoga in this unique manner. Prior to this moment, he had no inkling of what lay in store for him nor had he sought any spiritual goal. A young boy with no previous interest in yoga was suddenly asked, that day, to sit for an exceptionally difficult form of tapas, which would transform him into a yogi of iconic stature.

1950 – After about   1952   1953
one year of tapas

The strange drama took place in a flash and none of the other boys noticed anything extraordinary till Sathyaraju sat down in the yogic posture, a little away from them. Their reaction was that he was play-acting by pretending to be a holy man. They tried to wake him up, at first by teasing and then through rough treatment, which included plastering of mud on his body and a dip in the canal. After a little while, Sathyaraju's friends got alarmed because there was no response from him to their rather violent behaviour. Some boys then informed Sathyaraju's family. As it happened, his mother and grandfather were away to Kakinada but his uncle, accompanied by four or five persons, went to the canal bund to investigate the matter. Apprehensive that ghosts possessed Sathyaraju, one of them struck him, a few times, with a wooden staff. This brought Sathyaraju to semi-consciousness of his surroundings but even that was obscured by the vision of the lingam. He was, however, forcibly carried to his home but his uncle and others could not, despite many determined attempts, take him inside through the door. His legs would get stuck with the doorsill. He was then made to sit in the outer veranda of the house. By now the news had spread to the village and a large number of people gathered around the house. Many tried to talk to Sathyaraju; most thought it was play-acting or a spirit had entered his body. However, it was an old man named Peddakamaraju who divined Sathyaraju's state and advised everyone to leave him in peace. Most people dispersed to their homes by about 8 p.m. leaving Sathyaraju alone with the family, who, concerned that he had not eaten since the morning, forced him to gulp a glass of milk. After everyone had retired for the night, Sathyaraju, still in divine inebriation, went back to the canal bank to continue his samadhi. He spent the entire night completely absorbed in it, despite the heavy monsoon rain. The faith that ordinary rural folk have in holy men was evident the next morning when a few kindly souls decided to physically lift him and placed him under a palmyra leaf umbrella constructed under a bodhi tree, which is still standing at almost the end of the village street, to protect him from rain. However, the derision and taunting continued but Sathyaraju was totally indifferent to what was happening around him. On the night of 8th August, some villagers also heard the sound of Omkar emanating from the spot where Sathyaraju was sitting. Again, some people carried him to his house. Tired by the events of the last two days, he went to sleep, after a light repast of milk. It was the last sleep that he was to have for the next few years. The morning of third day again saw him on the canal bund to continue with his tapas. He was worshipped there, for the first time, with incense and flowers by a lady from the village. The offering that she made of a coconut was distributed to others as prasad (consecrated fruit or food). Later in the afternoon, on the request of a few villagers, Sathyaraju shifted to the protection of a canopy made by them of palmyra leaves under the bodhi tree. That evening, his mother and grandfather returned from Kakinada. They were deeply disturbed by what they had heard about Sathyaraju's state. His mother was particularly inconsolable; she cried and wailed loudly and beseeched him to return home. It had no effect on Sathyaraju. It was then that his wise grandfather, seeing the boy's resolve, blessed him to continue with his quest. His mother was gradually reconciled to her son doing tapas and decided to serve him as best as she could. She would stay near him as much as her household chores permitted. Sathyaraju sat under the bodhi tree for the next three months or so. But, it was by no means a comfortable and trouble free stay. Some quarrelsome boys who used to get a thrashing from Sathyaraju earlier now took it on themselves to take their revenge. They had observed that Sathyaraju had not reacted to snide remarks nor to any physical assaults. Emboldened by it, some vicious youngsters would beat him with sticks till some passer-by or a neighbour would chase them away. Once, some nasty boys threw a piece of burning cloth on him. He was saved from serious burn by the ministration of a village elder. Although at times Sathyaraju had a vague awareness of the harassment yet it did not deter him from continuing with practice because he was so deeply and completely absorbed in the supreme Silence and detached from the body even at that very stage of the tapas. On 18 November 1949, he shifted to the small burial ground, adjoining the village, to escape from his tormenters who had continued to harass him relentlessly. Before that, he even tried to stay at an ashrama in the neighbouring village, Pasalapudi, but had to return after a day due to hostile reception from its incharge. The burial ground became his tapas sathana (place of tapas) for the next twelve years. A small two storey building (ashrama) has now come up there and Sri Balayogi used to stay in it whenever he visited Adivarpupetta. He was buried in the same ashrama when he shed his body on 29 March 1994.

1955   1955

1956   1957 after 8 years of
tapas with his mother

The news of Sathyaraju's tapas soon spread to neighbouring towns and villages. In January 1950, the district collector of the area, Sundram Pillai, accompanied by Narsimahamurthy, the tehsildar (revenue official), visited Sathyaraju during his midnight break and asked him if he could render any service. Sathyaraju asked for a tiger skin to sit on to continue with his tapas. This was provided and the tehsildar had a wooden platform constructed in a thatched hut for Sathyaraju to sit on. Later, in October 1950, a 12 feet by 12 feet room was built, on a piece of land next to the burial ground, due to the efforts of Pillai and Narsimahamurthy, for Sathyaraju to continue with his tapas undisturbed. It was kept locked and the key to it was in the custody of his mother, who had taken it upon herself to oversee his welfare, specially feed him properly. She would open the room daily a little before midnight and offer him a glass of milk. The tehsildar also organised a village committee to look after Sathyaraju. He also started sending regular donations to Srimati Parvathamma to buy fruit and milk for her son. A well was also dug close to the room for Sathyaraju's daily bath. The room now forms part of a small temple, dedicated to Sri Shankar Bhagwan, which was constructed in the area after completion of the tapas. Apart from his mother, Narsimahamurthy was one of the earliest devotees who rendered lifelong service to Sathyaraju. In January 1951, Tapaswiji Maharaj, a holy man of the Udasi order, came to visit Sathyaraju. Tapaswiji was a prince (of Patiala State) but had renounced the world, at the age of fifty years, in search of God and when he died in October 1955, he was 187 years of age. He had an ashrama (hermitage) at Kakinada and when he heard of Sathyaraju's tapas he went to visit him. During the meeting, Tapaswiji realised by the power of his yogic vision that the former was a great saint who had taken birth to perform a divine mission. He also came to know that Sathyaraju was, in a previous incarnation, Sri Chand, son of Guru Nanak, who had founded the Udasi sect and Tapaswiji was a disciple of his at that time. After talking to him for some time, he advised Sathyaraju to take milk regularly; otherwise, the body would not remain fit for the severe penance (of tapas) that he was practising. He bought a cow and left it with Sathyaraju's mother for providing him with milk diet. Sri Tapaswiji visited Sathyaraju on a few occasions subsequently. Once in March 1951, Tapaswiji applied medicated oil that he had prepared on Sathyaraju's body to relieve him of the agonising pain caused by a burning sensation all over the body. Tapaswiji had learnt many an ayurvedic (Indian system of medicine) cure from yogis when he had lived in the Himalayas. One of the unique formula that he knew was of kayakalpa that rejuvenates an aging body and makes it young. That was the secret of Tapaswiji's longevity. Sri Sivabala Yogi was to try thrice the same technique of kayakalpa under the guidance of a disciple of Sri Tapaswiji, though with somewhat indifferent results, in later years.

The tapas yoga practiced by Sathyaraju is associated with the four cardinal directions. The essence of this yogic discipline has been explained in Chapter 4 (Answer 96). He began his tapas with the eastern direction and attained its siddhi (successful completion) on 28 October 1953. Thereafter, he did tapas of the northern direction till August 1955. The siddhi of the western direction was attained on 25 June 1956 and southern direction in May 1957. The last four years were spent doing tapas of the eastern direction again and during this period Sathyaraju was in samadhi for only twelve hours a day. The remainder of the time was used to give darshan (i.e. devotees could meet him), rest etc. Sri Shankar Bhagwan used to give instructions to Sathyaraju every time he sat for tapas facing a different cardinal direction. He would also manifest in between when the need arose. At the end of Sathyaraju's tapas, the divine Guru appeared before him on 01 August 1961 and complimented him on his unwavering devotion and firm resolution to accomplish his goal. He gave him certain instructions for his divine mission. He also named Sathyaraju as Sivabala Yogeshwara. Sathyaraju later changed this to Sivabala Yogi since the word, Yogeshwara, means Lord of the yogis and it is an appellation for God. He did not want to create any misapprehensions in the minds of his devotees by laying any claim to divinity. The name, Sivabala Yogi, signifies a boy yogi devoted to Siva and His consort, Bala. But, his devotees always referred to him as Swamiji. He began to initiate devotees in meditation (dhyana) during the last four years of tapas.

1961 - Dhyana Mandir   Tapaswiji Maharaj

The completion of Sri Swamiji's tapas was celebrated by thousands of his devotees on 07 August 1961. Thereafter, he started regular initiation of devotees into meditation that was always followed by kirtan (devotional singing). It was done near the dhyana mandir (i.e. the room in which Sri Sivabala yogi had done tapas). Sri Swamiji left Adivarpupetta for the first time on 21 Mar 1963 to propagate his mission. He visited the ashramas of Sri Tapaswiji Maharaj at Kakinada and Mysore. He also paid short visits to Madras (now renamed as Chennai) and Doddallapuram. A large number of people were initiated into meditation at these places. On the request of Sri Kasetti Srinivasalu, Sri Swamiji visited Bangalore for the first time in the summer of 1963. The former donated an acre of land for establishment of an ashrama on Bannerghatta Road,

Bangalore, which was opened by Sri Swamiji on 07 August 1963. It became his headquarters till it was shifted to another ashrama on a four-acre plot in JP Nagar, a couple of kilometres away from the old ashrama, on 07 August 1977. Sri Swamiji spent most of his time in this ashrama except when he was touring other parts of the country. He visited north India for the first time when he came to Dehradun, in May 1965, on the invitation of Bhag Singh Lamba. The Maharaja and Maharani of Patna were his devotees and they donated their house on Rajpur Road in Dehradun for conversion into an ashrama. After suitable modifications it was opened on 13 February 1972. It became the chief centre of his activities in the north. After 1965, Sri Swamiji toured various parts of the country, mostly by road, on a regular annual basis. He usually spent his birthday at Bangalore, Mahashivratri (a festival devoted to the worship of Sri Shankar Bhagwan, the divine guru of Sri Swamiji), in February/March, at Adivarpupetta and the early part of the summer at Dehradun. 07 August, the day he sat for tapas and also the day of its completion, was invariably celebrated at Bangalore. Sri Swamiji had, during his lifetime, visited practically every part of the country. Some of the other ashrams are located at Sambhar Lake, Farrukabad, Hyderabad and Ananthpur. He also visited Sri Lanka a number of times. Sri Swamiji embarked upon a tour of the western world for the first time in the summer of 1987 with a visit to London. He went to the USA in 1988 and also to the UK. His last visit to USA was in the autumn of 1990. He initiated a number of devotees into meditation in both countries.

Sri Swamiji had developed diabetes in the late seventies. He took medication off and on but did not bother to continue with regular treatment for any length of time. This led to an aggravation of his condition and it started to deteriorate sharply in the early part of 1991, on his return from USA. His kidneys were affected. Gradually, diabetes struck practically every organ in the body, reducing his activities to the minimum. Though he was gravely ill he did not give up the habit of being present for the daily kirtan. Devotees could approach him, as before, to solve their problems or seek guidance. During the last couple of years of his life Swamiji was confined to the ashrama at Bangalore, except for an occasional visit to nearby places. In the beginning of March 1994, he left for Adivarpupetta to celebrate Shivratri (a night given to the worship of Sri Shankar Bhagwan), as was his wont every year. His condition became very serious from the third week of March onwards and he shed his body on 28 March 1994 at Kakinada in a devotee's house. He was interred, as per custom, in the ashrama at Adivarpupetta on 02 April 1994.

1963 – After 12 years of tapas   1964 – At Madras (now Chennai)

Sri Sivabala Yogi and his mother

Practice of tapas yoga in this age (kaliyuga) is extremely rare because of its uncongenial and often harsh conditions. It is fraught with dangers that may prove even fatal. Some of the extraordinary hurdles that Sathyaraju encountered during his twelve years long tapas are recounted below to give serious aspirants some idea of its uniqueness and severity. As a spiritual feat, it is unparalleled in modern times. Performance of tapas, in the gross body, is not an ordinary spiritual phenomenon. Its successful completion depends on an iron resolve and divine grace that ensures overcoming of almost insurmountable obstacles, which a yogi invariably encounters during practice of tapas yoga. To succeed, a yogi requires exceptional courage and unusual mental strength, especially in one's determination to go ahead, no matter what the cost. Besides that, one must have purest form of devotion and total detachment from sensual experience. Lastly, the body must be strong and have enough tanmatras (i.e. subtler than neutrinos) of ether in its constitution to bear the torturous hardships to which it is subjected during the tapas. All these factors are very well illustrated in the tapas that Sathyaraju did. His sadhana was beset with unusually perilous and daunting difficulties, hindrances and excruciating bodily suffering right from the beginning. Many misguided people tried to disturb his tapas through ridicule, physical beating and harassment of all kinds. It was specially so during the first three months and, although a few persons from the village began to serve him out of devotion, yet it did not prevent some miscreants to continue troubling him in whatever way they could. The move to the burial ground put a stop to the deliberate interference from mischief-makers because of the fear that such a place causes in the minds of the ignorant. Although it was no more than 40 x 25 metres or so and very close to the village on its south west, yet those who bore enmity with Sathyaraju were mortally afraid of venturing into it because it was known to be an abode of snakes and pests. It had overgrown grass and the eerie silence of dark nights struck fear even amongst the most stout hearted of them. But it did not end Sathyaraju's pain and agony, which continued in a different form and, in fact, became much worse. A few of the inflictions that he suffered during the tapas period, especially during the first eight years, are as much a proof of the exacting nature of tapas yoga as of his strong will power to bear them. Snakes, including venomous king cobras, bit Sathyaraju on a number of occasions. Rodents nibbled at his flesh, hordes of mosquitoes bit him at will and colonies of ants and insects crawled over his body as he sat motionless in samadhi in an enclosed space of a few square meters in that humid and energy sapping climate. His constantly perspiring body was covered with dirt and bird droppings. At least for the first eight years he had practically no or little rest or sleep, as he was in constant tapas, except for a half hour break prior to midnight for a bath and normal bodily functions. Even that was discontinued for several months, at times, when he remained in uninterrupted tapas. During the last four years, he used to rest for a couple of hours, which included some sleep. Throughout the period of tapas he suffered agonising stomach aches many times. Sathyaraju lived on just a glass of cow's milk (or Horlicks) for the first eight years and thereafter it was supplemented by small quantities of fruit. For many months, when he was in deep continuous samadhi, he did not eat or drink anything. Sathyaraju was totally oblivious of his body as he sat motionless, hands firmly clasped with each other, in padamasana, day in and day out, month after month and year after year (except for the daily half hour break at midnight). Time itself stood still, as he had transcended its very notion. There was a time, after a few years of tapas, when he could not separate his hands from each other, as their flesh had glued together, due to constant clasping, and his fingers became stiff and permanently bent at the middle. Once, Sathyaraju's body suffered intense burning sensation when an evil person practised black magic on him. The agony was so great that it brought tears in his eyes. All such happenings had their toll on his body, which was reduced to an emaciated state. But, he did not give up his tapas. His filth covered hair grew long (upto the waist level) into matted locks (jatas) and he retained them (including a beard) even after the tapas was completed. For almost three years, he lost control over his limbs, due to constant sitting in one position and, also, by the wounds on his body caused by the venom of cobras and the bites of rats etc. He used to experience excruciating pain (even after tapas for a few months) when he had to attend to his basic bodily functions because they had become weak due to lack of wholesome diet and rest. At times, during tapas, he used to drag himself to a bucket of water, placed outside his hut to take a bath. Sathyaraju was a very healthy child with a sturdy build, which, in normal course, would have developed into a robust and vigorous constitution. But, the growth of his body was affected by the continuous tapas and, more particularly, by the lack of a proper diet. Throughout his later life, his body lacked the vitality that he would have otherwise had but for the tapas. The saga of Sathyaraju's tapas is too recent a phenomenon (there are many eye witnesses who are still alive) to be dismissed as a fraudulent myth even by the so called rationalists. As a spiritual accomplishment, it is of epochal importance, which is marked by rare courage and unmatched devotion that no ordinary yogi, leave alone an aspirant, could have displayed. It is an awe inspiring epic that is scripted by the Lord only for the greatest yogis as part of the wondrous divine drama. It is a shining example of a disciple's (i.e. Sathyaraju's) steadfastness to do his guru's (i.e. Sri Shankar Bhagwan's) bidding in a desireless and fearless manner, despite the great suffering. Although ordinary aspirants do not undergo hardships on the scale described above, yet there is a lesson for them to hold Sri Sivabala Yogi's pure devotion, sincerity and determination as an example to succeed in their quests.

It is difficult to find a rational way to explain how the body lived through such unsparing distress for such a long time. In later years, Sri Sivabala Yogi used to say that he would pass off into samadhi, after the break at midnight, with the greatest ease, in-spite of his bodily afflictions. One can only marvel at such stupendous detachment, because, it must not be forgotten, the general feeling of bodily suffering does not cease even in a state of Realisation. Sri Sivabala Yogi was once asked if he did not feel the bodily pain when he sat in meditation, as he used to during the evening kirtan (devotional singing). His answer was revealing and instructive. Yes, he replied, the pain is there but he accepts it as a challenge (to fight and overcome it). He had a similar resolve during his tapas. More than all that was the extraordinary divine grace that ensured that he would not falter. Sathyaraju had surrendered to his Guru from the moment of his initiation and it was His grace that made it possible for him to succeed.

1970 – By the River Ganges
near Rishikesh

Circa mid 1970 – At
Dehradun Ashram

Shrimati Parvathamma
Sri Sivabala Yogi's mother

Circa 1988 – At Jhansi

There was only one instance when Sathyaraju's firm resolve to practise tapas yoga wavered a little. A deadly cobra bit Sathyaraju in December 1949, as he was going from the burial ground to the canal, for his daily midnight bath. So deep was his detachment from the body that he ignored the bite and went back into samadhi after the bath. However, the venom had its effect on the body in the form of discoloration of the skin and gangrene set in after a few days. The bodily pain was intense and excruciating. This coupled with the mental and physical agony of the past few months almost made Sathyaraju give up tapas. Fed up with the increasing suffering, he decided to return home but met his Guru on the way. He told him not to give up tapas and assured him of divine grace and protection. He gave him a mantra, which cured him of his bodily afflictions. This apparent show of weakness spurred Sathyaraju to vow that he would not ever succumb to any doubt nor would he accept defeat at the hands of evil forces ranged against him. He thus converted a momentary loss of faith into an abiding source of impregnable strength. He was to be bitten by cobras again but the mantra given by his guru ensured that their venom was ineffective on his body. All through his tapas, he went through unimaginable physical torture in a body impoverished by lack of proper diet but he never ever thought of giving it up again.

Sri Sivabala Yogi's story would be incomplete without a mention of his mother, Srimati Parvathamma. There was an unbreakable bond of love between them, which transcended their relationship of the current life. She was a simple and unassuming motherly figure who served Sri Swamiji during the entire period of tapas and later at the ashrama at Bangalore. She was very tender hearted, pious and full of all-pervasive love, especially for the poor and the needy and would serve cheerfully all those who came to see Sri Swamiji. Although she displayed no outward spiritual tendencies, yet she was not an ordinary lady. It is borne out by Sri Swamiji's revelation, made many times that his mother protected him from many dangers after her death. She passed away on 15 Jun 1976 at Bangalore and a small shrine was constructed in her memory, in the premises of the Bannerghatta ashrama. Knowing her divine stature, the Guru would invariably seek her blessings there before embarking on any important venture. Before her death, she had requested him to look after the family, which he did till his end.

Of a stout built with medium height and a dusky complexion, Sri Swamiji wore only a loin-cloth in the summer months but covered himself with a shawl in winters. He had a lovable and childlike nature with a great sense of humour. There was hardly any time, except during meditation and kirtan, when he was not in a jovial and frolicsome mood. He would always be cracking jokes and enjoyed a hearty laugh. He had a bewitching smile, which came to him readily. For a person of no formal schooling, he had an astonishingly good knowledge of politics, economic problems, technical details about cars and electrical appliances, construction of buildings, income tax laws and host of other similar subjects. Being firmly established in absolute Silence, he would often mix up the past with the future while talking. Sri Swamiji had picked up a number of languages, mainly from hearing from others. Besides all South Indian languages, he could speak Hindi and had a working understanding of English. He had a quaint manner of speaking, which was altogether charming and endearing in its effect. For example, he would speak in Hindi with a liberal mix of words from other languages and a new comer would often find it difficult to understand him initially. But, once one got used to it one found that it was a very expressive way of talking. He had an excellent memory; he would not forget a person even if he had met him or her once casually. Possessed of an incisive intelligence and a keen sense of observation, he would always have the last word on any subject that was being talked about in general. Sri Sivabala Yogi did exhibit some marked personal qualities. Chief amongst them was his all-pervasive love that permitted everyone to approach him easily. He could not say no to any request nor turn anyone away. When told once that he was very compassionate, he corrected the person concerned that his sole motivation for acting was love. He did not ever forget those who rendered him some personal service and they were recipients of his abundant grace. Although very soft hearted yet he could be very firm with devotees if it was for their benefit. He had a never die spirit and was invariably in an upbeat mood. Be that as it may, Sri Sivabala Yogi's most distinctive trait was fearlessness. He could not have gone through the very demanding nature of tapas without it. He had this attribute even as a small boy; once, he stood his ground facing a furious cobra when all his playmates had run away and it was the snake that beat a hasty retreat. This was one characteristic that no one failed to notice in his conduct in his life after completion of tapas.

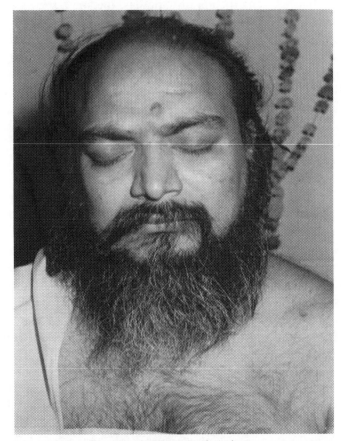

Circa 1988 – At Jhansi

1987 – At West Wickham, London   1988 – At Seattle, USA

A typical day in Sri Swamiji's life would begin in the early morning by a thorough and vigorous bodily massage with a generous dose of coconut oil (almost a small bottle) mixed with lemon juice. This was carried out by devotees, who often numbered four or five, and would last for an hour. Daily oil massage was essential as the internal yogic heat (brahman agni), generated as a result of tapas, was so intense that it caused dryness in the body. Apart from that, it exercised the muscles. More often than not, he found the massage so relaxing that despite the vigour with which it was done he would fall asleep. He would ask his masseurs to have breakfast in his presence before he went for a bath in lukewarm water. This was followed by breakfast. Sri Swamiji used to rest after that and then, prior to lunch, talk to some of his disciples who wanted guidance privately. This period was also spent in sorting out administrative problems in the ashrama where he was staying. The afternoon was spent in a similar fashion and it was also used by him to give instructions for replies to be sent to the letters from devotees, meet aspirants and tell them stories from the Puranas and other scriptures. Sometimes he would talk about the current situation in the country and how it affected the poor for whom he had a special concern. He gave initiation for meditation to everyone who sought it from 5.30 p.m. onwards. It lasted for an hour, which was always followed by kirtan (devotional singing) for an hour or so. Devotees could sing hymns composed by saints in any language. Thereafter, they could approach him to seek his blessings or seek his advice to solve personal problems. This would carry on till 8.30 p.m. or so. After that, Sri Swamiji would retire to his private quarters. Some of his close disciples were then permitted to sit in his company and could ask him questions. Sri Swamiji would always insist that they have dinner with him, though he himself would eat alone after everyone had done so. Every visitor to the ashrama was invited to have his or her food there. He was very particular about this and once a week, on Sundays, and on special occasions like his own birthday and that of other saints (of all creeds and religions), mass feeding of devotees was organised. He would be present throughout the occasion to insure that everyone was fed well. Similarly, visitors to the ashrama were looked after on his personal directions. Sri Swamiji was not a heavy eater and took simple food. Usually, breakfast and lunch consisted of rice based South Indian preparations (with plenty of chilies) and dinner was of chapattis (made of wheat flour), dal (cooked lentils) and vegetables. Sometimes, he would visit the homes of close devotees, on special requests, and then partake of whatever was offered. He was very fond of cooking and would often cook for his devotees. Sri Swamiji used to sleep around mid-night, though he seldom slept for more than two to three hours at a stretch. He would make up his sleep by short naps prior to or after lunch.

Sri Swamiji's method of teaching was simple but very efficacious for those who practised it earnestly. He taught primarily in absolute Silence for which no formal instruction was required. His initiation was enough to set an aspirant on the right track to attain liberation, provided he or she put in the required effort. After deeksha (initiation), physical contact with him was not at all essential. However, this path requires a certain degree of spiritual maturity and a willingness and ability to surrender one's self to the guru. There are very few seekers of this calibre, specially in this age (kaliyuga) that is characterised by extreme selfishness. Sri Swamiji, therefore, modified the path of Silence to make It work through that of atman dhyana (meditation on the self), which has been briefly explained in Chapter 4. Even the latter discipline is not an easy one to pursue for most aspirants. He used to, therefore, give only preliminary initiation for meditation on the self and, depending on one's spiritual progress, capability and temperament, would impart further instruction subsequently. This was also done in Silence, which often manifested by giving directions during meditation or through dreams. Some aspirants were given a divine name or a mantra for repetition in this manner; an odd one was initiated into self-enquiry while the others carried on with meditation on the self. But, in all cases, guidance came from within, specially through the medium of bhava (sadly, this phenomenon was badly misunderstood by most devotees), which implies that the Guru's tapas shakti manifested temporarily in a seeker's mind to answer doubts, remove hurdles and keep his or her quest alive. Unfortunately, there were not many aspirants who cared to understand the Guru's teaching and fewer still who practised it at all. Mesmerised as ordinary jivas are with material gains, all that they could request Sri Swamiji was for promotions in their jobs, good health, birth of male children and so on. Rarely did anyone ask an intelligent question on spiritual matters. It was like going to a limitless ocean of wealth and walking back with a pebble picked up from its shore. Such is the state of spirituality in kaliyuga. It must, however, be emphasised that the adorable Guru himself was not despondent with this attitude of devotees and was invariably most gracious to everyone who sought his blessings for whatever reason. He encouraged all of them to do as much service (sewa) as they could. Ritualism played no role in the practice of meditation as taught by Sri Sivabala Yogi and formal rites, when performed, were mainly to celebrate certain occasions (e.g. birthdays of saints) in a traditional manner. Sri Sivabala Yogi did not ever give sermons nor did he advise seekers to read any particular scripture. Everyone was free to do so according to his or her mental proclivity. There was no ceremony involved during initiation. It was a simple affair in which a devotee of Sri Sivabala Yogi would apply vibhuti (sacred ash), consecrated by the latter, on the brikuti (space between eye brows) of aspirants. They were then told, in a few sentences, how to meditate. His greatest stress was on practice and more practice. He did not ever enter into disputations on the doctrinal aspects of Reality nor did he criticise other saints' teachings. He regarded all sages of the past with respect and celebrated their birthdays by distribution of food to the poor and singing of kirtan (devotional music), which was undoubtedly an essential element of his teaching. People came to him from all corners of the world; everyone was welcome, no matter to which denomination, caste, gender, race etc. one subscribed to. He made it specially clear that women were as capable of attaining liberation as men. The earliest and well known example of teaching in absolute Silence is that of Sri Dakshnimurthy, who instructed some highly evolved souls in this method at the beginning of the present time cycle. Sri Sivabala Yogi's unique contribution to spiritual heritage of mankind is to revive and keep alive this most effective of all disciplines in this dark age. To conform to its spirit, he generally discouraged questions from students who were not pursuing their quests seriously. He would advise everyone to meditate to know the answer to doubts because Silence alone can resolve them. It must not, however, be concluded that he did not ever entertain questions. He would readily reply to a query if it was raised by an earnest disciple or give some instruction on his own if he felt that it would help the latter. His replies were invariably one liners pregnant with profound meaning and the questioner had to be very discriminative to understand it. Many an answer would contain a reply to a doubt that was likely to arise in a devotee's mind later. Although he had not studied any scripture, yet he could elaborate their teaching, for the benefit of devotees, on certain esoteric and obscure aspects.

1989 – At Bangalore Ashram   1991 - At Portland, USA

A discerning reader of this work would have been struck by the liberal and catholic nature of its teaching. Its primary message is that all tenets in a spiritual discourse are valid and relevant for those who seek liberation and want to put an end to their ignorance; also, that religious dogma and bias have no place in it. Further, one need not necessarily be religious, as commonly understood by most people, to pursue a spiritual quest, which, in its essence, deals with control of mind. A rational person with a scientific nature is even more suited to conduct such an enquiry. The great yogi personified an approach like that as a guru. He did not accept pre-destination of actions and declared emphatically many times that jivas have the will power and intelligence to change fate provided they do sadhana (practice). He used to advise seekers to be mentally strong to progress in spiritual or worldly life. He clarified many times that he did not subscribe to any religion or sect or creed and the sole purpose of his coming was to show people the way to God and freedom. He was specially concerned about the poor and the deprived and said often that it gave him immense peace to feed them. His grace was, and still is, all pervasive and it was, and still is, available to anyone who sought it (or seeks it now). Most gurus are selective in accepting devotees but Sri Sivabala Yogi's uniqueness was that his initiation was not denied to anyone. He was an ideal guru for those who were prepared to practice his teaching. He imposed no restrictions of any kind on aspirants, i.e., in matters of diet, posture, timings of meditation, conduct, celibacy and so on. They were free to develop spiritually by self-effort made in the privacy of their homes, without any change in their life styles and in their own ways. He taught that any undesirable habit (e.g. drinking) would be given up on its own once one begins to practices meditation regularly. Similarly, silent guidance, an effect of his tapas power imparted at the time of initiation, would take care of matters such as diet, posture etc. that has variations for each individual. He would often tell devotees to educate their children well so that they could adapt themselves to conditions of modern life and make an honest living. He could never, out of infinite love, say no to an aspirant's request, even when it pertained to worldly matters. Many people gained materially through his grace. The great suffering that he went through in the last few years of his life was for the sake of devotees, many of whose karma he expiated through his body. Not only that, his incredibly severe tapas and, in fact, his entire life was devoted to save all those who took (or take) refuge in him. Most gracious of the yogis, the beloved Guru said once that he would carry a truly devoted disciple on the palm of his hand to the Lord. What greater assurance does a genuine devotee need? Can there be an easier way to attain the goal?

Sri Sivabala Yogi was one of the supreme teachers of the world. The highest class of teaching contained in this work is a testimony of the above assertion. No praise is too high for the venerable divine Guru who was none else but the Lord. It is Gurprasad's firm conviction that the holy Sri Sivabala Yogi was an embodied form of Ishwara (God) and there is enough evidence of this in the preceding Chapters. More than that, who else but a divine incarnation could have gone through the mind boggling and awe inspiring tapas? Who else could have spent an entire life time in Turiyatitta (the State beyond the Fourth)? It must, however, be stated that he did not ever affirm his divine status and usually kept silent when questioned on it. His past history, revealed in meditation, leaves no scope for doubt that he has been amongst the greatest gurus and avtaras (incarnations) since the beginning of time. He was the embodiment of pure love, divine knowledge and power of yoga, and was a real spiritual giant of our times. Blessed indeed are those who had his darshan (i.e. met him) but who can count the blessings of those who practise his teaching? When comes another like him?

For a serious sadhak (aspirant), Sri Sivabala Yogi's saga is a fascinating account of how earnest practice is done. There is much to learn from the way he conducted his tapas, specially the role that divine qualities like fearlessness, devotion, faith, determination, perseverance and so on play to succeed in any spiritual quest. The more advanced one wants to be in a spiritual discipline, the more of the above attributes one should have. Sri Sivabala Yogi was very reluctant to talk about himself or his tapas. There are many aspects of his life, mission and the exceptionally sublime experiences that he had during tapas, which are generally not known. He has been gracious enough to reveal some of them in the answers to the questions asked in the pages that follow. They supplement the brief biographical sketch outlined in the earlier paragraphs. Some of the so called modern minded readers might perhaps be sceptical about a few of the extraordinary events that would be brought out later. They are not asked to suspend their disbelief but at the same time they ought to keep their minds open to accept that even scientific research is generally viewed incredulously by some people initially. Galileo was persecuted by ignorant persons who had closed their minds to any new discovery. There is still a large number of people in and around Adivarpupetta who were eyewitnesses to the story of Sri Sivabala Yogi's tapas. A doubting Thomas is advised to investigate and enquire things rationally rather than jump to hasty conclusions arrived at with inadequate knowledge of spiritual matters. Let a reader be not like a blind man who doubts the existence of the sun because he cannot see it. Many readers are likely to find some answers, given in succeeding pages, hard to understand, specially those related to Swamiji's tapas. It is not possible to do so without some spiritual growth. It is not essential to know every nuance of spirituality to appreciate fully Swamij's life story. One should read Swamiji's saga in that light. Sri Sivabala Yogi was addressed as Swamiji by the devotees and he would also refer to himself in the third person (i.e. as Swamiji) while talking. This scheme has been adhered to in the questions and answers that follow. Many of Sri Swamiji's replies have a general spiritual significance and they complement some of the points made in earlier chapters. Although Sri

Sivabala Yogi is no more in the physical sense, yet he lives in the subtle body till the final dissolution of the universe. Some of the questions and their replies are reflective of this premise.

Gurprasad

Saga of Sri Sivabala Yogi

Q1. Generally, some extraordinary events or so-called miracles are associated with the advent of great yogis. Swamiji took birth in a most non-spiritual environment. In fact, many persons were hostile to him while he was in tapas. There were no indications of Swamiji's eminence as a teacher till the time of tapas. How does one understand this aspect of his life?

A1. The so called unusual occurrences connected with the birth and early childhood of saints take place in the minds of individuals due to their deep love for them, which matures through an association with them lasting over a number of lives. Events like the ones mentioned in the question are manifestations of devotion and only those who have purified their minds generally experience them. That is why ordinary people regard them as miracles etc. The yogis themselves do not cause any unusual happenings. Everything happens in the mind of a seer to fulfill a deeply felt desire (vasna). All such incidents come to pass due to the prarabdha (present life's) karma of a sage and a devotee. The life of every seer is unique in its own way, to suit the times and circumstances prevailing at the time of his or her advent. What happened during Sri Krishna or Sri Jesus Christ's time cannot be repeated now because peoples' attitudes and karma are no longer the same. The present age is characterised by cynicism about spiritualism and, hence, very few so-called miracles take place because vasnas (latent desires) of individuals manifest in accord with prevailing times. Kal (time) decides the overall nature of karma to be performed during any period. Even divine incarnations do not go contrary to the natural scheme of things; rather, they come to uphold it. Swamiji's life must be understood in this context. He did not determine his prarabdha karma. His Guru told him to take birth in his family at Adivarpupetta and he had no idea of his mission prior to his birth. It was revealed to him during the tapas. Sages assume human body to help devotees to work out their karma and in the process make spiritual progress, which is not dependent on manifestation of supernatural happenings. It must also be remembered that every devotee need not be spiritually advanced to come in contact with a saint. Karmic association between two individuals is based on factors like attachment, desire etc. A jiva meets a holy being due to past karma and the type of effort made by him or her in the previous lives. Swamiji's devotees at Adivarpupetta did not lack devotion but their own prarabdha karma forced them to act in the way that they did. Many of them had good spiritual tendencies while a few were evil minded. Swamiji bears no ill will towards those who maltreated him during the tapas. All of them realised their mistake in due course of time. It is good for them, in a way, because Swamiji, by accepting their hostility, has expiated their bad karma of many lives. In normal course, actions that cause pain to others bring their own retribution, as per the law of karma that is based on the cause and effect theory. But, those who were ill disposed towards Swamiji will not suffer the consequences of their actions. Moreover, the very nature of tapas, as explained previously, is to overcome obstacles of various kinds. The pain that was inflicted on Swamiji by a few people, as also by reptiles, insects etc. was part of karmic hindrances, which he had to remove to complete his tapas successfully. Thus, events relating to Swamiji's life, before, during and after tapas, must be regarded as part of his prarabdha karma.

Q2. It is generally said that great sages take birth through parents who have worshipped the Lord for a long time. It is a reward of their devotion. Swamiji's own family did not exhibit any signs of spirituality either before or after his tapas. Is this not quite unusual?
A2. Such doubts arise in the minds of devotees due to their ignorance of the law of karma. They have some preconceived notions about what spirituality is all about on account of their limited knowledge. They feel that everyone connected with a saint should be dripping with love and honey. This is not borne out by the lives of many incarnations of the past. Sri Krishna's uncle was his greatest enemy; Sri Jesus was betrayed by one of his own close disciples and there are innumerable instances where the saints were opposed by their family members. All these things take place due to the law of karma, which is based on the pair of opposites. There are good and bad people everywhere; they take birth together to bear the fruit of their karma, which is a mixture of pain and pleasure. Sages come to this earth to fulfil this divine law. If some people from Swamiji's family have shown lack of spirituality, it is part of their karma. One should not imagine that spirituality consists of doing meditation only. To come in close relationship with a yogi and live in his or her company is in itself a mark of grace based on past karma. Many members of Swamiji's family have been devoted to him for many lives and had rendered him selfless service in the past. Some of them were attached to him through previous karma but that does not imply that they had to be advanced spiritually also. Swamiji's maternal grandfather was a highly evolved soul; so was Swamiji's father. His mother was the embodied form of the Devi and Swamiji worshipped her as such. Their inherent spiritual leanings were not apparent to others due to their prarabdha (present) karma but they bloomed fully at the time of death. The explanation for this phenomenon is that potency of non-spiritual karma does

not allow manifestation of some divine attributes, which then takes place either at an appropriate time during a person's life time or at the end of it.

Q3. Swamiji's mother did not do any spiritual practice. She was attached to him like any other mother is to her child. Nor did she display any spiritual attainment. How can she be regarded as the embodiment of the Devi?

A3. She needed to do no practice (sadhana), as she was already perfect. It needs to be pointed out that many divine beings who take birth as avtaras (incarnations; an aspect of the Lord) do not indulge in any spiritual practice; they take birth for a specific purpose, which is their mission. This aspect is covered in Chapter 4, under Tapas, in this work. Swamiji's mother was an incarnation (avtara) of the Devi who had taken the karma of some of Her devotees to appear in human form to give birth to him. Her mission was to look after Swamiji during tapas and protect him then and later from many dangers. She did that with love to fulfil the divine will. But for her, Swamiji's tapas would have been even harder than what it was. Swamiji loved her with his heart and soul. Her role was similar to what the holy Virgin Mary had played in the life of Jesus Christ. If she appeared ordinary to other people, the fault lies with their ignorance. Are they in any position to judge the spiritual status of even average seekers, leave alone divine souls? Swamiji's mother's seeming attachment was part of her prarabdha karma, which does not affect her spiritual stature. Has it not been emphasised earlier that the Self Realised also laugh and cry like others (for the benefit of casual observers) without causing a ripple in their minds?

Q4. Has Swamiji granted salvation to his family?

A4. The familial connection with a yogi is a form of sat sangha (holy company). Its benefits are immense provided one takes advantage of it. The karmic connection extends to the past and future generations. In the latter case, it is established through a saint's progeny. Swamiji's family will derive benefit according to their motive in rendering him service.

Q5. It is said that satgurus and yogis do not ever lose memory of their divine nature. Did Swamiji have it as a child (i.e. prior to tapas)?

A5. It is essential to have some knowledge of how the yogis assume a human body to understand fully the answer to the above question. One should remember that some divine incarnations are in perpetual tapas in the subtle world. That is a state of total thoughtlessness. A pure thought wave flashes in a sage's consciousness when he or she is required to take birth by the divine will. It may also reveal the nature of one's mission and its memory is the seed that sprouts in the embodied form. This memory is embedded in one's pure consciousness but remains dormant due to an overload of the samaskaras of one's prarabdha (present life) karma. It manifests on its own at the appropriate time, i.e., when the mission is to begin. The question alludes to this latent state of memory and a yogi is like any other jiva before it materializes. There are a number of ways in which it happens. In some very rare cases, a divine being retains the memory of his or her divine mission from birth onwards. Sri Shankracharya and Guru Nanak were two such unique incarnations. Swamiji was in a state of absolute Silence in the subtle sphere when a lightening like flash passed through his consciousness, directing him to take birth. No other detail of the mission was revealed nor did it occur to him to inquire about it. It is not possible to convey, in words, the state of Silence. Suffice it to say that it leaves no scope for asking questions. Swamiji took birth as a result of what transpired in his consciousness. He had absolutely no desire to become embodied nor did he crave to perform any mission. It is only the memory of the divine will's direction that brought him into this world but it was submerged in his prarabdha karma. Swamiji was in a state of total desirelessness in the subtle world and retained the same state throughout his life after the completion of tapas. Prior to it, the memory of the divine ordination was dormant in his mind, which became alive on 7 August 1949. Swamiji was not thus consciously aware of his real nature as a child but its latent memory impelled him to undergo tapas on the above date.

Q6. Is not the state of desirelessness, mentioned above, common to all yogis who do tapas in the subtle world? How did Swamiji's state differ from others?
A6. Tapas in the subtle world is done with a purpose. Usually, it is in response to the prayers of the devotees. The awareness of the latter's karma impels a saint to do a specific form of tapas (in the subtle world prior to human birth), to help them. In that sense, some ever- free souls have a prior knowledge of their missions and then they do tapas to fulfil it. Swamiji was already doing tapas for tapas's sake (i.e. not for carrying out any special divine task) in the subtle world, when he was asked to take birth. He was not aware then what he had to do in the world. He had, therefore, no desire to do tapas in the physical body.

Q7. Did Swamiji retain this attitude in the embodied form?
A7. Yes. Swamiji regained his memory (of being in absolute Silence) on 07 August 1949 and he remained in that state throughout his life. This is an aspect of Swamiji's life, which, perhaps, many devotees cannot understand or appreciate. Those who wish to understand why Swamiji acted in the manner that he did need to know that he had absolutely no desire to perform any mission. Whatever he did was at the behest of his Guru and as a service to Him. There was no other reason.

Q8. Does the above answer imply that Swamiji did not specifically incarnate for the sake of his devotees?

A8. No. It does not. All that it means is that Swamiji was not aware of his devotees' prayers in the subtle world because he was irrevocably established in absolute Silence. The all-knowing divine will responded to devotees' prayer by asking him to take birth. Swamiji came to know of his devotees' entreaties only when his Guru revealed his mission, towards the closing stages of his tapas.

Q9. Is desireless tapas superior to tapas with desire? Did the divine Guru have a purpose in making Swamiji act in this manner?

A9. Tapas is neither high nor low. It is done either with the knowledge of the mission or without it. The power attained in tapas is according to the requirements of the divine mission. Towards that end, it does not matter whether the purpose is revealed or not before it begins. The divine Guru's will is inscrutable and Swamiji never questioned Him about the object of his tapas. However, one lesson for the devotees is that total self-surrender, which implies complete subservience to the guru's will, is the best form of guru-disciple relationship. Leave all your burdens, including doubts, for the guru to carry or answer, as he deems best. Swamiji's Guru never failed him in anything nor will Swamiji for his devotees (i.e. those who surrender to him). Swamiji will do everything for such seekers and they can attain the supreme goal of liberation very easily.

Q10. What was the nature of spiritual relationship that Swamiji adopted with his Guru during or after his tapas?

A10. Swamiji's consciousness was so utterly absorbed in the voidless void of supreme Silence, after the first hour or so of his initiation, that he had no memory left (i.e. of his prarabdha karma) to form any relationship. He did not even know that he had a guru. The divine will ensured that Swamiji followed the latter's instructions whenever He appeared during the tapas. Shankar Bhagwan revealed His identity to Swamiji just a week before the tapas ended. Thereafter, Swamiji regarded his Guru as the embodied form of the supreme Lord and considered himself as His disciple. In addition, he established a relationship of a child with his parents; he regarded Shankar Bhagwan as his Father and Parvati as his divine Mother. It was not a conscious decision on Swamiji's part and happened on its own when the Guru and His divine consort gave him so much of their blissful love and protected him like a child. Swamiji regarded his Guru in that light throughout his life.

Q11. What was the distinguishing feature of Swamiji's relationship with the Lord?

A11. It was of total self-surrender and of absolute dependence on Him. Swamiji surrendered all the power that he had gained in tapas to his divine Guru, out of pure love for Him. All his actions were motivated by the divine will.

Q12. If Swamiji had given up all his spiritual power, how did he then help his devotees?
A12. Swamiji accepted aspirants on behalf of the divine Guru and placed them in the Lord's lap. What more could they want or desire? The Lord Itself looks after Swamiji's devotees.

Q13. Who was Swamiji's guru?
A13. Swamiji's guru is the disembodied pure and infinite consciousness that is firmly established in the indescribable Silence and yet manifests the world appearance as an act of its omnipotent will.

Q14. But, Swamiji was initiated into tapas by a holy form and he used to refer to his Guru as Shankar Bhagwan. He used to worship him as such. How does it reconcile with the above answer?
A14. The absolute Reality has no connection with anything because It alone is. All relationships that exist in the dual plane have their origin in the relative nature of the supreme consciousness (i.e. they are formed by the mind), which is omnipotent, omniscience and omnipresent. The infinite (i.e. formless consciousness) becomes finite (in the form of objects) to indulge in its sport (leela). A satguru is an embodiment of the infinite consciousness but in becoming so he or she does not cease to be so because his or her own individualised consciousness is irrevocably merged in it. This point may be hard to understand but it should be enough to say that the embodiment of ordinary jivas is somewhat different. They are born as human beings because of their samaskaras and vasnas and attain Realisation by destroying them along with the 'I'-sense. Their consciousness can never become infinite. Unlike jivas, a divine incarnation's assumption of samaskaras is temporary in nature (i.e. only for a particular birth) and, hence, their effect on the infinite consciousness is minimal. Compare this with a jiva's samaskaras (an individual's mental record of past karma) which are almost a permanent feature of his or her consciousness because of the numberless births that he or she takes. Just as the mind of a jiva imbibes knowledge (body being inert cannot lay claim to have knowledge) so also the real guru is the relative form of pure consciousness (and not the body that one sees, which appears temporarily and then disappears). No devotee can see a divine form all the time, unlike the consciousness of which one is always aware. It is in this sense that Swamiji regards the divine consciousness as his Guru. Ishwara is an amorphous form of consciousness but its embodiment becomes apparent to a seeker according to his or her nature and maturity.

Some see It as the yogic flame whereas others experience It as the sound of Omkar. Some have visions of their ishta deva (chosen divine form of worship) or their guru. Swamiji saw the Lord in the form of Shankar Bhagwan who was the ishta deva of his family for many generations. Swamiji regarded the latter as the former's embodied form. Swamiji also had the experience of the divine sound (of Omkar) as well as of divine light (of the yogic flame). The sound and light became embodied in the form of Shankar Bhagwan.

Q15. Swamiji had, during the tapas, regarded his guru as being a member of the Jangam Devar (a sect of holy men) and not as Sri Shankar Bhagwan. How is it that Swamiji did not recognise his own guru till almost the end of his tapas? A15. Swamiji's mind had become totally silent within the first hour after initiation. He had no desire to know anything, not even who his guru was. The holy being who appeared on 7 August to initiate him looked as though he was from the Jangam Devar community. Swamiji had seen these sadhus (holy men) earlier and he, therefore, concluded that he was one of them and it did not ever occur to Swamiji to question his identity. Swamiji found out who his guru was only when a sudden impulse arose in his consciousness to enquire about His real nature and that happened just a week before the tapas ended.

Q16. Swamiji worshipped Ishwara (God) in the form of Sri Shankar Bhagwan. Do his devotees have to do the same? A16. Aspirants should worship Ishwara in the form that appeals to them the most. All Its forms are the same and it is only ignorant people who grade them in a pecking order. No devotee is required to change his or mode of worship. The important point is to remember the Lord at all times. It is immaterial in what form and manner it is done.

Q17. Did a yogi of Swamiji calibre require a guru? A17. Swamiji was not a yogi on 7th August 1949 when he was initiated by the divine Guru. He became one only after the completion of tapas. Yogihood lies in upholding the divine law, ordained for the natural order, in which guru-disciple relationship has been accorded prime importance. Swamiji only followed the principles laid down for embodied souls.

Q18. Although Swamiji did desireless tapas, yet the yogic power that he acquired must have had some purpose. What was it? Did he have to do tapas at all since he was already a perfect yogi in the subtle world? A18. To practise tapas yoga continuously and always is Swamiji's nature. There is never a time when he is, either in this or the other (i.e. subtle) world, not engaged in it. Tapas shakti is a divine power of intelligence that exercises total control over the cosmic mind (i.e. in its general aspect). It is the most sublime and superior form of yoga shakti, the power of self-control that is effected through mental concentration. The tapas that Swamiji was doing in the subtle world was of a general nature. The tapas that he did after 7 Aug 1949 was of a specific nature i.e. to help aspirants overcome ignorance. It is potent enough to obliterate the last vestiges of ignorance and grant complete freedom to an aspirant.

Q19. What was Swamiji's first reaction when he saw the light emanating from the palmyra fruit and he heard the sound of Omkar?
A19. Initially, Swamiji was surprised and bewildered because of the novelty of the experience. But, it was very soon replaced by wonder at seeing the enchanting light (brighter than many suns but very soothing) and hearing the divine sound of Omkar. It is not possible to describe how blissful and captivating this experience was.

Q20. What was the nature of this experience? How long did it last?
A20. It was an experience of having a vision of the Lord's form. It is a precursor of the sahaj nirvikalpa (highest) samadhi state. The above experience is granted at the end of higher (nirvikalpa) samadhi. Swamiji's experience was in this state and it did not last more than a minute. A similar experience may occur even in earlier stages of samadhi but it is not of the same grade.

Q21. What happened after that?
A21. Shankar Bhagwan, who Swamiji thought was a Jangam Devar, initiated him and he passed off into samadhi.

Q22. But, Swamiji continued to see the light and shivalingam for quite some time after his initiation. How is that possible in samadhi?
A22. Swamiji saw that vision only when other people disturbed his samadhi and he regained partial consciousness of the body. The process involved in the attainment of samadhi has been briefly touched upon earlier in Chapter 4. The Lord's vision appears intermittently till the final (effortless) stage of sahaj nirvikalpa (highest) samadhi is achieved.

Q23. Swamiji had once said that he had destroyed his mind in the first hour after initiation and had darshan (vision) of the Lord within three hours of it. Could you please, Swamiji, describe this phenomenon and its significance?
A23. Immediately on hearing the divine mystic sound of Omkar, Swamiji regained memory of the tapas that he had been doing in the subtle world prior to his birth. Swamiji attained samadhi as soon as he was initiated by Shankar Bhagwan due to the sudden awareness of the above memory but it was superimposed with samaskaras and vasnas of his prarabdha karma. This point maybe a little hard to understand because highest samadhi is normally achieved only after all mental impressions (samaskaras) and the 'I' is destroyed.

The above mentioned memory refers to its latent state, described in Answer 5 earlier, and it manifested suddenly when a very potent current passed through Swamiji, soon after the initiation. The current was of the tapas shakti and it engulfed Swamiji like a mighty wave that shook him badly. But, it stabilized in a minute or so and in the process purified his mind totally (i.e. of samaskaras and vasnas) in an hour's time. Swamiji's playmates got worried on seeing his state and did their best to bring him back to the world. Swamiji would at times regain partial consciousness for periods not lasting more than a few seconds. He would then become aware of the divine sound and light, as related earlier. The moment Swamiji's mind ceased to exist (i.e. after the first hour), he passed into the deepest samadhi, of which there is no memory. It cannot, therefore, be described except to say that it is state of absolute Silence of a voidless void (sunn) in which even the pure consciousness ceases to be aware of itself. How can it be put in words? Swamiji then lost awareness of his body and the world; it was as though they did not exist. After that, he did not know what his friends and relatives did. He continued to remain in that state for another couple of hours and then he was brought out of it by Shankar Bhagwan. He told Swamiji to resume his tapas that he had been doing in the subtle world but which had been interrupted due to his birth. The above incidents took place on the bank of Godavari canal.

Q24. The state described above appears to be of maha (great) samadhi, from which only the Lord can arouse an aspirant. Does it imply that Swamiji attained Turiyatitta (state Beyond The Fourth) as explained in Chapter 4 under the heading, Samadhi?
A24. Swamiji remained silent on being asked the above question. After repeated requests he said, it is not for Swamiji to say what state he had attained that day. He was not aware of anything. Let a discriminative seeker form his or her own opinion about it. Swamiji is relating events as they occurred from prarabdhic memory. There is nothing more to be said on the subject.

Q25. It has been stated above that Swamiji lost awareness of the world? Did he continue with tapas in the same state?
A25. That state formed the substratum of Swamiji's subsequent tapas and he would pass into it completely off and on. Although Swamiji had destroyed his own mind, yet some portions of the samaskaras and vasnas of his would be devotees needed to be eliminated to make it easier for them to pursue their quests. This is inherent in the guru-devotee relationship and is based on the law of karma. A part of Swamiji's tapas for the next eight years (i.e. till August 1957) was done for this purpose. It was achieved by gaining tapas power. Swamiji had awareness of the world through the samaskaras of devotees and this state was superimposed on the substratum of Silence. Swamiji would then

become aware of the body and the world only when the devotees alluded to them while conversing with him. This is an effect of the interconnection of karma between a group of people.

Q26. What did the experience of regaining memory of the tapas denote?
A26. It made it easier for Swamiji to proceed with tapas in his gross body. It appeared to him that he was merely carrying on with something, which he had begun earlier.

Q27. Swamiji's body had begun to shake even before he heard the sound of Omkar. What was that due to?
A27. It was a precursor of what was to follow. The body started to vibrate because of an intense and violently potent current that coursed through it, as brought out in Answer 23, which set in motion a cyclic flow of currents of tapas shakti, which were not so vehement. The nature of yogic currents has been explained briefly in Chapter 4 in the discussion on the path of yoga. They ceased temporarily after the vision of the Lord. Swamiji felt them many times in his tapas when he regained awareness of the body, for reasons explained in Answer 25.

Q28. Swamiji's body used to pulsate with currents, even in later life, specially when he sat for dhyana (meditation) during the time devotional singing (kirtan) was done in the evenings. Could not Swamiji control them?
A28. There is no need to control a natural phenomenon, which is a manifestation of cosmic prana (motion) that inheres in the consciousness. Its individualised form is felt in the body when the mind is purified to a certain degree. Swamiji had no desire to counter what exists in the divine scheme of things.

Q29. Swamiji had the vision of the divine Guru after he saw the sacred light (jyoti). It was not seen by any of the other boys who were present there nor did they hear the divine sound of Omkar? Why was it so?
A29. It was an experience of the subtle body. The subtle eyes and ears of the other boys were shut and, hence, they did not know what was going on. The divine Guru can assume a physical form, if required; however, Swamiji's experience was on the subtle plane though he saw his Guru with open eyes.

Q30. What instructions did the divine Guru give?
A30. He asked Swamiji (in Telegu) to sit down in padamasana (lotus posture), which was not known to the latter. The Guru then demonstrated how it is adopted. Swamiji then sat in it but found it a bit difficult due to the bodily pain that it caused. But, Swamiji forgot about the pain soon after initiation.

Q31. What happened after Swamiji adopted the padamasana?

A31. The Guru initiated Swamiji by pressing the right hand thumb on his brikuti (space between the two eyebrows) and told him to concentrate his mind on it. Swamiji did, as instructed, and instantly felt a powerful current (of tapas power) pass through his body. It travelled, from the brikuti to the Heart, in a flash, and without any effort on his part. Swamiji then passed into samadhi.

Q32. Does the above experience imply that Swamiji passed through various stages of samadhi described in Chapter 4.
A32. No. The highly potent current coursed through his body like a lightning strike that obliterated all forms of awareness; then there was only absolute Silence.

Q33. What happened after that?
A33. After about three hours, Swamiji had a sudden vision (darshan) of divine light, more powerful than billions of suns. Out of it emerged Shankar Bhagwan, in a form different from the one that Swamiji had seen at the time of initiation. It was a very blissful experience. It took place just before Swamiji was forced by his uncle and others to go home.

Q34. What is the significance of the above experience? Did Sri Shankar Bhagwan give any instructions to Swamiji?
A34. It was a marvelous and wondrous experience whose mystic nature cannot be described. Although there was no verbal exchange, yet the power of Silence communicated lucidly to Swamiji to do tapas. There was no other direction. Swamiji did not at that time realise its significance. It now appears to Swamiji that it was to fulfill his prarabdha (present life's) karma.

Q35. Did it not occur to Swamiji to question the Guru on the purpose of his tapas?
A35. No. Swamiji's mind had already ceased to exist. There was, therefore, no thought in his consciousness that wanted to know anything. Swamiji's prarabdha karma enjoined on him the duty of being a disciple of the Lord. Swamiji was born in that bhava (divine mood) and it never occurred to him, neither then nor later, to ever ask his Guru for anything. He merely did what the Lord wanted him to do. Another point worth noting is that an experience like the one narrated above leaves only a mark of wonderment in the consciousness and there is no scope of asking questions. Inquisitiveness is an attribute of the mind but what is there to ask in the absence of the latter?

Q36. Swamiji had visions of his Guru (as Jangam Devar) and Sri Shankar Bhagwan a number of times during his tapas. This was specially so before the commencement of tapas of a particular direction and then on its successful conclusion. Were all these experiences in the subtle plane? How were their instructions communicated to Swamiji?

A36. At times, Swamiji saw them in their gross forms when they would talk in the physical sense. At other times, it was an experience of subtle body and instructions were given in the subtle language (i.e. directly in the consciousness), which is really wordless (i.e. it impels the consciousness to act in the desired manner). On some occasions, Swamiji was spoken to in Telegu.

Q37. How did Swamiji proceed with his tapas after he was forced to return home?

A37. There was a lot of interference from many curious people who did not understand Swamiji's state. Swamiji wanted to concentrate on tapas undisturbed. But, for the first few days many mischievous persons hounded him mercilessly. But, Swamiji did not bother about them and continued to do his tapas as best as he could. He was greatly helped by a few kindly souls who provided him a makeshift shelter from the monsoons, under a bodhi tree on the edge of the village.

Q38. Swamiji's mother and grandfather were not present in the village when he began the tapas. How did his first meeting with them go? Was not Swamiji moved by the tearful entreaties of his mother to give up tapas and return home?

A38. Swamiji's mother and grandfather came to see him on the evening of 9th August, after their return from Kakinada. Swamiji loved them both dearly and was very much attached to them. Swamiji was in deep tapas when they came but became aware of their presence due to divine intervention (that interrupted his concentration). They were both very upset and anguished because they thought Swamiji would renounce the world and leave them and the family. Swamiji's mother was totally heartbroken and cried inconsolably. She pleaded with him to return home and look after the family. Swamiji grandfather was initially quiet but later intervened to remind him that it is a son's duty to care for his mother when the father is no more. Swamiji listened to them but remained unmoved since he was totally established in the Silence. He told them that he had begun the quest on God's instructions and there was no way that he could violate the divine will. He assured them that they need not worry about the family which would not face any problems in the future. After a little while, Swamiji's grandfather appreciated his grandson's firm resolution and blessed him by saying that he must not fail (in doing tapas). He advised Swamiji's mother not to insist on his giving up tapas. He also added the entire family would support Swamiji to the best of its capability. Swamiji's mother was initially reluctant to leave and was then persuaded by his grandfather to return home. Swamiji realised his mother's spiritual status the moment he saw her that evening. He also came to know that she had been his mother in many previous lives and would look after him, this time, with love and care. It also dawned on Swamiji that her wailing and crying was part of her prarabdha karma but that was on the surface of her consciousness, which was very calm underneath. Swamiji was, therefore, not taken in by her hysterical behaviour because he knew that she would come around soon to accept that he had embarked on a divine mission. She was also reassured somewhat that day when she saw a vision of the ancient sage, Dattreya, known as the trimurti (literally, three faced; implying the Lord as the creator, preserver and destroyer) and he assured her that Swamiji was under divine protection.

Q39. How did she realise that Swamiji was on the right path?
A39. It was not difficult for her to gain conviction that Swamiji was doing the proper thing. A few days after the first meeting, the divine will gave her an indication of who she was. She had a vision of Dattreya again and he revealed to her that she was Swamiji's divine mother and she need to have no worry about her son. After that, she decided to serve Swamiji with her heart and soul. She did that during the tapas and later on as well.

Q40. There was a severe cyclonic storm, in November 1949, which caused widespread damage in the area but left Sri Swamiji's place of tapas, under the bodhi tree, untouched. How did this miraculous event take place?
A40. Swamiji was in deep tapas and he did not know about the tempest till he saw his mother there. It could be another way by which the Lord wanted to reassure her that the anxiety that she felt for Swamiji was inconsequential.

Q41. Did Swamiji initiate his mother on the path of yoga?
A41. No. She did not need a guru because she was already perfect. Only ignorant people are fooled by judging such souls only by their karma. Swamiji loved her as the Divine Mother.

Q42. What role did Swamiji's grandfather play during the tapas? What were the reactions of the family to Swamiji's tapas?
A42. Swamiji's grandfather, after initial misgivings, supported him fully. He was the first person to tell Swamiji not to give up tapas till he achieved success. He bolstered Swamiji's resolve by frequent visits and gave him words of encouragement. Swamiji would listen to him (when he was not in tapas) but did not speak to him. Swamiji did greatly appreciate his blessings. He was a very sincere and fearless person who had done service (sewa) to Swamiji in the past. He died before completion of Swamiji's tapas. The other members of the family were either too innocent of spiritual matters or too young to play any significant part in his tapas. Later, they tried to serve him as best as they could, according to the law of prarabdha karma.

Q43. Why did Swamiji shift to the burial ground, which must have been an awful place to do tapas?

A43. Swamiji was quite happy practising tapas under the bodhi tree. He lost all attachment to the body nor was he aware of it. The unceasing harassment that some people caused did not bother him. However, knowing them, his grandfather advised him one night to change his place of tapas from the bodhi tree to the burial ground. He told Swamiji that miscreants would be too scared to disturb him there. Swamiji accepted his suggestion and moved there during the next night. His grandfather's word came true as no one bothered him there. Although very close to the village, people avoided going near it, specially at night when it was plunged in utter darkness. It was quite damp and was covered with thick outgrowth of weeds, grass and shrubs; it had plenty of rodents, insects and reptiles. Swamiji did not bother about any of them and went to the burial ground's centre to continue with tapas.

Q44. Swamiji was in continuous tapas except for half an hour's break before midnight. Was this done on the divine guru's instructions?

A44. No. It happened on its own without Swamiji's desire to have a break. Swamiji's tapas used to be interrupted automatically at 11.30 p.m. every night and his consciousness would remain at a slightly lower level for performing essential bodily functions. It was a divine way of preserving the body.

Q45. What was this lower state like? Was it like the normal waking state of jivas?

A45. No. The intensity of the state of tapas is difficult to describe. A mere thirty minutes break, in a day, hardly made any difference to Swamiji's submergence in the Silence. However, the body continued to act according to its prarabdha karma, which would bring about a vague and an undefined bodily awareness. Swamiji was like a chronic drug addict who, despite being in a world of his own, continues to perform normal bodily functions.

Q46. Swamiji underwent terrible suffering during the tapas. Besides the physical harassment caused by mischief mongers, venomous cobras, rats, worms, insects of all kinds etc. bit him. At various times, the body had festering wounds and once even gangrene had set in. Swamiji could not use his limbs for some time; his fingers were bent permanently, from the middle, due to constant clasping while he was in uninterrupted samadhi for many months, thus making them almost of no use. What did Swamiji feel when he was going through it all? How could he cope with such excruciating pain and continue with tapas?

A46. Swamiji did not feel the pain as long as he was in samadhi because he was merged in the absolute vacuity of Silence. That state is like a vortex that draws everything around it by a powerful and irresistible pull into the centre of an unspecified voidless void. There is neither pain nor pleasure nor this nor that in that state. Swamiji did not ever come out of that state fully after his initiation. But for that, he could not have carried out the tapas. Swamiji's consciousness was inextricably fixed in the unfathomable void even when he was not in tapas, as, for example, during the half an hour break at midnight. Yet, he felt the acute suffering due to the bodily awareness that he had on account of the devotees' samaskaras, as explained in Answer 25. It was the magnetic attraction of the void, which allowed Swamiji to carry on with the tapas in-spite of the unbearable agony that he used to feel intensely during the break. An hour or so before the time for the break, Swamiji's consciousness would begin, very gradually, to gain an indistinct and undefined general awareness. It was pure awareness of the bodily prarabdhic (i.e. present life's karma's) memory and its interconnection with samaskaras of devotees. Swamiji felt the body's suffering through this memory. The pain would become sharp as the consciousness would withdraw, as it were, from the Silence, though without losing it entirely. It would be excruciating by the time he had to leave his seat for the break, which made it worse because of the movement of the body. It used to be a real ordeal then. It was the divine Guru's grace alone that made it possible for Swamiji to go through the entire span of tapas. Swamiji was also determined not to give in to any sign of admission of defeat in his quest.

Q47. How is it that Swamiji felt the pain intensely in samadhi when the general impression is that it is a state above the pair of opposites?

A47. The above observation is right but it is applicable to the absolute Self that an aspirant becomes in samadhi. But, one must remember that the relative consciousness in general (i.e. of God as also of other jivas) survives the above experience. A Realised person's body along with its prarabdha karma (i.e. its memory) is integral to that consciousness till its death. Body's actions and their consequences (e.g. pain) are felt by the relative consciousness but its impact is not so great because it is experienced in a general way, just like an infinite ocean's awareness of a ripple that rises in it.

Q48. If the pain is felt in a general way in samadhi, does it not imply that its effect on the consciousness is minimal?

A48. The general sense signifies that the pain is experienced in a potential form by the consciousness but it does not imply its absence. Its acuteness depends on the prarabdha karma of the person concerned but the consciousness itself contains all degrees of it in ideation form.

Q49. How did Swamiji overcome the experience of pain?

A49. Swamiji bore it as well as he could during the break and, thereafter, quickly passed into samadhi. He felt no pain in that state. In general, all saints do that when their bodies are subjected to inhuman treatment. Sri Jesus Christ went into the highest form of samadhi when he was being crucified. So did Guru Arjun Dev when he was tortured on a burning iron plate and hot sand was poured over his body.

Q50. Swamiji almost gave up tapas once because he was fed up with the suffering his body was undergoing. How did that happen?
A50. It took place in the burial ground in the third week of December 1949. A deadly cobra bit Swamiji when he was going for his usual midnight bath to the canal. The entire area was engulfed in darkness but Swamiji was able to see the snake wriggle away, after having bit him, through a clearing in the grass. But, it did not strike Swamiji that he should do something about it since his consciousness had not come out fully from the state of Silence. Swamiji went back to samadhi after his bath. The next night he found that he could not get up from his seat for the daily break. His body was in great agony as he could not breathe properly and he felt unbearable pain in the chest. He could not see properly. It was almost being in the throes of death. Swamiji did not know what had struck him till he remembered the snakebite. His legs were swollen and he could move his arms only with great difficulty. Not knowing what to do, Swamiji made a supreme effort to go back into samadhi. He remained in that state intermittently throughout the next twenty-four hours. After every few hours, Swamiji's samadhi would be interrupted by the difficulty in breathing but he would exert himself determinedly to plunge into it again. This state of affairs continued for three days or so after which gangrene set in Swamiji's leg and it started emitting a foul smell. By this time, however, the breathing had normalised somewhat and Swamiji could move about a little with great effort. It was during this period that Swamiji was visited, by a young boy of almost his (i.e. Swamiji's) age. He told Swamiji that he had seen Swamiji writhing in pain and offered to help. He took hold of Swamiji's hands and began to massage them gently; then, suddenly applied pressure on his fingers and cracked them; thereafter, he disappeared. Swamiji had felt some pain in the fingers but did not bother about it. These cracks healed over a period of time but the fingers remained bent due to constant clasping of hands in Samadhi. Many years later, the Guru revealed to Swamiji that the boy was actually Kal (i.e. the embodied form of time) who had come to deter Swamiji from doing tapas. That is the time Swamiji felt frustrated and resented the torture he had suffered all along since 7th August. On the spur of the moment, Swamiji decided to give up tapas and return home. It was about midnight when he left his seat and set out for home. Enroute, he was intercepted by his Guru (in the form of Jangam Devar) who asked him what was he upto. Swamiji narrated all the problems that he had faced in the last four months and how the cobra bite had worsened his suffering. Swamiji told the Guru that he was quite fed up and since he had no desire to

do tapas nor, for that matter, had he any inclination to do so on 7ᵗʰ August, he was giving it up. The divine Guru was very solicitous and gracious towards Swamiji then. He explained to Swamiji the nature of his tapas and also the reasons for the problems that he had faced. He told Swamiji that desireless tapas was its highest form and it was being done as service to the Lord. Further, He assured him of his grace and told him not to abandon the path of tapas because it was a sign of weakness, not expected from Swamiji. In conclusion he said to Swamiji, ` 'you have much work to do for the Guru. Continue with the tapas of the East, as you are doing now. The Guru would visit you off and on to give further directions. Remain firm in your resolve (to do tapas) and all would be well'. Swamiji's Guru then gave him two mantras; one, to counter the effect of the venom of the cobra and this was to be repeated for a couple hours daily at midnight. Two, a mantra for the tapas of the eastern direction, which was to be repeated for eight hours daily. The Guru disappeared thereafter. Swamiji was cut to the quick when his Guru had implied that he (Swamiji) was a weakling since he had decided to abandon practice of the divinely inspired tapas. Swamiji had always considered himself strong and he vowed there and then that he would never succumb to any desire to give up tapas and he would do his Guru's bidding. He also decided to surrender himself to the care of his Guru. Swamiji then walked back to his seat and repeated the mantra to effect a cure for the poison infected by the cobra. There was a marked improvement in his condition on the very first day and he became all right within a couple of days.

Q51. What did Swamiji's Guru reveal to him about the nature of the tapas and the reasons for the difficulties that he had faced?
A51. In essence, He told Swamiji to do tapas for the sake of devotees to counter the power of the gods, Brahma, Vishnu and Shiva and Kal (time), who have created the illusory sensual phenomenon through maya (ignorance). He also explained that such tapas entails many problems and one has to face many serious obstacles which can only be conquered by fearlessness. He told Swamiji that the harassment that he had received from many people was part of his prarabdha (i.e. present life's) karma. In retrospect, Swamiji thought that the cobra bite was a blessing in disguise because his resolution to do tapas became very firm and he learnt a little about its nature.

Q52. Swamiji was semi-paralysed for nearly a week after the incident described above. Did not your mother or anyone else from the village notice it?
A52. Once Swamiji shifted to the burial ground, he had told his mother that he should not be disturbed but she could leave a glass of milk for him every night. Accompanied by someone from the family, she would do that around sunset. No one from the village dared to approach Swamiji's tapasthana (place of tapas) during the night as it used to be so dark. Some curious bystanders would

come to see Swamiji during daytime but only from a distance. No one noticed Swamiji's condition because he continued to sit in padamasana (lotus posture) as he used to do normally and, also, he continued to have milk, despite the physical effort involved in doing so. To all outward appearances, except for the discoloration of the skin, there was nothing wrong with Swamiji. Fortunately, his mother did not notice his skin due to the semi-dark conditions at the time of her visits. Even the foul smell of gangrene escaped her notice. After the above incident, Swamiji told his mother, by sign language, to leave a torch with him.

Q53. Swamiji, throughout the tapas (except during the last four years), you lived on a glass of milk. Even that was given up when you sat in continuous samadhi for many months on a number of occasions. In August 1955, you had to switch to Horlicks for about a year because you developed an allergy to milk. How did you survive on such scanty diet and hardly any water in that hot and humid climate, especially when you were growing from adolescence to manhood?
A53. The body's requirement of food and water is dependent on the nature of work it is engaged in. The metabolic process is slowed down, almost to a standstill, during tapas. The individual prana, held within the body, vibrates in consonance with its cosmic counterpart, which provides the body the subtle energy composed of all basic elements. The body is thus able to live without much food and water. The growth of Swamiji's body took place according to its samaskaras under the control of the cosmic pranic wave, which is centred in the region of the diaphragm. However, the lack of proper diet did affect the development of Swamiji's bone structure as well as some of his internal organs. Its effects became quite pronounced during the last three years of his life.

Q54. In Answer 89, Chapter 4, it was mentioned that kumbhak (retention of breath for some time after inhalation, prior to exhalation) takes place in samadhi and it requires a great deal of practice to acquire mastery over it. How did Swamiji attain it for nearly eight years (except for the daily breaks and a few minor interruptions) continuously from August 1949 to May 1957 (i.e. during the time he sat in tapas of all the four directions) without any previous preparation?
A54. Swamiji had been doing tapas, in his subtle body, even before he was born. His physical body contained that subtle body and Swamiji was able to carry out tapas due to it. It was the strength of the subtle body and its impact on its gross counterpart that allowed Swamiji to attain sudden kumbhak on 7th August 1949 and later continue with it through the subsequent years.

Q55. It appears that cobras and other serpents had a special fascination for Swamiji. They bit him at least five times from 1949 to 1958. Why was it so and what effect did it have on him?

A55. Swamiji faced many obstacles, interposed by Kal (time) and the trinity of gods, in order to force him to give up tapas. The snakebites were part of the overall scheme of the forces (of ignorance) that Swamiji had set out to conquer. The divine Guru gave a mantra to Swamiji to overcome the venomous effect of their bites. That is how Swamiji survived. Incidentally, serpents bit Swamiji at least ten times during the first eight years, which includes four cobra bites during the western tapas. Swamiji's nervous system was affected the most by them, specially those of cobras. As a result, he had difficulty in breathing, swallowing and speaking (except when he was observing silence). Swamiji also experienced dizziness, numbness of the body, particularly of the limbs, nausea, convulsions, blurred vision, burning sensation in the body, discoloured patches of skin, muscular pain and so on. At times, they were so severe that Swamiji could not even sit in samadhi and lay writhing on the ground. Their effects were much worse prior to the time the Lord gave Swamiji the mantra for snake bites. The powers of the mantra reduced Swamiji's suffering and usually he would become alright in a few days. Swamiji survived due to divine grace.

Q56. But, the mantra did not work when Swamiji was bitten twice by an amber coloured nag (king cobra) on 12 October 1955 when he was going to the well (dug for him in the burial ground) for his daily bath. Swamiji remained unconscious for four days. Why was it so? How was it that Swamiji's condition was not discovered by anyone?

A56. The above incident happened during the early stages of tapas of the western direction. The nag that bit Swamiji on that night was not really a cobra. It was a siddha purusha (a person having supernatural powers; a class of highly evolved souls who live in the subtle world to perform divine missions) who had assumed the form of a nag. He was sent by Swamiji's Guru to test his fearlessness for carrying out the tapas of the western direction, which is the most difficult of all its forms to master. The nag was only meant to frighten Swamiji but bit him in anger when Swamiji stepped on it. Being a siddha purusha, its venom neutralised the immunity enjoyed by Swamiji from poison of snakes. Swamiji's Guru upbraided the siddha purusha for exceeding his brief and revived Swamiji after four days. There was a positive development of this incident. A little of the poison injected by the nag remained in Swamiji's body throughout his life. It was enough to counter the unhealthy and undesirable vibrations of many people who touched Swamiji's body. There were a number of evil-minded persons who visited Swamiji with impure intentions. The venom of the nag was like a protective shield against the vibrations of such people. No one discovered Swamiji's condition because he had, at the start of western tapas, instructed the committee constituted (in mid-1950) to look after him that its members could visit the dhyana mandir (i.e. the room in which tapas was practised) only once a month to clean up the place. Otherwise, his glass of

Horlicks was to be slipped through the door every night. As it happened, the appointed day (the last Saturday of the month) fell after four days of the above incident, by which time his Guru had revived him. Swamiji then related (in sign language) to his mother all that had taken place.

Q57. Swamiji had almost lost control over his limbs from July 1950 to June 1953. How did that happen? How did you cope with this disability?

A57. It was a very difficult period in Swamiji's tapas because his legs and arms were almost crippled for almost three years. The body had to endure torturous suffering. Most of the time Swamiji could not lift his arms more than a foot and that too with great exertion. He used to crawl to the bucket of water placed near the entrance of the dhyana mandir (the room in which he was doing tapas) and splash some water on his body. At times, Swamiji used to drag himself, in sitting position, with the help of his hands, to the bucket. He would do the same to relieve himself, in a sitting position, a little away from the hut. It was with the greatest difficulty and considerable pain that Swamiji could separate his hands, clasped together for practically the entire time (except during the breaks) that he was in tapas. At times, Swamiji would take more than an hour to attend to his bath and other bodily needs. On occasions, he would skip bathing. All this came about because of the lingering effects of the venom that was injected in Swamiji's body by the cobra bite in December 1949. The lack of proper diet, no rest for the body and a host of other ailments that affected him during this period compounded it further. Swamiji suffered from excruciating stomach aches frequently; sometimes, his body was subjected to intense burning sensation. Some evil-minded people (i.e. with rakshakic or demonical natures) tried their tricks of black magic and tantric (tantra is also a spiritual discipline that is badly misunderstood and misused; one of its lowest forms is to inflict pain on others) practices to deter Swamiji from the path of tapas. It was all a part of the overall scheme of Kal (time) to prevent Swamiji from succeeding in his mission. Swamiji was oblivious of the agonising pain as long as he was in samadhi but it used to be terrible for an hour before the break and during it. Swamiji had already vowed that he would not give up tapas but he was totally frustrated with this crippling handicap. By mid-1953, Swamiji felt desperate enough to discontinue his tapas for a few days. He just stayed in the room and would, off and on, do mental japa (repetition) of Omkar. This would take Swamiji's mind away from the afflictions. Taking advantage of Swamiji's dejection, the embodied form of Kal (time) visited him one night and offered to restore him to full health provided he gave up tapas. Swamiji paid no heed to Kal's exhortations and threats. He simply closed his eyes and it disappeared after a little while. But, before doing that, he cursed Swamiji that his hands would remain incapacitated for the rest of his life. The next night (i.e. 15 Jan 1953), Swamiji's Guru came (in the gross body) and enquired from him the reason for his not practising tapas. Swamiji, fed up as he was with his state, gave vent to his feelings and pointed to his arms and legs. The Guru complimented Swamiji for not falling into the trap of Kal and assured him of His continued grace and protection. He then lightly moved his hands over Swamiji's limbs and they were restored to their normal functioning, except the fingers of his hands, which were already bent in the middle due to the earlier fracture and tight clasp in which they were held during the samadhi. He, thus, partially undid Kal's curse. The Guru then told Swamiji to resume his tapas and mentioned that he would attain the tapas siddhi (successful completion) of the eastern direction in the next few months. He made Swamiji sit in tapas and disappeared after that.

Q58. What did the embodied Kal look like? How did it appear?
A58. Swamiji's room was in utter darkness when it appeared to descend into it from a vast black hole. It became so dark that Swamiji could not even make out his own body but he could vaguely see a grotesque shape, near the door, in shiny black colour. It had two tiny slits for eyes with red-hot fire in them. It had two large protruding teeth, again of gleaming black colour with splashes of blood on them. Swamiji could not make out the rest of its body but it appeared to be quite large. It was an awful and unpleasant sight. Kal visited Swamiji thrice again but it had a different loathsome form, every time. Its progeny, who also attempted to disrupt Swamiji's tapas, are equally revolting to look at.

Q59. How often did Swamiji relieve himself during the first eight years of his tapas?
A59. The quantity of excreta and urine, formed in the body, is dependent on the amount of food and water taken by it. One's intake of food and water is reduced considerably during the samadhi state but the little that one takes is converted into prozas (the subtle essence of food used to sustain the subtle body) due to the currents of divine power (ad shakti). Therefore, there is very little excretion of waste material from the body. Swamiji used to take a glass of milk (or Horlicks) daily and a couple of small glasses of water. Most of the water used to evaporate during the perspiration of the body. Swamiji needed to clear his bowels once in fifteen or twenty days and his bladder once in four to five days. This period would extend to almost a month when he was in continuous samadhi. All of this was possible because Swamiji's body was being sustained by tapas shakti (divine power) through the subtle essences of the basic elements (i.e. air, water, earth etc.).

Q60. How did Swamiji manage with practically no sleep for the first eight years of his tapas?

A60. It was not a problem at all because samadhi state is one of yoga nidra (yogic sleep), described in Chapter 4, Answer 8(d). Swamiji did not feel sleepy during this period because the body was not involved in any physical activity. It used to feel quite rested except the time when it was undergoing pain. Sitting in one position (in a yogic posture) in the confined space of a small room, without any ventilation, caused its own problems for the body but at no stage did Swamiji suffer for lack of sleep.

Q61. Why did Swamiji observe mauna (silence) from October 1953 to May 1957?
A61. It was done on the divine Guru's instruction. It was a means to prevent a break in the state of Silence in which Swamiji was established. It was essential to do so because of the impending (7 August 1955 to 25 Jun 1956) tapas of the western direction. It is a very strenuous and troublesome form of tapas and it drains out a yogi's last ounce of energy. The Guru prepared Swamiji for this ordeal in many ways and restrain from speech was one of them. After it was over, Swamiji did not utter a word for more than a year because he was in the process of regaining his energy.

Q62. Swamiji suffered a lot during tapas and even later, specially in the last three years of his earthly sojourn. Could he not alleviate his pain through the power that he had gained in tapas?
A62. Swamiji had set out to perform a divine mission for his Guru. What sort of a yogi would Swamiji have made if he had wanted to apply the tapas shakti (power) on himself? The power was earned for the sake of the devotees. It is a sign of immaturity to even consider using such power for oneself because it implies that the 'I', in which desires inhere, is still in existence. In any case, at no time, either during tapas or later, did Swamiji become aware of any such power that he had. It never even occurred to him that he should cure himself. Swamiji had surrendered everything to his Guru and He could do with his body as He pleased. That was Swamiji's attitude throughout his life.

Q63. Narsimha Murthy, the tehsildar (revenue official), could arouse Swamiji from samadhi. How could he do that? How did he meet Swamiji?
A63. One night, in the third week of January 1950, Sundram Pillai, the District Collector, accompanied by the tehsildar came to see Swamiji just as he was preparing to go to the canal for his bath. They were carrying torches. They asked Swamiji a few questions about tapas and enquired how he had survived the cobra bite (in December 1949). Swamiji told them that he was doing tapas as per his Guru's will and it was His grace, which saved him from the venomous cobra. They were with Swamiji for about fifteen minutes and, before leaving, the collector asked Swamiji if he could do anything for him. Swamiji asked for

a tiger skin to sit on during tapas. The collector promised to send one and, in fact, the tehsildar brought one the very next day. He came a little before sunset but waited till mid-night to meet Swamiji during the break (from tapas). He told Swamiji that it was not proper to spread the tiger skin on the damp ground on which he (Swamiji) was sitting, as it would rot very soon. He said that he would have a thatched hut with a wooden platform made and he (Swamiji) could continue the tapas there. Swamiji agreed to this proposal and shifted to the hut by end of January 1950. Later, the tehsildar was instrumental in getting a pucca (i.e. made from baked bricks) room constructed for Swamiji's tapas in the land adjoining the burial ground. Narsimha Murthy was also responsible to have a well dug near the room. Swamiji shifted to his new abode in the first week of October 1950. He also assured Swamiji's mother of all help in looking after him and exhorted the villagers to show him reverence. He would send her some money, off and on, for this purpose. Soon thereafter some people began to visit Swamiji to do namaskara (pay obeisance) from a distance. Some bold ones would come at night also. Swamiji was struck by Narsimha Murthy's devotion and permitted the latter to serve him. He would pay frequent visits to Swamiji at night and sometimes, even during daytime but without disturbing him. On a few occasions, he would relate to Swamiji some of the spiritual experiences that he had after coming in contact with the latter. Apart from Swamiji's mother, he did the most to look after him during the tapas. Swamiji had decided to sit in uninterrupted samadhi for a month without a break prior to the completion of eastern tapas, which was due by the end of October 1953. Obviously, no milk or water could be taken during this period. Swamiji had mentioned this to Narsimha Murthy prior to sitting for tapas. He was visibly upset to hear that Swamiji would go without any food and drink for so long and felt that the latter's body (already quite weak) might not survive. Swamiji then told the tehsildar that he could arouse him (i.e. Swamiji) from samadhi, by touching him, in case of any emergency. Swamiji's mother could also break his samadhi by uttering the word, Omkar, in his right ear. But, they used this power very rarely. The first time they did so was in early October 1953, after about ten days of the continuous samadhi, when they both came together to enquire how Swamiji was doing. Swamiji did not talk to them but he indicated that he was all right and they should leave him alone. It took less than a minute to send them away. During the last four years of tapas (from May 1953 to August 1961) Swamiji's mother and the tehsildar aroused him from samadhi on a few occasions. This was mainly to cure people from sudden afflictions, like snakebites.

Q64. Why did Swamiji need a tiger's skin to do tapas on? Swamiji continued with this practice even after its completion. Why?

A64. Tapas generates very powerful pranic currents (of tapas power) in a yogi's body. A tiger's skin absorbs them and in the process the yogi gets some relief from them. It is an aid but not an indispensable one. Swamiji used the tiger skin for this purpose both during and after tapas.

Q65. Some aspirants use a deer's skin to sit on during practice. How does it differ, in its effect, from a tiger's skin?
A65. A deer's skin absorbs currents of a lesser intensity. It is an aid (not an essential one) for those who are in the advanced stages of higher (nirvikalpa) samadhi.

Q66. What was the purpose of Swamiji's tapas?
A66. Swamiji did not sit for tapas with any aim in mind. The story of his sudden initiation on the path of tapas yoga has been recounted earlier. Beyond that, Swamiji did not know his mission till the divine Guru revealed it towards the end of the twelve years tapas. Swamiji began the tapas at the Guru's behest and continued to sit in it as a service to Him.

Q67. Swamiji, please be gracious now to explain the nature of your tapas, starting from the eastern direction. How does this tapas affect an aspirant?
A67. Beginners may not fully appreciate the real import of teachings given here. They are advised not to dwell too much on it. Their understanding would improve if the mind is purified with practice of meditation. Swamiji started the tapas on 7ᵗʰ August 1949 facing the east. It happened on its own because, before birth, Swamiji was doing the eastern tapas in the subtle world and it was, as such, a continuation of the previous effort. However, till the divine Guru's visit in the third week of December 1949 (recounted previously), Swamiji was in samadhi most of the time. It is a state that cannot be described in words. But, for purposes of teaching, one may say that it is the state of being the absolute bliss, pure knowledge and unconditioned yogic power. Swamiji was not aware of anything in samadhi. The tapas for Swamiji's mission really began after the divine Guru revealed its nature and imparted a suitable mantra during His appearance in December after the cobra bite. Swamiji did the eastern tapas till 28 October 1953 when he attained its siddhi (successful completion). It is too esoteric a subject for easy comprehension without some spiritual growth; suffice it to say that the preservative power (whose embodied form is Vishnu), signified by the ring around the brahman chakra (this chakra or centre of consciousness is located in the subtle body and conforms roughly to the centre of the brain; the ring revolves around it along the cranium), moves in a clockwise direction. The expansion of the brahman chakra into the ring is the function of the power of creation (Brahma is its embodied form) and its contraction onto the centre (of brahman chakra) is done by the power of dissolution (represented

in embodied form by Shiva). In simple words, Brahma's tapas expands the brahman chakra to give it a clockwise impetus to create the phenomenal world, which is then sustained by Vishnu and Shiva's tapas power contracts it to its centre again (i.e. into brahman chakra) to make the creative process dormant till the next creation (by Brahma). The world and its objects are preserved because they are in motion and creation comes to a temporary end when it becomes latent. The creative process originates in motion (prana) and is also sustained by it in the same manner as a small pebble tied to a swinging string that stays afloat, at a fixed circular distance from its centre, due to the kinetic energy imparted to it. The motion must cease before it is pulled back to the centre (i.e. into the hand of the person swinging it). Similarly, the movement (i.e. prana), which brings about subtle creation and its sustenance, is centred in the brahman chakra. Thus, the first step in the dissolution of creation and of mind is to counter or stop the clockwise motion mentioned above. One should try to understand Swamiji's tapas in the context of the above teaching. Swamiji did tapas of the east by repeating the mantra that the divine Guru had given him and he also followed certain other yogic techniques to control divine power and prana. Its effect was to create an anti-clockwise movement in the ring (of creation) mentioned above. It did not stop its clockwise motion (which represents creation in general) but produced a sufficiently strong counter current in the form of a new ring that ran below the first ring. The anti-clockwise ring was created by the tapas power that Swamiji had gained while facing the eastern direction. This ring was further strengthened when Swamiji completed the tapas of the other directions. It was the above mentioned phenomenon that enabled Swamiji to perform his mission. Its practical effect for the devotees is as follows. The clockwise movement of the ring (or the tapas power of Vishnu) sustains the vibrations of an extroverted mind, both in its general and individual aspects, and one cannot control the mind till a contrary kinetic energy counters it. The tapas power that Swamiji gave to the devotees, at the time of initiation, contained the anti-clockwise currents in latent form and they are activated through meditation. All that an aspirant is required to do is to attach his or her mind to Swamiji's power and it would automatically control it. The power that Swamiji earned in the eastern tapas helps a devotee in the first three stages of control of mind (i.e. self-discipline, self-purification and self-abidance). Apart from its effect on individual mind, Swamiji's tapas power (of the east) had a bearing on certain other aspects of his mission. It would be discussed separately. It was but natural that Swamiji would face problems whilst doing tapas. Rationally speaking, it should be obvious that change of direction of motion through a hundred and eighty degrees (i.e. from forward to reverse) is bound to be resisted, just as a flying aircraft counters the retarding force. The drag is much worse when the motion is changed from clockwise to anti-clockwise. The opposition of Vishnu to Swamiji's tapas (or tapas in general of the eastern direction) should be understood in the light of this explanation. The primary obstacle that Swamiji faced during this phase of tapas was the effect that counter clockwise pranic motion had on his body. Prana holds the bodily structure intact by combining the tanmatras (neutrino like essences) of various elements according to one's karma, which is based on the clockwise motion set into being by Brahma. The combination of tanmatras (the basic building blocks of elements; much like the neutrinos that the physicists talk about) began to be disrupted when Swamiji's tapas produced the anti-clockwise movement. It produced a severe pranic imbalance in his body in the first few months of the tapas and it persisted to a lesser degree for nearly three years. It was the main cause of Swamiji's bodily suffering, which resulted in many serious afflictions. The inability to use his limbs was the result of pranic malfunctioning. So were Swamiji's allergy to milk and some stomach problems. The divine Guru by running His hands over Swamiji's body (in June 1953) restored the pranic balance but the damage done to the internal organs did not completely disappear. An aspirant who practises any of the yogic disciplines need not worry about facing the same bodily problems that Swamiji did. They manifest in tapas only because a yogi endeavours to control cosmic forces (i.e. of the trinity of gods) of creation and they oppose any change by interposing obstacles of the types mentioned above. Vishnu tried to disturb Swamiji's tapas through the seductive charm of many heavenly looking damsels. On quite a few occasions in 1952 and 1953, exceedingly beautiful girls would dance in provocative postures in front of Swamiji. They would also sing in divine voices. This would happen during breaks at mid- night. Swamiji would invariably close his eyes and pass off into samadhi to avoid looking at them. God Vishnu, a very impressive and bejeweled personality with a kingly bearing dressed in regal robes, visited Swamiji in February 1953. He ordered Swamiji to give up tapas, failing which he would cause more damage to his body. When ignored, he offered to make Swamiji the emperor of the world. He went away when Swamiji refused to listen to him and went into his samadhi. Later, in May 1953, kal (personified form of the idea of time) came calling again on Swamiji and addressed him, 'O Lord, I know that you are a great yogi. I have a daughter who has done more tapas than you. If you marry her, the combined power of both of you would produce a son who would be mightier that the united power of the trinity of gods (Brahma, Vishnu and Shiva). Consider it carefully.' Swamiji did not even look at the repulsive Kal. Later, on another day in August 1953, Kal threatened Swamiji with death if he continued with tapas. Swamiji remained firm and resolute and did not even enter into conversation with him. There were many other similar hindrances, which were placed on his path to disturb his samadhi, by some of the lesser gods and demons. A few of them pronounced curses.

Finally, by end of September 1953, Swamiji went into continuous samadhi for about a month. He was aroused from it by Shankar Bhagwan on 28th October 1953. It was the same form, but much more luminous, than the one Swamiji had seen on 7th August 1949, three hours after his initiation. At that time, Swamiji had not enquired who He was. But, this time he did and learnt His real identity. He was tall (six feet plus), slim and sharp featured (broad forehead, large almond shaped eyes, a roundish face), without hair and appeared to be eternally young. He wore a lion cloth and looked dazzlingly snow white and merely beholding Him sent Swamiji into a rapturous divine ecstasy, which is hard to describe. He looked so different from Swamiji's Guru, who was more human looking with a darkish complexion. That they were both the same Being was unknown to Swamiji then. Shankar Bhagwan complimented Swamiji for the fearless and steadfast manner in which he had done tapas. Swamiji gave a negative reply when asked if he required anything. Bhagwan then told Swamiji that his Guru would give him further instructions and disappeared. Swamiji then rested for a day totally engrossed in the divinely blissful experience of the vision of Sri Shankar Bhagwan. The next night, around midnight, the god Vishnu came to do namaskara (pay obeisance), as a sign of surrender to Swamiji. The divine Guru (as Jangam Devar) appeared at about 0200 hours on the same night and expressed happiness for the successful conclusion (siddhi) of the eastern tapas. He exhorted Swamiji to remain true to his purpose for the next phase of the tapas, which was to be of the northern direction. The Guru revealed an appropriate mantra and a special yogic technique to control prana that originates in the north and with that ended the first four years of tapas.

Q68. Were the experiences given above in the subtle plane?
A68. The experiences relating to Kal and the trinity were of their subtle bodies. They took place when Swamiji was about to emerge from samadhi. So were the experiences of other gods and demons. Swamiji saw the girls in their physical forms. Swamiji's Guru appeared in human form but Sri Shankar Bhagwan came in His subtle body.

Q69. How did Swamiji escape the effects of the curses mentioned above?
A69. Some of them Swamiji took on his body and they were worked out through the pain that he suffered. There are some eternal companions (i.e. ever free souls) of Swamiji who do not ever leave his side, i.e., they come with him in every birth. Sometimes they assume a gross body while at others they serve him in their subtle forms. At least two of them hovered around Swamiji in their subtle bodies to protect him from gods, demons and celestial girls throughout the tapas. They did so on the command of the divine Guru. Some of the curses these boys took on themselves; but for that, Swamiji's condition during tapas would have been much worse.

Q70. How is it that the eternal companions of Swamiji could not prevent the gods etc. from harassing him in tapas? Could they not do anything when Swamiji was writhing in pain or had been physically incapacitated?

A70. They were instructed by Shankar Bhagwan to ensure that Kal and other gods etc. do not come in physical contact with Swamiji because they could go to any extent, including causing permanent damage to the body or even its death, to stop him from succeeding in tapas. Both the boys, mentioned above, are great tapaswis (i.e. highly accomplished tapas yogis) themselves and one of them is specially blessed by the Lord with a lot of extraordinary powers. Even the siddha purushas (those who have mastered certain paranormal powers for divine purposes) show him reverence and take instructions from him. These boys kept Kal and others at bay by using their powers. They were eminently successful in preventing the latter from coming close to Swamiji and thus rendered him great service. Swamiji would not have succeeded in tapas yoga but for them. They could not alert Swamiji's mother and others in the village when he was in great physical agony because they knew, through their divine knowledge, that Swamiji's suffering is a means to overcome some of the obstacles that he would encounter in carrying out his divine mission. Besides that, karma of many devotees was expatiated in the process. The two boys and a few of Swamiji's other companions have a part to play in his mission. The boy with the most powers is the chief of Swamiji's companions and he played a leading role in tackling Kal etc. He has a fiery temper and would invariably quarrel with Kal in particular to invite his wrath so that he (Kal) could not come close to Swamiji. Once Kal got enraged with him because he prevented the former (i.e. Kal) from assaulting Swamiji who was immersed in samadhi. The boy picked up Kal and, using his powers, threw him (i.e. Kal) out of Swamiji presence. Kal was so incensed that he pronounced a curse on the boy. The above incident took place during one night in the summer of 1953.

Q71. When did the above mentioned boys join Swamiji in his tapas? Did they stay with him throughout his earthly journey? Did Swamiji see and talk to them during tapas?

A71. They were detailed by Sri Shankar Bhagwan to protect Swamiji in Dec 1949, after the incident of the cobra bite. They were with him till the completion of the tapas and would thereafter meet him off and on throughout his life. In fact, they were present when Swamiji shed his body (on 28 Mar 1994) and accompanied his subtle body to the sacred hills, located in the subtle world. Swamiji was not aware of their presence during tapas as he was totally and utterly established in the absolute Silence. Nor did the boys reveal themselves to him on Sri Shankar Bhagwan's orders. Swamiji came to know about them on one evening, many years after the completion of the tapas, during his dhyana (meditation), which he used to do daily, just before the kirtan (musical rendering of sacred hymns) was sung by the devotees.

Q72. How did Swamiji proceed with the tapas of the northern direction? What was its purpose and experience?

A72. This phase lasted from 29th October 1953 to 1 August 1955. Its object was to neutralise the power of germination in the seeds of creation to a limited extent. As explained above, the creative process restarts after its (previous) dissolution. Swamiji's tapas was not meant to undo the natural law and, therefore, it did not affect Brahma's power to recreate. Its effect was confined to the individual mind. The creative power (of Brahma's tapas) makes a jiva's samaskaras to sprout into palpable thoughts and Swamiji's did tapas to counter it for his devotees. The implication is that the use of this power prevents individual samaskaras from turning into thoughts, which includes the basic 'I' thought. In other words, it helps an aspirant to reach the manolaya (subsidence of mind) stage. Brahma resisted Swamiji's tapas since it affected his power (of creation of thoughts) but being a creator, he is more compassionate than other gods, just as parents are for their children. He did not impose any serious obstacles as such but tried to deflect Swamiji from his path by offering to gratify his desires. Brahma appeared twice and asked Swamiji to ask for a boon but since the latter had no wishes to fulfil, he declined the former's offer. Swamiji was otherwise not troubled in this phase and enjoyed the bliss of being in samadhi. Swamiji sat in continuous samadhi for 15 days prior to 1 August 1955 when, again, he had darshan (vision) of Shankar Bhagwan. This time His consort, the divine Mother Parvati, accompanied Bhagwan. The Mother was tall (about five feet and nine inches) and was wearing a white sari. She looked in Her mid-twenties with a longish but square face and had doe eyes. There was something extraordinarily ethereal about Her and She exuded motherly divine love. Swamiji saw them in their gross forms, which in the case of Bhagwan was not as glowing and luminous as in the previous vision. They blessed Swamiji and warned him of the difficult times ahead but assured him of their grace. Shankar Bhagwan told Swamiji to rest for some days, after which the Guru would initiate him for the next phase of tapas. Swamiji rested till the mid-night of 7th August 1955. During this period, Swamiji used to sleep for three hours or so daily and for the remainder of the time, he would hum the sound of Omkar, which gave him immense peace and rest. Swamiji had a vision of the subtle form of Brahma during the early hours of 5th August. He was accompanied by a number of sages. They all did namaskara (i.e. greeted) to Swamiji and sought his blessings as a sign of surrender. The divine Guru appeared at mid-night on 7th August 1955 and initiated Swamiji, by touching his brikuti (space between the eyebrows), for the tapas of the west. He imparted a mantra for it and generally outlined the obstacles that he would face in the western tapas.

He mentioned to Swamiji that no one could become a true yogi (or a satguru) unless one can vanquish the dark forces that operate in this direction. The Guru gave His blessings and told him, 'no matter what happens, don't give up tapas. A defeat from god Shiva leads to a yogi's destruction and much harm accrues to his family and devotees. Remain fearlessly firm in your resolve. Whenever you need help, hum the sound of Omkar, and the Guru will look after you.'

Q73. What is the nature of the tapas of the western direction? What was its practice like?
A73. The gods, Brahma, Vishnu, and Shiva had done their tapas, before creation came into being, facing north, east and west respectively. The sun, for example, rises in the east and sets in the west because of the tapas of Vishnu (who is only sustaining the motion created by Brahma) and Shiva respectively. The western direction signifies, in general, the power of the consciousness to withdraw its own projected images in tamoguna (i.e. gross form of objects) into satoguna (i.e. into their satva form). In other words, Shiva's tapas power dissolves the gross world into its causal form at the appropriate time. To do it, Shiva (or the power of dissolution) annihilates the gross and subtle worlds by disintegrating the basic elements, whose various combinations create different forms of objects, by withdrawing the prana, which holds them together. It is a cataclysmic process on a cosmic scale, which, in effect, contracts the ring of creation (i.e. expanded brahman chakra) into the centre of brahman chakra (located roughly in centre of the subtle brain) and then sink it in the Heart for its recreation in the next time cycle. A similar phenomenon takes place during the control of the mind up to its subsidence (manolaya) stage. For an individual, the process in not painful (in fact, it is blissful) because a guru's tapas power does not allow Shiva to cause an upheaval in the mind, as he would in the normal course of destruction. The process of dissolution (of the world) is not confined to its physical aspect alone but its more crucial part is to make latent the ideas, from which objects are created, in the consciousness. The purpose of the western tapas is to help the devotees subside and destroy their minds. It takes off from tapas of the north in which a yogi gains power to stop thoughts from erupting, as explained in the previous answer. The western tapas ensures that the power of transforming samaskaras into thoughts (i.e. the power of Brahama's tapas or of the northern direction) is not only neutralised but also made dormant. In simpler words, the western tapas allows the mind to withdraw all thoughts into the basic 'I' thought and make the latter dormant. That is the state of manolaya (subsidence of mind). The distinction between the tapas of the north and west is that while the former creates conditions for manolaya, the latter actually puts it into effect. Extinction of the mind implies emancipation of the individual from the grip of ignorance, created by the trinity of gods. Any attempt to do so (i.e. by attaining samadhi) is strongly resisted by Shiva's tapas power because it is

his role to ensure that the mind remains intact; if it was not so, it would have been much easier to reach the samadhi stage to attain liberation. That is why success in samadhi is so hard to achieve. At the time of dissolution, the world (of ignorance) assumes its latent or causal form but it is not completely destroyed. Similarly, any attempt to kill the mind (or go beyond manolaya) is opposed by the most powerful of all gods, Shiva, because he is divinely ordained, in the natural order of things, to ensure that subsidence of mind is followed by its extroversion again. The opposition begins after the abidance stage, which, as pointed out in Answer 67, is achieved by the anti-clockwise motion of the mind. To subside it, the mind is first concentrated on the centre of brahman chakra and then made to sink in the Heart prior to its destruction. The resistance to mind's subsidence and destruction becomes progressively worse as one goes into the final stages of one's quest. One should try and understand the nature of Swamiji's western tapas in the light of above explanation. He had already created, through the eastern tapas, sufficiently strong currents to counter the power of Vishnu. It means that Swamiji had earned enough tapas power for the consciousness (of his devotees) to break loose from the ring of creation and be ready to move to the centre of brahman chakra. The tapas of the north and east thus prepared Swamiji to undertake the more arduous western tapas. The aim was to help devotees transform their subtle minds (i.e. the state achieved during the ascent of consciousness to brahman chakra) into their causal forms and their subsequent destruction. It might appear that the transformation of consciousness from subtle to causal should actually be assisted by Shiva since it conforms to his nature (of making it causal at the time of dissolution). But, it is not so because Shiva has to dissolve the world, including its objects, at some undetermined time in the future. An individual's attempt to subside the mind invites Shiva's wrath because it is being done prior to the time fixed for general dissolution. Swamiji did western tapas through the repetition of the mantra given by the divine Guru and he concentrated on the centre of brahman chakra whilst doing so. The mantra created strong pranic vibrations, which were more potent than Shiva's power. This gave Swamiji the power to help his devotees pull their minds away from the subtle phenomenon onto the centre of brahman chakra. Then, Swamiji concentrated on the Heart, which made the above power to descend to It. In other words, it helps the devotees to achieve manolaya. After that, Swamiji concentrated on the yogic flame and gained enough divine power to help devotees destroy their minds. Thus, Swamiji did the western tapas in the stages described above. The tapas lasted from 7th August 1955 to 25th June 1956 and Swamiji spent roughly a third of the time in each stage. Out of it, the last stage (of concentrating on the yogic flame) was the hardest.

Q74. What were Swamiji's experiences during the western tapas?

A74. Swamiji suffered the most during this phase of the tapas. His body was racked with pain, disease, incapacitation and extreme enervation. A brief account of some of the problems faced has already been touched upon. Swamiji encountered many threats and serious obstacles and would not have survived but for the Guru's grace. On 7th August 1955, after the Guru's departure, Swamiji had barely begun the repetition of the mantra, when he felt the rumbling of the earth, beneath his seat, as though a mighty and frightening earthquake was taking place and also that the earth was about to open up to devour him. Swamiji opened his eyes and found the hut swaying perilously. Swamiji was quite taken aback by this unexpected development and was wondering what to do when he was confronted by the god Shiva, who revealed his identity on enquiry (by sign language since Swamiji was observing silence) by Swamiji. Shiva's body was made up of fire, which flooded the room with a red glow. Swamiji could feel the heat emanating from him. He spoke to Swamiji as follows, 'look boy', he said, 'you are too young to know what you are doing and its harmful effects. You are embarking on a dangerous path. It can lead only to your destruction, as also of your family. Don't even begin the tapas; otherwise you will suffer its dire consequences; not only you but even your mother would pay for your ill-advised venture. Rest assured that you cannot succeed. Get up and go home; you do not know my power that permits no one to go against it. Take my warning seriously. If you do, I will grant you any boon that you want; otherwise, be prepared for a terrible time ahead'. There was a sudden surge of anger in Swamiji on hearing this threat and he wanted to tell Shiva that he accepted his challenge. But, he controlled himself when he remembered of the vow not to give up tapas, no matter what it takes to succeed. Ignoring Shiva, Swamiji promptly went into samadhi with the help of the mantra. Although the trinity of gods regards the Devi as its divine mother, yet Shiva conveyed to Swamiji's mother, in a dream, that his son's life was in danger. But, the Lord assured her of His protection. Swamiji's experience, related above, was localised to the room in which he was doing tapas. He saw the physical form of Shiva who looked a little like he is depicted in calendars. It became apparent very soon that he intended to carry out his evil intent and a series of painful events took place. Within a day of the commencement of the tapas, Swamiji was afflicted with severe stomach-ache, which continued off and on for a number of months. Swamiji also felt a burning sensation in the body, especially in the upper part, and the skin was badly discoloured. The cow that was supplying milk for Swamiji died suddenly. Its replacement did not last for more than two weeks. Swamiji developed an allergy to milk. He would throw it up the moment he took it. Finally, he gave up milk and went without any diet for a number of days till Horlicks was substituted in its place. Swamiji's mother fell ill which was a source of worry. The story of how Swamiji was bitten by an amber coloured snake during October 1955 has already been narrated. Almost till the end of January 1956, every time Swamiji went out for a bath at the well, during the mid-nightly break, the earth used to shake as he walked making it difficult to keep balance. The agni god (idea of fire in corporeal form or the embodied form of fire element) appeared in subtle form, one night in September 1955, and aroused Swamiji from samadhi by creating unbearable heat in the room. He warned Swamiji that the intensity of heat would increase if he persisted with his tapas. Swamiji, with utmost difficulty, ignored the agni god and the heat and hummed the sound of Omkar in consonance with the pulsation of the cosmic wave in the area of the diaphragm. It is a pranayamic exercises to control the universal prana. Although Swamiji had neither learnt nor practised pranayama, yet its knowledge existed in his prarabdhic memory that was activated on its own at that time. Its vibrations brought the room temperature to normal and Swamiji did not suffer the ill effects of this experience. After a few days, the wind god (the embodied form of the air element) tried to create havoc in the room. This happened around mid-day. Swamiji was lifted up in the air by about two to three feet and then suddenly left to drop down on the ground. It broke Swamiji's samadhi but he did not see the god. The most serious disturbance was caused by Kal (time), sometime in the third week of March 1956. After Swamiji had ignored its warnings, it started to disintegrate the basic elements that constitute the body. It did so by withdrawing the pranic forces that holds the basic elements together in the body. It was an extremely torturous experience, so bad, in fact, that Swamiji could not go back into samadhi, despite his best efforts. At times, Swamiji felt that his bones had been reduced to pulp and he could not see or hear for a day or so. His emaciated body was on the verge of collapse. It was then that Swamiji passed out and remained unconscious for about forty-eight hours. When he came to, he saw his Guru administering some water (amrit, the divine nectar) in his mouth. The Guru was extremely pleased with Swamiji's sense of purpose and advised him to carry on regardless. He reassured him of His protection and grace. The Guru told him that the worst is almost over and his troubles would end soon. Swamiji regained his strength soon after the Guru's visit. Swamiji was shaken by the above experience and decided that the only way to overcome the external interference was to remain in samadhi continuously without any break. The next night, he informed his mother and other members of the committee (set up to look after him) of his firm resolve. He told them not to disturb him under any circumstances till he either attains success in tapas or dies in the endeavour to do so. In the latter event, Swamiji's body was to be interred as per rites performed for yogis. This was communicated in sign language as Swamiji was still observing silence on the Guru's direction. Swamiji would make a sign and his mother or someone else would confirm their understanding of it through speech. In the dim light of the lantern (Swamiji's mother used to carry it during the visits at night), it took quite some time to convey the gist of what Swamiji proposed to do. Swamiji's mother was visibly upset and one or two members tried to change Swamiji's mind. But, Swamiji indicated to them to leave and soon passed into samadhi. Swamiji's Guru aroused him from it, one night, after ten days. He gave Swamiji a mantra to overcome the tapas power of Kal and told him, to start taking the glass of Horlicks again. The next day Swamiji's mother came to know that he had got up from samadhi when she met him near the well. She would come to see Swamiji two to three times a day to see that all was well. Swamiji indicated to her that he wanted Horlicks, which she quickly brought from the house. Swamiji did not have to repeat the mantra for long. On the night of 15th April 1956, Kal came and prostrated before Swamiji, just as he was about to get up for his daily bath. He sought Swamiji's blessings and promised full co-operation for his (Swamiji's) mission. It was an experience in the subtle plane. After that Swamiji did not face any more hurdles in the western tapas. There were, however, a few interferences of a minor nature. After Kal's visit, Swamiji reverted to the repetition of the original mantra given for the western direction. One night, in the second week of May, Swamiji was having a bath at the well when an old man accosted him and asked for some water. After quenching his thirst, the old man tried to engage Swamiji in a conversation by asking him his name and a few other questions. The man got quite angry when Swamiji replied in sign language and then he demanded that Swamiji see him off till his house in the village. On Swamiji's refusal, he caught hold of his left arm in a vice like grip to physically drag Swamiji to the village. On a sudden impulse, Swamiji delivered a hard blow on the old man's shoulder with his yoga danda (the wooden staff carried by yogis, which Sri Tapaswiji had given to Swamiji in 1951. He had also presented a kamandulu, a small vessel to carry water). It was enough to release Swamiji but the impact of the hit on the old man made Swamiji fall down because of the lack of energy in his body. By the time Swamiji recovered the old man had disappeared. Swamiji did not bother to find out who he was till his Guru, on His visit on 25th May, revealed to him that it was god Shiva. The latter wanted to physically highjack Swamiji in order to put an end to the tapas. Meneka, the goddess of seduction, tried to entice Swamiji on the night of 24th May. Swamiji was having a bath at the well when an exceedingly beautiful girl made a request (in Telugu) for water to drink. She was tall and alluring and wore a bright orange sari. She was not particularly fair. Swamiji ignored her when she tried to talk to him and made indecent gestures. The girl then walked away from the well but encountered Swamiji again when he was on his way back to his room. Playfully, she tried to block Swamiji's movement; again, she made lewd gestures and gave bewitching smiles. It was then that Swamiji realised who she was. Swamiji managed to bypass her but he saw her in the room, which was bathed with ethereal light emanating from her. As the girl broke into a sensuous dance, Swamiji quickly moved to his seat and passed off into samadhi by concentrating on the sound of Omkar. It was the last major obstacle that Swamiji faced during his entire tapas. Thereafter, Swamiji's health began to improve and he gained some of his vitality. Swamiji had a vision of the divine Guru on 25th May who expressed his happiness and appreciation at the way Swamiji had overcome the various hurdles. The Guru then told Swamiji to sit in continuous samadhi till Shankar Bhagwan roused him from it. That happened on 25th June 1956. Shankar Bhagwan was accompanied by Mother Parvati and they both looked radiantly beautiful, much more than in their earlier visions, and Swamiji could not take his eyes off them. He was wonderstruck with divine joy and experienced infinite bliss to see them. It took some time for Swamiji to recover from the supernatural sight. Both the divine Beings then conversed with Swamiji (as always in Telugu) for a few minutes. They told him that the most difficult part of the tapas was over and he could look forward to an easier period ahead. Bhagwan expressed his desire that Swamiji continue his tapas for another six years for which the Guru would give him further directions. It was in this manner that Swamiji brought to a successful conclusion (i.e. gained siddhi) the tapas of the western direction.

Q75. Did not the two eternal companions of Swamiji, mentioned in Answer 69, stop Kal and others from causing physical harm?
A75. The boys were extremely courageous and took on Kal fearlessly in a fierce fight to block him from physically touching Swamiji. It made Kal furious and he pronounced a curse on Swamiji, which led to the incidents described in the previous answer. He also cursed the boys who suffered for a number of years, even after Swamiji had left the world. The boys also made sure that neither fire god nor wind god nor Meneka come close to Swamiji. Incidentally, this was not the first encounter that Swamiji had with Meneka. She had come (in physical form) to disturb his tapas some days after the cobra bite in December 1949, related in Answer 50. At that time, she looked like a Brahmin girl of sixteen years or so and was radiantly beautiful. She was dressed in a white sari. It was a moonlit night and Swamiji had just sat down for tapas when she tried to attract his attention by singing a bawdy song in Telegu. Swamiji closed his eyes and passed into samadhi. It was then that one of boys assumed his gross body and picked her up and threw her in the canal. He threatened her with dire consequences if she returned. She withdrew but not before cursing him. She came again a couple of times but was chased away by the boys. The incident of god Shiva, related above was the only one when there was a physical assault on Swamiji. The clever Shiva came to know about the presence of the boys

with Swamiji through his yogic vision (kal in his pride did not bother to use his power to discover them). He, therefore, sent some nymphs to keep them busy while he tackled Swamiji. It were the boys who ultimately forced Shiva to withdraw from the scene after Swamiji had hit him with the stick. Both the boys did great service to Swamiji throughout the tapas.

Q76. Swamiji saw a vision of Ishwara (God) in the form of Sri Shankar Bhagwan and also saw the god Shiva. Popular opinion regards them as being the same. Was there a difference in their appearance? How could such an experiences arise when Swamiji had already destroyed his mind?

A76. Swamiji had the above experiences through his prarabdhic (i.e. it exists due to present life's karma) memory. Although the mind had ceased to be, yet the memory of the prarabdha karma (the experiences that the body had to undergo) remained intact in pure form in the general consciousness. In fact, Swamiji's entire tapas and the subsequent life were only an unfolding of his prarabdha karma. Shankar Bhagwan is a form of the infinite Ishwara whereas god Shiva represents only one aspect (i.e. of dissolution) of Ishwara's limitless powers. They, thus, differ in their characteristics and divine power. The differences arise because the relative consciousness (of Reality) has two different ideas in it; one of the limitless Ishwara and the other of the finite god of destruction. Their relationship is similar to that exists between a limitless ocean and a drop of its water. The manifestation of these ideas, like all other notions of the consciousness, in tangible form takes place in the reflecting surface of maya, as discussed in Chapter 2. However, a seer sees the reflection through the prism of his or her samaskaras that are superimposed on the consciousness. In other words, an idea is concretised to fulfil one's desires (vasnas) and, therefore, its perception varies accordingly. Gross objects appear similar to all jivas because their commonness is inherent in their ideas (objects are formed from them) held in the divine consciousness, which is reflected in every individual's mind. Although the above is applicable to the subtle and causal spheres for the same reason, yet an embodied jiva does not perceive them similarly due to mental extroversion. The memory of normal gross sensual perception overshadows, due to its superimposition on the consciousness, the sameness of subtle and causal objects when their cognition arises in yogic practice (sadhana). In simpler words, the subtle and causal objects appear, during spiritual experience, in the light of one's sensual experience of the gross world. Ishwara, gods, goddess's etc. have no particular form. They are seen in visions according to what one imagines them to be. That is why they are said to be a creation of the mind. Each seer sees them differently. Usually, they are seen in the form in which they are worshipped. Swamiji saw Shankar Bhagwan and the god Shiva in almost similar forms because they existed like that in his prarabdhic memory, which was formed during visits to temples.

Swamiji was not discriminative enough before his tapas; as such, he did not make any distinction between Ishwara and other gods. He did not, for example, know the difference between the infinite God and a finite god. That is why Swamiji saw them looking alike. However, there is a very vital difference between the two forms. Shankar Bhagwan's divine luminosity and brilliance is incomparable and matchless. It is so great that even billions of suns appear like its pale shadow. The god, Shiva, on the other hand, is just like the sun that we see everyday. However, Swamiji's power of discrimination had reached the absolute level during tapas and on that account he could know instinctively the nature of the form that appeared before him. Thus, Swamiji enquired about Shankar Bhagwan's identity, on 28th October 1953, only to confirm what he felt deep within him.

Q77. How can aspirants draw such fine distinctions between the visions of Ishwara and gods during their spiritual experience? Is there no way one can make out the difference in such visions?
A77. One should learn to reject all such experiences as false rather than getting involved in trying to establish the identity of such apparitions. That is the best course of action. However, in the advanced stages of lower samadhi (bhava and savikalpa) the knowledge of the form seen in a vision arises on its own in the consciousness. The vision of Ishwara, in any of Its forms, is blindingly dazzling. No god or goddess can match its radiance (tejas). One can know the difference only through repeated experience in the light of one's power of discrimination.

Q78. What was the tapas of the southern direction like? How did it go?
A78. It was the most blissful period of Swamiji's tapas. His entire being was saturated and drowned in divine joy, which is hard to describe. Swamiji began the southern tapas on the night of 26 June 1956 when the Guru gave a special mantra for it. The uniqueness of the mantra was that Swamiji remembered and worshipped the Devi (embodied form of supreme power in female gender), who dwells in the south, in all Her beneficence. The Devi has innumerable aspects; wrathful, terrible, destructive, protective, boon giver, wish fulfiller, embodiment of divine power, repository of divine knowledge, sustainer (like a mother), source of love and bliss and so on. Although one can approach Her in any aspect, yet it is best to avoid doing so through non-beneficent ones. One has to follow a very severe and hard discipline, involving many elaborate rites, to please Her in the wrathful or terrible aspects. It is time consuming and may even turn out to be dangerous for an aspirant. Many tantrics (followers of tantra) try and do it but most of them end up achieving nothing worthwhile. Swamiji's mantra expressed his love for the Divine Mother and sought Her blessings. The Devi was pleased with Swamiji and gave Her darshan (vision)

on 7th August 1956. Swamiji was roused from samadhi, around 9 o'clock that night, by the brilliance of an unearthly light, which penetrated the core of his being. It was extraordinarily dazzling and very, very peaceful. It sent Swamiji into divine ecstasy of pure love. He felt as though his body was melting in the infinitely blissful glow of that marvelous light which pervaded not only the room but also the area around it. Then, in a flash the Devi appeared in physical form and Swamiji knew instantly that She was Durga Devi. Swamiji was initially dumbfounded to see such a captivating, beautiful and benign form. She did not look like Her image seen in temples nor was she riding a tiger. Dressed in a white sari, She was of medium height with an ivory complexion and exuded divine love. She blessed Swamiji by putting Her hand on his head and asked if he knew who She was. Swamiji nodded his head but indicated that he could not talk because he was observing silence. Visibly pleased with the answer She enquired from Swamiji about the many hardships that he had faced during the tapas. Swamiji narrated (in sign language) all that had happened in the tapas and the Mother was extremely solicitous about Swamiji's welfare. She told Swamiji, My child, you will have no problems now. I shall look after you and protect you from all evil forces. You have much hard work to do for Me, which your Guru will reveal later. For the present continue with tapas. Do you need anything? On Swamiji's saying no (by moving his head) She gave Her blessings and walked out of the room. The ethereal light persisted even after the Mother's departure. She stayed with Swamiji for nearly an hour. Swamiji's heart overflowed with the bliss of divine love after the above experience and he remained immersed in it till it was time for his nightly ablutions at the well. The divine light enveloped Swamiji for quite some time even after the bath and he bathed in its glow. It was a wonderful experience and Swamiji felt a heavenly peace within. The Mother gave Her darshan twice again. Once in February 1957, and the second time at the end of April 1957. They were both brief visits. The Mother told Swamiji, on her last visit, that he had attained the siddhi of the southern direction but he should continue his tapas till the darshan of Shankar Bhagwan. She also said, ` On completion of tapas, offer one thousand and eight coconuts to each direction.' Accordingly, Swamiji warned his mother and other members of the committee to arrange for the coconuts. Swamiji sat in continuous tapas till 18 May 1957 when he had darshan of Shankar Bhagwan. The Lord expressed His pleasure at the unflinching devotion displayed by Swamiji during tapas. He pronounced Swamiji a yogi since he had completed tapas of all the four directions. The divine Guru appeared a little later and told Swamiji that he could break the vow of silence (mauna) on the following day and further instructions would follow after that. He also told Swamiji that he could meet people the next day and act on the instructions given by the Divine Mother.

Q79. Swamiji's tapas came to an end on 7th August 1961. Kindly complete its story after the visit of the Guru on 18 May 1957.

A79. Swamiji had effectively completed tapas of the four directions on 18 May 1957. He had not, however, been given any instruction for the future. On 19th May 1957, a small number of people (mostly from the village) assembled near the tapas room. Around 7 o'clock (in the evening) Swamiji came out of it and the ceremonial offering of coconuts began thereafter. They were offered to the various directions (i.e. symbolic of God's all pervasiveness) in the same order as Swamiji's tapas i.e. east, north, west and then south. A few women present there sang some sacred hymns. The ad-hoc kirtan (devotional singing) was rendered after the rite for the offering of coconuts had been completed for each direction. The ceremony was gone through till midnight when Swamiji broke his vow of silence by chanting Omkar for about 30 minutes or so. Swamiji then stayed with his mother and assembled people for some time. That night and the next day, Swamiji rested by being totally absorbed in the infinitely blissful sound of Omkar. The next night, Swamiji had darshan of his Guru who blessed him for successful completion of the tapas. He told Swamiji to continue tapas, for another four years, facing the east. Swamiji was to do tapas for twelve hours a day (4 am to 4 pm). The rest of the time was to be devoted for the darshan of the devotees (4 pm to midnight), ablutions, bath, rest etc. (midnight to 4 am). The Guru advised Swamiji to have milk and fruit diet twice (before and after tapas) a day. The divine Guru authorised Swamiji to initiate aspirants on the path of yoga during the darshan period. However, the Guru made it clear that the grace (of initiation) was not to be denied to anyone, irrespective of caste, creed, race, gender, nationality, and other man made differences. After the Guru had finished giving directions, Swamiji, on a sudden impulse, asked the Guru to reveal His identity; on being asked who he thought He was, Swamiji replied, 'although you look like Shankar Bhagwan minus His divine glow, yet you appear more like a member of the Jangam Devars. Is that right'? The Guru was rather amused at Swamiji's query and replied that he would clarify his doubt at the end of the twelve years tapas. Swamiji continued with the tapas as directed by the Guru. The next four years passed off peacefully and Swamiji's health improved considerably. Swamiji did not face any problems during the second phase of the eastern tapas since the god Vishnu had already (after the first four years) submitted to him. Vishnu, in fact, fully co-operated with Swamiji this time and many of his minions (lesser gods and goddess) sought Swamiji's blessings in order to work for him (in performance of the divine mission). A notable experience that Swamiji had during this phase of tapas concerned Ravana. He is the chief of demons (of a particular type) and is the embodied form of wickedness, in the pair of opposites of virtue and evil. In January 1958, he appeared (in gross form) before Swamiji, one night, and, after doing namaskara (greeting), said, `O! Lord, just as your nature is to uphold virtue, mine is to create disturbance for those who follow the path of truth. I take birth whenever you do to fulfil my nature. Bless me to play my role in the divine drama.' Swamiji then conversed with him for a few minutes after which he went away. The form of Ravana that Swamiji saw was at least six feet tall, well built and fair complexioned. He had a regal bearing and his face had luminosity (tejas). The only conclusion that Swamiji could draw from the above experience was that evil would increase in the world and it would have to be put down by virtuous people. Another experience of a similar nature was the subtle vision of the Kali Devi in Her wrathful aspect. Swamiji saw Her in the second week of June 1958. She was dark to look at and had blood shot eyes. Swamiji did namaskara to Her and the Devi said, ` I am pleased with your devotion. Some evil-minded people would want to harm you after your tapas is over. Be rest assured they will meet a just end from Me.' Apart from the above experiences, Swamiji also received assurances of support (for the divine mission) from many other gods and goddesses. Swamiji used this period of tapas to evolve a procedure for initiation of devotees. Swamiji initiated about ten people from Adivarpupetta on the day following the divine Guru's directions, given above. Initially, Swamiji used to initiate devotees himself in the tapas room but as the word spread to the neighbouring villages and towns their number swelled beyond the capacity of the room. Sometimes, the number of prospective aspirants would be between two to three hundred or even more. It was then that Swamiji evolved the system of deputing one of his close devotees to initiate aspirants. Swamiji would bless such a person to impart his power (only for the day of initiation) to others. Around the middle of 1958, Swamiji began the distribution of vibhuti (consecrated clump of clay) when a large number of people started requesting him for blessings to solve their health and other personal problems. In the beginning, Swamiji had not fixed any time limit for doing meditation (dhyana) in his presence after the initiation. Some people would sit for a few minutes whereas others would carry on for an hour or so. But, even then, Swamiji made it a practice that anyone who came for initiation should participate in kirtan (devotional singing) and only then could they talk to him. Some devotees began to exhibit signs of bhava (mood of devotion induced by the subtle presence of a deity) a week after Swamiji had started to give initiation. Its novelty became a talk of the villagers and it resulted in people coming for Swamiji's darshan in thousands. On Swamiji's mother's suggestion, it was decided by the committee organised to look after him to celebrate the days on which Swamiji sat for tapas (7th August) and his birthday (24th January). To this Swamiji added Shivratri, a day in February/ March devoted to the worship of Lord Shiva. Tapas day was first celebrated in 1959 and the other occasions in 1960. Traditional rituals accompanied by prayers and kirtan were performed during the celebrations. Swamiji also introduced mass feeding of the devotees on all these days. Thus, the genesis of what Swamiji did after completion of tapas was laid during the period May 1957 to August 1961. Swamiji's work began on a small scale and it evolved gradually on its own without any preconceived notions of doing this or that. With the coming in of devotees in large numbers, Swamiji was kept quite occupied and it did not take long for the last four years to pass. From the beginning of 1961, Swamiji had begun to lose interest in the meagre diet that he was taking. He stopped taking fruit and even the glass of milk was consumed occasionally, after a gap of a few days. The time spent in samadhi was increased to sixteen hours or more. From February onwards Swamiji stopped giving initiation and did not go out of the tapas room except for his midnightly bath. However, devotees were permitted to do kirtan for one hour around the time of sunset. By end of May 1961, Swamiji was so overcome by the power of Silence, in which he was established, that he sat in continuous samadhi throughout the months of June and July. Sometimes in the third week of July, the Guru revealed that the tapas would formally end on 7 August. On the midnight of 1 August 1961, Swamiji had darshan of the divine Guru when he aroused him from samadhi. The Guru gave a bewitching smile when Swamiji did namaskara (i.e. greeted) to Him. He inquired from Swamiji, `how do you feel, now that your tapas is coming to a close'. Swamiji replied, ` I had sat in tapas by your grace. It is your divine grace, which has brought me to this stage. I do not seek the fruits of tapas and I surrender them at your lotus feet. Be gracious to accept them.' The Guru was visibly pleased with Swamiji's answer. The Guru then told Swamiji that since he had a doubt about Him, He would reveal His identity and asked him to look at His form intently. He had barely finished speaking when a lightening flash issued from His body. Momentarily, Swamiji was blinded by the dazzlingly brilliant light but recovered soon enough to see the marvelously snow white form of Shankar Bhagwan who was accompanied by the divine Mother in the form of Parvati. The doubt about the Guru's identity had arisen because, apart from His height and dark complexion, He resembled the form of Shankar Bhagwan that Swamiji had seen during the tapas. Swamiji was thrilled to no end by the above experience. Shankar Bhagwan and Mother Parvati then sat down on the platform on which Swamiji was sitting. They chatted with him for some time and complimented him on his devotion to his Guru and unwavering faith in His word. Bhagwan then told Swamiji that he could from then on act on his own with total freedom. Swamiji's answer was that he had no particular desire to do anything and would do whatever his Guru willed. After that, Shankar Bhagwan said, ` If you have a wish, it will be granted. You can ask for anything now.' Swamiji declined to ask for anything. The Guru was delighted with the above replies and said, 'My son, I am most pleased that you have attained siddhi (success), in kaliyuga (the current age), of the most sublime and difficult form of yoga (i.e. tapas yoga). It would inspire generations of devotees in the future. It would forever remain a watershed in the spiritual history of the world. You have set an unique example of a disciple's love for his Guru and the desireless manner in which He should be served. Go forth now and re-establish dharma (the moral law based on truth) in the world in which selfishness abounds. Display the same resoluteness in your endeavour, as you did in tapas. You will succeed despite many difficulties. For this purpose, awaken the latent spirituality in all those who seek your grace. Teach them how to control their minds through the power of absolute Silence. Do not confine yourself to any known religion, dogma or ritual nor should you propagate them. Accept them all as equally good. Let the devotees progress according to their own creedal beliefs. You may accept worship from them. Let your ashramas (centres to propagate the mission) be free from any ill will or prejudice. Develop them as centres of love and service. You may initiate aspirants on any path. Not only that, you may also initiate disciples on the path of tapas yoga. Give solace to all those who are sick in spirit and body. Anyone you bless will have My blessings. You may grant liberation to anyone you please. Any devotee of yours who displays even one hundredth of your zeal (during the tapas) would attain automatic salvation. Henceforth, be known in the world as Sivabala Yogeshwara and you will have the power of Mahakal (Destroyer of time). My blessings are always with you and I shall give further directions for your mission from time to time'. After Shankar Bhagwan had finished speaking, the divine Mother said, 'My child, you had to endure a lot of suffering because Kal and others had cursed you, which could imperil the success of your mission. I will take birth now to undo the evil effects of the mischief done by Kal. The latter regards Me as his Mother and My mere presence in the world would mitigate all that he has done. Rest assured of My protection and love'. On hearing these wonderful words, Swamiji was astounded and overwhelmed with great love for the Lord and the divine Mother. Regaining his composure Swamiji prostrated before Shankar Bhagwan and Mother Parvati and addressed them, 'O Lord! O Mother! I had no desire to come into this world. It was your divine will that brought me here. Tapas was done on your command and I was able to go through it entirely by your grace. My sole desire is to fulfil your will. As you order, so shall it be. But, for that, I pray for your continued grace and protection for my devotees.' They departed after assuring Swamiji that they dwell in his heart and would always look after him and his devotees. It was an infinitely blissful experience and for a long time that night Swamiji felt its marvelous effect. The next few days were spent in rest and preparation for the ceremonial celebrations, on 7th August, for completion of twelve years of tapas. Swamiji had become quite weak due to the lack of diet during the continuous samadhi for the last two months. Nevertheless, he spent the whole of 7th August, from 8 am onwards with his devotees, who numbered almost three hundred thousand. Apart from some religious rites, kirtan was performed throughout the day. Mass feeding of devotees started around mid-day and finished late at night. It was around midnight that Swamiji went to his tapas room for rest. Although Swamiji had taken frequent breaks (for rest) during the day, yet he was quite tired by the end of it. Swamiji then rested for the whole night. Thus concluded the twelve years tapas of Swamiji. What has been revealed here is only a gist of some major experiences that he had during that period. Swamiji has done this only with one purpose and that is to inspire aspirants to ponder over his quest and draw suitable lessons from it for their spiritual advancement.

Q80. What are the suitable lessons, which would benefit the devotees?
A80. It is for aspirants to deduce what they ought to learn from Swamiji's tapas. Swamiji does not want to say anything more on the subject except make some general remarks. A spiritual quest can bear fruit only through determined self-effort and divine grace. There are always ups and downs in one's practice (sadhana). That is but natural because it is all a play of the mind, which plays tricks according to one's samaskaras and vasnas. There are many times when one gets fed up, as Swamiji did on a few occasions, because of external factors (part of one's karma) or lack of apparent progress. It is then that one's resolution to go ahead assumes crucial importance and one should learn to be ruthless with mind's whims and fancies. Such determination is invariably rewarded with divine grace. Devotees must have total faith in themselves and in the guru. Doubts always crop up when this or that does not happen. Be certain it is not the guru's fault. It is the weakness of one's own mind or part of one's karma. Be equally certain that divine grace manifests only when one is ready for it. Swamiji realised very early (i.e. during the first three or four months) in the tapas that devotion to his Guru was going to be the single most important factor to reach his goal. Swamiji loved the Guru and did tapas as a service to Him in a spirit of self-surrender and without any desire.

Q81. Swamiji went through unimaginable sufferings during the tapas and faced many serious obstacles. Many aspirants may apprehend similar problems for themselves. Would their fears be justified?
A81. The answer is a big NO. The precise reason for Swamiji's tapas was to remove difficulties that his devotees might encounter during their practice. Swamiji would consider his tapas a failure if any aspirant initiated by him was to face any problem of the type that he did. Swamiji's tapas protects his devotees from all dangers and they are certain to have a smooth passage till the end. Swamiji wants to assure his devotees that they need to entertain no

misapprehensions about such matters. All that Swamiji asks his devotees is to do meditation regularly and sincerely. Swamiji will take care of any hurdles that might arise in it.

Q82. What did Swamiji attain at the end of his tapas? What was his state and its experience?
A82. Swamiji had not set out to accomplish anything during the tapas. He merely followed his Guru's directions and surrendered his self to Him. Swamiji is, therefore, not aware of any achievement as such. The main events of tapas have been related previously and readers may draw their own conclusions about it by using their power of discrimination. As for Swamiji's state is concerned, there was no change in it after the first hour of the commencement of tapas. Swamiji was then established in the supreme state of inexpressible Silence and remained in it throughout his life. All actions of Swamiji, after the first hour, took place due to his prarabdhic memory, as explained in Answer 76. Swamiji's awareness of his actions and his surroundings was akin to the memory of a forgotten dream. Everything happened on its own without Swamiji's participation. What is it that exists in the Voidless Void? The experience of the state of Silence cannot be put in words and, hence, it is not possible to describe it.

Q83. Swamiji has described his state, during the tapas, as of being in samadhi. Could you kindly elaborate a little on it?
A83. The answer to the above question can be known only in the Silence of one's heart. It is a waste of effort to try and understand a transcendental (i.e. beyond the mind) spiritual state through the intellect. Aspirants are advised to meditate as much as they can and they would have all their queries answered in it.

Q84. How could Swamiji have the experiences, narrated above, when his mind had ceased to be? Were they all subjective in nature? For example, what was the source of the dazzling divine light that formed the body of Shankar Bhagwan?
A84. It was briefly discussed in Answer 10 of Chapter 4 of this work that all spiritual experiences are basically subjective and take place due to one's samaskaric vasnas (deep rooted desires formed from samaskaras or mental impressions). Swamiji's experiences are no exception to this rule and they occurred due to his prarabdha (present life's) karma. Just as a person established in the Reality continues to have sensual experience (according to one's samaskaric memory) till the body lasts, so does he or she sees visions etc. in the same manner. The divine light emanates from the yogic flame (or the conditioned Heart) and the Lord is its embodied form.

Q85. The account of Swamiji's tapas reads like an ancient tale from Puranas (books written in ancient times; they elaborate teachings difficult to understand by illustrating them in story forms). A modern minded reader may find it hard to believe it. What would be a more rational explanation of the tapas and the various problems that he had faced in it?

A85. The sufferings that Swamiji underwent in tapas represents the evil effects of samaskaras and vasnas (mental impressions and desires) of his devotees (i.e. those who had fully or partially surrendered to him in the past). They had accumulated them over innumerable previous lives and were to discharge them in their present or future lives. Some of their worst aspects were or are to be expiated in this dark age (kaliyuga). Swamiji did the tapas to work out the most harmful part of their prarabdha (current life's)karma and to that extent it would be easier for the aspirants to traverse the spiritual path. Swamiji has not only removed the bodily afflictions of many of his devotees but has also empowered them, through the act of initiation, to introvert their minds. Swamiji gained this power through tapas. The divine consciousness manifests as the world when its clockwise vibrations, induced by maya, are reflected in it. By doing tapas, Swamiji had created sufficient quantity of anti-clockwise pulsations, in the consciousness, for the devotees to detach themselves from the objective world and introvert their minds. For that to happen, seekers are required to attach their minds, through meditation, to the power that Swamiji gives at the time of initiation. The clockwise and anti-clockwise vibrations represent the ignorance and wisdom (or knowledge) aspects of the consciousness. Thus, Swamiji's did tapas to gain the power of divine knowledge, which would destroy individual ignorance of his devotees. Knowledge and ignorance are ideas of a contrary nature. An ignorant mind is characterised by extroversion caused by its own inherent centrifugal force and supplemented by individual samaskaras. It is but natural for the latter to resist when it is sought to be controlled by its countervailing centripetal force that lies dormant in every individual mind and which is activated by the knowledge that a guru imparts. This is the real nature of impediments that one faces in practice. Swamiji encountered major hurdles because he was trying to control the centrifugal force of the cosmic mind for a large number of devotees. The imagery of gods (i.e. Kal, Brahma, Vishnu, Shiva etc.), drawn earlier, is meant to explain this basic phenomenon and is used to make instruction simpler for ease of understanding. In a state of duality, existence of gods etc. appears to be as real as one's own individuality and both represent embodiment of ignorance. The obstacles that Kal (time) and other gods interposed on Swamiji's path should, in the rational sense, be understood to imply the difficulties that one encounters in overcoming ignorance. The trinity (of gods) has been charged by the divine will to create the sensual phenomenon and then perpetuate it in a cycle of sustenance and dissolution followed by recreation in the matrix of time (kal). They are thus duty bound to create hurdles for yogis to prevent them from granting liberation to jivas. They submit only to the divine power of the Lord who indulges in Its sport (of creating seeming bondage and freedom for individuals) for Its pleasure. Swamiji faced more problems because he was doing tapas for the collective benefit of many aspirants, unlike an individual devotee who does sadhana (practice) for his or her own self. Incidentally, one should not imagine that Puranic events could take place only in the ancient times. Such a view betokens a closed mind that cannot appreciate that the divine play takes place according to Ishwara's inscrutable will, which regards the division of time into past, present and future as of no relevance. Divine scheme of things has its own logic, which exists in the Puranas also, provided one reads them with discrimination. A modern mind is open to fresh ideas and is discriminative. One should reflect over Swamiji's tapas in that light.

Q86. Swamiji was given mantras to repeat by the divine Guru. How could he do that when he was in the highest state of samadhi most of the time? How did Swamiji gain their powers?

A86. The root of every mantra lies in its idea in the pure consciousness. A mantra is repeated in order to purify the individual mind and attain its ideation form in the relative consciousness. Swamiji would do mental repetition of a mantra for less than a minute and he would pass off into samadhi. Swamiji's prarabdhic consciousness (i.e. his memory) was then automatically concentrated on the pure idea of the mantra in the divine consciousness. The power of mantra accrued in Swamiji's prarabdhic consciousness as long as it was concentrated on its root. Its siddhi (complete empowerment) was attained when Swamiji had gained sufficient power for purposes of his mission.

Q87. Swamiji's Guru had told him to counter the power of the trinity of gods (Brahma, Vishnu, and Shiva) during his tapas. Was it neutralised totally?

A87. The trinity represents ignorance in general in an embodied form. Its power cannot be countered completely because it has earned it due to divine will to last for a certain fixed time cycle. That is the period for which the present universe will remain in existence. Tapas done by yogis is for a specific mission and is meant primarily to help aspirants to attain liberation. In other words, tapas, being an individual act, removes ignorance in particular for a certain number of people. Total neutralisation of the power of trinity would imply destruction of ignorance in general, which would be contrary to the divine scheme of things. A yogi performs tapas to counter the power of trinity for a limited purpose. The same is true of Swamiji tapas.

Q88. How did the repetition of mantras counter the power of trinity (of Brahma etc.)? Swamiji had mentioned in a previous answer that he had also practised some other yogic techniques during tapas. What did they involve?

A88. The trinity of gods had acquired its tapas power through repetition of mantras and practice of certain yogic disciplines to control prana in the consciousness (i.e. to extrovert it by creating clockwise motion in it). These mantras were revealed to Brahma, Vishnu and Shiva during their tapas by the divine guru. The power of a given mantra can be countered by a contrary mantra that is more potent than the former. The Lord (i.e. divine guru) revealed to Swamiji the counter mantras and their repetition created contrary (i.e. anti-clockwise) vibrations to render the trinity's power ineffective (to the extent required for Swamiji's mission). The power of a mantra increases when its repetition is combined with the practice of tapas yoga facing various directions. Another method adopted by Swamiji was to control the cosmic prana, whose vibration is felt in the region of the diaphragm. Swamiji achieved success in it by synchronising the flow of prana with the naturally existing rhythmic pulsations of Omkar at a cosmic level. It is a special yogic technique for which a yogi needs initiation by the divine guru. More effective than these methods was the yogic technique to control the divine power (ad shakti) to employ it effectively for the benefit of devotees. For this purpose, Swamiji used to concentrate prarabdhic consciousness (i.e. the memory of his prarabdha karma that had been destroyed) on the divine flame to empower it for transmission to aspirants. The divine power given to seekers, during initiation, sharpens their intelligence and strengthens their minds. Swamiji's bhava leela (the technique of imparting instruction, in silence, without physical interaction between the Guru and a disciple) took place due to this power.

Q89. Did Swamiji practice all the above methods for each cardinal direction? How did he know which technique to adopt during various stages of the tapas? A89. Swamiji was revealed and, in fact, initiated to practise the above methods by the divine guru. Swamiji spent most of the time to exercise control over the divine power and a little less on restraining prana. Repetition of mantras was done for the least time. Swamiji did that for each direction and there was no set procedure to divide the time amongst the three yogic techniques. It was all done on the instructions of Shankar Bhagwan who would tell Swamiji what was to be done during tapas of each direction. Sometimes, He would ask Swamiji to change his method after the tapas of a particular direction had begun. In general, Swamiji would begin tapas of a direction with repetition of the given mantra for a few days and then practise control of prana for some weeks. He would always end the tapas (of a direction) with concentration on the divine flame. It has been related earlier that Swamiji had sat for continuous samadhi for a few months in various phases of the tapas. All that was done in the blissful glow of the divine flame (i.e. a yogi becomes part of it).

Q90. How is it that Swamiji sanctioned the worship of Brahma, Vishnu and Shiva, despite their opposition to his tapas and the fact they are agents of ignorance?

A90. The question of antagonism between two forces arises from an egocentric point of view. The intellect tries to rationalize actions that take place in the divine sport according to its own limitations. But, in a state of non-mind concepts like enmity lose their meaning. While in tapas, Swamiji did not feel that the trinity was interposing any obstacles. The gods were merely acting according to their nature and so was Swamiji. He saw his own tapas and the opposition of the trinity as part of the divine play. Swamiji did not feel that Brahma, Vishnu, Shiva and Kal were apart from him. Notwithstanding the above explanation, all gods and goddesses have to act according to their natures even if they are Self Realised. They acted the way they did in Swamiji's tapas to fulfil their duties laid down by the divine will. They reveal knowledge of their natures if they are worshipped with devotion. It is really a play of the mind (i.e. its own creation); it encounters no problems from the trinity as long as it acts within its ambit. Any attempt to break out of it completely is resisted by it because that is its nature. Worship of Brahma and others cannot release one from ignorance but it has value as a preliminary practice, which was brought out in the earlier instruction also. Some people in India are habituated to worship the trinity and Swamiji encouraged them to continue with it as a means to express their devotion.

Q91. Cobras bit Swamiji a few times during the tapas. A number of other saints have similar experiences. How is it that cobras (nags) have so much association with yogis?

A91. The path of yoga, in its elementary form, is associated with the arousal of the kundalini shakti (it empowers the subtle mind after one learns to exercise some degree of self-control through practise of a spiritual discipline) in the subtle body. For purposes of teaching, this power is said to be dormant in ordinary jivas, just like a serpent in hibernation lies coiled up. The subtle power of kundalini exists in all forms of life but remains latent in them. Apart from human beings, it becomes active the most in nags (cobras) when they come out of hibernation or at the time they spread their hoods to strike jivas. It happens involuntarily but for a temporary duration. It is almost akin to the phenomenon that takes place in human beings when kundalini awakens due to spiritual effort. The mind has been conditioned to associate the kundalini power with snakes and, hence, one has their experience when it awakens. A cobra is feared because of its poison, which is symbolic of all that is evil and painful. The association of serpents with yogis exists because there is a natural unfelt attraction between two objects whose subtle bodies are empowered by kundalini. There is a karmic connection between a snake and a person bitten by it. The former accumulates poison to repay others for the pain it had suffered previously from them. It is a natural consequence of the cause and effect of the law of karma. A yogi has no karma of his own but has assumed that of his devotees. A yogi accepts the poison of a cobra for the sake of devotees in order to mitigate their suffering.

Q92. Even Swamiji's Guru, Sri Shankar Bhagwan, is depicted in images etc. with a cobra around his neck. What does that signify?

A92. Swamiji's Guru is the formless Ishwara (God). The Lord can be depicted in any form in an image or a picture to fulfil the needs of an aspirant. That is a creation of the mind. The Lord appears to a devotee in whatever form He is worshipped. Swamiji saw Shankar Bhagwan with a cobra around His neck because his family worshipped him in that form. The depiction of Shankar Bhagwan with a cobra is based on an ancient legend given in one of the Puranas. It is meant to convey that He takes on Himself the poisonous effects of the karma of those of his devotees who worship and love Him. Also, in teaching, maya is said to be like a venomous cobra but it is a power of the Lord that does not affect It but is poisonous for only those who are blind (ignorant) enough to be bitten by it. Maya (represented by a cobra) serves the Lord but is the reigning queen of the ignorant.

Q93. Many may regard the above explanations as mumbo-jumbo. Can such view be rationalised?

A93. The instruction given above falls within the realm of relative knowledge. The mind has limitless aspects and its experiences are equally so. What one considers as mumbo-jumbo may appear as perfectly normal to another. Such is the nature of relative knowledge and those who have grasped this vital point view the phenomenal world and its experience as mumbo-jumbo. What is there to rationalise in a false appearance? Notwithstanding the above, those who question Swamiji's experience are advised to learn to control their minds. Only then would they be able to judge its veracity. What can be more logical than the law of karma which says that as one sows, so shall one reap? Evil deeds bring pain to their doers. Such suffering may take any form. A snakebite is just like any other karma that one has to undergo to pay for some misdeed done in the past. The guru absolves devotees of all the harmful effects of their karma by assuming their suffering on himself or herself. Such is the power of grace and self-surrender. Even in the field of relativity, the law of karma is not hocus pocus, though to some it may appear so due to limited understanding.

Q94. Tapaswiji Maharaj had Swamiji's darshan (i.e. meeting with him) in January 1951. He is reported to have said that he had come to know through his spiritual knowledge that Swamiji was Jesus Christ in one of his earlier incarnations and later as Sri Chand, Guru Nanak's son, whose disciple he (i.e. Tapaswiji) was in the previous life. Is that true? What was Swamiji's impression of him?

A94. Swamiji has no comment to make on what an individual's spiritual experience reveals. Swamiji was struck by Tapaswiji's imposing appearance and although he had renounced being a prince a long time back (he was already more than 180 years old when he met Swamiji) yet he looked like one and deported himself accordingly. He would talk to Swamiji through one of his Telegu devotees. Swamiji accepted his offer of service because it was made in a spirit of love and sincerity. Swamiji was at that time too deeply involved in tapas to know if Tapaswiji had a past connection with him. Swamiji is indeed indebted to him for his service, specially for his advice on taking milk, during a difficult phase of the tapas. (Guruprasad's Note. On being told, in 1988, by Gurprasad that he saw a vision and also had a dream in which Swamiji appeared as Jesus Christ, Swamiji merely replied, Tapaswiji had a similar experience. But, a couple of years later, in a conversation about divine retribution for those who betray holy sages, Gurprasad asked Swamiji casually, what punishment did Judas get; his answer was, 'Swamiji forgave him'. Swamiji often talked to Gurprasad about him being Guru Nanak's son. He said once that he would like to go to Pakistan. On being asked why, he replied, 'so that Swamiji could see his old place of birth').

Q95. Swamiji was given the surya (sun) mantra by Tapaswiji Maharaj in October 1952. Although Swamiji's Guru approved of him doing its japa (repetition), yet He changed it a little. Why was it so? Did Swamiji regard Tapaswiji as his guru, since he accepted his (i.e. Tapaswiji's) initiation?

A95. Swamiji had only one Guru whose embodied form was Shankar Bhagwan. Tapaswiji had a past karmic connection with Swamiji. He had a desire in his mind to help Swamiji in his tapas. Tapaswiji had an experience, sometime in the middle of 1952, in which he felt that impartation of the surya mantra to Swamiji would benefit the latter. Swamiji was going through a tough phase in his tapas then and, he, therefore, decided to repeat the mantra after Tapaswiji explained its beneficial effects. The mantra given by him was incomplete because some words were missing in it. He had given it from memory and the Guru corrected it and told Swamiji to do its japa for two hours daily. Tapaswiji had not given the mantra in guru bhava (in the form of a guru). Rather, he was trying to repay a karmic debt and Swamiji had accepted it in that mode.

Q96. Why did Swamiji repeat the surya (sun) mantra? What benefit was it supposed to give?

A96. Surya (sun) should not be confused with the physical sun seen by the eyes. There are billions of such suns in the universe. All of them are a gross appearance of the heat and light principles (or ideas) inherent in Reality. The nascent manifestation of these ideas is the yogic flame described in Answer 54, Chapter 4. Surya in the causal and subtle sense refers to the divine flame, which is the source of relative knowledge. The mantra given by Tapaswiji related to the gross and subtle aspect of surya whereas the one given by the divine Guru took Swamiji directly to the yogic flame in its causal aspect (i.e. its nascent reflection is satoguna of maya). Swamiji derived many benefits from the surya mantra. The chief of these was that Swamiji's causal and subtle bodies were tempered in surya's yogic heat, which made them fit for the rigours of the tapas, especially of the western direction. Swamiji would not have survived the tapas but for this mantra. The sufferings of the physical body was borne, to a large extent, by the subtle body, which had been strengthened by the surya mantra. Swamiji's subtle body, impregnated with surya's power (of heat and light), is still intact (i.e., after his departure from this world) and continues to perform its divine mission. Surya shakti (the power of the divine flame) forms an ingredient of the tapas power that Swamiji gives during initiation and it helps devotees in their meditation and other pursuits. The light aspect of surya's power relates to its ability to reveal divine knowledge. Those who meditate seriously would have their minds enlightened by it. Similarly, the yogic heat, inherent in surya shakti, cleanses the mind of its impurities by burning them.

Q97. Swamiji had gone to the region of the sun (surya mandal) sometime in October 1954. Why did you do that and what was its experience like? When did Swamiji gain siddhi (success) of the surya mantra?

A97. Swamiji gained siddhi of the mantra on a full moon night in October 1954. The surya devta (the sun god) appeared before Swamiji just before he was to get up for his daily break. He did namaskara (i.e. greeted him) to Swamiji and assured him of his full support for Swamiji's mission. Swamiji saw the subtle body of the sun god and it was more dazzling (of white light) than many other forms of gods etc. that Swamiji saw. He was a young man without any beard or hair on the head. He had an eternal youthful look and very potent vibrations emanated from his body. He is a great tapaswi (yogi) and even Kal (time) cannot match his power. He is the embodiment of divine knowledge and yogic power and helps all those who seek his blessings for their sadhana (practice). Swamiji had darshan of the divine Guru on the night following the above experience. On a sudden impulse, Swamiji requested Him to take him to the surya mandal in order to test whether the body could, after the siddhi of mantra, withstand its heat. The Guru agreed with a smile and asked Swamiji to close his eyes and in a jiffy Swamiji was in surya loka (region). It was intensely hot and blindingly bright, but, at the same time, very blissful. After a little while, the divine Guru brought Swamiji back. The above experience was of the subtle body that travelled to the region of the sun located in the brahman chakra, a little to the east of the sacred hills, touched very briefly upon in Answer 54 of

Chapter 4. An experience like this is not easy to bear and it requires a great deal of yogic preparation (in sadhana). Swamiji was able to do so because of the Guru's grace. Devotees are advised not to attempt practice of such a difficult yogic sadhana (practice) in this age. Even in Swamiji's case, his subtle body would have been burnt by the sun's heat but for divine grace. On the return journey from the surya mandal, the Guru made sure that Swamiji took a dip in many rivers (in the subtle region) to cool it down.

Q98. Swamiji spent maximum time in tapas facing the east. Did that have any significance? Why did Swamiji do tapas of the western direction for the least time (07 Aug 1955-26 June 1956) as compared to the other directions when it is said to be the most difficult to attain success in?
A98. Swamiji followed his guru's directions in all matters related to his tapas. He spent maximum time in tapas in the eastern direction because of the divine mission assigned to him is to re-establish dharma. It implies that predominance of virtue over evil should be restored in the natural order. That is best done through the preservative power that dwells in the east. As far as the west is concerned, Swamiji's guru had given him some very potent mantras that neutralised Shiva's power quickly. One should not prolong western tapas for too long because it gives time to Shiva to cause more and more obstructions, specially for the survival of the body.

Q99. Why was it that Swamiji did tapas for only twelve hours a day in the last four years?
A99. The tapas had been very severe for the first eight years, which had weakened Swamiji's body considerably and it was in no state to do any physical work. Swamiji needed time to recoup. Also, one cannot give up severe tapas suddenly because the body requires time to stabilize, just like a car engine running at a high temperature is allowed to cool down a little before switching it off. The additional four years of tapas with its reduced timings served this purpose. The eastern tapas done in the bargain was a bonus.

Q100. There are not any recorded instances of a yogi undergoing severe suffering on the scale that Swamiji did while doing tapas. Even the great gurus and sages of the past did not apparently sit in tapas in the physical body. Why did Swamiji have to go through such a torturous practice (sadhana)?
A100. Many yogis have done tapas in the physical body in the past and they succeeded despite determined opposition by Kal (embodied form of time) and others. Their suffering was no less than Swamiji's. Notable amongst them was Sri Vashista (guru of Sri Rama), the celebrated author of Yoga Vashista. In general, tapas in the physical body is practised whenever an epochal change is imminent (e.g. a minor or a major dissolution of the world affecting a large

number of people). Destruction of Ravana (a demon king; his destruction by Sri Rama is narrated in Ramayana) was one such great event of ancient history. People in general suffer a lot of pain whenever such cataclysms take place. Yogis do tapas in the physical body to minimise it; besides that, they gain power to exterminate evil forces to ensure a smooth change over. Evil in the modern world is represented by tyrants, selfish rulers, corrupt officials, a callous administration and so on. A gross effect (e.g. an uncaring government that affects millions of people) is best tackled by doing tapas in the physical body. Tapas of this type has greater relevance for those yogis whose divine mission also involves the functions of an avtara (divine incarnation that restores the superiority of virtue over evil in the world). Swamiji's tapas should be viewed in the context of above explanation. Swamiji has revealed some of his experiences only to assure devotees of his protection in the future. Yogis in the earlier days did not disclose the nature of their tapas to more than their close circle of disciples. Times and circumstances were different then. Swamiji would earnestly exhort all his devotees to practise meditation regularly and seriously to awaken the dormant tapas shakti given at the time of initiation. It would look after them in this and the next world.

Q101. Swamiji advocated the path of meditation (dhyana) although the divine guru had authorized him to initiate aspirants on all disciplines. Why was it so?
A101. The answer to the above question will be best understood if one knows the basic method of Swamiji's teaching.

Q102. Could you please elaborate on it?
A102. Swamiji's primary instruction is to control the mind through the power of Silence (or tapas), which he imparts at the time of initiation. Tapas shakti is a divine power of self-control and is regarded as the most superior form of yoga shakti (i.e. the power of concentration). Swamiji emphasises meditation on the self (atman dhyana) as a means to control the self. The essence of meditation is to concentrate one's mental energy on an object for a certain length of time. It is not possible to follow any path till the mind develops the ability of concentration. In that sense, to do meditation is a basic requirement for any aspirant, no matter what path he or she wishes to pursue. Swamiji stressed the importance of meditation in that respect for all devotees. But, this does not mean that meditation by itself cannot lead to the final goal. Meditation, in any form, is a fundamental means to obtain liberation, which has been brought out in Chapter 4, on the path of yoga. The point to understand is that Swamiji gives a preliminary initiation in meditation in order to attain a certain degree of mental discipline and stabilisation. Having achieved that, an aspirant can either continue on the path of meditation or follow a different discipline according to one's mental predilection based on one's samaskaras. The changeover takes

place on its own under the impact of the power of Silence and a devotee gets appropriate instructions from Swamiji. A number of devotees have had their paths changed in this manner. Besides the path of meditation that the majority of the seekers pursue, Swamiji has revealed the divine name or suitable mantras on the path of devotion to many aspirants. He has also initiated a rare few on the path of self-inquiry (Gurprasad is one of them). Of course, Swamiji's fundamental principle is that every devotee must learn to do selfless service (sewa) conjointly with meditation or any other path that one is following. Swamiji is most pleased with those who do desireless sewa, even if they do not practice other paths seriously. But, the best results are achieved if service is done in addition to the practice of one of the other paths.

Q103. How does Swamiji teach in Silence?
A103. The relative Self (Atman or mind in general of God) in its general aspect is the best teacher of all because in It dwells infinite intelligence. The same Self exists as the jivatman (the modified self as the individual mind or the 'I' that imagines itself to be the body) of an individual. The samaskaric dross conceals the purified nature of the jivatman and an individual is, therefore, unable to use its inherent purified intelligence to control his or her mind. To rely on this indwelling intelligence, which is of the nature of Silence, as the internal guru is the essence of Swamiji teaching. Swamiji's tapas power is the quintessential form of divine intelligence that is a derivative of relative Silence and it embodies the principle of self-control. Swamiji transfers this power to a devotee during initiation and it inheres in the individual 'I' consciousness (or the centre of one's mind). Tapas shakti is so over powering that an aspirant who surrenders his self ('I'-ness) to it is not required to do anything else but there are few persons of this calibre. The individual 'I' has a causal, subtle and gross form; depending on one's spiritual maturity, Swamiji's initiatory power maybe felt in any of them. The most pure hearted would feel its impact in the causal 'I' consciousness immediately and they may even attain samadhi suddenly. Less ripe ones experience it in the subtle 'I' and raw beginners in their gross 'I'. Swamiji's tapas power then acts as the indwelling guru in one's own self (jivatman or the individual mind). All that a seeker needs to do is to be aware of this power and it would provide all the guidance that one seeks. It would clear all doubts. This power works intangibly and often without a seeker's awareness. It manifests palpably in lower samadhi (i.e. when the causal 'I'-current is felt), specially in its bhava aspect in which guidance becomes more demonstrative. The vast majority of aspirants have impure and extroverted minds, which impairs their ability to feel this power in the initial stages of practice. One of the reasons why Swamiji gives the preliminary initiation for atman dhyana (meditation on the self) is for a devotee to develop the power of concentration to become aware of the tapas shakti (due to mental purification). Once that

happens, one should retain its awareness and it would do the rest, including give the supreme reward of liberation. No other effort is required.

Q104. How does this power work in an aspirant from the time of initiation onwards?

A104. Swamiji's preliminary initiation is for atman dhyana (meditation on the self or the 'I') for reasons given in the previous two answers. The omnipotent tapas power is given to aspirants in seed form at the time of initiation and once it is developed by self-effort, there is nothing that it cannot achieve. Each devotee receives it according to individual capacity. A highly mature disciple may attain instant samadhi, in any of its variants, through it. But, in most cases, it develops gradually, just like the germination of a seed into a tree takes time. It is so due to the impurities of individual mind and, hence, the initiatory tapas shakti is given in a latent form. Just as a seed does not grow in an unprepared soil, so does the awareness of tapas shakti not arise immediately in an impure mind. Swamiji transfers his power to the brikuti (the point in the subtle body, which corresponds to the space between the eyebrows) of an aspirant. The individual consciousness is thus potentially joined with the tapas shakti (of Swamiji), which originates from the divine consciousness. There is, therefore, a link between the individual mind and pure consciousness (of Ishwara) through Swamiji's tapas shakti from the time of initiation onwards. A student is only required to make this link stronger, firmer and more intimate, which would introvert the mind on its own. It is done through self-effort made in meditation on the self (atman dhyana) or any other discipline (provided one is initiated in it). Swamiji's power dwells in the centre of the mind (in which inheres the 'I') and the brikuti is one of its reflected forms. Its impact maybe felt instantly if one can concentrate on it with a certain degree of one pointedness of the mind. Some may see it in the form of light or hear some divine sound; others may feel it as a current. Its presence may also be experienced in the form of mental peace, calmness, and heaviness in the brikuti area or any other spiritual experience. The dormant power of Silence turns into its active state as one's ability to concentrate improves. The power begins to ascend to the sahasrara chakra (centre of subtle consciousness located at top of head in subtle body) if one can concentrate on the brikuti, without extraneous thoughts, for approximately an hour. The ascension in the initial stages is experienced in the form of purifying currents and it carries with it the individual mind. The tapas shakti assumes a subtler form when further exertion is made in meditation on the self. It then descends from the sahasrara chakra, to the outer periphery of the Heart (general area below the right nipple) via the brahman chakra (located in the centre of head). It is a slow process and it requires constant effort to keep one's mind concentrated on the space between the eyebrows (brikuti). One may concentrate on the sahasrara chakra or brahman chakra or on the Heart, depending upon how far the mind has reached, as an additional aid. The point to note is that concentration of the mind activates the tapas shakti, which then guides it to move towards the Heart. All forms of spiritual experiences or thoughts are distractions, which detract the mind from meditation and slow down its journey to the Heart. One must reject them as utterly undesirable. The subtle mind abides in the tapas shakti when it descends to the brahman chakra and subsides in it when it reaches the outer core of the Heart, i.e., the state of causal mind in manolaya. Effort made thereafter converts the tapas shakti into the divine flame that destroys the mind in its yogic heat and light. This is a very general and brief account of how the tapas shakti operates. It is the sole guide that a devotee needs but one has to be aware of it by self-effort. It dissolves all infirmities of the mind and leads it to its source on its own. Awareness of tapas shakti serves the purpose of hearing and contemplation of instruction, the first two steps prior to practice; in other words, meditation on the self (atman dhyana) gives their benefits. A devotee need not come in physical contact with Swamiji nor have a verbal exchange with him because it gives all the benefits of sat sangha (holy company). Tapas power is like a magnetized light, which attracts the mind to itself. The only self-effort required is to keep one's mind oriented towards it through meditation. It removes fear and doubt from the mind. The divine qualities develop through it. All this is possible if an aspirant does regular practice with devotion, faith and sincerity and at the same time learns to use his or her power of discrimination.

Q105. How should an aspirant do meditation to come in contact with tapas shakti?

A105. Seekers are advised to study the section on atman dhyana given in Chapter 4, Path of Yoga, which explains the method of meditation in detail. Some salient points are given below. A devotee's consciousness is in potential touch with the tapas shakti from the moment of initiation. However, seekers do not become aware of it because of the extroversion of their impure minds. To attain its awareness, the outward tendencies of the mind have to be arrested and then brought to bear on the brikuti, where the power of tapas dwells. It is achieved in the preliminary phase of meditation, which consists of self-discipline and purification. The mind is able to fully concentrate on the brikuti only after it has achieved a certain degree of purification and discipline. Regular practice, prescribed by Swamiji, is of atman dhyana (meditation on the self, i.e., 'I') as enunciated in Chapter 4. It was brought out there that the mind has a centre around which it revolves. It is the point of origin of the mind into which it merges before its destruction. The mind has three forms; causal, subtle and gross. Similarly, the centre (or the 'I' of a jiva) appears in causal, subtle and gross aspects and they are all reflections of the Heart. Swamiji's tapas power is transmitted in the causal centre (around the Heart) for highly evolved souls at the time of initiation. But, an outward looking mind cannot feel the presence of tapas shakti in the Heart and that is why Swamiji plants its seed in the brikuti, which is a point in the subtle body. A seeker is required to concentrate his or her gross mind that functions through the physical senses on this subtle point. Meditation on the brikuti introverts the outgoing consciousness on itself; further practice purifies the mind, first, to its subtle aspect and, then, to its causal form, as described in the previous answer. The initial stage of atman dhyana is done as follows. An aspirant should apply vibhuti (consecrated piece of clay given at the time of initiation) on the brikuti, which protects one from evil and hostile forces. It also establishes a link with the power of tapas. Devotees are advised to pray to their ishta deva (the deity chosen for personal worship) or to Swamiji or to both prior to commencing meditation. An aspirant should concentrate on the brikuti in a relaxed mode by adopting a comfortable posture. As an aid to concentration, one should look at the brikuti without moving the eyeballs. It may cause a little strain in the beginning but disappears with practice. The head, neck and chest should be kept in an upright position. Those who are not used to sitting in this position may find it difficult to do so in the beginning. Regular practice overcomes such problems. In any case, every effort should be made to keep the head erect, failing which one may fall asleep during meditation. The brikuti is a very tiny point (it is smaller than one billionth of a hair's width) and a beginner cannot locate it straightaway. One should, therefore, look in the general area of space between the eyebrows and concentrate the mind on it. One may, as an additional aid, imagine the point of concentration to be the centre of one's mind. As one meditates, thoughts are bound to erupt in rapid succession, causing a distraction in practice. The essence of one's self effort lies in preventing the mind to run away with thoughts by being aware of the brikuti only. That is best done by ignoring thoughts and keeping one's consciousness concentrated (on the brikuti) and to feel that all one's senses, specially of seeing and hearing, are located there. One should bring one's mind back to the brikuti every time it strays from it. It is a constant mental struggle and takes time before an aspirant achieves a modicum of success in keeping the mind concentrated on the brikuti. But, one should not get disheartened by lack of apparent success because every single attempt that he or she makes in controlling the mind leads him or her closer to tapas shakti. The power of tapas is activated a little, every time one makes even the smallest effort to restrain mental motion. A beginner is not likely to become aware of it but its silent influence is felt in the mind unknown to oneself. A student's only duty is to practice regularly and Swamiji's power will bring the mind to it on its own. One would notice, after a little practice, that the mind is entertaining thoughts that it never had before or could possibly have (e.g. some may even be of evil nature). It is a sign that the mind is regressing into memory (of past lives) and has taken a small step on the journey to introversion towards its centre. Continuous practice disciplines and purifies the mind. A sincere devotee who does at least one hour's practice daily should be able to notice a fair degree of improvement in these aspects in about six months. The mind gets closer to the tapas shakti (at the centre of brikuti) as concentration gets better. The latter's power of guidance improves as the spatial separation between the two is reduced. As one progresses, endeavour should be made to concentrate on the inner side of the space between the eyebrows rather than on its external physical aspect. But, no force is to be used for this purpose. The internalised concentration takes the consciousness to the centre of brikuti. After reaching that point, an aspirant should concentrate on it in order to absorb one's mind in Swamiji's power. Once this process begins, one may feel heavy pressure in the area of the brikuti. After earnest and serious practice, one may experience the currents going up to the seventh chakra (located on top of the head); an aspirant may also feel peaceful or see light, or hear some divine sound or notice gaps between thoughts. One should then concentrate on the spot where the mental current ends. The method of meditation for the other charkas or points is similar to the one described above. Aspirants may have various kinds of experiences during meditation but they are to be rejected by using one's power of discrimination. A beginner should set a goal, in terms of time, for meditation and ensure that one sticks to it as a matter of self-discipline. One should try and reach the target of one hour as soon as possible and then extend the period further according to one's capacity. The above is a general account of one method of doing meditation. Individual variations are possible but one can keep the above as a guide and have firm faith that the power of Silence will direct one's self effort on the right lines.

Q106. It was said earlier that Swamiji gives a preliminary initiation on the path of atman dhyana (meditation on the self) to all those who seek his grace. Do the devotees require a subsequent initiation? If so, what is the difference between the two?

A106. Swamiji's may give just one initiation or more according to the requirements of a seeker. The latter course is for the benefit of a student, whose spiritual development takes place in graduated steps and is controlled by Swamiji. That is the best way to go forward for most devotees who need to temper their impure minds gradually in the fire (brahman agni) of tapas shakti. A single initiation is enough for very mature disciples. The preliminary initiation is given by Swamiji as a well-wisher of a devotee and it is given in mitra bhava (i.e. as a friend in general) to prepare him or her for a spiritual quest. As a general rule, it sets in motion the process of mental discipline and purification. Generally, Swamiji used to give the first initiation according to the procedure described in Answer 79. Subsequent initiation was mostly done by his subtle body during meditation and, in some cases, in person also. The effect is the same in both cases. Depending on the mental attitude and spiritual progress, the second initiation is given to a devotee in any of the relationships that he or she forms with Swamiji (e.g. father, mother, master etc.). By and large, Swamiji does not initiate aspirants in guru bhava (i.e. in the guru-disciple relationship) or in the beloved-lover relationship in the first or second initiation, except in the case of ripened seekers, because they are difficult to form and sustain as brought out in discussion on guru in Chapter 2, Answers 14-33. The type of subsequent initiation depends on an aspirant's spiritual maturity and mental propensity. In general, the difference between the first and the second initiation (which may be followed again by more initiations) is that the tapas shakti is more potent and active in the latter case. It is for one's benefit that tapas power acts gradually because most seekers cannot bear its full impact straightaway due to mental impurities. The release of tapas shakti happens on its own as one practices earnestly. Swamiji may initiate a student into any path (including revelation of divine name and mantras) at a suitable time, which maybe applicable even to the first initiation and he may also do it in any relationship. It all depends on an aspirant's spiritual level. Physical presence of Swamiji is not required for any of the initiations mentioned above. This is more so now that Swamiji is not in gross form. In general, Swamiji's initial and subsequent initiations are potent enough for an aspirant to reach lower samadhi. Swamiji initiates in guru bhava (guru-disciple relationship) only those capable of attaining higher samadhi. Special initiation is required for tapas.

Q107. Does it mean that the less mature devotees should not regard Swamiji as their guru?
A107. No; they may do so in a general way but it is better if they regard him as a parent or a loving master in the initial stages of practice. The implication is that Swamiji regards his devotees as children and looks after them accordingly. In that aspect, he is tolerant of their faults and does not insist on a very strict regimen for them because they are, in their present state, incapable of adhering to it. They would be able to do so as they progress. The relationships mentioned above are good for gradual progress. But, to regard Swamiji as a guru implies that one should follow each and every instruction of his in letter and spirit, in a state of surrender without any desire, just as Swamiji did during the tapas. It requires great spiritual strength and maturity. The tapas power to remove ignorance totally is given by Swamiji only if a disciple has attained a high degree of self-control and has acquired divine qualities in good measure. That power is too potent for ordinary devotees to bear. It is for their benefit that Swamiji advises them to adopt the guru-disciple relationship only after an apprenticeship in other relationships. Incidentally, guidance for it also comes from within through meditation. Similarly, beloved-lover relationship

is extremely difficult to sustain unless one is very pure hearted and has a high degree of mental detachment. It is best to form this relationship only after attaining the early stages of lower samadhi.

Q108. The path prescribed in this age (kaliyuga) is nama-japa (repetition of the divine name) done with love and devotion. Many scriptures confirm this. However, Swamiji has laid emphasis on meditation. Why has he preached a different viewpoint?

A108. It is true that remembrance of the Lord with love and devotion is highly suitable for this age, dominated as it is by material and selfish tendencies amongst jivas (human beings). Most people are unable to make a serious spiritual effort in kaliyuga because of the latter factor. The path of divine love is indeed laudable because those who have pure love and devotion, in their hearts for the Lord, require little effort to attain It. These attributes lead to self-surrender to the Lord and once that happens, He or She does everything for a true devotee. The main problem in kaliyuga is the short life span of jivas, which mitigates against a prolonged practice of a spiritual discipline. Divine love is ideally suited to overcome such a difficulty. Be that as it may, it does not imply that other paths are not suitable or cannot be followed in kaliyuga. Jivas having varying types of mental tendencies and temperaments are born in every age and the divine will keeps all paths alive at all times to help them improve spirituality. The present age is characterised by great scientific advancements and educated people tend to be rational. The modern mind does not easily accept ritualistic form of worship, which is the starting point for most people on the path of love. People today are rather skeptical of traditional and dogmatic religious practices. The path of meditation on the self (atman dhyana), as taught by Swamiji, is highly suitable for present day aspirants because it deals with an entity (i.e. one's 'I'-ness) whose existence is not in doubt and which is accepted by everyone as the root cause of one's unhappiness, worries, tensions etc. The mind, based on the 'I', is in constant turmoil and there is no salvation unless one controls it. The analogy of deep sleep is relevant in this context; one feels happy in it because the mind is at rest. Thus, the core of Swamiji's teaching lies in making the restless mind restful. Swamiji's method of meditation is very simple; it has absolutely no religious connotation nor is it associated with any sect or creed nor does it require anyone to perform rituals, rites etc. It is totally scientific and is suitable for believers as well as agnostics. Swamiji promises eternal happiness to those who learn to control their minds. The stress and strain suffered by most people these days due to the competitive and fast life disappears if they critically examine their selves to determine the cause of their worries and unhappiness. If the mind is the villain, the power to destroy its vile nature also lies in it. Swamiji stresses the importance of self-effort to control the mind. It is a method of self-reliance, without dependence on any outside agency including that of an external God. Swamiji gives initiation for control of mind through meditation. That is all there is to his teaching. One need not go to a temple or a church etc. to perform any worship or listen to sermons or even read scriptures. Swamiji has not laid restrictions of any kind on his devotees. Meditation can be done anywhere and at any time. What can be easier to overcome one's suffering? However, this should not be construed to mean that Swamiji does not emphasise the need for love and devotion or, for that matter, decries any other path. In fact, Swamiji always advises his devotees to develop love for the Lord, in addition to doing meditation. A combination of meditation, as taught by Swamiji, love and service (sewa) is the most effective method for modern day devotees. It leads to attainment of true knowledge. Swamiji integrates other paths with meditation and love if a seeker's mental makeup requires it for his or her spiritual growth.

Q109. How does the practice of other paths result in the growth of tapas shakti? A109. Divine love is the quintessential form of tapas power. Notwithstanding the path that one follows, every seeker should try to feel, in the heart, love for the Lord. There is no better, safer and easier way to awaken the dormant tapas shakti given at the time of initiation. Remembrance of the Lord through repetition of Its divine name or a mantra is an excellent means to develop and nurture love for It. Japa (repetition of divine name) done properly, as described in Chapter 4, Answers 45-48, activates the tapas shakti, which then draws the mind to Silence. Path of self-enquiry, like atman dhyana (meditation on the self), is the most direct way to feel the Silence by knocking down the false existence of the 'I'. The search for the elusive 'I' through constant enquiry of 'who am I' awakens the latent tapas shakti. After that, it guides a seeker to look for the 'I' in a silent and an unobtrusive way. The path of service is best pursued in combination with the practice of other disciplines. Worship and prayer done with real devotion are very good aids to arouse Guru's tapas shakti. Its initial manifestation might not be as palpable as it is on other paths because actions are done by an extroverted mind. However, its silent guidance is assured if a jiva learns to ponder over the actions that he or she does in a spirit of self-surrender. Tapas shakti gives positive help if one is discriminative in performing actions and tries to remain unattached to their fruits. A major effect of the germination of tapas shakti is the growth of divine qualities in an aspirant and they bring about a complete spiritual transformation, if used discriminatively. There are many other disciplines that lead to spiritual growth. Swamiji's advice to aspirants is to regard them as subsidiary ones. They are not easy to practise and require a long time to show results after strenuous effort.

Q110. How can a student make rapid spiritual progress? In what does the essence of doing meditation lie?

A110. Meditation aims to control the mind, i.e., destroy all thoughts to make it motionless. A serious aspirant ought to realise that the benefits of meditation accrue according to a number of factors. It is desirable that one should do meditation for as long as one can but equally important is its quality. Thoughts are eliminated from the mind only if the root 'I' thought is first identified and then destroyed. One should, therefore, make every effort to become aware of the 'I'-current as soon as possible. It is a long and a slow process for most devotees and its awareness is attained only in lower samadhi. Prior to it, a seeker needs to develop the ability to concentrate on an object (e.g. brikuti) for a certain length of time without extraneous distractions, such as thoughts, visions and experiences. That should form the index of judging the quality of one's meditation. Progress in meditation depends on how well the qualities of devotion, detachment and discrimination are developed in an individual. One should pay special attention to them right from the beginning. Detachment from thoughts is the goal and is achieved through devotion and discrimination. The mind dwells on the brikuti more easily if one has devotion for the Lord. Devotion is like a homing device, which propels the jivatman (individual self) to a union with the power of Silence. It is a very powerful aid. Discrimination is the quality that rejects (or ignores) thoughts. It is developed on its own every time one tries to concentrate on the brikuti while paying no attention to thoughts. The task of discrimination becomes simpler if the mind contemplates the Guru's teaching with devotion. An aspirant should consciously and deliberately apply the sense of discrimination to his or her daily affairs during non-meditation hours. Always try to do those actions that earn divine grace and bring one closer to God. There is no action that is more purifying and brings greater reward than selfless service (sewa). Nothing pleases Swamiji more than motiveless sewa. Every devotee must do it in one form or the other. Above all Swamiji's advice to all devotees is to learn to do everything, including meditation, in a spirit of self-surrender, out of love for the Lord, and without desire for anything. An aspirant will progress fast if he or she combines the above features with meditation. Swamiji is pleased most with those seekers who have love for the Lord in their hearts, are humble and have surrendered their desires.

Q111. Is the path taught by Swamiji of Silence or a composite of all disciplines based on It?
A111. Swamiji's primary method of teaching is in Silence and in its secondary form the Silence empowers other disciplines to fructify them faster and with much less effort than they would otherwise require. All paths lead in the end to Silence. Swamiji has made the ultimate goal within the reach of everyone from the beginning of one's practice. Swamiji teaches in absolute Silence in which no physical or verbal contact with an aspirant is required. Those who

are fit to receive initiation in this manner need only to pray to Swamiji with a yearning heart and he would impart the tapas shakti to them. This may be done in a silent way in the mind (it would leave no doubt that initiation has taken place) or through Swamiji's subtle body, which may appear in a dream or otherwise. However, there are very few aspirants who are suitable to receive grace in this manner because of their extroverted and impure minds. Thus, the path of absolute Silence, by itself, is applicable only to a selected number of disciples and in this age (kaliyuga) they are likely to be ever free souls. Keeping this factor in view, Swamiji has modified the basic path of Silence to make it inclusive of all other disciplines to ensure its easy availability to everyone including raw beginners. It implies that Swamiji's tapas shakti is an integrated power that pulls the individual mind, to itself, of any devotee irrespective of the path that he or she follows. In other words, Swamiji has made all other disciplines as derivatives of the path of Silence (or they are superimposed on It) and their practice is done in its matrix. Swamiji advocated atman dhyana (meditation on the self) because it is the quickest way to feel the presence of tapas shakti. Practice of other paths (e.g. of love, devotion, service, meditation on a form etc.) would also lead to it but would take a longer time. Self-enquiry is the only other path that leads directly to the power of Silence given by Swamiji. Thus, for a majority of devotees, Swamiji's path of Silence is a composite one in which all paths have been integrated. It is similar to the lanes on a road (i.e. aspirants move on the road of Silence only no matter which lane they traverse; each discipline is a superimposition on the substratum of Silence that draws the mind to Itself). The path of Silence is the best of all because it requires the least effort on the part of a seeker and Swamiji has opened its gates to everyone, including those who have impure and extroverted minds and, also, for those who have no previous background in making spiritual effort.

Q112. How can a sincere devotee make use of such extraordinary grace during practice?

A112. The ideal way to practice is as pointed out above in a spirit of self-surrender, love and desirelessness. Practice as much as one can and as best as one can. Spiritual benefits that accrue from such effort would be manifold more than what its (i.e. effort's) just rewards ought to be.

Q113. Many gurus are said to teach in silence, although they adopt a particular path to do so. How does Swamiji's method of imparting instruction differ from them?

A113. All satgurus have the tapas power to teach in the way that Swamiji does. However, in practice, they modify it to suit the needs of their devotees in the milieu prevailing at the time of their advent. Teaching in silence has an important aspect that needs to be noted. Is it a path by itself or is it being used in combination with others? If the latter, how much of the tapas power of Silence is used to make them (i.e. other paths) effective? There is no difference in the teaching of gurus if the path of silence is followed independently (i.e. it is not combined with the practice of other disciplines). Variations arise only in case it is pursued conjointly with other paths (e.g. of love and devotion, meditation etc.). Some gurus explain their subsidiary paths in detail when questioned about it whereas the others have minimal verbal contact with aspirants. This difference in approach is a reflection of the power of Silence that is grafted on the secondary path, i.e., gurus who talk little about the latter empower it to greater degree. Obviously, the last mentioned is easier to practice because it requires less effort on a student's part. Satgurus use both methods; Swamiji's tapas shakti was used primarily in the silent mode, even when it was employed conjointly with other disciplines.

Q114. Who all have, in the past, used Swamiji way of teaching?
A114. Sri Dakshnimurthy is the original and foremost satguru who used omnipotent tapas shakti to teach in absolute Silence. That was in the beginning of the present time cycle. The same power has since then manifested in some gurus of the highest class but they do not take birth too often. Notable amongst them are Vashisht in ancient times, Jesus Christ and Shankarchayara in the first millennium, Kabir and Guru Nanak in the middle ages and Raman Maharishi in the last century.

Q115. Why did Swamiji use vibhuti (consecrated piece of clay) for initiating devotees and conferring blessings on them for various other purposes (e.g. health problems)? How does it affect an aspirant?
A115. Swamiji gave consecrated vibhuti to aspirants at the time of initiation and even to people who were not devotees if they sought his blessings to solve their personal problems or made a request to alleviate their anxieties, worries etc. Distribution of vibhuti was integral to Swamiji's method of teaching in Silence. It helps an aspirant to awaken the dormant tapas shakti temporarily, during meditation, and, also, wards off evil forces from interfering with it. It should be applied on the brikuti (space between eyebrows) before doing meditation. It functions similarly for other purposes; its power removes obstacles to satiate some desires, cures diseases and improves health by restoring pranic imbalances and gives peace of mind to make it stress free. Swamiji began to use vibhuti when a large number of people started to approach him for initiation or other reasons. At times, they came in thousands and to deal with them individually would have involved too much talking, besides the enormous time required to do so. Swamiji state was not conducive to indulge in such acts and, moreover, it was contrary to the spirit of teaching in Silence. Swamiji, therefore, devised the system of giving vibhuti; it used to be distributed freely to anyone who wanted

it. In individual cases, Swamiji would listen to their requests and gave them the vibhuti without getting into frills and unnecessary elaboration. Similarly, Swamiji did not give any lectures or sermons during initiation; his empowered vibhuti served the same purpose.

Q116. Why is it that Swamiji's grace given through the vibhuti did not work in some cases?
A116. Vibhuti given at the time of initiation is invariably effective for spiritual development provided the persons concerned makes the requisite effort. Its latent power is still intact in those who were initiated but did not begin practice; it would manifest instantly, if they follow Swamiji's teachings and do meditation. Vibhuti was ineffective for some people who had asked for it for personal purposes. There are many reasons for it; one, they did not use it according to instructions; two, did not ask for more of it once the original stock was exhausted; it is specially so when used for purposes of health; three, the efficacy of vibhuti is related to one's karma; change of very potent samaskaras could have had adverse effects on the person concerned and sometimes it is better to go through pain rather than avert it.

Q117. It is a general observation that not many devotees of Swamiji have taken to meditation seriously. Even those who have shown the inclination to do so have failed to make substantive progress. Is it not surprising that the omnipotent grace of the power of Silence has not evoked or impelled them to spirituality in a more meaningful manner?
A117. The above remarks are not unusual in the sense of their being peculiar to Swamiji's devotees. The question assumes that every unhappy person seeks solace in detachment from the world. It is not so because the insidious effects of maya (ignorance) are so powerful in enslaving the mind to a life of pleasure that most people do not even want to forsake them. They may suffer but they do not want to give up ignorance. The majority of the people who go to a guru do so to solve their personal problems of worldly nature, which usually relate to health, children, money, property disputes, promotions etc. They have no idea of the nature of Reality or, at best, have vague notions about the goodness of a personal God who they expect to look after them without their doing anything in return. The largest number of devotees who came to Swamiji (or go to other gurus) comprised this category. Swamiji blessed them out of love for them. For, it must be understood, neither divine grace nor true love can be all pervasive if it is given selectively. Swamiji looks alike at everyone and all were (and still are) welcome to partake of his grace and blessings. That is why no one was (or is) ever turned away and initiation was (or is) not denied to anyone. Fulfilment of minor wishes, due to Swamiji's blessings, built/builds up faith in many devotees. Such small gains often resulted in some of them to turn to spiritual

life in due course. Very few amongst those who practice have the curiosity for divine knowledge that would help them to grow spiritually. That is why most devotees fell/fall by the wayside. Many amongst even the mature seekers are waylaid by their egos and only a rare few reach the highest state and that too at the time of death. Those who are liberated while living are generally the ever-free souls in this dark age. Those who do meditation in fits and starts cannot be considered to have begun their quests seriously. Many give it up after the initial enthusiasm wears off. Some make progress of varying kinds. This is the broad picture of the overall state of seekers in this age (kaliyuga). The reason for this is not far to seek. Practically everyone is looking for magical formulae to achieve this or that without lifting a finger on their part. It was explained earlier that the nature of the mind and the body is to act. The mind attains whatever it desires with self-effort. It should be obvious, even to the meanest intelligence, that one cannot develop spirituality without striving for it. This is where the majority of aspirants fail. They are unable to detach themselves from the world due to mental weakness that prevents them from breaking the bonds of attachment, desire, greed, pride etc. For the same reason, they are content to rot in the quagmire of ignorance and make no effort to get out of it. Swamiji's tapas shakti, given during initiation, is in seed form and it must be nurtured for its growth by self-effort. To expect otherwise is to go against the natural order of things in which primacy has been given to self-struggle to achieve anything. Swamiji's power of Silence has made it infinitely easier for seekers to reach the final goal but the impetus to do so must come from them. Is it the fault of the seed if the gardener does not water it regularly for it to germinate?

Q118. Does it mean that initiation given by Swamiji has gone waste in the majority of cases?
A118. No, it can never be so. Swamiji has planted a seed of his grace in the mind of the devotees. It will sprout some time or the other, even if it takes many lives to do so. All those who came to Swamiji did so, not so much by accident, but because of their past karmic connection with him, a process which began many lives back. Every time, they have gained a little by his company (sat sangha) and they will do so again by his present initiation.

Q119. Is it applicable even if they do not make the effort?
A119. The seed of tapas shakti cannot dry up even if no effort is made. Such is its power. If nothing else, it would ensure that such people come back to Swamiji in their new births. Even otherwise the mere presence of tapas shakti in one's mind makes some difference to the person concerned (could even be without his or her awareness), just as a candle does in the darkness of a vast jungle.

Q120. What is the best mental attitude towards practice (sadhana) for an aspirant? What relationship should one establish with Swamiji?

A120. One may adopt any relationship with Swamiji according to one's maturity and he would respond accordingly. However, it should be kept in mind that guru-disciple and lover- beloved relationships are suitable only for those who are very pure at heart. To accept Swamiji as a guru implies that one has implicit faith in him and one is prepared to sacrifice everything to practise his teaching through pure devotion that does not seek to gratify any desire. It is difficult to find a disciple of this calibre in this dark age. Aspirants are advised to do meditation out of love for Swamiji and in the spirit of self-surrender and service to him. Do meditation as a service to Swamiji, just as he did for his Guru. Swamiji then takes extra care of such devotees. To regard the Guru as loving father or mother is the best form of relationship for majority of the devotees.

Q121. How many of Swamiji's devotees have made real spiritual progress?

A121. All those who have made the effort, even if it is a little bit, have benefited, although they may not be aware of it. Effort here does not mean meditation (dhyana) only; it includes service (sewa), sat sangha, development of qualities like love, remembrance of Swamiji and so on. They have been recipients of Swamiji's grace and they are assured of a better birth next time. A few have made very good progress and, in due course, a few rare souls amongst them may even attain liberation.

Q122. Swamiji did not elaborate the method of doing meditation at the time of initiation and consequently many devotees did not even know how they should set about their practice. Some of them claim that they are not even aware that they have been initiated. Why is there confusion on this point?

A122. These doubts arise in the minds of those seekers who lack faith, devotion and discrimination. They need an excuse to explain their own lethargy for not practising meditation. Such people are unable to overcome the effects of their karma, which propels them to a life of sensual pleasure. At the time of initiation, the method of doing meditation (dhyana) is brought out in outline, which conforms to the spirit of teaching in Silence. An aspirant is expected to follow these instructions in the beginning. Later, the power of tapas, imparted at the time of initiation, reveals on its own further steps to be taken. In fact, a seeker is only required to concentrate on the brikuti (space between the eye brows), while ignoring thoughts, for the prescribed period of one hour and the rest takes place on its own. But, most devotees do not even do that. Swamiji was always ready to clarify any doubts on meditation but very few students asked him any questions. It is but natural that seekers of this type cannot make any substantive spiritual progress. An aspirant who does not even know that he or she has been initiated must have very strong tamasic (mentally lethargic) tendencies. It is like a patient, on the deathbed, having been revived by a lifesaving injection, denying that he was ever administered any such drug. What can one expect from such a devotee? Self-improvement requires effort, which most aspirants do not make. They expect miracles (from the guru) without themselves lifting a finger. Know it for certain that there is no other way to earn divine grace except through self-effort.

Q123. There is also an impression that Swamiji did not encourage questions on spiritual subjects because he seldom spoke on such matters. His usual answer to every question was to meditate. Devotees would have liked to hear about the Truth from Swamiji and, perhaps that would have enthused some of them to take to spiritual life more seriously. Would they have not benefited more if Swamiji had followed the more traditional method of instruction?
A123. The highest and most effective form of teaching is in Silence. The guru is one's own Self. Everything apart from It is unreal. An external guru is the manifestation of the Self and his or her role is over once he or she puts a seeker in contact with the in-dwelling guru. That is what Swamiji does. All that an aspirant is required to do is to attach his or her mind to Swamiji's power and the rest follows on its own, including clarification of doubts. It would have been contrary to the spirit of teaching in Silence if Swamiji had gone around giving discourses or encouraging aspirants to indulge in talking unnecessarily because that would have led to the creation of many more doubts. Make the mind silent and ignore all doubts. That is the best course of action. But, it requires a certain degree of spiritual maturity to follow it. Less mature students have their doubts resolved in meditation through the exercise of the power of discrimination. The ability to obtain answers to one's questions from within (from the Self) by the use of discrimination is a superior form of teaching. Such doubts can be on any subject like food, sex, sleep, and nature of Reality etc. A doubt resolved through personal effort leads to self-confidence (atman vishvash) and in the bargain improves one's power of discrimination. To stop dependence on an external guru right from the beginning is a very effective method of inner development of an aspirant. Immature seekers do not understand it and want to hear about the Truth from an outside source. Who can talk about Truth when its nature is that of Silence? An aspirant can obtain all the benefits of hearing and contemplation (sravana and mannana) by practice of meditation as taught by Swamiji, who was aware of nothing except the Silence. To whom could he speak and talk to? Notwithstanding the above, Swamiji realised that most aspirants were not ripe enough to follow the above method in its entirety. He was always ready to clarify genuine doubts of devotees but they seldom asked him. Those who did got the answers. Swamiji discouraged some seekers to query him because they were doing so to show off or were not yet ready to understand the answers to their questions. Most people asked Swamiji about their personal and worldly

problems and he replied to them accordingly. Swamiji's advice to devotees, who entertain genuine doubts, is to make sincere effort to do as much meditation as they can. Their misgivings will be dispelled on their own.

Q124. Swamiji was very liberal in giving blessings for solution of all kinds of problems that devotees faced in their worldly life. He would also give vibhuti (consecrated piece of clay) for this purpose. Many devotees have the impression that despite Swamiji's grace many of their wishes were not gratified. Quite a few of them lost their faith that way. What is the explanation for such a phenomenon?

A124. Doubts like this arise due to immaturity. A doctor prescribes medicine for all types of patients who seek his attention. He does not turn a patient away, just because the latter's disease is incurable. Some patients are cured and some are not; some even succumb to their disease, despite the treatment. A saint is an embodiment of love and compassion and is very much like a doctor; he or she cannot turn away anyone who seeks refuge in him or her. His or her grace is all-pervasive, like the wind, and is available to all equally. A person who gives blessings selectively is not a sage. Swamiji used to (and still does) bless a devotee out of love whereas the motive of the latter is to satisfy a desire. Wishes are fulfilled only when one's samaskaras (mental impressions of past karma) are ready to give fruit for one's labour. Depending upon their strength and purity, fructification of some desires are hastened by the blessings of a yogi. It may not take place in some cases because either the student is not sincere or the samaskaras relating to a particular wish are too strong or unsuitable for gratification. Thus, utterance of blessings should be seen in the context of the law of karma. Swamiji's blessings solved the worldly problems of many devotees but they did not do so in some cases. It is not a reflection on Swamiji's power but the effect of their own karma and lack of faith in him. Many aspirants do not realise that non- satiation of desires is at times a blessing in disguise. A sick child does not know what is good for him to eat. In the same way, an immature devotee does not understand that fulfilment of a wish can, at times (depending on one's karma), lead to consequences, which are worse than the satisfaction of a desire. Blessings given by Swamiji should be understood in the light of this answer.

Q125. Could not Swamiji use his yogic power to change the karma of an aspirant?

A125. Karma can change gears only if the bonds of samaskaras (mental impressions) inherent in the mind are loosened through sadhana (practice). The supremely intelligent tapas shakti brought about such changes automatically in a few cases because they were beneficial for their spiritual upliftment. Swamiji's blessings inhere in the power of tapas given during initiation. It alters the karma of an aspirant, if it is going to aid in spiritual growth. But, for it to be effective one must do meditation sincerely and regularly in a spirit of self-surrender.

Q126. Many people sought Swamiji's blessings for various purposes. Did they go waste if some of their wishes were not fulfilled?
A126. No. Blessings of a yogi can never remain barren. If they do, the person who utters a blessing is not a yogi. Swamiji's blessings invariably helped devotees in a number of ways. To some it gave the strength to bear disappointment of having a wish unsatisfied; others realised their own inadequacies and put in more effort; many were saved from suffering the consequences of their actions; a few had their desires fulfilled in a different manner; some will realise their hopes later and so on.

Q127. It is often said that a satguru is like a wish fulfilling tree. How should a devotee regard Swamiji in the light of this statement?
A127. The above saying is true, but, its understanding by average jivas is defective. It refers to a mahatma's (great soul's) grace to grant liberation, which fulfils all hopes and expectations. But, ignorant people interpret it to imply satiation of worldly desires. The law of karma governs the functioning of the gross world. As one sows, so one reaps. A yogi upholds such divine laws. Self-effort and divine grace are integral to the law of karma. Saints bless those people who have earned karmic merit due to past and present effort. The nature of such blessings has been explained earlier. The karma of any individual can be changed by a yogi's grace, provided the self-effort is prolonged, sincere and done with devotion. There are few aspirants who meet this criterion. If a saint was to grant every worldly wish of devotees, even when they do not deserve it (due to past karma), who would ever make the effort to attain liberation? Everyone would be content to remain caught up in the net of maya. A yogi like that would be proclaimed God and the whole world would then line up to get their worldly desires gratified! Would such a yogi be ever able to impart instruction to seekers to detach their selves from the world in order to attain the Reality? Who would ever want salvation? No saint in the past has ever granted every wish of a devotee nor would it happen in the future. It is against the functioning of the natural order of things, which runs on the principle of acquiring fruit of one's labour according to its merit (or the lack of it). It is illogical to think that even the omnipotent Lord would violate Its divine law to satiate every whim and fancy of a seeker. Aspirants are advised to apply themselves to the practice of meditation rather than waste time in entertaining immature doubts.

Q128. Devotees often asked Swamiji many questions on the worldly affairs in general. Some of his comments turned out to be true whereas a few did not.

How does one understand this in the context of the general impression that a yogi's word is sacrosanct?

A128. It is an unexceptionable view that a mahatma's (great soul's) word is inviolable since it is an expression of the divine will. But, one must try to understand how and why such blessings are uttered. Saints have their individual prarabdha (present life's) karma to perform and they speak and act according to it. Some of them are serious by nature; others are full of humour. Some indulge in light banter and so on. Moreover, karma is invariably an interaction between two or more individuals. Veracity of a yogi's word depends on the mood (bhava) in which it is uttered. Obviously, something said in a light-hearted manner should be understood in the same light. A remark made in the divine mood of being a guru or boon giver or as a protector has the stamp of inevitability (about its occurrence) on it. An utterance like that is made in sahaj, which implies that it was impelled by the divine will. In such a state, a pure thought suddenly flashes in a yogi's consciousness and he or she speaks out naturally without any prompting or a request from the devotee. A saying like that has divine sanction. It is always true and cannot be undone. At times, Swamiji made some remarks to test a devotee's power of discrimination or faith. Sometimes, he would speak in a playful mood out of love for a devotee and in jest. Some comments of Swamiji made in a mood of anger were inviolable because they were uttered without deliberation.

Q129. Many of Swamiji's utterances were warped as far as time factor was concerned. It was difficult to make out whether he was talking about the past or the future. Why was it so?

A129. Swamiji was aware only of the indescribable Silence after the tapas. He had no memory of his prarabdha karma in that state. Swamiji would attain a very dim and a vague general awareness of his surroundings when devotees interacted with him but it did not break the Silence. Swamiji spoke as people do in sleep. This was Swamiji's state throughout his life. Time and space factors are non-existent in the supreme Silence. Thus, whatever Swamiji said was without any sense of time and he could not, therefore, make a distinction between the past and the future. It was Swamiji's way of teaching the devotees to transcend the limits of time. Many aspirants wanted to know about the future. Usually, Swamiji discouraged people asking such questions. At times, however, he would respond because of the earnestness of the questioner. Swamiji's answer would be based on what the tapas shakti revealed to him. All actions have already taken place in the matrix of that power and Swamiji's perception would conform to it. Some devotees were confused by Swamiji's utterances on these matters because the perception of time is relative to nature. Time is only an idea in the modified consciousness, which separates events into past, present and future but it is not so in the pure consciousness. Swamiji always perceived events as having occurred already and he would reveal them as such to a questioner. However, the latter's impure consciousness would superimpose his or her own idea of time on these revelations with the resultant confusion.

Q130. Why did Swamiji drop the word Yogeshwara from the name given to him by the divine Guru?
A130. Yogeshwara means the Lord of yogis and is a term applied to Ishwara. It also refers to Shankar Bhagwan; obviously, Swamiji could not equate himself with his Guru. Swamiji performed his mission out of devotion for his divine Guru and love for his devotees. It would have been inappropriate to add an appellation to his name, which might have suggested to the devotees a connotation contrary to the spirit in which Swamiji did his work.

Q131. Swamiji exhibited in his body the characteristics of ardhnarishwara (half male, half female). When did he have its experience for the first time and what did it signify?
A131. Swamiji became aware of being the form of ardhnarishwara within the first hour after initiation on 7 August 1949 but lost it there afterwards since he had no bodily consciousness. Male and female principles form the basic foundation of the pair of opposites in which the knowledge of one is obtained in relation to the other. They form the basis of relative knowledge and are applicable to all objects and not merely human beings. A male body can never fully understand the attributes of the female because of their relativity. The absence of one results in the manifestation of the other and vice versa. The concept of ardhnarishwara is applicable to Ishwara in whose general (causal, subtle and gross) body male and female genders exist in equal measure. It is so because Ishwara is able to hold contrary ideas in their totality, in Its consciousness, due to Its tapas shakti. Male and female characteristics manifested in Swamiji's causal and subtle (karan and linga sarira) bodies to give him the knowledge of both forms including their feelings, emotions, experiences etc.

Q132. Swamiji has said above that he had practically no awareness of the body either during or after tapas. How did he then talk or answer questions of aspirants? How was his body sustained?
A132. A drum is silent till it is struck. In the same way, Swamiji's Silence was slightly tampered with, temporarily, when he was asked a question or when he was in the company of devotees. It made the memory of Swamiji's prarabdha (present life's) karma active without his awareness. The tapas shakti's interaction with the prarabdha would make Swamiji talk. It did not affect the Silence. A drum produces sound because it exists in it already; similarly, what Swamiji uttered in speech pre-existed in his consciousness based on his

prarabdha karma. A person in deep sleep talks without being aware of what he is saying. Swamiji was in the same state of deep Silence. A sleeping child is fed by his mother. In the same way, Swamiji's body was maintained by his devotees due to their own prarabdha karma. Above all, the divine Guru looked after Swamiji like His child. Swamiji went through the tapas similarly.

Q133. Swamiji's answers (to his devotees' questions) were usually one-liners, profound in wisdom but difficult to understand. The replies needed to be interpreted correctly to obtain a full comprehension, which many failed to do. Why did not Swamiji give detailed explanations to individual queries? Did his answers have a general application or were they meant for the questioner only?
A133. To give long-winded explanations is against the spirit of teaching in Silence. The answers served the purpose of hearing (about the Truth) as well. The purpose of contemplation is to gain conviction through discrimination, which must come from within. Detailed explanations often makes a listener mentally lazy and one tends to become non-discriminative in contemplation. Moreover, Swamiji's state of Silence did not permit him to talk too much. Swamiji gave answers according to the level of understanding of a questioner. In that sense, they were applicable to particular individuals only. However, some answers were general in nature; their relevance (general or individual) depended upon the type of question asked.

Q134. Swamiji was quite fond of talking on matters other than spiritual. Why was it so?
A134. All such things are determined by one's nature formed from one's prarabdha (i.e. present life's) karma.

Q135. Swamiji has stressed the importance of meditation and its combination with other paths. Some devotees are fond of ritualistic forms of worship. Should they continue doing so?
A135. They may perform any kind of worship to which they are used to, based on their religious beliefs, customs, traditions etc. But, it should be done with love and devotion. Aspirants should also continue with their customary codes of conduct; it is also applicable to matters of diet. There is no need for any devotee to change his or her religious denomination. Control of the mind, through meditation, as taught by Swamiji, is not affected by any such acts. Those who are not attracted by rituals may avoid them if they so wish. It would not detract from their practice. Any change that one ought to make would come on its own as one progresses spiritually. One can then decide one's course of direction.

Q136. Swamiji often told Gurprasad that he belongs to no sect or religion. What did he imply by that?

A136. Swamiji had merged in the great Silence during the tapas itself and all his life he remained immersed in it. He was not aware of his body to which labels of being from this or that religion, sect or creed are applied. Of what avail are the sectarian beliefs and religious traditions in that inexpressible bodiless state? A sage only teaches how to attain Self Realisation through control of mind. Conformance to existing forms of worship and faith in traditional religious beliefs are used only as a means to make spiritual progress in the beginning. None of them, by itself, has any particular merit for spiritual advancement. Their practice falls off on its own with spiritual development. For a beginner, they are a help since one is used to them but gradually as one progresses one must learn to regard the entire creation as a manifestation of the Lord. If one can do that, all sects and religious beliefs appear to be equally true. God has no religion except that of universal love. Yogis take birth to affirm the unity of creation. To what religion, as practised and understood by ignorant people, can they belong? They are above all forms of differences and distinctions. In case they have not arisen above them, they are hardly saints.

Q137. Swamiji used to make a distinction between religious leaders and yogis. Why was it so?
A137. A saint, to be called as such, must be Self Realised whereas a religious leader wears the garb of a holy man, speaks the language of scriptures and does not practice what he preaches. Such people organise movements in the name of gurus and sages and pretend to speak for them. They do so to boost their egos and exploit the ignorant to gain authority over them by becoming their leaders. Some of them are learned and know the scriptures well. Intellectual understanding like that only swells their pride. Some are politicians who exploit the religious sentiments of the people for their selfish ends. Many become heads of temples, churches, mosques and other holy places founded in the name of saints. People like them become community leaders and pretend to be the voice of gurus, often by misinterpreting their instructions. In short, religious leaders are those who in the guise of serving others serve themselves first. Most of the heads of traditional religious movements fall in this category. After a holy person's departure from this world, his or her teachings are usually codified by some of his or her devotees (excluding those authorised by a seer) who then begin to preach them to others according to their limited understanding and become their guides. For this, they lay down their own rules and procedures to perform worship. Being devoid of any spiritual knowledge, the religious leaders lay stress on external forms of worship consisting of rites and rituals made by them. They become more elaborate with the passage of time, with each new leader adding his or her bit to them. In due course, a priestly class springs up to conduct various laid down (by them) religious ceremonies because ordinary people have no understanding of their complex procedures. Such a show of

piety befools most people. This is the general way in which the legacy of prophets is treated. The teachings of gurus lay emphasis on development of the inner self through practice of a spiritual discipline based on universal love and divine knowledge but this aspect is ignored by religions leaders because it requires hard labour to make a success of it. It is easier, on the other hand, to indulge in externalised forms of worship and, hence, ordinary jivas become addicted to it. Most of the religions that are followed these days have evolved in this manner after the departure of their so called founders. The essence of teaching of all prophets and seers is the same but some of their followers, in the garb of religious leaders, misinterpret it (deliberately or due to ignorance) to create creedal differences with others. All gurus teach their devotees to give up notions that create distinctions between created beings to realise that all are equals because the same Lord dwells in each heart. The religious leaders, on the other hand, create differences by proclaiming the superiority of their adherents over others. Thus are born new sects and denominations in the names of saints, gurus and prophets. Their followers then proclaim that their sects are better than others and claim them to be the only way to achieve salvation. Most of the religions today are distinguished from each other, in the popular imagination, by their external rites and rituals and not by the teaching of their founders. Such degeneration takes place in all spiritual traditions after the saints, who established them, have shed their bodies. Religious leaders are usually the cause of strife rather than harmony. They contrive to make their gurus exclusive to their religions. They proclaim them to be either Hindus or Muslims or Sikhs or Christians etc. Thus, in their eyes, Sri Rama was Hindu, Guru Nanak was a Sikh, Sri Jesus was a Christian, and Prophet Mohammed was a Muslim and so on. The truth is that these holy beings had transcended distinctions of all kinds and they saw no difference between men and women anywhere. They took birth for the sake of their devotees and having given them spiritual ministration, they went back into tapas for the next phase of their advent. But that does not prevent the religious leaders from labelling them as being a member of this or that sect or community. They do this to incite people for their own personal benefit. Swamiji wants to caution gullible devotees not to fall in their trap. They should rather concentrate on developing spiritually. Swamiji's path is of universal love and harmony based on equality. Swamiji's devotees should rise above differences created by the religious leaders and they can do so through divine love and meditation.

Q138. Apart from meditation, Swamiji laid a lot of stress on kirtan (devotional singing of hymns set to music). Swamiji would always insist on the performance of kirtan wherever he went. Why did he single out kirtan for special emphasis amongst many other aids available for spiritual advancement?

A138. It is everyone's experience that listening to even pop music transports a person into a mental mode of feeling happy. Music brings out the finer sensibilities in an individual. Kirtan is very potent catalyst to create a mood of devotion in a person. Songs sung in the praise of the Lord makes the mind calm and touch chords of love in the inner most recesses of the heart. It has been brought out earlier that no matter what path one follows, spiritual progress is not possible without true devotion (to Reality). Of all the aids to develop and express devotion, kirtan is the best. That is why Swamiji gave it a pride of place in his teaching. Meditation and kirtan help an aspirant to control the mind. Bhakti (devotion) and meditation are the same. Meditation done in a mood of devotion is very efficacious, much more so than without the assistance of the latter.

Q139. Does that not imply that meditation should follow kirtan rather than precede it, as was the case during Swamiji's time?
A139. Kirtan can be performed at any time, before or after meditation or at any other convenient opportunity. Swamiji used to initiate new aspirants around 5.30 p.m. and kirtan was done after that to suit the convenience of a large number of people, especially office goers and ladies busy in household chores, to participate in it. Listening to kirtan with a one pointed mind itself is meditation.

Q140. Why did Swamiji fix the time in the evening for initiation?
A140. These days most people go to work in the mornings or are otherwise busy throughout the day in their daily chores. It was to suit their convenience that Swamiji fixed the evening time for imparting initiation. Swamiji initiated aspirants in the morning whenever it was required.

Q141. Swamiji also lays a lot of stress on service (sewa)? Why is it so? What can one hope to achieve through service which meditation cannot give?
A141. It was brought out earlier that selfless performance of one's karma is a basic path for everyone, irrespective of what other discipline one follows. Karma is integral to one's life and there is no escape from carrying it out. Some devotees find meditation difficult to practise because their rajasic (extroverted) natures mitigate against it. For them, performance of their karma, without expectation of a reward and done as service to the Lord, is enough. Swamiji's initiation helps such aspirants to do so. The benefits from desireless service are the same as from meditation. Performance of motiveless sewa is a primary and fundamental means to attain salvation. Ideally, it should be combined with the practice of meditation or any other path to make rapid spiritual progress. Even if no other discipline is followed, performance of sewa compensates for it provided it is done selflessly. The test of one's attainment in meditation lies

in doing one's karma without a desire. Similarly, the true measure of service is to entertain no thoughts of the self. For these reasons, Swamiji would like all devotees to do sewa (service) whether they practise meditation or not.

Q142. What type of sewa would Swamiji like his devotees to do?

A142. Firstly, every devotee, in whatever status or relationship he or she has been placed, should perform his or her karma in a spirit of motiveless service to the Lord. Secondly, one must regard every other being, nay all forms of life, as manifestations of the Lord and one should love and serve them as such. Thirdly, try to alleviate pain from everyone's heart, especially those who are poor, infirm, old, sick etc. because very few people really care for them. There is so much misery in this world that one does not have to go far to look for people in distress. Fourthly, do every act including meditation as worship of the Lord without wanting to get anything in return. Fifthly, do not attempt to shun action because no embodied soul can do so. It is against the divine law. One should, therefore, regard going through one's karma as an opportunity to do service for the sake of service. Sewa performed in this manner will assuredly lead a devotee to the highest stage.

Q143. Swamiji made a liberal use of bhava (inducing the presence of a deity in a devotee's mind) in instructing a number of devotees. Is there any special reason for doing so? What is the nature of bhava?

A143. Swamiji makes extensive use of bhava to give instruction in Silence for the spiritual upliftment of some aspirants. The supremely intelligent tapas shakti induces bhava so that a student knows that there is a higher power that controls his or her actions for his or her benefit. The importance of devotion has been stressed often enough in this work. Bhava refers to either a gradual or a sudden manifestation of devotion for a particular deity in an aspirant. Usually, such an upsurge occurs on its own when a seeker, through self-effort, purifies his or her mind to a certain degree. True devotion for an object (one's guru, a saint or any other deity) leads to its manifestation in the mind. An aspirant is transported into a mood (bhava) of divine joy felt due to the presence of the subtle body of the deity in one's consciousness. Bhava is a temporary state and its manifestation on a permanent basis occurs in bhava samadhi, described in Chapter 4 of this work, under Samadhi. Swamiji gives the experience of bhava to a number of devotees in order to give them a little taste of the divine bliss that could be theirs provided they make an effort to attain it. Swamiji uses it as an incentive to draw them into the vast ocean of divine bliss (ananda). The experience of bhava usually takes place after a certain degree of mental purification and development of divine qualities like love. Swamiji brings it about deliberately at an early stage for some students so that they have an inner urge to improve spiritually. The experience of bhava can take place during any stage of meditation or while listening to kirtan or at any other time.

Q144. How is it that some devotees have the experience of bhava whereas the others do not?
A144. A spiritual experience occurs according to one's nature. Bhava is generally attained by those in whom devotion takes the form of a deep attachment to an object (like a saint or a deity) and one wants to feel its presence. It is a result of either the current effort or of the previous one (i.e. of past lives). Swamiji confers the experience of bhava on those devotees who will benefit from it. Those who do not get it either do not need it or are not yet ready for it. Sometimes, Swamiji may give bhava to a raw beginner to encourage him or her to realise his or her spiritual potential. It is not essential for everyone to have bhava to make further progress.

Q145. Many devotees get bhava during the time devotional singing (kirtan) is carried out. Some of them dance around; others do pranayama (breathing exercises) or adopt yogic postures etc. Some aspirants can talk to Sri Swamiji in the subtle plane. What is the difference between these states?
A145. Kirtan is an excellent aid to develop a mood of devotion and that is why most devotees get into bhava when it is sung. Bhava of this kind is a low grade transitory experience induced by the presence of a deity's subtle body in a devotee's mind. One acts under its influence as an expression of joy on being so near to one's object of worship. Dancing in a mood of devotion falls in this category and so does practising pranayama, which is good for one's health and it results in purification of nadis (channels for flow of spiritual energy in the subtle body). Such experiences last for some time and then they disappear on their own. Those who can talk to Swamiji or other saints have attained a high degree of devotion. It is a more mature form of bhava and is often induced by Swamiji as an act of grace. However, the full impact of bhava is felt in the lower (i.e. bhava) samadhi stage only.

Q146. How does the experience of normal bhava differ from its samadhi form?
A146. Samadhi implies a state of permanency and effortlessness. It is applicable to all forms of samadhi. A state attained temporarily is not samadhi but only its forerunner. Thus, merely talking to Swamiji is not a sign of a person being in bhava samadhi. Such an experience indicates bhava (a temporary eruption of devotion for an object), which takes place in meditation when the mind becomes somewhat calm and purified. Bhava samadhi is a state of intimacy with the object of worship and it is a sign of deep devotion, pure love and self-surrender. It cannot be attained easily unless the mind is purified of the samaskaric dross. Bhava samadhi indicates a high state of self-control, unlike

bhava's experience that takes place in an uncontrolled mind. The spatial difference between a devotee and an object of devotion is pronounced in ordinary bhava whereas it is practically non-existent in bhava samadhi. The experience of bhava culminates in bhava samadhi when it matures due to hard practice of meditation. The difference between the two states should be obvious. Bhava maybe experienced even if the mind has still not been purified of pride, attachment, desire, greed etc. In other words, the ego is fully intact in ordinary bhava whereas it is very much under control (i.e. it is in its causal form) in bhava samadhi. The experience of bhava, in effect, denotes a student's temporary nearness to Swamiji (or any other deity) in the subtle plane. In the early stages of bhava, one may be vaguely aware of Swamiji's presence (i.e. of his subtle body) but it becomes more definite as one progresses. The effects of bhava on an aspirant improve in consonance with one's advancement. The beginning of bhava samadhi is like clasping Swamiji's hand (in the subtle body) without any intention of leaving it. Its middle stage is like embracing Swamiji whereas its end is reached when one surrenders one's 'I' to him (i.e. Swamiji does not then let a disciple out of his clasp).On the other hand, one is miles away from Swamiji in ordinary bhava. The 'I' is not destroyed in bhava samadhi but all its impurities assume a latent form, which does not take place in ordinary bhava. The Realty lies beyond this state and is attained when a seeker rejects the experience of bhava samadhi as false. It is difficult to do so because the mind becomes addicted to the bliss felt in this last tenuous state of duality. One has to then use one's power of discrimination to attain the higher samadhi. From the description given above, it should be clear that the experience of bhava is of an impure mind and, hence, unreliable. A devotee's samaskaras are a barrier between Swamiji and him or her. That is why one can never fully feel his presence. Nor is one able to distinguish properly between what Swamiji says (i.e. when he gives instructions or speaks otherwise) and what one's mind dictates (according to its vasnas or desires). In the majority of cases, devotees pretend to speak for Swamiji to please their own egos. More often than not, Swamiji's bhava triggers off a chain reaction of thoughts in the mind and one then feels that it is Swamiji who is doing the talking. In fact, it is a play of the mind, which creates thoughts for its pleasure to boost its vanity. It happens to practically every devotee because one fails to use one's power of discrimination. Bhava samadhi is attained if one learns to reject the experience of bhava as unreal. It is only in that state that a disciple feels Swamiji's real presence but even then one has to be very discriminative in apprehending his instructions and putting them to practice. In simple words, bhava samadhi is akin to the beginning of the ascent to the last steep slope of Mt Everest where normal bhava is like making preparations for the climb to the base camp. Experience of bhava is a common phenomenon that is granted to many people while attainment of bhava samadhi in the dark age (kaliyuga) is real achievement gained by a few rare genuine aspirants.

Q147. The experience of bhava has been badly misunderstood by most devotees and some have misused it to exploit others. For example, a few amongst them claim to speak for Swamiji. They say that they are acting under his directions and pretend to teach others. Some even accept some sort of worship from others on the grounds that it is Swamiji who is being worshipped in their person. Many devotees copy his mannerism and speech. Are such gestures and acts a genuine manifestation of Swamiji's bhava?

A147. The state of devotees, mentioned in the question, indicates two things; immature devotion and poor sense of discrimination. It is also a commentary on their ignorance as well as on the gullibility of those who regard them as another form of Swamiji. The nature of bhava that they experience has been explained in the above answer. It is their own ego, which makes them believe that Swamiji acts through them. The true measure of a spiritual state is the degree of self-control that one attains in it. It is only unripe minds that get bowled over by minor experiences. In some of the cases mentioned above, Swamiji's bhava does provide an initial impetus to their minds but then their egos take over, once that impulse disappears due to samaskaric impurities. They then claim to reveal to others Swamiji's instructions. They are unable to discriminate between the assertion of their egos and Swamiji's bhava. There is no reason to accept such revelations. Swamiji's method of teaching is to make the mind silent through one's self effort. Why would he pass instructions to devotees through others when he can do it himself through tapas shakti? It has been emphasised earlier that a seeker should never equate oneself with one's guru. It is a serious dereliction and its consequences cannot be anything but harmful. Swamiji is very indulgent with his devotees but on this point would like to caution them to give up the pretence of being his form. It is only ignorant fools who pretend to be Swamiji or speak for him and bigger fools are those who accept such nonsensical claims as true.

Q148. What is Swamiji's advice to these devotees?

A148. They should learn to discriminate their experience and then reject them as unreal because they are an obstacle to their further progress. They must exercise greater control over their minds and egos. Any desire to have a following is self-destructive because no one can teach others without divine sanction and that comes only after Self Realisation. They should realise that the test of spiritual improvement lies in attaining self-control and not in blabbering and putting up a façade. The goal is far for them and they should practice more meditation in a spirit of self-surrender and desirelessness.

Q149. How many disciples have Swamiji initiated into tapas yoga?
A149. There is no need for Swamiji's disciples to do tapas. Swamiji has initiated a few mature seekers in the higher practices of yoga, which lead to samadhi.

Q150. How many devotees did Swamiji initiate during his lifetime?
A150. Fifteen lakhs (i.e. one and half million).

Q151. Out of this number, how many have really made it to the lower (savikalpa and bhava) samadhi? Has anyone attained higher (nirvikalpa) samadhi or its sahaj state (nirvikalpa sahaj samadhi)?
A151. Samadhi is the culminating stage of one's practice. It is attained only by those who are really devoted to God (or the guru) and have a highly developed sense of discrimination. Samadhi is indicative of an advanced state of spiritual growth that is reflected in detachment from sensual phenomenon. It is acquired through divine grace only; it is not at all easy to attain, for it entails hard and dedicated practice lasting for a long time. Although even lower samadhi is difficult to come by, yet to reach the higher (nirvikalpa) samadhi stage and to go beyond it is particularly hard in this age (kaliyuga). Swamiji will himself make known to those of his devotees who attain the highest (sahaj nirvikalpa) samadhi. However, numbers are not important in these matters. A seeker's duty is to make effort and the guru does the rest. Swamiji does not perceive spiritual progress in terms of time or the number of people he saves, as ordinary people are apt to do. He sees who is sincere and genuine; he keeps pushing such seekers forward. Every devotee of Swamiji is assured of his grace. It needs to be remembered that those who attain the higher states mentioned above are hardly likely to proclaim it to the world. If someone did, it would be obvious that such a person is nowhere near his or her claimed attainment. For, it should not be forgotten, that the essence of spiritual development is how well and effectively has one controlled one's ego and to talk of one's achievements is contrary to its spirit. To know the spiritual condition of another devotee, one must attain at least an equivalent or higher state. For that reason, Swamiji does not like to talk about such matters. But, there should be no doubt that some close disciples of Swamiji have made good progress in exercising control over their minds. How many of them will reach the highest state of liberation cannot be predicted because it depends upon their continued self- effort. The ever-free souls, who are Swamiji's eternal companions, would reveal themselves through Swamiji's grace at the appropriate time.

Q152. Swamiji, during his lifetime, used to initiate devotees through the medium of vibhuti (consecrated piece of clay). He would also give vibhuti, specially blessed by him, for meditation and other purposes. In the absence of Swamiji's physical form, how can aspirants obtain fresh stocks of vibhuti?

A152. All those devotees who have been initiated by Swamiji can procure vibhuti from any of his ashramas. They should then pray to Swamiji, holding the vibhuti in their hands, to bless it for meditation or for any other purpose for personal use only. Swamiji's subtle body, present in tapas shakti imparted at the time of initiation, would then bless it. Swamiji's blessings are with his devotee, regardless of his physical absence.

Q153. Some new devotes may wish to be initiated on the path of mediation? Can Swamiji initiate them even now (i.e. without his embodied form)?
A153. Yes. Swamiji may initiate some aspirants in the subtle form through the medium of dreams etc. It depends on their desire, sincerity, past effort and devotion. All those desirous of Swamiji's grace should pray to him earnestly and as often as they can. Swamiji would assuredly show them the way forward. Be certain that no one's prayer remains unheeded by him for long. Swamiji may authorise some very close disciples, of the ever-free category, to initiate new devotees. They are destined to continue Swamiji's mission.

Q154. There are a lot of pretenders in the field of spirituality, which has become a business these days. They may fraudulently initiate people in Swamiji's name in order to exploit the gullible to have a following of their own. How would an average new devotee distinguish between a genuine disciple (i.e. the ever-free soul mentioned above) and a fake one who claim to speak on behalf of Swamiji?
A154. Know it for certain that Swamiji has not authorised anyone, either in India or abroad, to act on his behalf except for one disciple (in India) who has attained a very high degree of self-control and he will never proclaim himself to be a guru or have a following; he neither seeks publicity nor money. He enjoys Swamiji's complete trust and has his authority to disseminate divine knowledge. All others who speak falsely in the name of Swamiji and pretend to be gurus will meet the consequences of their pretentious conduct. It should be obvious to any reader of this work that only a liberated being can be a guru and that too with divine sanction. Even Self Realisation does not warrant a person to act as a guru till the Lord ordains it so. Only a jeevan mukta (liberated while still in embodied form) can enjoy such a status. It was pointed out in the earlier teaching that an ordinary aspirant is unlikely to attain this state in this age (kaliyuga). It is only the spiritual accomplishment of an ever free soul that marks him or her out for that exalted position. It is from this category that Swamiji may authorise one or two persons to initiate fresh devotees on his behalf. A false guru's initiation for meditation has no effect on the control of mind because he or she lacks the spiritual power that can be transferred to others. On the other hand, a true guru's initiation must invariably result in some form of experience or impact at the time it is carried out, provided a devotee is genuinely seeking freedom from ignorance. In some cases, it may not happen

immediately but one should experience the effects of initiation soon afterwards, within a month or so, provided one does meditation, by feeling a little peace within. An average aspirant is generally a gullible one whose object of meeting a guru is to achieve a selfish goal. A person like that does not usually practise meditation. He or she is more interested in knowing the future or gratify a desire. One's own immaturity and non-discriminative nature misleads one to go astray and seek blessings from frauds. A sincere aspirant is guided from within and is saved from falling prey to false messiahs. Besides all this, it is one's karma, which brings one in contact with the right people. Swamiji's advice to new seekers is to learn to use their heads in these matters.

Q155. Many devotees have the impression that Swamiji does not use his power to bring about a change in their lives as some other holy men do. Some others feel that he has not given them the grace that they deserve for their effort in meditation. How would Swamiji respond to such perceptions?
A155. Those who entertain such doubts are not aware of their own inadequacies created by their samaskaras (mental impressions of past karma). They expect miracles to take place in their worldly conditions, especially in matters of becoming rich or having sons or gaining rapid promotions or removal of bodily afflictions etc. Swamiji's mission is to enlighten the minds of the ignorant. How would the satiation of worldly desires help such people to turn to God? More often than not, grant of wishes leads people to indulge in them with greater vehemence. Notwithstanding this, Swamiji has brought about subtle changes in the lives of many aspirants even if they do not acknowledge it. He has fulfilled the hopes of large number of them. But, this must be seen in the context of their own karma. Swamiji has not fulfilled every wish of his devotees because that would run counter to the natural order of things. An unanswered prayer of a seeker is either due to his or her own insincerity or the inappropriateness of the time for its grant or the karmic obstacles whose removal would not bring the desired effect. As for Swamiji's grace is concerned, it is not for an aspirant to judge what he or she deserves. The mind raises doubts like this to protect its identity. A wise student should not fall prey to such misgivings because effort cannot be but rewarded by grace. More the effort, more the grace. Effort done sincerely and in humility earns infinite grace. Swamiji has showered his grace on everyone who has made the effort, whether big or small. Let no aspirant suffer any misapprehension on this score. Every devotee who makes the effort gets more than his or her deserved share of Swamiji's grace.

Q156. Some aspirants experience violent forms of currents at times either during meditation or otherwise. Sometimes the currents run in the body for prolonged periods causing headaches etc. Is there any harm in all this?

A156. It is perfectly safe to experience currents running for long period. It indicates that the mind is getting attuned to a higher yogic power. One should continue with practice of meditation and currents will automatically stabilise. Conditions like headaches etc. disappear as the mind is purified. Currents may, at times, open the various knots in the subtle body signifying spiritual progress.

Q157. Some devotees, after being initiated by Swamiji, have been to see some other holy men and have accepted initiation from them. Is the potency of Swamiji's initiatory power lost in such cases?
A157. No; Swamiji's tapas shakti, given at the time of initiation, can be countered only by a more potent power. It is only then that meditation would be affected. Anyone who is prepared to initiate a devotee of Swamiji is obviously not aware of his power of tapas. No true guru will initiate a devotee of Swamiji again. Aspirants who have been initiated twice can practise meditation but without combining the two methods. If desired, they can be practised separately. Swamiji's tapas shakti will gradually neutralise the other power through improvement in meditation.

Q158. A few devotees have come under the influence of some ordinary tantrics (those who have gained lower powers through practice of tantra) and have suffered on that account, despite Swamiji tapas shakti. How is it that it could not counter the evil influence of these so called holy men?
A158. It is due to lack of faith in Swamiji that some devotees turn to some godmen. It is a sign of a wavering, weak and indecisive mind. The frauds mentioned above earn a little bit of low grade merit through mantra shakti (power of mantra) and then they set about beguiling and exploiting ignorant people. They cannot counter the power of tapas given by Swamiji. The ill effects suffered by some devotees, due to their contact with certain tantrics, is because they have not nurtured the tapas shakti, imparted at the time of initiation, by practice of meditation. It was pointed out earlier that it is given in seed form and it stays that way if one does not practise meditation. No evil force can touch a devotee of Swamiji, provided one does meditation regularly. Those who are still suffering from some harmful effects are advised to practise meditation to neutralise it.

Q159. Swamiji initiated a large number of people yet he could remember them, even if he had met them once. How did he have such a perfect memory?
A159. It is the effect of tapas done by Swamiji. Tapas shakti is excellent in every way and it remembers everything, of past and future, in its pure memory form.

Q160. Swamiji made remarks, at times, about the past lives of some devotees and even obliquely hinted at his own previous births. How did this memory arise when he was totally engulfed in the great Silence?

A160. Although the state of Silence is sans memory, yet the body has to do its prarabdha (present life's) karma as long as it lasts. Swamiji's pure prarabdhic memory used to become active when he had to talk to devotees. Whatever Swamiji revealed was in response to a seeker's expressed or unexpressed doubts. It was always said for the benefit of an aspirant's spiritual upliftment.

Q161. The Bhrigu and Kumar Nadies (works dealing with predictions based on astrology) reveal that Swamiji had taken seven births in the past. Swamiji himself never confirmed or denied the veracity of such revelations, although a few disciples have learnt, in meditation, a few of Swamiji's past incarnations. Are the revelations in the above Nadis true? Should the aspirants believe their own experiences in this regard?

A161. Swamiji has had innumerable births in the past and will continue to incarnate in the future as long as all his devotees do not attain salvation. Astrology is a branch of physical science and very few of its propagators achieve any great proficiency in it because it requires hard and long study lasting a life time. Even then it cannot reveal the future hundred percent because astrological knowledge is relative in nature and is gained by the mind, which is itself imperfect. Normally, predictions are made based on the movement of planets; but there are millions of other objects, like stars, which influence life on earth. No one can possibly make a full study of the impact of such objects on an individual's life. Besides that, a jiva's karma is interconnected with many other people (e.g. family, friends etc.). Astrological predictions are, therefore, never fully reliable, though an astute astrologer may be able to predict a fair amount. The Nadis mentioned above contain some elements of truth but not the whole of it. Revelations made in meditation are due to purification of memory. To know the former lives of a saint requires a very high degree of introversion and stillness of the mind. Disclosures made to certain close disciples of Swamiji, about his past, is due to their karmic connection with him. Some of them have served him for a very long time and they get to know about Swamiji's past lives in a regressed state of purified memory. Sometimes, Swamiji may, out of grace, reveal his past connection with an earnest disciple. In general, one should accept such disclosures only after reaching the state of savikalpa or bhava samadhi.

Q162. It is said that some of the nadies are based on divine revelations made to sages. Some claim Brighu to be a saint. What is the truth in such assertions?

A162. The reliability of such claims lies in knowing the spiritual state of the so-called sages. Ordinary people tend to proclaim someone a saint if something said by him or her turns out to be true. That is not a test of a person's spiritual status. Knowledge of future events is gained in various stages of meditation. It is relative in nature and can never be fully trusted. Those who have written nadis and claim their predictions are based on divine revelations have gained such knowledge or ability to foresee the future in meditation. That is why some sayings of the nadies are true whereas the others are false. The proportion depends on the level of purity and one pointedness of the mind attained by the person making such revelations, which allows one to go back into memory of past lives. To regress into memory implies that one can know the samaskaras and vasnas (mental impressions and latent desires) of another person and, based on them, one can predict the course that his or her present life is likely to take. But, it should be remembered that performance of karma is based on various options to do it. Hence, it is not possible to predict the future accurately. Some persons obtain boons from gods and goddesses to foresee the future whereas some others attain siddhis (powers) through repetition of mantras. But, all such knowledge is relative and partial. Devotees should bear in mind that sainthood lies in overcoming notions of time. What sort of seer is he or she who goes around proclaiming the future to the world? Saints make remarks about the future for the benefit of devotees. Such sayings are not astrological predictions but divine revelations made in the context of a seeker's karma and they are made only once a while to help an aspirant overcome some concern affecting his or her spiritual growth.

Q163. Rakhta Kali (i.e. manifestation of the Devi) in the person of a girl sucked blood, for two hours, from Swamiji's palms in January 1962. Is that not a bizarre incident, which one would normally associate with tantrics or ordinary godmen out to dupe the gullible? What is its rational explanation?

A163. Devi is a generic term for the embodied form of ad shakti (divine power). It has many aspects encompassing its countless attributes. She is known as Kali Devi in one of her forms. It is a popular misconception that Kali is the embodied form of the Devi in Its terrible aspect only. But, the truth is that She is also a symbol of love and protects Her devotees, like a mother does her children, from persons of demonical natures by meting out divine retribution. Evil and wickedness are very much part of the world as any rational mind would accept. She is depicted in black colour because it is symbolic of tamoguna (the dark aspect of maya), which is the predominant trait of demons and evil forces. For example, Kal (the embodied form of time) is black by nature. She absorbs everything tamasic in Herself to protect those who love Her. Good and bad must co-exist in the pair of opposites, as explained earlier in Chapter 3. The Kali Devi's subtle embodiment is for the purpose of upholding virtue and destroying evil. Ignorant worshippers only remember Her later aspect and not the former one. Many of Kali's devotees in the subtle world (i.e. lower type of goddesses) are of demonic natures and they worship Her only in Her terrible form. They do so to gain power to spread evil and wickedness in the world, that being their nature. They usually look for weak willed persons to possess them (i.e. their subtle bodies take an abode in such jivas) and force them to cause harm to others. A lower form of tantra deals with this aspect and many of its evil minded practitioners propitiate goddesses of this type through mantra shakti (power gained through mantras) and then misuse this power to frighten others for selfish gains. The girl in question had fallen prey to a tantric in the past and its harmful effects manifested in her at the time she came to Swamiji. Rakhta is a goddess of the lower type who possessed the girl and demanded sacrifice of blood. As an act of grace, Swamiji allowed Rakhta to suck his blood through that girl so that she could overcome her sinful nature. Otherwise, she would have hurt many other people. Swamiji absolved the girl of her fear by letting Rakhta taste his blood. She was otherwise destined to act through the girl to do many more wicked acts. Incidentally, the girl in question became his devotee later. The subtle form of Rakhta came once again, in February 1962, on the Maha Shivratri Day, to demand a sacrifice of blood. Swamiji allowed her to suck his blood for some time and then forbade her from entering his ashram or causing harm to his devotees.

Q164. How could Rakhta drink Swamiji's blood for two hours without causing him physical harm?
A164. All such experiences take place in the subtle plane. Although the effects of subtle body are felt by its physical counterpart, yet Swamiji did not allow Rakhta to do so by the power of his tapas. Swamiji let her suck his subtle blood but its physical effect was no more than worth a drop of it. Swamiji did not use his tapas shakti deliberately to prevent Rakhta from causing him physical damage. It was done by Swamiji's Guru who protected him by His grace.

Q165. Could not Swamiji order Rakhta to leave the girl, mentioned above, without going through the blood sucking incident?
A165. The physical body has to suffer the consequences of its past karma. That is the only way to expiate it. The girl, in question, had certain evil tendencies at the time she was possessed by Rakhta and she came to Swamiji as part of her karma. What Swamiji did was part of his karma and he saved the girl from acting wickedly in future through the sacrifice of blood. This is all part of the natural order of things in which the consequences of a devotee's karma are expiated by the guru through certain actions. The above incident is an example of how Swamiji protects his devotees from evil doers. Normally, Rakhta would not have dared come near Swamiji due to his tapas power but by permitting her to do so, he saved many more devotees from suffering at her hands.

Q166. Swamiji had visited the court of Dharmaraja (the god of death and justice) sometimes in early 1969. How did it come to pass and what was its purpose?
A166. It happened during the tapas, which Swamiji undertook on Shankar Bhagwan's directions, from 7th August 1968 to 7th August 1969. Swamiji came

to know during the course of tapas that some minions (jamdoots or agents) of Dharmaraja had come to take his mother away. It is the normal function of these agents to force the subtle bodies of jivas to go to Dharmaraja at the time of death. Swamiji's mother, being of divine nature, was not subject to Dharmaraja's reign. She could shed her body at will. The jamdoots were hovering around Swamiji's mother by mistaking her for another similar looking lady. Even gods and their agents act in error at times, especially those who are not Self Realised. Swamiji's subtle form, therefore, visited Dharmaraja and advised him to tell his minions to desist from troubling his mother. An agent of Dharmaraja hit Swamiji with a stick before he entered his court. He thought that Swamiji had come to Dharmaraja's court, after death, to hear the award of his karma. The jamdoots maltreat the subtle bodies of jivas, after death, before Dharmaraja passes his judgement on their karma. It is their nature to act thus and punish people for their misdeeds. As soon as Swamiji entered the court, Dharmaraja immediately recognised Swamiji by his yogic vision and came forward to receive him by prostrating before him. He requested Swamiji to sit on his throne. Swamiji declined his offer and told him the purpose of his visit. He readily apologised for the conduct of his assistants, including the one who had hit Swamiji. Dharmaraja sought Swamiji's blessings, which brought an end to this experience. Swamiji did not go deliberately to Dharmaraja. It happened on its own during tapas with great suddenness. Swamiji's mother lived for a few more years and shed her body when its karma had exhausted itself. It should also indicate to devotees the sort of treatment that they are likely to get after death if they do not attain salvation.

Q167. Some of the incidents related earlier are likely to cause disbelief in a rational mind. They read more like a tale of fantasy and their occurrence might even appear rather farfetched to a materialist. How should a discerning student view them?

A167. The theory of rationality is applied, these days, by thinking people only to what the gross senses perceive and experience. This is due to ignorance of things that exist beyond the material world. A so called rationalist sees objects in a dream every day and yet denies the existence of subtle eyes. One should, therefore, not be too concerned about sceptics who make it a habit to doubt all that their limited visions do not reveal. A really intelligent person should have an open mind that accepts the possibility of things existing beyond one's narrow sensual experience. Further, one should reject the assertion of others' experience only after a thorough investigation based on reason and knowledge (of things not perceived by the senses). Swamiji's advice to the cynics is to study the subtle phenomenon through control of mind and see how the subtle bodies function according to the laws applicable to them. Swamiji's poser to a doubting Thomas is to reflect on how a jiva travels from Delhi to London in a dream to experience objects there without leaving one's bed. There is nothing more to be said on the subject.

Q168. Swamiji was very fond of organising mass feeding for all comers on certain days, especially on Sundays and holidays. Swamiji would eat only after all the devotees had been fed. What was its significance?

A168. To feed a hungry person is the best of all meritorious acts (punya). There is no greater merit than feeding the poor because their craving for food is never satisfied. Prolonged hunger is against the natural order, which gives pre-eminence to preservation of the body as a means to be free of ignorance. Satiation of hunger is a basic desire and it causes pain if it remains unfulfilled for long. A hungry person is incapable of acting well and least of all would he or she seek liberation. Practice of spiritual discipline is best done when one is neither hungry nor thirsty. Poor people always leave behind vibrations of contentment and happiness after they are fed. It is an aid in creating a spiritual atmosphere. It always gave Swamiji a great degree of peace when mass feeding of devotees was organised in his presence. The subtle essence of food is a fuel to burn the yogic flame and its divine heat brings waves of bliss when the hunger of others is satisfied. Swamiji used to feel the pain of hungry people (as he did of all types of suffering) in his heart. Mass feeding was a means to remove it. Swamiji used to organise it on holidays and Sundays to have maximum attendance. One must appease the hunger and thirst of another before satisfying one's own. That is selfless service. Besides that, eating together, in large numbers food cooked in the same kitchen removes caste consciousness. Swamiji wanted to set that as an example. Service is a two-way traffic; the guru serves a devotee and, in turn, the latter should serve the former. Remember, to leave a person hungry when one is in a position to do something about it is to incur a sin. That is the divine law.

Q169. Swamiji used to celebrate, in his ashramas, birthdays of many saints who are generally associated with various sects, creeds and religions. Why did he do that?

A169. People of various religious denominations and races came to Swamiji and he regarded them equally. Swamiji himself did not subscribe to any creed as such. He, however, wanted to establish that all saints are equally holy and worthy of everyone's worship. No true guru or seer is really associated with any religion as is commonly supposed by ordinary people because he or she transcends all man-made differences created on the basis of sects, castes, languages, races etc. He or she merely accepts customs and traditional forms of worship followed by the family in which he or she is born. Devotees must live in harmony amongst themselves and learn to overcome feelings of being different from others. Even the most spiritually ignorant person likes to participate in festivals connected with anniversaries of saints. It is one of the ways for them to worship and remember the Lord, even though if it is for a fleeting moment. There is some merit earned by such participation. Swamiji used to celebrate such occasions to establish equality of all traditional religions, as also to encourage devotees to revere all saints and gurus equally.

Q170. Why did Swamiji sit for meditation during kirtan (devotional singing) since he had already achieved a much higher state during tapas?
A170. It was meant to set an example to devotees to listen to kirtan with one pointed mind. The divine mood of devotion sets in only when the mind is stilled. That is the purpose of kirtan. Swamiji's state did not change during the time he sat for meditation, which was as part of his prarabdha karma to impart teaching to devotees. At times, Swamiji's Guru would give him some directions during this period. Also, very often Swamiji's subtle body, in many forms, would leave his gross body to help seekers in various ways.

Q171. Did the subtle body of Swamiji help all devotees? How could one body multiply into so many at one time?
A171. A yogi's subtle body can assume any number of forms due to the omnipotence of tapas shakti. Swamiji's subtle body is generally present wherever his devotees are. It goes to help aspirants who pray to him earnestly and remember him with love. It gives them protection against evil forces and provide subtle guidance during meditation. Swamiji during his life time did not consciously detach his subtle body while he was alive. It happened on its own due to the power of tapas in response to the prayers of his devotees.

Q172. Does this phenomenon still take place?
A172. Swamiji's subtle body will continue to exist for the present time cycle due to his tapas. This is true of the subtle bodies of all yogis who do tapas. The subtle body of Swamiji will continue to guide devotees as long as they entreat him sincerely for his grace. It rushes to the help of those who love him with pure devotion.

Q173. Does Swamiji's subtle body transfer to an aspirant's body at the time of initiation?
A173. Tapas shakti, imparted at the time of initiation, has within it Swamiji's subtle body. But, it manifests only when devotees have attained a certain steadiness of their minds through practice of meditation. It manifests fully in the final stages of bhava samadhi, when the mind is purified of its samaskaric dross.

Q174. Why did Swamiji need frequent periods of rest?
A174. Swamiji's body had become healthy after tapas due to wholesome diet and rest. But, it still lacked the vigour and vitality, which a person of his

age should have had. Swamiji's adolescent years were spent in tapas without adequate diet, which had severely affected the body's growth. It was made worse by the venom of snakes. Swamiji could not fully recover from this debility. After the tapas, Swamiji's body used to experience constant currents of tapas shakti, which used to feed off the subtle essences of the food taken by him. That is why Swamiji advises disciples in the advanced stages of practice to take good and wholesome diet. The above factors were responsible for Swamiji's general physical weakness and the requirement of frequent rests.

Q175. Swamiji had carried out kayakalpa (a yogic technique to rejuvenate an ageing body) on three occasions. Did it not improve Swamiji's health?
A175. It did but the efficacy of yogic techniques like kayakalpa has to be judged in the context of an individual's prarabdha (present life's) karma. The inherent weaknesses of one's body are overcome by it to a certain extent but it cannot remove them completely. The same thing happened when Swamiji did kayakalpa. It was most effective the first time (done immediately after the completion of tapas) and least effective the last time (1992). The one done in 1982 produced medium results.

Q176. When did Swamiji's health begin to deteriorate?
A176. Swamiji maintained a reasonable level of health till he was fifty years of age. Thereafter, his body began to lose its vitality gradually.

Q177. Swamiji's health had worsened after the summer of 1991 and practically all bodily systems were affected. What was the cause for such deterioration?
A177. Serpents, including cobras, bit Swamiji, a number of times during the tapas. Their poison had enfeebled his body and traces of the venom injected by cobras remained in it throughout his earthly life. The poison had affected some of the vital bodily organs. Later, Swamiji developed diabetes, which led to a lot of complications, resulting in the malfunctioning of most of the organs.

Q178. How is it that a body of a yogi like Swamiji, infused with tapas shakti, could be affected by a disease like diabetes?
A178. The physical body is subject to growth and decay. That is its nature established by the divine will, which makes no distinction between the body of a yogi and that of an ordinary jiva. Some hatha yogis (i.e. practitioners of the physical aspect of yoga) follow a yogic discipline, which prolongs the body's existence but even they cannot prevent its eventual decline. Swamiji did not do tapas for the sake of the mortal body. Rather, he did it to destroy the notion that one is the body. Swamiji, therefore, did not bother if the body survived or was healthy or unhealthy. Swamiji's body was made up of the samaskaras of his devotees, which he had taken upon himself to expiate for them. In doing so, Swamiji did not take only the healthy karma of devotees. He took on

their burden, which included their diseases and illnesses. Besides that, many aspirants who came for Swamiji's darshan (i.e. to see him) used to pray to him to remove their bodily afflictions. Some sick persons wanted Swamiji to cure them. In some cases he restored them to health by taking their sufferings on his self. All jivas emit vibrations of their samaskaras and vasnas and they affect the bodies of those who come close to them. Thus, Swamiji's body was subjected to the vibrations of all those who came in contact with him. Some of them were of evil nature and their vibrations affected Swamiji's health adversely. Even the retention of venom of snakes in his body was to atone for the ill deeds of his devotees. The cumulative effect of all these factors affected Swamiji's health. He developed diabetes in the late seventies, which caused malfunctioning in his kidneys and other organs. Swamiji accepted all this out of love for his devotees and as his service to them.

Q179. Many saints do not allow their devotees to touch their bodies because of their adverse vibrations. But, Swamiji allowed everyone to touch his holy feet when any of them prostrated before him. Why did he sanction it? What effect did his vibrations have on others?

A179. The exchange of bodily vibrations is the maximum during physical contact. Swamiji's vibrations also affected the bodies of his devotees. Their effect was according to the samaskaric purity of the devotees. Those who stayed in Swamiji's company for long benefited more than the others. However, it would be wrong to conclude that such contact is a substitute for meditation. It brings about minimal changes. All those who came to Swamiji and touched his body did so to carry out their karma and he allowed them to do so as part of his karma. Swamiji had no desire to change either his or others' karma in this respect. His state of supreme Silence was not affected by what the body did. Why should he have bothered whether anyone touched him or not?

Q180. Many devotees prayed to Swamiji to cure himself with his tapas power and he always gave an impression, in normal conversation, that he would live to be an old man, implying thereby that his disease would disappear. The reality turned out to be otherwise. How is it that Swamiji who was so compassionate otherwise did not heed their prayers?

A180. As stated earlier, Swamiji had no desire to take birth. He only complied with his Guru's directions to do so. Similarly, Swamiji had no desire to keep the body or discard it. He gave up the body on his Guru's orders as per his prarabdha karma. There was, therefore, no question that Swamiji would use his tapas shakti to prolong his life. If a yogi uses his power on himself, it implies that the feeling of 'I'-ness still exists in him. Self Realisation destroys all notions like 'I am the body or I have the power to cure' etc. How can a yogi then use a non-existent power to cure an unreal body? The best way to do one's karma is to submit to the divine will cheerfully. Swamiji wanted to set that as an example for the devotees to follow. There was thus no way that Swamiji could accede to the requests of devotees in this regard. At the same time, he did not want to cause them any distress and he would make light of his health problems, whenever they raised such topics.

Q181. Did Swamiji know, in advance, of the time of his departure from this world?

A181. Swamiji did not seek any such knowledge. The idea of time (kal) had already disappeared from his consciousness during the tapas. To become aware of a limitation like that again would have implied that Swamiji had not been able to maintain the state of great Silence. Swamiji had neither any attachment nor concern with the body. In fact, he was not even aware of it. He had, therefore, no desire or need to know the time he would shed the body.

Q182. Swamiji could ignore bodily suffering during tapas because he was totally immersed in the great samadhi. But, he went through an equally harsh period during the last three years of his life when he could neither eat nor drink water in adequate quantities. He had very serious health problems and, yet, when asked, he would deny that he was undergoing pain. He also never changed his routine, specially coming out for daily darshan (i.e. meeting the devotees). How could he cope with so much bodily punishment despite leading a fairly active life?

A182. Swamiji's condition was akin to that of a half awake person who has just got up from sound sleep. In that state, one is not immediately aware of the body because the mind is immersed in the memory of blissful sleep, which makes one feel refreshed. A bystander thinks that the person is awake, but, in reality, he is not yet aware of his surroundings. In the same way, devotees saw Swamiji suffering but did not realise that he was totally absorbed in the bliss of Reality. He became partially aware of the pain only when devotees reminded him of it; otherwise, he did not suffer at all. Swamiji was not attached to the body and, hence, food and water did not bother him. The body had to atrophy because of malfunctioning of various organs according to its prarabdha karma, which also impelled Swamiji to follow his routine. Swamiji would have failed as a guru if he had not given darshan (grace) to devotees till the end.

Q183. There is a feeling that perhaps devotees did not do enough to look after Swamiji when he was sick. It is possible that better treatment could have prolonged his life. How does Swamiji respond to such misgivings amongst some disciples?

A183. Swamiji was very happy with the way he was looked after by his devotees throughout his earthly existence, especially in the last three years. Everyone served him well. Swamiji has utmost love for his devotees and none of them should entertain the feelings expressed in the question. Time had come for Swamiji to discard the body and there was no way that it could be altered.

Q184. What were Swamiji's last moments like before leaving the body?
A184. Swamiji felt like a person falling off to deep sleep after a tiring day. About three hours before Swamiji discarded the body, he began to recede into the innermost core of his being, characterised by ineffable peace and unconditioned bliss, which the superimposition of his prarabdha karma on the fathomless Silence gave. Gradually, Swamiji lost even the slight memory (due to prarabdha karma) of the supreme bliss. The body went through its last throes as per its karma, without in any way affecting Swamiji. He had no awareness of how and when he shed the body. The explanation given above relates to his prarabdhic experience, i.e., it refers to the recession and disappearance of the memory of his prarabdha karma held in the general consciousness. It did not affect the state of supreme Silence.

Q185. Where does Swamiji dwell now?
A185. Where can Swamiji go? There is nowhere to go to. The incomparable Atman alone is and Swamiji is immersed in Its Silence. All objects exist in it in a unitary and non-dual manner. For those who find this hard to understand, suffice it to say that Swamiji inheres in the heart of every devotee. He dwells there beckoning all those who love him. Swamiji's subtle form went back to its eternal abode, after leaving the gross world, in the sacred hills in the subtle world. He lives there in the company of his devotees who serve him as they used to here. He instructs them in meditation and other disciplines. Many more will join him there after their deaths. Swamiji also does tapas in the subtle body on the directions of his Guru.

Q186. When would Swamiji take birth again?
A186. It depends on the prayers and needs of the devotees. Swamiji would be reborn sooner if they seek his grace with love and learn to surrender to him.

Q187. The activities of various ashramas (centres set up to propagate Swamiji's mission) have suffered a setback after Swamiji's departure from the world. There have been some bickering in the management of few centres. The attendance of devotees has come down. Does this indicate loss of faith? Why should it have happened so soon after Swamiji's departure?
A187. Chaff and grain are separated at the time of harvest. Similarly, how much do the devotees understand a guru's teaching is known only by their conduct after the latter is no more in bodily form. People who have not controlled their egos often claim his or her legacy. Something similar has happened in Swamiji's ashramas. Many are asserting their right to speak for him and propagate his

mission. Know it for certain that Swamiji has not authorised anyone to do so. His mission can prosper only through spiritual power. How many of those who pretend to act on his behalf have it? The problems mentioned in the question are mostly about the property of the ashramas. It is an example, in its incipient stage, of how religious leaders, described earlier, come into being to assert their egos and mislead gullible people. It has happened because of the prarabdha karma of some of the devotees. They pretend to serve Swamiji in their own limited and ignorant way. Actions of some of them indicate immaturity in devotion and faith. The problems being faced by ashramas are a passing phase and they would be set right soon. Genuine aspirants should not bother about these matters. They should continue to practise meditation and do sewa (service) as explained earlier.

Q188. What is Swamiji's advice to those who manage the various ashramas?
A188. The routine set by Swamiji of meditation and kirtan (devotional singing) must continue unabated daily. The management must look after and keep the ashramas neat and clean. Mass feeding of the poor is not to be discontinued and it should be organised as it was done during Swamiji's time. Devotees must perform service (sewa) in the ashramas according to their physical capacity. The management must ensure that no new practice or ritual, except the ones prevalent during Swamiji's time, is introduced in any ashrama. It must not be forgotten that Swamiji ashramas are spiritual centres for propagation of meditation and there is no place for propagation of any religion or politics of any kind in them. The doors of the ashramas are to be kept open, at all times, for everyone, irrespective of caste, creed, religion, race and gender. In times to come, some of the ashramas would become important centres of spiritual learning.

Q189. Now, a word about the future. Swamiji's divine mission, revealed by the Lord, had a twin purpose; one, to awaken latent spirituality in those who seek his grace and, two, to re- establish dharma (i.e. destruction of evil for virtue to predominate). Swamiji has undoubtedly succeeded in the first part; the divine teaching given in this work as also the large number of people initiated into meditation bear witness to it. But, the other aspect does not appear to have taken off. Dark forces rule the roost in much of the world and it is specially so in India. Now that Swamiji is no more in the physical body, would it be a correct assumption that he failed to accomplish what his Guru had ordained?
A189. No! No! It can never be so. How can the word of the divine Guru go unfulfilled? It is immaterial whether Swamiji is in this or that form. It is his all-pervasive and omnipotent tapas shakti, which acts and it is not confined in any particular body. Swamiji still lives in the subtle body. The power of tapas will remain effective for the time for which it was earned. Kal (time) and the

trinity of gods are powerless against it. That shakti (power) is operative today and would remain so for a long time to come. One cannot assess the success or otherwise of Swamiji's mission in a very narrow and limited time frame. Divine missions are not subject to such conditions and most of them outlast the physical presence of their propagators. They unfold according to the divine will operating in the context of cosmic plan of action. Individual jivas are only bit players in the divine drama that is enacted according to its own time plot. The work of Sri Jesus, Sri Shankracharya, Guru Nanak, Sri Raman Maharishi and other yogis of a similar stature is still going apace, though not through the so called religious leaders who pretend to speak for them. The same is true of Swamiji's mission. Swamiji has laid the foundation and many of his disciples would build over it in the future using his power of tapas. Know it for certain that Swamiji's mission has just begun and it would fructify in due course as per divine ordination. Nothing more needs to be said on the subject for the time being.

Q190. All great gurus and yogis are invariably accompanied by some ever free souls to help them to propagate their divine missions. How is it that a yogi of Swamiji's exalted status has not been accompanied by his eternal companions (i.e. ever free souls) to help him in his mission?
A190. It is a superficial comment. Ignorant people tend to judge the state of ever-free souls by their own notions of what such beings ought to be. Spiritually immature persons judge the holiness or otherwise of a people by their garb that they wear or marks on their forehead or how much they quote from scriptures and so on. Estimates of their natures are based on one's knowledge, gained through books, of past saints and their companions. It does not occur to them that the divine drama is never repeated because the circumstances are different in every age. Is it possible for an ignorant person to form an estimate of who an ever free soul is? It is true that some ever-free souls always accompany satgurus and avtaras to disseminate their teachings or assist them in carrying out their divine missions. Examples of Sri Christ and Sri Ramakrishna are well known in this regard. The number of such disciples that accompany a holy sage varies according to the requirement of the mission. It is not essential that they must always take birth along with him or her. Some may even precede him or her or be born after the departure of the holy being from this world. The assumption in the question that Swamiji did not bring any such souls is incorrect. It is not possible for ordinary people to know them unless they reveal themselves through some spiritual or other act. They may do no spiritual practice nor show any outward signs of being holy. Some may even remain unknown and indulge in only silent work. Casual observers cannot appreciate that they act without any selfish motive. All free souls take birth after doing tapas in the subtle world. Usually, they need not do any tapas in the gross body. They draw their power and authority to perform their work from the saint they come to

serve. Sri Ramakrishna's close disciples did not perform any great penance to gain spiritual power. It was his grace that made Swami Vivekananda and others do his work. There are a number of Swamiji's close disciples who are destined to continue his mission. Some of them are his eternal companions and are inextricably connected with his tapas. A few are of the sapt rishis (i.e. the seven sages who are the alter ego of the Lord) class. Some of them had taken birth during Swamiji's time and some would come later.

Q191. Who amongst the current set of seekers falls in the above category?
A191. Embodied souls function according to their prarabdha (present life's) karma. These disciples will reveal themselves by their deeds at the appropriate time. Ordinary devotees cannot, in any case, recognise them nor is there any requirement to do so at present. Everything will become clear in due course of time.

Q192. It is the spiritual experience of Gurprasad that Swamiji was an incarnation of God. Is it true?
A192. Swamiji was a yogi who did service (sewa) for his Guru and his devotees. Personal experiences of aspirants are their own convictions. Beyond that, it is not Swamiji's policy to talk about these matters.

Q193. Can Gurprasad proclaim his personal conviction to the world at large?
A193. It is for him to decide; guidance for such things comes from within the heart. Swamiji's advice to all aspirants is to attain liberation first; only then would they know the real Swamiji.

Q194. It is for the first time that an Indian sage has revealed upanishadic knowledge, which alone gives liberation, directly in English language. Is there a reason for it?
A194. Swamiji is not bound or confined by any language, religious belief, caste prejudice, national boundary, racial discrimination, gender bias and so on. The teachings given here are based on his knowledge of the Truth attained by him in tapas. Its expression is suited to the current scientific age. English is an international language today and is known in most countries. Swamiji wants that the teaching given here has a wide readership amongst intelligent and rational people, cutting across man made barriers of every kind. English language is the most suitable medium for this purpose at present. In due course, this work will be translated into many other languages.

Q195. Swamiji's monumental word, given in this work, may appear to lack divine sanction, now that he is no more present in the embodied form. Also, some people, not conversant with spiritual matters, may question its method of revelation in bhava samadhi. What would be Swamiji's answer to such doubts?

A195. Divinely inspired works need no certificates of authority, least of all from ignorant people. The revelation itself (of the instruction) carries the stamp of authority. Those who practice any form of spiritual discipline and have even a little knowledge of matters of spirit will instantly recognise the merits of the teaching given here. Intelligent persons who give primacy to reason will find it hard to criticize Swamiji's teaching because it is based on a rational analysis of spiritual experience. Those with half-baked knowledge gathered mostly from books might raise some objections to this work. Their motive would be to show off their cleverness and so called learning. Any such criticism is invalid because it is not backed by actual experience of Reality. It is best ignored. No one needs to accept this work merely on faith. Every reader is advised to use his or her power of discrimination to do so. One must first practise what has been set forth here to know its merit. The power that has revealed the teaching would remove their doubts. Then, and only then, would they know its divine source.

Q196. Swamiji has been most gracious and patient to satiate a humble disciple's (i.e. Gurprasad's) hunger for knowledge. By your blessings alone has it been well understood. What is Swamiji's final advice to the devotees?

A196. Swamiji wants to emphasise that human birth is very difficult to obtain in the divine scheme of things. It is due to the accumulated merit (good karma) of many lives that one is born as a man or woman. To earn the grace of a guru (i.e. to be initiated) is even more difficult. Having earned this merit, Swamiji's advice to his devotees is that they should not waste this precious opportunity. The only worthwhile activity of a jiva is to know the Truth; the rest is all worthless. A moment spent in remembering the Lord is far more rewarding than a lifetime wasted under the influence of maya. More specifically do the following: -

(a) Learn to control the mind. There is no other way to know the Reality and to live in eternal bliss.

(b) Practise meditation as much as possible. Let practice be a devotee's religion, caste, creed and duty.

(c) Let the Lord or Guru bear your burden. There is nothing higher than to do all actions including meditation in the spirit of self-surrender.

(d) A spiritual journey is long and full of obstacles, created by one's own mind. Do meditation fearlessly with complete faith that the Guru will remove all hurdles with his grace.

(e) Remember, quality of self-effort is as important as time spent in doing so.

(f) To make rapid spiritual progress, one should practise meditation with devotion and love. Meditation combined with devotion, love, discrimination and sewa (service) is even better. Progress then will be faster and more rewarding. Better than all these is to do meditation desirelessly with devotion, love, discrimination, detachment and do service at the same time in a mental mode of self-surrender and fearlessness. That is the best and the quickest method to control the mind. Those who have been initiated by Swamiji in other paths should practise them in the spirit indicated above.

After the previous answer, Swamiji said, **'the teaching given in this work is complete now. All those who study it earnestly and discriminatively will have his blessings. It would confer on them the benefits of hearing (sravana) and contemplation (mannana) of Truth. One should reflect on the teaching throughout one's sadhana (practice). Anyone who practises it with a firm resolve not to give up till the goal to know the Reality is reached is assured of Swamiji's grace. Swamiji will never forsake a devotee; that is his promise. Know it for certain that all those who have real devotion for Swamiji have his protection and he would give them a far greater reward than what their effort deserves. Remember, if a devotee takes one step towards Realisation Swamiji will take a hundred or more steps to bring him or her closer to the Goal. Finally, keep in mind that the Lord Itself looks after Swamiji's devotees.'**

> *O Beloved Guru! Who can measure thy limitless grace that has revealed the divine knowledge given in this work! It is the key to the treasure-trove of liberation. Pray be gracious to those who want to know its secrets. It cannot be known otherwise. Bless them with its true understanding.*

Gurprasad

Glossary

A

Ad Shakti	Divine or primordial power that creates, sustains and destroys the universe; principle of supreme intelligence and omnipotent will.
Advaita	Non dual; neither a subject nor an object.
Agni Devta	Idea of fire in corporeal form or embodied form of fire.
Agni	Fire; one of the basic elements that constitutes creation.
Aham Brahmanasmi	'I Am Brahman'; one of the great sayings that sums up divine wisdom.
Aham Sphurana	'I' pulsation;the experience of 'I' felt as a vibration in the Heart
Ahankara	Feeling of I-ness; pride.
Akasha	Space; ether; one of the basic elements out of which creation manifests.
Amrit	Divine nectar; confers immortality.
Ananda	Divine bliss.
Anhad Shabda	Unstruck sound; the divine sound of Om heard in advanced stages of practice.
Anthakarna	Inner or invisible organ of perception; the mind that is centred on' I'- sense and in which inheres intelligence, memory and roving mind including senses.
Ardhnarishwara	Half male half female.
Asanas	Physical yogic postures.
Asat	Unreal; false.

Ashrama	Place where hermits and sages live.
Asthoola	Gross; physical.
Atman Dhyana Yoga	Union through meditation on the self ('I'sense).
Atman Vichara	Self-inquiry.
Atman Vishvash	Self confidence.
Atman	Self; the absolute Reality.
AUM	The word, Om, is pronounced as AUM.
Avarana	Veiling power (of maya).
Avtara	Divine incarnation.
Ayam Atman Brahman	This Self is Brahman; one of the great sayings that proclaim the ultimate Truth.
Ayurveda	Indian system of medicine

B

Bala	Shankar Bhagwan's consort.
Bhakti	Devotion; expression of divine love.
Bhava Leela	Experience that a devotee has of the presence of a higher power or a deity in one's self.
Bhava Samadhi	Lower samadhi in which there is intimacy with object of worship
Bhava	Mood; inducing of the presence of a deity in a devotees' mind.
Brahaman Agni	Yogic heat produced due to mental concentration or Heat that emanates from divine flame in the Heart.
Brahma Loka	Region where Brahma dwells.
Brahma	One of the trinity of gods; Brahma is said to be the creator of our universe.
Brahman Jnani	Knower of Atman or Brahman; the supreme state of Absolute Knowledge.
Brahman	The Supreme Being; the Absolute God.
Brighu Nadi	Works of Brighu dealing with predictions based on astrology.

Brighu	An ancient astrologer.
Brikuti	Space between the eye brows.
Buddhi	Intelligence.

C

Chakra	Centre of consciousness or power located in various parts of subtle body.
Chit	Consciousness

D

Dakshinmurthy	An aspect of God that imparts spiritual instruction in total Silence; Its embodiment manifested at beginning of time to teach some sages in Silence.
Darshan	Vision; school of philosophy.
Dattraiya	Ancient sage.
Deeksha	Initiation; the process by which a guru initiates a devotee into spiritual life.
Devanga	Name of Swamiji's community
Devi	Embodiment of divine consciousness as a female; God in the female gender; embodied form of Ad Shakti (Supreme Power).
Dharma	Moral law based on truth, righteousness, duty etc.
Dharamaraja	God of death and justice.
Dhyana	Meditation.
Drishti-srishti	Doctrine of sudden creation.
Dukha	Pain.
Durga Devi	Goddess of destruction of evil doers.
Dwaita	Dualism; doctrine of Reality being a subject as also an object but both being two separate entities; seer and seen.
Dwapar Yuga	The second age; precedes Kaliyuga.

G

Gunas	Attributes; qualities.
Gurprasad	By the grace of the guru.
Guru	Spiritual master; teacher; one who has the power to remove ignorance by imparting divine knowledge.
Guru Bhava	Relationship of a disciple with a guru.

H

Hans	Heavenly bird; signifies power of discrimination.
Hath Yoga	In popular perception, a system of physical postures (asanas) and set of breathing exercises (pranayama or science of breath) to keep good health.
Havan	A ritual performed to please deities with fire.

I

Ishta Deva	Object of worship; one's favourite saint or deity to whom one prays.
Ishwara	God as the Lord of all creation.

J

Jal	Water; one of the basic elements of creation.
Jamdoot	Minions; agents of god Dharmaraja.
Jangam Devar	Sect of holy men devoted to god Shiva.
Japa	Repetition of a divine name or mantra.
Jata	Matted locks.
Jiva	An individual; a person; a man or a woman.
Jivatman	Individual soul; the 'I' that imagines itself to be the body.
Jiwan Mukta	Realised while still living.
Jnana Marga	Path of knowledge.

Jnana Yoga	Knowledge as a means to know the Reality.
Jnana	Divine knowledge.
Jyoti	Divine light.

K

Kal	Time; it is divided into four yugas or ages called satya yuga, treta yuga, dwapar yuga and kali yuga. It can also manifest in an embodied form.
Kama	Craving; desire; feeling of lust.
Kamandulu	Small vessel to keep water; carried by holy men.
Karan	Causal.
Karma	Any action of the mind and body done with 'I' sense.
Karma Yogi	One's who does karma without 'I'sense.
Kayakalpa	A yogic technique comprising meditation and taking of some Ayurvedic preparations that rejuvenates an aging body to become young.
Kiryamna Karma	Karma to be done in future.
Kirtan	Devotional singing
Kosa	Sheaths that are said to cover the Atman; they are annamaya (physical body sustained by food) kosa; pranamaya (subtle sheath empowered by prana) kosa; manomaya (mental sheath or roving mind) kosa; vijnanamaya (sheath of intellect or of intelligence and will power) kosa; anandamaya (sheath of bliss) kosa.
Krodha	Anger.
Kuccha	Earthen.
Kumar Nadi	Work dealing with prediction based on astrology.
Kumbhak	Retention of breath.
Kundalini Shakti	Subtle power that dwells in subtle mind and body; also, called serpent power that lies coiled up (i.e. dormant) at the coccyx.

L

Lakshmi Devi	Goddess of wealth; god Vishnu's consort,.
Leela	God's play; the sensual world.
Lingam	Stone symbol of Shiva.
Lobha	Greed.

M

Mahatma	Great soul.
Maha Samadhi	Great samadhi; the highest form of samadhi.
Mahashivratri	Festival devoted to worship of Sri Shankar Bhagwan.
Maha Yogi	Great yogi.
Maha Vakas	Four great maxims or sayings that encapsulate divine knowledge.
Manas	Roving mind.
Mann	Mind; more specifically roving mind.
Mannana	Contemplation; reflection.
Mantra	A word or a group of words specially blessed by a guru for repetition by a devotee.
Mantra shakti	Power of mantra.
Mauna	Silence.
Maya	Ignorance; the power of illusion that is used by the Lord to create the universe
Manonash	Destruction of mind
Manolaya	Self-subsidence; a spiritual state prior to attaining samadhi.
Meneka	Goddess of seduction.
Mitra Bhava	Feeling of friendship.
Muni	Seer.

N

Nadis	Channels for flow of energy in subtle body.

Nag	King cobra
Nama	Divine name (of God).
Nama-japa	Repetition of a divine name.
'Neti','Neti'	'Not this','Not this'.
Nirguna	Attributeless(Realty)
Nirvikalpa Samadhi	Higher samadhi in which the 'I' thought is finally destroyed.

O

Omkar or Om	God conceived as the mystic symbol of sound.

P

Padamasana	Traditional yogic posture adopted for meditation for long periods.
Pappa	Demerits.
Paramatma	The Supreme Self or Reality.
Para Bhakti	Devotion to formless Reality.
Parbrahman	Absolute Brahman
Parvati Devi	Consort of Shankar Bhagwan; also, god Shiva's consort.
Patanjali	Ancient sage, author of Yoga Aphorisms.
Pawan	Air; one of the basic elements of creation.
Prarabdha Karma	Current life's karma.
Prajnanam Brahman	Absolute knowledge is Brahman; one of the great sayings.
Prana	Yogic word for motion; breath.
Pranayama	Control of prana by breathing exercises.
Prasad	Consecrated fruit or food.
Prithvi	Earth; a basic element of creation.
Prozas	Subtle essences of food used to sustain subtle body.
Punya	Merit.

Puranas	Scriptures written in ancient times to simplify teaching for ease of understanding; many of them are in story form.
Purusha	Indwelling God in human body; a male being.

R

Rajasic	Active
Rajoguna	An attribute of maya that signifies activity.
Rakshakic	Demoniacal nature.
Rakta Kali	A goddess with a demoniacal nature.
Ravana	A demon king who was killed by Lord Rama.
Riddhi	Paranormal power of a lower order.
Rishi	Sage
Rupa	Shape; form.

S

Sadhaka	Aspirant
Sadhana	Serious spiritual practice
Saguna	Relative form of Reality
Sahaj	Natural and effortless state.
Sahaj Samadhi	Highest samadhi; state of Realisation.
Sahasra Chakra	Chakra located on top of the head
Sakshatkara	Realisation; the final experience that ends one's practice.
Samadhi	The transcendental and super-sensuous state in which the mind is destroyed; it has three forms; lower, higher and highest.
Samaskara	Mental impression.
Samkhya	One of the six schools of thought.
Sanchit Karma	Karma of past yet to bear fruit.
Sapt Rishis	Seven sages who are alter ego of the Lord.
Saraswati	God Vishnu's consort.

Sat	Real; Truth.
Satchitananda	Truth, consciousness, bliss.
Satguru	Divine incarnation in guru aspect.
Satoguna	An attribute of maya; signifies purity, equilibrium, calmness etc.
Satsang	Company of a saint.
Satvic	Purified.
Satya Yuga	Age of truth; first age in which selfishness is the least.
Savikalpa Samadhi	Lower samadhi
Sewa	Service
Shabda	Word; Omkar; guru' teaching.
Shakti	Power
Shivalingam	Stone symbol of Shiva
Siddha Purusha	Person having supernatural powers.
Siddhis	Paranormal powers of a higher order.
Smaran	Remembrance.
Smriti	Memory.

T

Tamoguna	An attribute of maya that stands for grossness, lethargy dullness, inactivity etc.
Tamsic	Impure and lethargic.
Tanmatra	Subtle (atomic) form of various elements.
Tantra	Spiritual discipline.
Tap, Tapas, Tapasya, Tapas Yoga	In general, practice of any spiritual discipline to control the mind through its purification. In particular, tapas is the highest form of yoga that can be practised only by divine incarnations.
Tapas Shakti	Yoga shakti's sublimated and cosmic form.
Tapas Siddhi	Successful completion of tapas
Tapasthan	Place of tapas

Tat	That
Tat Taum Asi	That Thou are; one of great sayings that signifies highest state of Realisation.
Tehsildar	Revenue officer.
Telegu	A South Indian language, Sri Sivabala Yogi's mother tongue.
Treta Yuga	Third Age
Trimurti	Three faced.
Trinity of Gods	Brahma, Vishnu, Shiva
Turiya	Fourth state; state of Realisation.
Turiyatitta	Beyond the Fourth State; state of Realisation.

U

Upanishadic	Knowledge that ends relative knowledge

V

Vashista	Celebrated author of Yoga Vashista
Vasna	Mental tendencies
Vedanta	One of the six schools of thought.
Vibhuti	Consecrated piece of clay
Vichara	Inquiry
Vidhea Mukta	Liberated after death
Visistadvaita	Qualified monotheism; doctrine that a subject is the object also; experienced in advanced stages of spiritual practice.
Vivek Shakti	Power of discrimination
Vritti	Mental vibration.

Y

Yaganas	Rituals involving sacrificial offerings to fire.
Yoga	Union(with God)

Yoga Danda	Wooden staff carried by yogis
Yoga Nidra	Yogic sleep experienced in manolaya and samadhi.
Yoga Shakti	Yogic power; power of mental concentration.
Yogeshwara	Lord of yogis.
Yuga	Epoch; age.

Index

References are to the chapters and question answers.
(For example 1.10 refers to Chapter 1, Question/Answer10)

A

Abhyasa 1.10, 1.14
Ad Shakti...3.10, 3.11, 3.12, 3.13, 5.59,
    5.88, 5.163
Advaita...3.70
Agami Karam...3.68
Agni...3.64, 4.10
Aham Brahamasmi...4.70
Aham Sphurana...3.53, 3.90
Ahankara...3.40
Akasha...3.62, 3.64, 4.10
Allah...3.10
Amrit...5.74
Ananda...5.143
Anandamaya Kosa...3.65
Anhad Shabda...3.67
Anthakarna...3.32
Annamaya Kosa...3.65
Ardhnarishwara...5.131
Asat...4.74
Asthoola...3.19, 3.63
Astrology...5.161
Atman...2.44, 2.73, 3.10, 3.30, 4.69
Atman dhyana...4.53, 5.102
Atman Vichar...4.76
Atman Vishvash...5.123
Aum...3.67
Avarana...3.19

Avtara(s)...4.42, 4.58, 4.96, 5.3, 5.100,
    5.190
Ayam Atman Brahman...4.70

B

Bhakti...5.138
Bhava...5.143
Bhava Leela...5.88
Bhava Samadhi ...1.23, 1.24, 4.90,
    5.143,5.146, 5.161, 5.173, 5.195
Brahma...2.25, 2.32, 3.59, 3.60, 3.61, 3.62,
    3.67, 5.67
Brahma Loka...2.25
Brahman...2.17, 3.11, 4.69, 4.70
Brahman Chakra...5.67, 5.73, 5.97, 5.104
Brahamin...5.75
Brahman Agni...4.54, 4.57
Brahman Jnani...4.92
Brighu...5.162
Brighu Nadi...5.161
Brikuti...2.21, 4.47, 4.58, 5.72, 5.104, 5.105
Buddhi...3.32

C

Chakra...4.53
Centifugal Force...5.85
Chit...3.23
Cobra...5.50,5.55,5.91

Cosmic Prana...2.63, 5.28, 5.53, 5.88
Currents...4.61,5.28, 5.156

D

Dakshinimurthy...4.81, 5.114
Darshan...2.18, 5.23, 5.33
Dattreya...5.38, 5.39
Deeksha...2.21
Deer Skin...5.65
Devi...3.12, 3.61, 5.2, 5.3
Dharama...3.68, 5.79
Dharamaraja...5.166
Drishti-srishti...3.59
Dukha...3.42
Durga Devi...5.78
Dwaita...3.70
Dwapar Yuga...3.62

E

Eternal Companions...5.69, 5.70

G

Gangerene...5.50
Godavri Canal...5.23
Gunas (Satoguna, Rajoguna,
        Tamoguna)..2.72
Gurprasad...1.21, 5.94, 5.192, 5.196
Guru Arjan Dev...5.49
Guru Gobind Singh...4.29
Guru Nanak...4.42, 4.96, 5.5, 5.94, 5.114
Guru Bhava......1.24, 5.95, 5.106

H

Hans...4.75
Hath Yoga...4.53, 4.54
Heart...1.7, 4.33, 4.35, 4.90, 5.31, 5.104,
        5.105
Horlicks...5.53, 5.56

I

Ishta Deva...4.10, 4.11, 4.20, 4.95, 5.14

Ishwara...2.7, 2.25, 3.5, 3.25, 3.26, 5.14,
        5.16

J

Jal...3.64, 4.10
Jamdoot.. 5.166
Jangam Devar...5.15, 5.21
Japa...4.47, 5.57
Jehovah...3.10
Jesus Christ...3.25, 4.85, 4.96, 5.1, 5.3,
        5.49
Jiva...2.1, 3.13, 3.28, 3.33, 3.60, 3.68
Jivatman...4.53
Jiwan Mukta...4.92, 4.94
Jnana...3.10
Jnana Marg...4.66, 4.67, 4.71, 4.77, 4.80
JnanaYoga...4.53
Jnani...4.77
Judas...5.94
Jyoti...4.54, 5.29

K

Kabir...5.114
Kal...3.62, 5.1, 5.50, 5.51, 5.55, 5.57, 5.58
Kali Devi...5.79, 5.163
Kaliyuga... 3.62, 4.92, 5.108
Kama...3.40
Kamandulu...5.74
Karma...2.1, 2.52, 2.59, 3.37, 3.58, 3.68
        Agami Karma...3.68
        Prarabdha Karma...3 68
        Sanchit Karma...3.68
Karan...3.19, 5.131
Kayakalpa...5.175
Kirtan...4.52, 5.79, 5.138
Kiryamna karam...3.68
Kosa...3.65
Krodh...3.40
Kumar Nadi...5.161
Kundalni...4.54, 4.61
Kundalni Shakti...4.54, 4.61, 5.91
Kumbhak...4.89, 5.54

L

Lakshmi...3.12, 4.42
Leela...2.20, 2.39, 3.17, 3.69, 5.14
Lobha...3.40

M

Mahatma...5.127, 5.128
Maha Samadhi...4.90, 5.24
Maha Shivratri...5.163
Maharishi...5.189
Maha Yogi... 4.96
Maha Vakas...4.70
Manas...3.32, 4.57
Meneka...5.74
Mann...3.32
Mannana...2.8, 5.123
Manolaya...4.8, 3.70, 5.72, 5.73
Manomaya Kosa...3.65
Manonash...4.8
Mantra...2.21, 4.8, 4.46, 4.47
Mantra Shakti...5.158
Mass Feeding...5.168
Mauna...5.61
Maya...2.35, 2.48, 2.90, 3.5, 3.6, 3.11, 3.15,
      3.16, 3.19, 3.21, 3.22, 5.76
Moha...3.40
Mother Parvati... 5.72, 5.74
Mumbo-jumbo...5.93
Munis...4.24
Mitra Bhava...5.106

N

Nadi...4.60, 5.162
Nag...5.56
Nama...3.5, 3.10, 3.55, 3.67, 4.45
Nama-japa...5.108
Namaskara...5.63, 5.79
Narshimhamurthy...5.63
Neti...4.66
Nirguna...3.6, 3.7
Nirvikalpa Samadhi...3.33
Nirvana...1.7

O

Omkar...3.10, 3.62, 3.67, 4.11, 4.12

P

Padamasana...5.30
Pakistan...5.94
Pappa...4.33
Paramatma...4.53
Para Bhakti...4.50
Parbrahman...3.10
Parvati...3.60, 4.42
Patanjali...4.53
Pawan...3.64, 4.10
Prajnanam Brahman...4.70
Prana...3.63, 3.64, 3.67, 4.81, 4.86, 5.28
Pranayama...4.8, 4.53, 5.145
Pranamaya Kosa...3.65
Pranic Energy...2.63, 5.53
Prarabdha Karma...3.68, 4.26, 4.81, 4.94,
      5.1
Prithvi...3.64, 4.10
Prophet Mohammed...5.137
Powers...4.84
Prozas...5.59
Punya...4.33, 5.168
Puranas...5.85
Purusha...3.10, 5.56

R

Rajasic Aspirant/Devotee/Person...2.66,
      2.67, 5.141
Rajasic Tendencies...2.66, 2.67
Rajoguna...2.72, 3.19, 3.24,
Rakshakic...5.57
Rakhta Kali...5.163, 5. 164, 5.165
Rama...3.10
Ramakrishan...2.25, 5.190
Raman Maharishi...2.25, 4.39, 4.96, 5.114
Ravana...5.79, 5.100
Realisation...4.88, 4.92
Religious leaders...5.137
Riddhi...3.43, 4.86
Rishi...4.24

Rupa...3.5

S

Sacred Hills...5.71
Sadhak...2.12
Sadhana...1.13, 1.20, 2.6, 2.11, 2.12, 2.13,
    2.58, 2.88, 4.8, 4.16, 4.52, 4.97
Saguna...3.5, 3.7, 3.8, 3.9, 3.22
Sahaj Samadhi...4.19, 4.89
Sahaj Nirvikalpa Samadhi...2.25, 4.90,
    5.20, 5.121, 5.151
Sahaj...3.59, 4.90
Sahasrara Chakra...4.54, 5.104
Sakshatkara...4.92
Samadhi...2.23, 2.24, 2.25, 3.33, 3.46,
    4.11, 4.89, 4.90, 4.91, 5.32
Samaskara...3.28, 3.31, 3.33, 3.36, 3.37,
    3.38
Samkhya...3.10
Sanchit Karma...3.68
Sapt Rishi...5.192
Saraswati...3.12, 3.60, 4.61
Sat...4.74
Satchitananda...3.10
Satguru...2.6, 2.7, 2.25, 2.26, 4.60, 4.83,
    5.72
Satoguna...3.19,3.24
Sat Sangha...2.6, 2.7, 2.8, 2.88, 4.8, 5.104
Satvic Aspirant...2.66
Satvic Attribute...2.66
Satvic Diet...2.61
Satya Yuga...3.62
Savikalpa Samadhi...2.25,4.90
Self Realisation...1.7, 4.8, 4.66, 4.81, 4.82,
    4.91, 5.148, 5.154
Sewa...2.31, 2.53, 4.8, 5.141, 5.142
Shabda...3.10, 3.67
Shakti...3.61
Shankar Bhagwan...5.10, 5.14, 5.15, 5.16,
    5.21
Shiva Shakti...3.11
Shiva...2.32, 3.57, 3.60, 4.21, 4.96, 5.67,
    5.73
Shivalingam...5.22

Siddha Purusha...5.56
Siddhis...3.43, 4.86
Silence...4.81
Sivabala Yogeshwara...5.79
Sivabala Yogi...Chapter 5
Smaran...4.41
Smriti...3.32
Sookshma...3.19, 3.63,
Sravana...2.8, 5.197, 5.123
Sukh...3.42
Sundram Pillai...5.63
Sunn...5.23
Surya Lok...5.97
Surya Mandal...5.97
Surya Mantra...5.95, 5.96, 5.97
Surya...5.96
Surya Shakti...5.96
Swamiji's
    Birth Date...24 January 1935
    Eternal Companions...5.69,5.70
    Final advice...5.196
    Guru...5.79
    Kayakalpa...5.175
    Mahasamadhi Date...28 March 1994
    Memory...5.132
    Mission...5.189
    Previous Lives...5.161
    Rebirth...5.186
    Subtle Body...5.171, 5.172, 5.173
    Tapas...5.17, 5.18, 5.51, 5.66, 5.67,
        5.72, 5.73, 5.74, 5.78, 5.81, 5.,82

T

Tamoguna...3.19,3.24
Tamsic Aspirant...2.66, 2.67
Tamasic Attributes...2.72
Tanmatra...3.64, 4.86, 5.67
Tantra...3.12, 4.21, 4.54, 5.158
Tap...4.96
Tapas...2,19, 2.25, 4.88, 4.96, 5.1, 5.9
Tapas
    Eastern Direction...4.96, 5.50
    Northern Direction...4.96, 5.72
    Southern Direction...4.96, 5.78

Western Direction...*4.96, 5.77*
Tapas Shakti...4.54
Tapas Siddhi...5.57
Tapasthana...5.52
Tapaswiji Maharaj...5.94, 5.95
Tapas Yoga...2.19
Tejas...5.77
Tempest...5.40
Tiger Skin...5.63,5.64
Trimurti...5.38
Trinity of gods...2.32, 4.96, 5.87
Turiya...4.90
Turiyatitta...4.90, 5.24
Tat...3.10
Tat Taum Asi...4.70
Treta Yuga...3.62

U

Upanishad...1.25
Upanishadic Knowledge...1.27, 5.194
Upanishadic Teaching...4.70

V

Vashista...5.100
Vasna...2.83, 3.3, 3.28, 3.31, 3.37, 3.38, 5.1
Vedantic Teaching...4.70

Vibhuti...5. 79, 5.105, 5.115, 5.116, 5.152
Vichara...4.73
Vidhea Mukta...4.92
Vijnanamaya Kosa...3 65
Visistadvaita...3.70
Vishnu...2.25, 4.21
Vishnu Loka...2.25
Viveka Shakti...4.74
Vivekananda Swami...5.190
Vritti...3.35

Y

Yagnas...4.24
Yoga...4.53
Yoga Danda...5.74
Yoga Nidra...4.8, 5.60
Yoga Shakti...4.3, 4.9, 4.17, 4.19, 4.54, 4.55, 4.96, 5.18
Yoga Vashista...5.100
Yogeshwara...5.130, 5.79
Yogi...4.53, 5.67, 5.78, 5.91, 5.126, 5.137
Yuga...3.62, 4.95

W

Waheguru...3.10
Wind god...5.74

Printed in the United States
By Bookmasters